Cross-Border Mergers in Europe

This discussion of the Cross-border Merger Directive and its implementing legislation in each Member State of the European Union and the European Economic Area provides companies and their advisors with useful insight into the legal framework applicable to, and the tax treatment of, cross-border mergers throughout the European Economic Area. Analysis of the Community rules laid down in the Cross-border Merger Directive and the Community rules on the tax treatment of cross-border mergers is complemented by chapters on the implementing legislation in each Member State, prepared in accordance with a common format and contributed by a practitioner from each state. Annexes contain the Cross-border Merger Directive (Annex I), the Parent–Subsidiary Directive (Annex II) and a list of the implementing legislation in each Member State (Annex III).

DIRK VAN GERVEN is a partner in the Brussels office of NautaDutilh (a leading Benelux law firm) and a member of the Brussels and New York Bars. He has extensive experience in all areas of corporate and financial law, including securities regulation. Dirk is in charge of continuing legal education for the Dutch-speaking Bar Association of Brussels and has published widely in the fields of corporate and financial law. Since 2003, he has also been a member of the supervisory board of Belgium's Banking, Finance and Insurance Commission.

Law Practitioner Series

The *Law Practitioner Series* offers practical guidance in corporate and commercial law for the practitioner. It offers high-quality comment and analysis rather than simply restating the legislation, providing a critical framework as well as exploring the fundamental concepts which shape the law. Books in the series cover carefully chosen subjects of direct relevance and use to the practitioner.

The series will appeal to experienced specialists in each field, but is also accessible to more junior practitioners looking to develop their understanding of particular fields of practice.

The Consultant Editors and Editorial Board have outstanding expertise in the UK corporate and commercial arena, ensuring academic rigour with a practical approach.

Consultant editors
Charles Allen-Jones, retired senior partner of Linklaters
Mr Justice David Richards, Judge of the High Court of Justice, Chancery Division

Editors
Chris Ashworth – Lovells LLP
Professor Eilis Ferran – University of Cambridge
Judith Hanratty – BP Corporate Lawyer, retired
Keith Hyman – Clifford Chance LLP
Keith Johnston – Addleshaw Goddard LLP
Vanessa Knapp – Freshfields Bruckhaus Deringer LLP
Charles Mayo – Simmons & Simmons
Gary Milner-Moore – Herbert Smith LLP
Andrew Peck – Linklaters LLP
Timothy Polglase – Allen & Overy LLP
Richard Snowden QC – Erskine Chambers
William Underhill – Slaughter & May
Dirk Van Gerven – NautaDutilh
Sandra Walker – Rio Tinto

Books in the series

Stamp Duty Land Tax
Michael Thomas; Consultant Editor David Goy QC

Accounting Principles for Lawyers
Peter Holgate

The European Company: Volume 1
General Editors: Dirk Van Gerven and Paul Storm

The European Company: Volume 2
General Editors: Dirk Van Gerven and Paul Storm

Capital Markets Law and Compliance: The Implications of MiFID
Paul Nelson

Reward Governance for Senior Executives
Edited by Carol Arrowsmith, Rupert McNeil

Prospectus for the Public Offering of Securities in Europe European and National Legislation in the Member States of the European Economic Area Volume 1.
General Editor: Dirk Van Gerven

Prospectus for the Public Offering of Securities in Europe: European and National Legislation in the Member States of the European Economic Area Volume 2.
General Editor: Dirk Van Gerven

Common Legal Framework for Takeover Bids in Europe: Volume 1
General Editor: Dirk Van Gerven

Accounting Principles for Non-Executive Directors
Peter A. Holgate and Elizabeth Buckley

The Law of Charitable Status
Robert Meakin

The Business Case for Corporate Governance
Ken Rushton

Cross-Border Mergers in Europe: Volume 1
Edited by Dirk Van Gerven

Cross-Border Mergers in Europe

VOLUME I

General Editor

DIRK VAN GERVEN

CAMBRIDGE
UNIVERSITY PRESS

CAMBRIDGE UNIVERSITY PRESS
Cambridge, New York, Melbourne, Madrid, Cape Town, Singapore,
São Paulo, Delhi, Dubai, Tokyo

Cambridge University Press
The Edinburgh Building, Cambridge CB2 8RU, UK

Published in the United States of America by Cambridge University Press, New York

www.cambridge.org
Information on this title: www.cambridge.org/9780521483278

First published 2010

Printed in the United Kingdom at the University Press, Cambridge

A catalogue record for this publication is available from the British Library

Library of Congress Cataloguing in Publication data
 Cross-border mergers in Europe / general editor, Dirk Van Gerven.
  p. cm. – (Law practitioner series)
 ISBN 978-0-521-48327-8 (Hardback)
 1. Consolidation and merger of corporations–Law and legislation–
 European Union countries. I. Gerven, Dirk van. II. Title. III. Series.
 KJE6467.C76 2010
 346.4′06626–dc22

ISBN 978-0-521-48327-8 Hardback

Contents

Contributors

AUSTRIA
Gottfried Gassner
Andreas Hable
Horst Lukanec
Binder Grösswang Rechtsanwälte

BELGIUM
Dirk Van Gerven
Jan Werbrouck
Philippe François
Julien Hick
NautaDutilh

BULGARIA
Anelia Tatarova
Raina Dimitrova
Yordan Naydenov
Borislav Boyanov & Co.

CYPRUS
Alexandros Tsadiras
LLPO Law Firm

CZECH REPUBLIC
Adam Jirousek
Jan Lasák
Kocián Šolc Balaštík

DENMARK
Vagn Thorup
Jeppe Buskov
Kromann Reumert

ESTONIA
Ahto Nirgi

Sven Papp
Raidla Lejins & Norcous

GERMANY
Andreas Wuesthoff
SJ Berwin LLP

HUNGARY
Jacques de Servigny
Zsófia Fekete
Szabolcs Erdős
Gide Loyrette Nouel

THE NETHERLANDS
Paul van der Bijl
Frits Oldenburg
Paul Storm
NautaDutilh

POLAND
Michał Barłowski
Wardynski & Partners

SLOVAK REPUBLIC
Michaela Jurkova
Čechová & Partners

UNITED KINGDOM
Ian Snaith
University of Leicester and Cobbetts LLP

NORWAY
Stig Berge, Herman Bondeson
Thommessen

Preface

The Cross-border Merger Directive is the next logical step in creating a unified European market within which companies based in the European Union will be able to do business across borders without restriction. Indeed, the Cross-border Merger Directive sets out procedural rules to permit and facilitate the merger of companies situated in different Member States of the European Union and the European Economic Area. It is a useful addition to the Third Council Directive (78/855/EEC) of 9 October 1978, which governs mergers of public limited liability companies situated in the same Member State.

The Cross-border Merger Directive defines the consequences of, and the procedure for, a cross-border merger. The main consequence is that all assets and liabilities of the acquired company are transferred by operation of law to the acquiring company. The Directive sets forth procedural rules for three types of mergers, i.e. the absorption of one or more companies into a surviving company, the merger of two of more companies into a newly formed company, and the merger of a wholly owned subsidiary into its parent company, for which a simplified procedure applies. With respect to procedural aspects, the Cross-border Merger Directive refers to a large extent to the Third Council Directive, which sets forth procedural rules for purely domestic mergers, i.e. between companies situated in the same Member State. Since the Third Council Directive has been implemented in all Member States, implementation of the Cross-border Merger Directive has been greatly facilitated.

It will be difficult to carry out a cross-border merger if the tax treatment of the merger is uncertain. In this respect, the Parent–Subsidiary Directive of 23 July 1990 on the common system of taxation applicable to mergers between parent companies and their subsidiaries in different Member States (as amended by Council Directive 2005/19/EC of 17 February 2005) provides for tax neutrality in the event of such a cross-border merger and is therefore a necessary complement to the Cross-border Merger Directive. Unfortunately, the application of this directive is limited to the European Union; in other words, it does not apply to the member countries of the European Economic Area (i.e. Norway, Liechtenstein and Iceland).

The Cross-border Merger Directive is intended to allow small and medium-sized companies to engage in cross-border cooperation by merging to form a company governed by the national law of a particular Member State (i.e. a national corporate form). In the Community legislature's view, the cross-border merger is an alternative to the formation of a European company (SE), which is intended to be used by larger companies. The latter can merge by first setting up an SE, which by definition is subject to uniform rules throughout the European Economic Area, set forth in a regulation which is directly applicable in all Member States. Of course, the reality is often very different, and practice indicates that several SEs have been formed by small companies that wish to benefit from the SE's European aura, while large companies tend to avoid the SE due to the difficult and lengthy procedures with respect to employee information and participation. A cross-border merger carried out in accordance with the Cross-border Merger Directive need not comply with these procedures if employee participation does not exist in any of the participating companies.

A book providing a comprehensive analysis of the European legal framework on cross-border mergers and the implementing legislation in each Member State of the European Union and the European Economic Area is a useful tool for those seeking to foster cooperation between companies from different Member States. This book will also be helpful to their advisers involved in preparing a cross-border merger. There are two volumes. Part one of the first volume explains the Community rules laid down in the Cross-border Merger Directive and the European tax rules applicable to cross-border mergers. The second part focuses on the implementing legislation of the Cross-border Merger Directive in each Member State. Volume I contains reports from fourteen Member States. The remaining reports will be published in the second volume.

Finally, I would like to thank the contributors to this book, esteemed practitioners from law firms throughout Europe, all of whom are well positioned to discuss the rules applicable in their respective countries. My thanks also go out to those whose names are not mentioned in the reports but whose work was essential to the success of this project, namely Katherine Raab and Bianca Porcelli as well as many others at NautaDutilh.

Dirk Van Gerven
Brussels, 17 February 2009

PART I

EC rules on cross-border mergers

1

Community rules applicable to cross-border mergers

DIRK VAN GERVEN
NautaDutilh

I   Introduction

1   Purpose

1.   Mergers between companies situated in different Member States are difficult. In certain jurisdictions, it is unclear whether a cross-border merger is even possible, especially if the company created through the merger will have its registered or head office in another state.

Directive 2005/56/EC of the European Parliament and of the Council of 26 October 2005 on cross-border mergers of limited liability companies (the 'Cross-border Merger Directive' or the 'Dir.')[1] is intended to facilitate this type of merger by providing procedural rules. A copy of the Directive can be found in Annex I of this book.

The Cross-border Merger Directive does not affect the applicable provisions of national law. Thus, each company taking part in a cross-border merger remains subject to the provisions and formalities of national law which would apply in the case of a purely domestic merger.[2] However, these national rules should be largely harmonised thanks to transposition of the Third Council Directive (78/855/EEC) of 9 October 1978 concerning mergers of public limited liability companies (the 'Domestic Merger Directive').[3]

2   History

2.   The Cross-border Merger Directive is based on a proposal by the European Commission of 18 November 2003 for a directive on cross-border mergers of companies with share capital.[4] In its Explanatory Memorandum, the Commission explains that European companies have been requesting for some time a legal instrument which will enable them to carry out cross-border mergers.

A first proposal for a directive facilitating cross-border mergers was adopted by the Commission on 14 December 1984.[5] This proposal was subsequently discussed in the European Parliament but the issue of employee participation in the decision-making process of the companies participating in the merger proved to be problematic. A report was prepared and presented to the European Parliament on 21 October 1987, but the Parliament was never able to reach an agreement on it. The adoption of a statutory framework for employee information and participation in the establishment of a European company ('SE') finally allowed the deadlock with respect to employee participation in

---

1 *Official Journal* L 310 of 26 October 2005.
2 Third recital to the Cross-border Merger Directive.
3 *Official Journal* L 295 of 20 October 1978.
4 COM (2003) 703 final.
5 *Official Journal* C 23 of 25 January 1985.

cross-border mergers to be broken by referring to the rules applicable to the formation of an SE by merger.[6]

The Economic and Social Committee formulated its opinion on the proposed directive on cross-border mergers on 28 April 2004.[7] Based on a report of its Committee on Legal Affairs of 25 April 2005,[8] the European Parliament approved certain amendments to the proposal on 10 May 2005 and sent the amended proposal back to the European Commission for finalisation.[9] The Commission accepted several of these amendments and incorporated them into the final draft of the Directive.

II   Application

3.   The deadline for transposition of the Cross-border Merger Directive into national law by the Member States was 15 December 2007 (Art. 19 Dir.).

Most Member States were late in enacting implementing legislation, and some have yet to do so. Currently, all Member States have transposed the Cross-border Merger Directive.

The Cross-border Merger Directive applies to the member countries of the European Economic Area (EEA), i.e. the EU Member States plus Norway, Iceland and Liechtenstein.[10] Therefore, all references in this report to the European Union or its Member States should be construed to include these three EEA countries as well, unless specified otherwise.

III   Scope

1   General

4.   The Cross-border Merger Directive applies to cross-border mergers of limited liability companies formed in accordance with the law of an EU or EEA Member State and which have their registered office, central administration or principal place of business in the European Economic Area. A merger is considered cross-border if at least two of the participating companies are governed by the laws of different Member States (Art. 1 Dir.). Consequently, the Directive does not apply to mergers between companies from the same

---

6 Art. 16 Dir.; see the Opinion of 28 April 2004 of the Economic and Social Committee, no 3.3.2; for a discussion of the rules applicable to the SE, see P. François and J. Hick, 'Employee Involvement: Rights and Obligations' in *The European Company*, D. Van Gerven and P. Storm (eds.), Cambridge University Press, vol. I, 2006, 77 *et seq.*

7 *Official Journal* C 117 of 30 April 2004.

8 A6–0089/2005 final.

9 *Official Journal* C 92 of 20 April 2006.

10 Further to the EEA Joint Committee's Decision of 22 September 2006, amending Annex XXII (Company Law) to the EEA Agreement (*Official Journal* L 333 of 30 November 2006).

Member State. Nor does it apply to a cross-border merger between a company established in the EEA and one governed by the laws of a non-EEA country.

In general, a company's central administration is considered to be its head office for purposes of applying the so-called real seat (*siège réel*) theory, which holds that a legal entity is governed by the law of the country where its head office is located. The terms 'head office' and 'central administration' are used interchangeably in the Community regulations and directives on company law,[11] in accordance with the European Court of Justice's case law. [12] The reference to the principal place of business being in the European Economic Area therefore seems redundant.

5.   The Cross-border Merger Directive is intended to regulate mergers between all limited liability companies, regardless of their corporate form. The scope of the Cross-border Merger Directive is broader than that of the Domestic Merger Directive, which sets forth uniform rules for purely domestic mergers of public limited liability companies. When implementing the Domestic Merger Directive, several Member States extended the scope of the rules set forth therein to other corporate forms.

Limited liability companies include the companies listed in Article 1 of the First Company Law Directive (68/151/EEC) of 9 March 1968 (Art. 2(1)(a) Dir.).[13] A list of qualifying companies in each Member State can be found in Annex II of this book.

Limited liability companies also include companies with share capital and legal personality which possess separate assets that serve to cover their liabilities and which are furthermore subject to guarantees provided for by national law, such as those described in the First Company Law Directive to protect the interests of shareholders and others (Art. 2(1)(b) Dir.).[14] This extension covers all companies with share capital whose partners or shareholders may be held liable only up to the value of their subscriptions or contributions, as represented by their shareholdings, provided these companies are subject to the provisions of national law implementing the First Company Law Directive. In other words, the term 'limited liability company' includes not only companies that take the corporate forms mentioned in Article 1 of the First Company Law Directive but also other companies, to the extent the rules set forth in the

---

11 In Regulation No 2137/85 of 25 July 1985 on the European economic interest grouping, the term 'head office' is defined as the place of central administration (Art. 4). The English-language version of Regulation No 2157/2001 of 8 October 2001 on the European company uses the term 'head office' (Art. 2), while the term *'administration centrale'* is used in the French version. The term head office is also used in Regulation No 1435/2003 of 22 July 2003 on the European Cooperative Society (Art. 2).

12 ECJ, *Daily Mail*, 27 September 1988, *ECR*, 1988, 5483.

13 *Official Journal* L 65 of 14 March 1968.

14 The English version refers to the protection of 'members'. The French version refers to *'associés'* and the German version to *'Gesellschafter'*, i.e. shareholders or partners, which is a better term to designate the holders of shares in such a company.

First Company Law Directive apply to these companies. These rules pertain to publication requirements, the validity of undertakings by a company in formation, the (un)enforceability of restrictions in the articles of association and the declaration of nullity of a company by the courts. It seems that the Cross-border Merger Directive is intended to apply to all companies with limited liability which are subject to a similar legal framework throughout the European Economic Area that provides sufficient protection for third parties when dealing with such companies.

The ultimate goal is indeed to extend the Cross-border Merger Directive to all small and medium-sized enterprises ('SMEs') that are not interested in forming an SE.[15] In the Community legislature's view, the SE is a form reserved for larger companies, which should be encouraged to create an SE when consolidating. The reality is, of course, more complex in that some SMEs may wish to set up an SE while larger companies may prefer merging rather than forming an SE.

The Member States may extend their rules of national law implementing the Cross-border Merger Directive to other corporate forms, such as companies with unlimited liability. However, in this case, these companies will only be entitled to benefit from the merger *ipso jure* if the national law of the Member States where the other companies participating in the merger are established so allows.

6.   The Cross-border Merger Directive is intended to authorise cross-border mergers without liquidation and the automatic transfer of assets and liabilities to the surviving or newly formed company.

Only companies that qualify as limited liability companies, as defined above, and that merge in accordance with the conditions and requirements of the Cross-border Merger Directive can benefit from the above rule. Furthermore, as explained below, such companies will only be entitled to apply the Cross-border Merger Directive if they are permitted to merge by national law (see no 13 of this chapter).

2   Excluded companies and mergers

7.   A Member State may decide not to apply the Cross-border Merger Directive to cross-border mergers involving a cooperative, even if that cooperative qualifies as a limited liability company as described above (Art. 3(2) Dir.). In this case, the cooperative shall still be entitled to participate in a merger to form a European cooperative society in accordance with the rules laid down in Council Regulation No 1435/2003 of 22 July 2003 on the Statute for a European Cooperative Society ('SCE').[16]

---

15 Explanatory Memorandum to the proposal for a directive, p. 3; Opinion of 28 April 2004 of the Economic and Social Committee, no 3.2.
16 *Official Journal* L 207 of 18 August 2003. A corrigendum has been published in the *Official Journal* (L 049 of 17 February 2007). For a discussion of the rules applicable to the SCE, see D. Van Gerven, 'Provisions of Community Law Applicable to the European Cooperative

The Cross-border Merger Directive does not define cooperatives. In its communication of 23 February 2004 on cooperative societies in Europe, the European Commission defined cooperatives as entities which

> [o]perate in the interests of their members, who are at the same time users, and (...) not managed in the interests of outside investors. Profits are received by members in proportion to their businesses with the co-operative, and reserves and assets are commonly held, non-distributable and dedicated to the common interests of members. Because personal links among members are in principle strong and important, new membership is subject to approval while voting rights are not necessarily proportional to shareholdings (one man one vote). Resignation entitles the member to repayment of his part and implies reduction of the capital.[17]

The significance of characterisation as a cooperative varies greatly from one Member State to another. In some countries, cooperatives operate as professional associations, providing services solely to their members, while in others they have evolved into commercial companies that present an alternative to other corporate forms.

8.   The Cross-border Merger Directive does not apply to cross-border mergers which involve a company whose corporate purpose is the collective investment of capital invested by the public and which operates on the principle of risk-spreading and whose units may be, at the holder's request, purchased or redeemed, directly or indirectly, out of that company's assets (Art. 3(3) Dir.). In this respect, actions taken by the company to ensure that the market value of its units does not vary significantly from its net asset value shall be regarded as a repurchase or redemption.

Such companies are governed by Council Directive 85/611/EEC of 20 December 1985 on the coordination of laws, regulations and administrative provisions relating to undertakings for collective investment in transferable securities (UCITS), as amended.

9.   Finally, the Cross-border Merger Directive does not apply to mergers to create a European company (SE) or a European cooperative society (SCE).[18] In this case, the merger will be governed by the rules laid down either in Council Regulation No 2157/2001 of 8 October 2001 (the 'SE Regulation')[19] or in Council Regulation 1435/2003 of 22 July 2003 on the Statute for a European Cooperative Society (the 'SCE Regulation').[20]

Society' in *The European Cooperative Society*, D. Van Gerven and P. Storm (eds.), Cambridge University Press, 2010, to be published.

17 See also the recitals to of Regulation 1435/2003 of 22 July 2003 on the Statute for a European Cooperative Society (SCE) (*Official Journal* L 207 of 18 August 2003).

18 Art. 18 of the SE Regulation and Art. 20 of the SCE Regulation.

19 *Official Journal* L 294 of 10 November 2001.

20 For a discussion of the formation of an SE by merger, see D. Van Gerven and P. Storm (eds.), *The European Company*, Cambridge University Press, vol. I, 2006, and vol. II, 2008. For a

IV   Definition of a merger and conditions

1   Definition

10.   The Cross-border Merger Directive distinguishes three types of mergers: (i) a merger whereby one participating company absorbs the other participating companies; (ii) a merger whereby all participating companies cease to exist and a new company is formed; and (iii) a merger of a subsidiary into its parent company (Art. 2(2) Dir.). The latter type of merger can be realised by means of a simplified procedure in which no new shares must be issued by the parent company (see nos 39 and 40 of this chapter).

11.   With respect to the first two types of mergers, the Cross-border Merger Directive regulates mergers whereby all the assets and liabilities of the participating companies are transferred to the surviving company in return for the issuance to shareholders of securities or shares representing the capital of the surviving company and a cash payment which may not exceed 10 per cent of the nominal value of the shares or, in the absence thereof, the accounting par value of the securities or shares (Art. 2(2)(a) and (b) Dir.). The term 'accounting par value' is not defined and must be determined in accordance with national law but, in general, should equal the amount obtained by dividing the share capital by the number of shares.

The reference to securities and shares representing capital is liable to cause confusion. It appears from the French version of the Cross-border Merger Directive[21] that the Community legislature considers both to represent capital. The term 'securities' (*titres*) seems to refer to freely transferable financial instruments, while 'shares' (*parts sociales*) are identified by the shareholder's name in a register or otherwise.

If the cash payment exceeds 10 per cent of the nominal value or, in the absence thereof, the accounting par value of the securities or shares representing capital, the merger can only benefit from the rules set forth in the Cross-border Merger Directive if at least one of the Member States concerned allows such a cash payment (Art. 3(1) Dir.). In this case, the merger will not benefit from the tax neutrality provided for by Directive 90/434/EEC of 23 July 1990 on the common system of taxation applicable to mergers (as amended by Directive 2005/19/EC of 17 February 2005).[22]

12.   In all types of mergers covered by the Cross-border Merger Directive, the assets and liabilities will be considered transferred on the date of dissolution without liquidation of the company. This seems to imply that a company which

discussion of the formation of an SCE by merger, see Van Gerven and Storm, *The European Cooperative Society*.

21   The French version refers to '*titres ou de parts représentatifs du capital social*', which confirms that both securities and shares represent capital.

22   See Chapter 3 of this book.

has already been dissolved and is in liquidation cannot participate in a cross-border merger. This is an important difference compared to domestic mergers. Indeed, the Third Council Directive of 9 October 1978 concerning mergers of public limited liability companies explicitly authorises the Member States to permit companies in liquidation to participate in a domestic merger, provided the company has not yet begun to distribute its assets to shareholders.[23]

2   Conditions

13.   Cross-border mergers governed by the Cross-border Merger Directive are subject to the applicable provisions of national law on mergers, unless the Directive provides otherwise. This fact is very significant.

Firstly, a cross-border merger in accordance with the Cross-border Merger Directive is only possible between companies that are entitled to merge under applicable national law (Art. 4(1)(a) Dir.).

Secondly, the companies participating in the merger must comply with the provisions and formalities of national law to which they are subject (Art. 4(1)(b) Dir.), including those relating to the decision-making process for a merger and, taking into account the cross-border nature of the merger, the protection of creditors, debenture holders, the holders of securities or shares and employees (Art. 4(2) Dir.). In this respect, national law may not introduce restrictions on freedom of establishment or on the free movement of capital unless these are justified in light of the European Court of Justice's case law, in particular by requirements in the general interest, and are necessary for, and proportionate to, achieving these requirements.[24]

The foregoing also implies that special legislation applicable to specific types of activities must be observed, such as Community and national legislation regulating credit intermediaries and other financial undertakings.[25]

In order to determine which national rules apply to each merging company, the Cross-border Merger Directive refers to the law to which the company is subject. In this way, the Directive avoids taking a position on the question of whether a company is governed by the law of the country where its registered office is located or of the country where its head office or principal place of business is situated. The head office is the place where the company is effectively managed and controlled, the place where its central management and administration are located.[26] Consequently, the law to which a company is subject will depend on national conflict-of-law rules. It is thus possible for a company to be subject to and governed by two sets of laws, i.e. if it has its registered office in a Member State which refers to the incorporation theory to

23 Arts. 3(2) and 4(2) Domestic Merger Directive.
24 Third recital to the Cross-border Merger Directive.
25 *Ibid.*, tenth recital.
26 ECJ, 27 September 1988, *ECR*, 1988, 5483.

determine the applicable law and its principal place of business in a Member State which applies the head office theory.

14.   The Member States can adopt legislation designed to ensure appropriate protection for minority shareholders who oppose a cross-border merger (Art. 4(2) Dir.; see no 28 of this chapter).

3   Opposition by national authorities

15.   The national rules of a Member State that allows its national authorities to oppose a domestic merger on grounds of public interest will also apply to cross-border mergers if at least one of the merging companies is subject to the law of that Member State (Art. 4(1)(b) Dir.). The concept of 'public interest' should be interpreted in accordance with applicable national law.

The national authorities can also oppose the formation of an SE or SCE by merger on grounds of public interest.[27] However, the national authorities cannot oppose a cross-border merger on grounds of public interest to the extent the merger is subject to scrutiny as a concentration under the EC Merger Regulation.[28] In this case, the European competition authorities will be competent, and the rules contained in the EC Merger Regulation will apply. Indeed, characterisation as a cross-border merger governed by the Cross-border Merger Directive is without prejudice to application of the rules on the control of concentrations set forth in the EC Merger Regulation and in national competition law.[29]

V   Consequences of a merger

16.   As a result of a cross-border merger governed by the Cross-border Merger Directive, the disappearing companies will be dissolved but not liquidated (Art. 2(2)(a) and (b) Dir.). Indeed, the assets and liabilities of these companies will be transferred without liquidation to the surviving company in the state in which they are located. This will occur by operation of law on this date. National law cannot provide otherwise.

In the event of a parent–subsidiary merger, all assets and liabilities of the subsidiary will be transferred without liquidation to the parent company holding all of its securities or shares representing capital. The subsidiary will then be dissolved but not liquidated (Art. 2(2)(c) Dir.).

The above-mentioned provisions regarding the consequences of a cross-border merger refer only to mergers between limited liability companies with

---

27 Art. 19 SE Regulation and Art. 21 SCE Regulation.
28 Art. 4(1)(b) of the Directive in conjunction with Art. 21 of Council Regulation (EC) No 139/2004 of 20 January 2004 on the control of concentrations between undertakings (*Official Journal* L 24 of 29 January 2004).
29 Ninth recital to the Cross-border Merger Directive.

a maximum cash payment, if any, of 10 per cent of the nominal value of the shares issued on the occasion of the merger. Nonetheless, the provisions of the Cross-border Merger Directive shall apply to mergers with a cash payment in excess of this amount if the national law of at least one Member State concerned allows the payment in question (see no 8 of this chapter). Consequently, such a merger will have the same legal consequences as explained herein.

17.   Once the merger is complete, the surviving company will be the sole owner of all assets and liabilities of the merged companies. The other companies that took part in the merger shall cease to exist by operation of law (*ipso jure*) (Art. 14(1)(c) and (2)(c) Dir.).

All assets and liabilities of the company that ceases to exist will be transferred by operation of law to the acquiring or newly formed company (Art. 14(1)(a) and (2)(a) Dir.) upon the entry into force of the cross-border merger (see no 34 of this chapter). If national law requires the completion of specific formalities before the transfer of certain assets, rights and obligations can take effect against third parties, the company resulting from the merger must complete these formalities (Art. 14(3) Dir.).

All rights and obligations of the merging companies arising from contracts of employment or from employment relationships existing on the effective date of the merger shall be transferred to the company resulting from the merger on that date (Art. 14(4) Dir.).

The shareholders of the merging companies shall become shareholders of the company resulting from the merger (Art. 14(1)(b) and (2)(b) Dir.) and shall receive shares in the surviving or newly formed company. However, no shares shall be exchanged for shares in the merging companies which ceased to exist held by the acquiring company itself or by the company being acquired and ceasing to exist. The same applies to persons acting in their own name but on behalf of a merging company (Art. 14(5) Dir.). This rule does not apply to shares in the acquiring company held by a merging company, which shall be transferred to the acquiring company, in which case the rules on acquisition of own shares will apply.[30]

VI   Merger procedure

1   General remarks

18.   The merger procedure shall be governed by the national law of the Member States where the merging companies have their registered or head offices, unless the Cross-border Merger Directive provides otherwise (Art. 4 Dir.). The national rules applicable to mergers between limited liability companies

---

30 These rules are an implementation of Art. 22 of the Second Company Law Directive of 13 December 1976 (*Official Journal* L 26 of 31 January 1977).

have been harmonised, to a great extent, due to transposition of the Domestic Merger Directive.

2   Common draft terms of cross-border merger

19.   The management or administrative organ of each participating company must prepare common draft terms of cross-border merger (Art. 5 Dir.). This is a single document prepared jointly by all companies involved in the merger.[31] It must include at least the following information:

    (i)   the corporate form, name and registered office of each merging company and of the company resulting from the merger and, where applicable, information on the proposed place of administration or the principal place of business of the latter company;[32]

    (ii) the ratio for the exchange of securities and shares representing capital and the amount of any cash payment; the reference to securities and shares should be interpreted to refer to both types of instruments representing capital (see no 8 of this chapter);

    (iii) the terms for the allocation of securities or shares representing the capital of the company resulting from the merger;

    (iv) the likely repercussions of the merger on employment;

    (v) the date as from which the holders of such securities or shares representing capital will be entitled to share in the profits and any special conditions affecting this entitlement;

    (vi) the date as from which the transactions of the merging companies shall be treated for accounting purposes as those of the company resulting from the cross-border merger;

   (vii) the rights conferred by the company resulting from the merger on shareholders enjoying special rights or on the holders of securities other than shares representing capital or the measures proposed concerning them;

  (viii) any special advantages granted to the experts who examine the draft terms of the cross-border merger or to members of the administrative, management, supervisory or controlling organs of the merging companies;

    (ix) the (draft) articles of association ('statutes') of the company resulting from the merger or, in the event of a merger by absorption, the amended articles;

    (x) where appropriate, information on the procedures by which arrangements for the involvement of employees in defining their rights to participate in the company resulting from the merger shall be determined pursuant to Article 16 of the Cross-border Merger Directive (see nos 41 and 42 of this chapter);

31 *Ibid.*, fourth recital.
32 *Ibid.*, eleventh recital.

(xi) information on the valuation of the assets and liabilities transferred to the company resulting from the merger; and

(xii) the (closing) dates of the merging companies' accounts used to establish the conditions of the cross-border merger; these need not be the annual accounts and can be interim accounts.

The merging companies are entitled to include additional information in the common draft terms of cross-border merger.[33]

20. The common draft terms of cross-border merger must be rendered public in the manner specified by the provisions of national law implementing the First Company Law Directive (Art. 6(1) Dir.). In accordance with this directive, publication must be accomplished by filing the terms with the appropriate commercial or companies register and by publication in the official gazette of the Member State in question of the terms in full or by extract or of a mention that they are available at the register. The publication in the official gazette may be replaced with equally effective means, which shall entail at least the use of a system whereby the information disclosed can be accessed in chronological order through a central electronic platform.[34] Each merging company shall ensure publication in its Member State, i.e. the state where that company is situated and to whose law it is subject. Interested third parties should be able to consult the register and obtain a copy of the common draft terms of cross-border merger in return for the payment of a fee.

The common draft terms of cross-border merger must be rendered public in the manner described above no later than one month before the date of the general meeting scheduled to vote on the merger (Art. 6(1) Dir.). National law or the articles of association of the merging companies, within the limits of national law, can provide for a longer period. In this case, however, any such longer period will only apply to the merging company governed by that country's law. However, the other companies will be required to prepare their draft terms of merger sufficiently far in advance in order to allow each company to publish them in accordance with its national law.

At least the following information must be published in the official gazettes of the Member States concerned: (i) the corporate form, name and registered office of each merging company; (ii) the register in which documents relating to the merging companies are filed in accordance with the provisions of national law implementing the First Company Law Directive and the entry number in that register for each merging company; and (iii) an indication, for each merging company, of the arrangements made to allow creditors and minority shareholders to exercise their rights and the address at which complete information on these arrangements may be obtained free of charge (Art. 6(2) Dir.). This information must be published in the official gazette together with the draft

---

33 *Ibid.*, fourth recital.
34 Art. 3 First Company Law Directive.

terms of cross-border merger (in full or an extract therefrom) or a mention of the fact that the draft terms may be consulted at the national register.

The Member States may specify additional information that must be included in the publication in the official gazette (Art. 6(2) Dir.). Any such additional information need only be published in the official gazette of that Member State.

Publication is intended to protect the interests of both the shareholders of the merging companies and third parties.[35]

3   Management report

21.   The management or administrative organ of each merging company shall prepare a report for the shareholders of that company explaining and justifying the legal and economic aspects of the cross-border merger and the implications of the merger for shareholders, creditors and employees (Art. 7 Dir.).

The report shall be made available to shareholders and the employee representatives or, in the absence thereof, the employees directly no later than one month before the date of the general meeting scheduled to approve the merger.

In the event the employee representatives issue an opinion in accordance with national law, this opinion must be appended to the report.

The management report on the merger shall be made available to the shareholders of each merging company before the date of the general meeting scheduled to vote on the merger (see nos 25 and 26 of this chapter).

4   Report of the independent expert(s)

22.   The draft terms of cross-border merger must be examined by an independent expert(s).[36] The expert(s) shall prepare a written report for the merging companies' shareholders.

The report should state whether, in the experts' opinion, the share-exchange ratio is fair and reasonable, indicating the method(s) used to arrive at the proposed share-exchange ratio; whether these method(s) are adequate; the value reached using each method; and an opinion on the relative importance attributed to these methods in arriving at the value decided on. The report must furthermore describe any special valuation difficulties which may have arisen.[37]

The shareholders of the merging companies can waive their right to an expert's examination and report. Furthermore, no report will be required if the shareholders of all merging companies agree that a report need not be prepared

---

35 Fifth recital to the Cross-border Merger Directive.
36 With respect to the simplified mergers see nos 39 and 40 of this chapter.
37 Art. 8(3) of the Cross-border Merger Directive refers to Art. 10(2) of the Domestic Merger Directive.

(Art. 8(4) Dir.). The waiver should be in writing, signed by all shareholders and must be produced at the general meetings of the respective merging companies in order to be confirmed in the minutes.

23.   The experts shall be appointed or approved by a judicial or administrative authority in the Member States of the relevant merging companies.[38] Although they are considered to act on behalf of the merging company and are therefore paid by it, the experts should be independent of this company and of all other merging companies (Art. 8(1) Dir.). The degree of independence can be defined by national law.

In general, one or more independent expert(s) should be appointed for each merging company further to a request of management (unless that company's articles of association or national law provide otherwise). Alternatively, if jointly requested by the merging companies, one or more expert(s) can be appointed to act on behalf of all companies involved and to prepare a single report on the cross-border merger (Art. 8(2) Dir.). This will help to contain the costs of the expert's investigation and opinion.[39]

The experts may be natural persons or legal entities, unless national law provides otherwise (Art. 8(1) Dir.). Any special advantages granted the experts must be defined in the draft terms of merger (Art. 5(h) Dir.), including their remuneration and any other financial advantages.

24.   The experts are entitled to request any information from each merging company they consider necessary to perform their tasks (Art. 8(3) Dir.). This means that if each merging company has appointed its own expert, the latter can request information not only from the company responsible for the appointment but also from the other companies involved. Such information includes copies of documents and access to books of account and other relevant documents of the merging companies.[40] The experts are entitled to examine, amongst other things, the report on the cross-border merger prepared by the management of each merging company.

25.   The experts' reports shall be made available to the shareholders of each merging company no later than one month before the date of the general meeting scheduled to vote on the merger (Art. 8(1) Dir.).

5   Shareholder approval

26.   In general, a cross-border merger must be approved by the general meeting of each merging company; the general meeting approves at such time the terms of cross-border merger (Art. 9(1) Dir.). Majority and quorum requirements are determined in accordance with national law. Under the Domestic Merger

---

38 Art. 10(1) Domestic Merger Directive.
39 Sixth recital to the Cross-border Merger Directive.
40 Art. 10(3) Domestic Merger Directive.

Directive (Art. 7) a majority of not less than two thirds of the votes attaching to the shares represented is required. Member States may provide that a simple majority is sufficient if at least half of the subscribed capital is represented. Moreover, the rules governing amendments to the articles shall apply. The general meeting is held at least one month (national law may provide for a longer period) after publication of the draft terms of cross-border merger (see no 20 of this chapter).

In the event of a merger by absorption, national law may provide that the approval of the general meeting of the acquiring company is not required if the following conditions are met: (i) the draft terms of cross-border merger are published in the Member State of the acquiring company at least one month before the general meetings of the companies to be absorbed; (ii) all shareholders of the acquiring company are entitled to inspect the corporate documents mentioned in no 27 of this chapter no later than the date mentioned in (i); and (iii) one or more shareholders holding a minimum percentage of the acquiring company are entitled to request that a general meeting be called to approve the merger. The minimum percentage is defined by national law, but may not be higher than 5 per cent. National law may exclude non-voting shares from this calculation (Art. 9(3) Dir.).

The general meeting of each merging company can resolve to make implementation of the cross-border merger contingent on its express ratification of the arrangements with respect to the participation of employees in the company resulting from the merger (Art. 9(2) Dir.). In this case, the arrangement on employee participation must be presented to the general meeting prior to final approval of the merger (see no 42 of this chapter).

27. The management and experts' reports must be made available to all shareholders before the general meeting scheduled to vote on the merger (Art. 9(1) Dir.).

The shareholders of each merging company are entitled to inspect these reports at its registered office at least one month before the date of the general meeting scheduled to vote on the draft terms of cross-border merger.[41] All reports of each merging company must be made available at its registered office.

Along with the above reports, the following information must be made available for inspection at each merging company's registered office: (i) the draft terms of cross-border merger; (ii) the annual accounts and management reports of the merging companies for the last three financial years; and (iii) an accounting statement prepared no earlier than the first day of the third month preceding the date of the draft terms of merger, if the latest annual accounts relate to a financial year that ended more than six months before that date.[42] The accounting statement must be prepared using the same methods and layout

41 Ibid., Art. 11(1).
42 *Ibid.*

17

as the last annual balance sheet. National law may provide, however, that this statement can be prepared without having to take a fresh physical inventory. Furthermore, national law may also provide that the valuation shown on the last balance sheet need only be altered to reflect entries in the books of account, provided interim depreciation and reserves as well as material changes in actual value not shown in the books are taken into account.[43]

Each shareholder is entitled to obtain copies upon request and free of charge of the documents made available at the company's registered office. Shareholders can also request copies in full or in part of these documents.[44]

6   Protection of minority shareholders

28.   The protection of shareholders in a cross-border merger is governed by national law (Art. 4(2) Dir.). The applicable provisions of the law of the Member State where the merging company is situated will apply. National law may contain special provisions designed to ensure *appropriate* protection of minority shareholders who have opposed the merger (Art. 4(2) *in fine* Dir.), including a right for such shareholders to claim reimbursement of their shares on the conditions defined by law and in the company's articles of association or to have recourse to the courts to challenge the share-exchange ratio or to obtain compensation for the loss of a right or value (see no 30 of this chapter for the consequences of such legal proceedings for the merger procedure).

Together with the draft terms of merger, any arrangements provided for the exercise of the rights of minority shareholders as well as the address where complete information on these arrangements may be obtained free of charge must be published in the national gazettes of the relevant Member States (Art. 6(2)(c) Dir.).

7   Pre-merger certificate and scrutiny of the legality of a cross-border merger

29.   The legality of a cross-border merger will first be scrutinised before the merger takes effect by a court, notary or other authority designated by the Member States concerned (Art. 10 Dir.).

The merger procedure will be scrutinised in each Member State concerned with respect to that portion of the merger which is subject to the laws of that state (Art. 10(1) Dir.). The authority designated to supervise cross-border mergers in each Member State will issue to each merging company subject to this state's national law a certificate conclusively attesting to proper completion of the requisite pre-merger acts and formalities (the 'pre-merger certificate'). This authority is bound to issue the pre-merger certificate without delay (Art. 10(2) Dir.). The pre-merger certificate is valid for a period of six months (see no 31 *in fine* of this chapter).

---

43 *Ibid.*, Art. 11(2).
44 *Ibid.*, Art. 11(3).

30.   In the event the law of a Member State of one of the merging companies provides for a procedure to scrutinise and amend the share-exchange ratio or to compensate minority shareholders, without preventing registration of the cross-border merger, this procedure will only apply to such merging company if the general meetings of the other participating companies, when approving the draft terms of merger, expressly agree to allow the shareholders of that merging company to have recourse to this procedure. In this case, the procedure must be initiated before the court with jurisdiction over the merging company whose shareholders are entitled to initiate this procedure (Art. 10(3) Dir.).

The decision to permit shareholders to have recourse to the above procedure(s) must be taken by the general meeting.[45] The majority required in this respect shall be defined by national law.

If national law allows shareholders to have recourse to the above-mentioned procedures or the general meeting has resolved to allow shareholders to have recourse thereto, the authority responsible for scrutinising the merger may issue the pre-merger certificate even if the procedure has commenced. In this case, the pre-merger certificate must mention that a procedure is ongoing. The procedure must be sufficiently described in the certificate to allow third parties to identify the procedure and the country in which it has been initiated. The decision ultimately taken in the procedure will be binding on the company resulting from the merger and on all its shareholders (Art. 10(3) Dir.).

31.   The legality of completion of the cross-border merger will in addition be scrutinised by the court, notary or competent authority designated by the Member State whose law governs the company resulting from the merger. Such scrutiny should cover the completion of the merger and, if a new company is formed, the formation of that company. In particular, the competent authority must verify whether the merging companies have approved the common draft terms of merger on the same terms and, where appropriate or applicable, that arrangements for employee participation have been determined in accordance with Article 16 of the Cross-border Merger Directive (Art. 11(1) Dir.) (see no 42 of this chapter).

Each merging company must submit its pre-merger certificate to the court, notary or competent authority of the Member State in which the surviving company is situated within six months of its issuance together with a copy of the draft terms of cross-border merger as approved by the general meetings of the merging companies (Art. 11(2) Dir.). The surviving company need not issue a pre-merger certificate, as its decision is part of the completion process monitored by the court, notary or authority designated to supervise completion of the merger, unless the general meeting of the surviving company is held before the completion of the cross-border merger is enacted.

---

45 Art. 10(3) of the Directive refers to Art. 9(1), not to Art. 9(3), thereof.

8   No prospectus obligation

32.   If the shares of a merging company are held by a large number of persons, this company must contact its shareholders (and the holders of other securities) through public means in order to ask them to approve the merger and to offer to exchange their shares for shares in the company resulting from the merger. This contact could qualify as a public offering within the meaning of Directive 2003/71 of 4 November 2003 on the prospectus to be published when securities are offered to the public or admitted to trading (the 'Prospectus Directive').[46] According to the Prospectus Directive, the offering of securities to 100 persons or more who are not qualified investors in any given Member State constitutes a public offering for which a prospectus, approved by the competent authority, must be published.

The Prospectus Directive, however, expressly exempts mergers carried out in accordance with the Cross-border Merger Directive and the Domestic Merger Directive from the prospectus obligation, provided a document is made available containing information which the competent authorities consider equivalent to that set forth in the prospectus required under the Prospectus Directive, taking into account the requirements of Community law, in particular the applicable directive (Art. 4(1)(c) of the Prospectus Directive). The same applies in the event the shares of the surviving company are admitted to trading on a regulated market simultaneously with the merger process (Art. 4(2)(d) Prospectus Directive).

The competent authority of each Member State where securities are offered to 100 persons or more (who are not qualified investors) will decide whether the information contained in the draft terms of cross-border merger is equivalent to the information required for the offering of these securities under the Prospectus Directive. If this is not the case, a prospectus must be prepared for that Member State in accordance with the provisions of national law implementing the Prospectus Directive (see no 33 of this chapter). The merging companies must put a question to the supervisory authorities of the relevant Member States in this respect.[47] In order to determine whether information is 'equivalent', the content of the offer document is compared to the information

---

46 *Official Journal* L 345 of 31 December 2003. For a discussion of the Prospectus Directive, see D. Van Gerven, 'General Provisions of Community Law Relating to the Prospectus to be Published when Securities are Offered to the Public or Admitted to Trading' in *Prospectus for the Public Offering of Securities in Europe*, D. Van Gerven (ed.), Cambridge University Press, vol. I, 2008, 3.

47 This is also the opinion of the informal task force of representatives of the supervisory authorities organised by the Commission (Summary record of the third Informal Meeting of 26 January 2005, 6). During this meeting the Commission stated that it has no immediate plans to adopt implementing measures with respect to the meaning of 'equivalence' in this provision of the Prospectus Directive.

required by the Prospectus Regulation.[48] There is no obligation to provide all the information required for a prospectus.[49]

An equivalence opinion issued by the supervisory authority of one Member State does not imply a passport in this respect. Consequently, the competent authorities in other Member States need not accept this opinion and are entitled to verify independently whether the information contained in the draft terms of merger is equivalent.[50] The supervisory authorities of the Member States concerned must, however, consult one another with a view to ensuring a common position on the issue of equivalence (Art. 4(4) Prospectus Directive).

33.   If the competent authority within the meaning of the Prospectus Directive reaches the opinion that the draft terms of merger do not contain equivalent information to that required by the Prospectus Directive, a prospectus will be required. In this case, the prospectus must be approved by the competent authority determined in accordance with the rules contained in the Prospectus Directive (see below), before the shareholders are called to vote on the merger and the prospectus is made public (Art. 3 Prospectus Directive).

In general, the authority competent to approve a prospectus is that of the Member State where the issuer's registered office is located, i.e. the state where the registered office of the company resulting from the merger is located (Art. 2(1)(h) Prospectus Directive).

Of course, it is possible to propose completing the draft terms of merger with the necessary information in order to avoid the need for a prospectus. This could be the best solution to avoid having to prepare, approve and publish a prospectus.

9   Entry into force, registration and publication

34.   A cross-border merger enters into effect on the date determined by the national law of the Member State to whose law the company resulting from the merger is subject.[51] In any case, this date cannot precede scrutiny of the legality of the cross-border merger (Art. 12 Dir.) (see no 31 of this chapter). The effects

---

48 Regulation 809/2004 of 29 April 2004 implementing the Prospectus Directive as regards information contained in prospectuses as well as the format, incorporation by reference and publication of such prospectuses and the dissemination of advertisements.

49 Summary record of the third Informal Meeting on the Transposition of the Prospectus Directive (26 January 2005) of the informal task force of representatives of the supervisory authorities organised by the Commission (available at http://europa.eu.int/comm/internal_market).

50 This has also been confirmed by the informal task force of representatives of the supervisory authorities organised by the Commission (see previous footnote).

51 The Domestic Merger Directive states that the Member States can provide in their national law when a merger in accordance with this directive shall take effect (Art. 17).

of the entry into force of a cross-border merger are discussed in nos 16 and 17 of this chapter. These effects are considered to have taken place on the date of dissolution of the merged companies.

In the event an arrangement on employee participation must be entered into which is different from the rules on employee participation applicable in the Member State to whose law the company resulting from the merger is subject, the merger can only be registered and take effect once such an arrangement has been concluded (see no 42 of this chapter).

Cross-border mergers in accordance with the Cross-border Merger Directive must, like any other form of concentration, meet the requirements of Community and national law on the control of concentrations between undertakings.[52]

A merger cannot be carried out if a competent national authority has opposed it and this opposition has not been retracted or revoked (see no 15 of this chapter).

35.   The completion of a cross-border merger is published in the Member States of the merging companies in accordance with the national rules implementing the First Company Law Directive of 9 March 1968. To this effect, a notice of completion shall be filed with the public register in which each merging company is required to file documents (Art. 13 Dir.).

Furthermore, a notice of completion shall be published in the official gazette of each Member State concerned in accordance with national law.[53] This requirement applies both to the companies that will disappear as a result of the merger and to the surviving company.

The public register with which the company resulting from the merger is required to file its corporate documents and information (in accordance with the provisions of national law implementing the First Company Law Directive) must notify, without delay, the public register with which each of the other companies is required to file a notice of completion that the cross-border merger has taken effect (Art. 13 Dir.). This notification should include the date of entry into effect of the merger.

The disappearing companies' registrations will be deleted only upon receipt of the above-mentioned notification from the surviving company's register (Art. 13 Dir.).

36.   The information regarding the company resulting from the merger which must be filed with the public register and published in the official gazette of the Member State where this company is situated shall be determined by the national law of that Member State.

37.   The information published is enforceable against third parties in accordance with the provisions of national law implementing the First Company Law

---

52 Ninth recital to the Cross-border Merger Directive; see also no 15 of this chapter.
53 Art. 3(4) First Company Law Directive.

Directive. Consequently, the cross-border merger will be enforceable against third parties after publication of the notice of completion.[54] The only exception to this rule is where it can be established that the third party in question had prior knowledge of the published information.[55]

Following publication, there is a transition period of fifteen days, during which time third parties can attempt to prove that they could not have known of the publication. If they can do so, the published information cannot be enforced against them.[56]

In general, third parties may rely on documents which must be published, even if they have yet to be published. However, to the extent that, in accordance with national law (see no 34 of this chapter), publication is required for a cross-border merger to take effect – which will normally be the case – they cannot rely on the notice of completion of the merger prior to the publication thereof.[57]

10   No avoidance of the merger

38.   As from the time a cross-border merger enters into effect, on the date defined by national law, it can no longer be declared null and void (Art. 17 Dir.). This rule is intended to ensure legal certainty.[58]

In the event of violation of the applicable provisions or formalities relating to a merger, the court before which the case is brought cannot avoid the merger. It can only award damages to the injured parties. The latter can in turn claim damages from the notary or authority that scrutinised the acts and decisions leading to the merger and failed to notice the violation in accordance with applicable national law.

This prohibition on avoiding a cross-border merger is the main difference with the rules applicable to internal mergers. With respect to the latter, national law can allow a domestic merger which has already taken effect to be declared null and void if the required judicial or administrative supervision of the legality of the merger was not properly performed or if the merger documents were not drawn up and certified in due legal form or if the general meeting's decision is void or voidable under national law.[59]

VII   Simplified merger procedures

1   Merger with a wholly owned subsidiary or subsidiaries

39.   In the event of a cross-border merger by acquisition by a company that holds all the shares and other securities entitled to vote at general meetings of the

---

54 *Ibid.*, Art. 3(5).
55 *Ibid.*
56 *Ibid.*
57 *Ibid.*, Art. 3(7).
58 Eighth recital to the Cross-border Merger Directive.
59 Art. 22 Domestic Merger Directive.

company or companies being acquired, the merger can be carried out by means of a simplified procedure (Art. 15(1) Dir.). In this case, a number of formalities designed to protect minority shareholders will not be applicable, since all shares and other voting securities are held by the (acquiring) parent company. Furthermore, when acquiring a wholly owned subsidiary, the parent company may not issue new shares in exchange for the transfer of all the subsidiary's assets and liabilities.

The common draft terms of cross-border merger must be prepared and rendered public in order to inform interested third parties, such as creditors. However, these draft terms need not include (i) the ratio applicable to the exchange of shares or securities representing capital and the amount of any cash payment; (ii) the terms for the allocation of shares or securities representing capital in the company resulting from the merger; or (iii) the date from which the holding of such securities or shares representing capital will entitle the holders to share in the profits and any special conditions affecting that entitlement. All other information described in no 18 of this chapter must be included.

An independent expert's report is not required. A management report on the merger will suffice. Furthermore, the general meeting of the subsidiary or subsidiaries being absorbed need not be convened to approve the merger.

The other formalities and rules applicable to a cross-border merger discussed in this chapter shall apply. The cross-border merger will enter into effect in accordance with national law.

2   Merger with a 90 per cent subsidiary

40. In the event of a cross-border merger by acquisition by a company that holds 90 per cent or more (but not all) of the shares and other voting securities in the acquiring company or companies, the report(s) of the independent expert(s) and the documents necessary for scrutiny of the merger shall be required only to the extent the national law of one Member State governing the merging companies so requires (Art. 15(2) Dir.). The term 'scrutiny' is not defined but is taken to refer to the scrutiny which national law may require for a merger with a 90 per cent subsidiary. Such scrutiny does not include the pre-merger certificate or completion of the cross-border merger in accordance with the Cross-border Merger Directive (see no 31 of this chapter). The rules of the Cross-border Merger Directive remain fully applicable, and national law cannot derogate from the scrutiny required by this directive.

Approval of the cross-border merger by the general meeting of shareholders of the subsidiary or subsidiaries is required.

VIII   Employee participation

41. In general, the company resulting from the cross-border merger will be subject to the rules of employee participation, if any, in the Member State where its

registered office is located (Art. 16(1) Dir.).[60] Employee participation implies participation in the decision-making process of corporate bodies of the relevant company[61] and is defined as a system permitting the 'influence of the body representative of the employees and/or the employees' representatives in the affairs of the company by way of the right to elect or appoint some of the members of the company's supervisory or administrative organ, or the right to recommend and/or oppose the appointment of some or all of the members of the company's supervisory or administrative organ'.[62]

42.   In the event that the national law of the Member State where the company resulting from the merger has its registered office does not provide for employee participation, the employees will not be entitled to participate in the management of the company, unless the rules of this Member State are set aside in accordance with the principles explained below.[63]

Even if the national law of the Member State where the company resulting from the merger has its registered office provides for employee participation, the rules on employee participation of this Member State will be set aside when at least one of the merging companies has employed, in the six months leading up to publication of the common draft terms of cross-border merger in the official gazette of the Member State concerned, more than 500 employees on average and provides for a system of employee participation (as defined above).

These rules will also be set aside if they do not provide for (i) at least the same level of employee participation as in the relevant merging companies, or (ii) an entitlement for employees of establishments of the company resulting from the merger situated in different Member States to exercise the same participation rights as employees employed in the Member State where the company resulting from the merger has its registered office (Art. 16(2) Dir.).

In these cases, employee participation will be regulated by the Member States largely in accordance with the principles and procedures set down in

---

60 It should be noted that reference is made to the law of the state where the company has its registered office and not to the state where the company's principal place of business is located.
61 See the thirteenth recital to the Directive.
62 Art. 16(2) of the Directive refers to Art. 2(k) of Council Directive 2001/86 of 8 October 2001 supplementing the Statute for a European company with regard to the involvement of employees (*Official Journal* L 294 of 10 November 2001).
63 It could also be deduced from a reading of Art. 16(1) in conjunction with the beginning of Art. 16(2): 'However, the rules in force concerning employee participation, if any, in the Member State where the company resulting from the cross-border merger has its registered office shall not apply', combined with the discussion of the proposal in the European Parliament (see p. 28 of the Report of the European Parliament of 25 April 2005 (A6-0089/2005) final), that in the event that the national law of the Member State where the company resulting from the merger has its registered office does not provide for employee participation, the employees will not be entitled to participate in the management of the company, regardless of whether employee participation existed in any merging company that ceased to exist due to the merger. But this

Directive 2001/86 of 8 October 2001 supplementing the Statute for a European company with regard to the involvement of employees (the 'SE Directive'). This issue is discussed in Chapter 2 of this book.

The merging companies must initiate negotiations with the employee representatives to reach an agreement on employee participation. If they fail to do so, the standard rules for participation contained in Part 3 of the Annex to the SE Directive shall apply. The merging companies can also decide to apply immediately the standard rules for participation without initiating negotiations. The special negotiating body has the right to decide, by a qualified majority, not to open negotiations or to terminate negotiations already started and to rely on the rules on participation in force in the Member State where the registered office of the surviving company will be situated. The procedure is discussed in Chapter 2 of this book. However, as long as an agreement on employee participation has not been reached or a decision taken to apply the standard rules, the completion of the merger cannot be registered.[64]

43.   The articles of association of the company resulting from the merger may not contain provisions that conflict with the arrangement for employee participation. In the event of a new arrangement or modifications thereto, the articles must be amended to reflect the new or modified arrangement. National law may provide that the board of directors or the equivalent management organ is entitled to proceed with the required amendments to the articles of association without having to call a general meeting of shareholders.[65]

44.   If one of the merging companies provides for an employee participation system and, as a result of the above rules, the company resulting from the merger shall be governed by that system, it must take a legal form that allows the exercise of employee participation rights (Art. 16(6) Dir.).

Furthermore, if the company resulting from the merger has an employee participation system it must take measures to ensure that the employees' participation rights are protected in the event of subsequent domestic mergers for a period of at least three years after the cross-border merger takes effect. To this end, it shall provide that the above rules of the Cross-border Merger Directive will apply *mutatis mutandis* to protect these rights (Art. 16(7) Dir.).

IX   Protection of creditors, debenture holders and the holders of non-equity securities

45.   The protection of creditors and debenture holders in a cross-border merger is governed by national law (Art. 4(2) Dir.). This means that the relevant

interpretation contradicts the Community legislature's intent, as described in the Explanatory Memorandum to the first proposal for the Directive (see no 2 of this chapter).
64 In this regard, Art. 16(3) of the Directive refers to Art. 12 of the SE Regulation.
65 In this regard, Art. 16(3) of the Directive refers to Art. 12(4) of the SE Regulation.

provisions of the law of the Member State where the merging company is situated will apply.

Further to transposition of the Domestic Merger Directive, the Member States should, at least for mergers of public limited liability companies, ensure adequate protection of the interests of the creditors of merging companies whose claims arose prior to publication of the draft terms of merger and which are not due at the time of publication. These creditors shall be entitled to adequate safeguards if the financial situation of the merging companies renders such protection necessary and if they do not already benefit from such safeguards. The protection of creditors of the company resulting from the merger may differ from the protection offered to creditors of the absorbed companies.[66] These rules will also apply to debenture holders unless the merger has been approved by the general meeting of debenture holders, if such a meeting is provided for by applicable national law, or by each individual debenture holder.[67]

Holders of securities which are not shares and which carry special rights must be given rights in the surviving company which are at least equivalent to those they held in the absorbed company, unless the change in their rights has been approved by a meeting of these holders, if provided for by national law, or, in the absence of such a provision, by each individual holder of such securities, or unless these holders are entitled to have their securities redeemed by the company resulting from the merger.[68]

46.   Together with the draft terms of merger, any arrangements provided for the exercise of the rights of creditors and the address where complete information on these arrangements may be obtained free of charge must be published in the official gazettes of the relevant Member States (Art. 6(2)(c) Dir.). The rights conferred on debenture holders or measures proposed concerning them shall be defined in the draft terms of merger (Art. 5(g) Dir.).

X   Conclusion

47.   The Cross-border Merger Directive is undoubtedly an important step towards a common market in which national law will not be able to prevent companies from moving from one state to another as they do business. There is indeed no reason not to allow cross-border mergers when a purely domestic merger is possible. This principle is already laid down in Article 293 of the EC Treaty, which provides that the Member States shall enter into negotiations in order to secure for their nationals the possibility of mergers between companies and firms governed by the laws of different Member States. The Cross-border Merger Directive makes this possibility a reality.

66 Art. 13 Domestic Merger Directive.
67 *Ibid.*, Art. 14.
68 *Ibid.*, Art. 15.

However, the possibility offered by the Cross-border Merger Directive to engage in cross-border mergers will remain largely elusive as long as the national tax laws have not been adapted to permit such mergers without the merging companies being taxed on their liquidation proceeds. Directive 90/434/EEC of 23 July 1990 on the common system of taxation applicable to mergers (as amended by Directive 2005/19/EC of 17 February 2005) requires tax neutrality in the event of a cross-border merger. This directive, however, has yet to be transposed into national law by all Member States. The tax implications of a cross-border merger are discussed further in Chapter 3 of this book.

48.   The European Commission will review application of the Cross-border Merger Directive by 15 December 2012 and, if necessary, propose amendments thereto (Art. 18 Dir.).

2

Employee participation: rights and obligations

PHILIPPE FRANÇOIS AND JULIEN HICK
NautaDutilh

I   Introduction

1.   Further to the creation of the European company (SE) and the European cooperative society (SCE), the Community legislature, as part of its efforts to unify European corporate law and allow the existence of transnational corporate entities, adopted a directive on 26 October 2005 setting out the

principles governing cross-border mergers within the European Union[1] (the 'Directive').

As with the SE Directive[2] and the SCE Directive,[3] the Community legislature bore in mind the issue of employee involvement, which is regulated by Article 16 of the Directive. However, whilst both the SE and SCE Directives regulate the involvement of employees in general (i.e. information and consultation procedures, creation of a representative body and participation), Article 16 of the Directive only governs employee participation. All other aspects of employee involvement shall continue to be regulated by the relevant provisions of national law.[4]

The Community legislature used the before-and-after principle as its starting point: insofar as possible, existing participation rights should be maintained within the company resulting from a cross-border merger.[5]

This chapter examines the Directive's provisions on employee participation. Firstly, the geographic scope and entry into force of the Directive are clarified, followed by the substantive scope of Article 16 of the Directive. We then turn to the provisions determining participation rules in the framework of a cross-border merger and the procedure to determine participation rights. Finally, we examine a few issues related to compliance with Article 16 of the Directive, reservation and confidentiality and the protection of employee representatives.

II   Geographic scope and entry into force

2.   The Directive entered into force on 15 December 2005[6] (Art. 20 Dir.).

With respect to the geographic scope of the Directive, it should be noted that the Community legislation on cross-border mergers is applicable in the twenty-seven Member States of the European Union as well as in the member countries of the European Economic Area (EEA).[7]

---

1 Directive 2005/56/EC of the European Parliament and of the Council of 26 October 2005 on cross-border mergers of limited liability companies, *Official Journal* L 310 of 25 November 2005.

2 Council Directive 2001/86/EC of 8 October 2001 supplementing the Statute for a European company with regard to the involvement of employees, *Official Journal* L 294 of 10 November 2001 ('SE Directive').

3 Council Directive 2003/72/EC of 22 July 2003 supplementing the Statute for a European Cooperative Society with regard to the involvement of employees, *Official Journal* L 207 of 18 August 2003 ('SCE Directive').

4 Twelfth recital to the Directive.

5 Thirteenth recital to the Directive; see also M. Evrard and E. van der Vaeren, 'Les fusions transfrontalières: un pas de plus vers une Europe harmonisée', *DAOR*, 2007, p. 118.

6 That is, the twentieth day following its publication in the *Official Journal*.

7 Further to the EEA Joint Committee Decision of 22 September 2006, amending Annex XXII (Company Law) to the EEA Agreement (*Official Journal* L 333 of 30 November 2006).

III   Substantive scope of Article 16 of the Directive

3.   As indicated above, Article 16 of the Directive only concerns employee participation within the company resulting from a cross-border merger. In other words, neither Article 16 nor any other provision of the Directive is aimed at regulating any other aspects of employee involvement in the company resulting from the cross-border merger, such as information and consultation rights. These issues shall continue to be governed by existing provisions of national law.[8]

   As for the system put in place, it should be noted that Article 16 of the Directive mainly refers to the SE Directive and the SE Regulation.[9]

IV   Determination of the applicable participation rules in the event of a cross-border merger

4.   In principle, the company resulting from a cross-border merger shall be subject to the rules in force concerning employee participation, if any, in the Member State where its registered office is located (Art. 16(1) Dir.). Consequently, if the Member State where the company resulting from the cross-border merger will have its registered office does not provide for employee participation rules, no such rules will in principle apply to the company.

5.   This rule is tempered, however, in three situations (Art. 16(2) Dir). In these cases, the rules in force concerning employee participation, if any, in the Member State where the company resulting from the cross-border merger has its registered office, shall be set aside and the procedure described in part V of this chapter shall apply (Art. 16(3) Dir.).

   These three situations are the following:

   (i)   At least one of the merging companies has, in the six-month period prior to publication of the draft terms of cross-border merger,[10] employed on average more than 500 employees and is operating under an employee

---

8 It should be noted that most of these provisions of national law in fact implement other Community Directives. In this respect, the twelfth recital to the Directive states that '[e]mployees' rights other than rights of participation should remain subject to the national provisions referred to in Council Directive 98/59/EC of 20 July 1998 on collective redundancies, Council Directive 2001/23/EC of 12 March 2001 on the safeguarding of employees' rights in the event of transfers of undertakings, businesses or parts of undertakings or businesses, Directive 2002/14/EC of the European Parliament and of the Council of 11 March 2002 establishing a general framework for informing and consulting employees in the European Community and Council Directive 94/45/EC of 22 September 1994 on the establishment of a European Works Council or a procedure in Community-scale undertakings and Community-scale groups of undertakings for the purposes of informing and consulting employees'.

9 Council Regulation (EC) No 2157/2001 of 8 October 2001 on the Statute for a European company (SE), *Official Journal* L 294 of 10 November 2001 ('SE Regulation').

10 As referred to in Art. 6 of the Directive.

participation system, within the meaning of Article 2(k) of the SE Directive, i.e. a system whereby the body representative of employees and/or the employee representatives are granted influence over the company's affairs by way of the right to elect or appoint certain members of the company's supervisory or administrative organs or the right to recommend and/or oppose the appointment of some members of these organs.

(ii)   The national law applicable to the company resulting from the cross-border merger does not provide for at least the same level of employee participation as operated in the relevant merging companies. The level of employee participation is measured with reference to the proportion of employee representatives on the administrative or supervisory organs or their committees or within the management group covering the company's profit units. This situation thus implies that the existing employee participation systems provide for employee representation within the above-mentioned organs or groups.

(iii)   The national law applicable to the company resulting from the cross-border merger does not provide for employees or establishments situated in other Member States the same entitlement to exercise participation rights as enjoyed by employees employed in the Member State where the company resulting from the cross-border merger will have its registered office.

As indicated above, in these three situations, the rules in force concerning employee participation, if any, in the Member State where the company resulting from the cross-border merger will have its registered office will not apply. In that case, employee participation in the company resulting from the cross-border merger must be determined further to a particular procedure, as described in part V of this chapter.

V   Procedure to determine employee participation rights

6.   This section discusses the procedure to determine employee participation rights in the event that the national rules on employee participation, if any, of the Member State where the company resulting from the cross-border merger shall have its registered office, are set aside. This procedure is thus only applicable in the three scenarios described above.[11]

This procedure is addressed by Article 16 of the Directive, which refers to various provisions of the SE Directive and the SE Regulation, which shall apply *mutatis mutandis* in the case of a cross-border merger (Art. 16(3) Dir.). In other words, the Directive does not create an *ad hoc* procedure in the framework of a cross-border merger but rather refers to an existing system, created for the SE.

---

11 See no 5 of this chapter.

This choice is regrettable for two reasons. Firstly, the cross-references render the system difficult to understand. Secondly, the substantive scope of Article 16 of the Directive differs from that of the SE Directive; the SE Directive is broader in scope (it covers all aspects of employee involvement, including information and consultation rights) while Article 16 of the Directive is limited to employee participation.

7. It should be noted that where these fall-back rules apply,[12] the cross-border merger cannot be registered or enter into effect as long as arrangements for employee participation have not been determined (Art. 16(3) Dir. and Art. 12(2) and (3) SE Reg.). The need to respect this procedure will obviously affect the projected timetable for the cross-border merger.

1   Preliminary information procedure and creation of an SNB

8. The Directive provides for a preliminary information procedure and for the creation of a special negotiating body ('SNB') representing the employees of the merging companies.

A   Preliminary information procedure

9. Where the management or administrative organs of the merging companies draw up a plan for a cross-border merger, they shall take the necessary steps as soon as possible, including the provision of information about the identity of the merging companies, concerned subsidiaries or establishments[13] and the number of their employees, to start negotiations with the merging companies' employee representatives on arrangements for employee participation in the company resulting from the cross-border merger (Art. 16(3)(a) Dir. and Art. 3(1) SE Dir.).

B   Creation of an SNB

10. As soon as the above-mentioned information procedure is complete, an SNB must be established.

(i)   **Composition**

11. In transposing the Directive, the Member States must ensure that members of the SNB are elected or appointed in proportion to the number of employees employed in each Member State by the merging companies, their concerned subsidiaries or establishments, by allocating in respect of a Member State one seat per portion of employees employed in that Member State which equals 10 per cent, or a fraction thereof, of the number of employees employed by the merging companies, their concerned subsidiaries or establishments in all the Member States taken together (Art. 16(3)(a) Dir. and Art. 3(2)(a)(i) SE Dir.).

---

12 That is, in the three situations referred to under no 5 of this chapter.
13 Namely, a subsidiary or establishment of a merging company which is proposed to become a subsidiary or establishment of the company resulting from the cross-border merger upon the completion thereof (see Art. 2(d) SE Dir.).

12.   Additional seats shall be allocated to certain Member States under particular circumstances.

Additional seats may be allocated to a Member State in order to ensure that the SNB includes at least one member representing each merging company which is registered and has employees in that Member State and which shall cease to exist as a separate legal entity following completion of the cross-border merger, provided:

(i)   the number of additional members does not exceed 20 per cent of the number of members allocated pursuant to the general rules;[14] and

(ii)   the composition of the SNB does not entail double representation of the employees concerned (Art. 16(3)(a) Dir. and Art. 3(2)(a)(ii) SE Dir.).

If the number of merging companies which shall cease to exist upon completion of the cross-border merger is higher than the number of additional seats available pursuant to the above rules, the additional seats shall be allocated to those merging companies in different Member States by decreasing order of the number of employees they employ (Art. 16(3)(a) Dir. and Art. 3(2)(a)(ii) SE Dir.).

13.   Take, for example, the case of a cross-border merger involving the following companies (all of which shall cease to exist following the merger):

(i)   company A, registered in France and employing 1,000 people;

(ii)   company B, registered in Luxembourg and employing 50 people;

(iii) company C, registered in Spain and employing 140 people;

(iv)   company D, registered in Spain, and employing 310 people.

The seats on the SNB shall be allocated as follows:

Member State	Company	Number of employees	Percentage of the total number of employees		Number of seats on the SNB
France	A	1000	66.66%		7
Luxembourg	B	50	3.33%		1
Spain	C	140	9.33%	30%	3
	D	310	20.66%		
Total		1500	100%		11

Since company A (France) employs 66.66% of the total number of employees, France will be allocated seven seats on the SNB (six seats representing 60% of the employees and one seat for the remaining 6.66%). As company B

14 See no 11 of this report.

(Luxembourg) employs 3.33% of the total number of employees, Luxembourg will be allocated one seat. Companies C and D employ 30% of the total number of employees, so Spain will be allocated three seats.

Assume the French SNB members are all employees of company A, whilst the Luxembourg member is an employee of company B and the Spanish members are all employees of company C. In principle, each company could claim an additional seat, since they will all cease to exist after the merger. Nevertheless, companies A, B and C will not be entitled to an additional seat, since this would lead to double representation (the French, Luxembourg and Spanish members on the SNB are employees of companies A, B and C, respectively). Consequently, only company D (which is not yet represented on the SNB) will be allocated an additional seat.

After allocation of this additional seat, the composition of the SNB will be as follows:

Member State	Company	Number of employees	Percentage of the total number of employees		Number of seats on the SNB
France	A	1000	66.66%		7
Luxembourg	B	50	3.33%		1
Spain	C	140	9.33%	30%	3
	D	310	20.66%		+1
Total		1500	100%		11+1 = 12

(ii)   **Appointment or election of SNB members**

14.   The Member States must determine the method to be used to elect or appoint the SNB members elected or appointed on their territory. Therefore, they must take the necessary measures to ensure that such members include, insofar as possible, at least one representative from each merging company with employees in that Member State, although such measures may not increase the overall number of SNB members (Art. 16(3)(a) Dir. and Art. 3(2)(b) SE Dir.).

In determining the methods used to nominate, appoint or elect representatives, the Member States must seek to promote gender balance.

Without prejudice to national laws and/or practice laying down thresholds for the establishment of a representative body, the Member States shall provide that employees in undertakings or establishments in which there are no employee representatives through no fault of their own, have the right to elect or appoint SNB members (Art. 16(3)(a) Dir. and Art. 3(2)(b) SE Dir.).

The Member States may provide that such members can include trade union representatives, regardless of whether they are employees of a merging company or a concerned subsidiary or establishment (Art. 16(3)(a) Dir. and Art. 3(2)(b) SE Dir.).

15. In the exercise of their functions, the SNB members shall enjoy the same protection and guarantees provided for employee representatives under national law and/or practice in their respective countries of employment (Art. 16(3)(f) Dir. and Art. 10 SE Dir.).

C Role and functioning of the SNB

(i) Role of the SNB

16. The SNB and the competent organs of the merging companies shall determine written arrangements for employee participation in the company resulting from the cross-border merger. To this end, the competent organs of the merging companies must inform the SNB of the merger plan and process, up to registration of the company resulting from the merger (Art. 16(3)(a) Dir. and Art. 3(3) SE Dir.).

   The SNB may also decide not to open negotiations or to terminate negotiations already under way and to rely on the participation rules in force in the Member State where the registered office of the company resulting from the cross-border merger will be situated (Art. 16(4)(b) Dir.).

(ii) Functioning of the SNB

17. The Directive sets forth a few rules regarding negotiations with, and the internal functioning of, the SNB.

(a) *Duty to cooperate*

18. The SNB and the competent organs of the merging companies must negotiate in a spirit of cooperation with a view to reaching an agreement on arrangements for employee participation in the company resulting from the cross-border merger (Art. 16(3)(b) Dir. and Art. 4(1) SE Dir.).

   The purpose of this rule is obviously to promote a consensual solution. In order to meet this goal, the parties must be willing to work together.[15]

(b) *Expert assistance*

19. The SNB may call upon experts of its choosing, such as representatives from appropriate Community-level trade unions, to assist it in its work. Such experts may be present at negotiations in an advisory capacity, at the SNB's request, where appropriate to promote coherence and consistency at the Community level (Art. 16(3)(a) Dir. and Art. 3(5) SE Dir.).

   The SNB may also decide to inform the representatives of appropriate external organisations, including trade unions, of the start of negotiations (Art. 16(3)(a) Dir. and Art. 3(5) SE Dir.).

---

15 In the framework of the SE, see P. Nicaise, 'La société européenne: une société de type européen!', *Journal des Tribunaux*, 2002, p. 489.

(c)   *Duration of negotiations*

20.   Negotiations should commence as soon as the SNB is established and can continue for up to six months thereafter (Art. 16(3)(c) Dir. and Art. 5(1) SE Dir.).
Nevertheless, the parties may decide by joint agreement to extend negotiations
for up to one year from the establishment of the SNB (Art. 16(3)(c) Dir. and
Art. 5(2) SE Dir.).

(d)   *Funding*

21.   In principle, any expenses related to the functioning of the SNB, particularly
negotiations, shall be borne by the merging companies in order to enable the
SNB to carry out its tasks in an appropriate manner.

    In accordance with this principle, the Member States may prescribe
budgetary rules for the functioning of the SNB. In particular, they may limit
funding to the costs of a single expert (Art. 16(3)(a) Dir. and Art. 3(7) SE Dir.).

2   Determination of participation rights

22.   The possible outcomes of negotiations are examined below.

A   Conclusion of an agreement on employee participation

23.   One possible outcome is the conclusion of an agreement on employee participation. Such an agreement is subject to certain requirements as to its form
and content. The Directive also sets out voting rules for conclusion of the
agreement.

(i)   **Content and form of the agreement**

24.   The following issues must be covered in the agreement on employee involvement concluded between the SNB and the competent organs of the merging
companies (Art. 16(3)(b) Dir. and Art. 4(2)(a), (g) and (h) SE Dir.):

    (i)   the scope of the agreement;

    (ii)   the substance of arrangements on employee participation, including (if
applicable) the number of members of the administrative or supervisory
body that the employees shall be entitled to elect, appoint, recommend
or oppose, the procedures as to how these members can be elected,
appointed, recommended or opposed by the employees, and the rights of
these members;

    (iii) the date of entry into force of the agreement and its duration, as well as
cases where the agreement should be renegotiated and the procedure for
renegotiation, including, where appropriate, the procedure in the event
of structural changes to the company resulting from the merger and
its subsidiaries and establishments which occur after formation of the
company.

The agreement between the SNB and the competent organs of the merging companies can also stipulate that the standard rules provided for by the Directive shall apply[16] (Art. 16(3)(a) and (e) Dir. and Arts. 4(3) and 7(1) SE Dir.).

(ii)   **Voting rules**

25.   The majorities required to conclude the agreement are expressly stated in the Directive.

The general rule is that a double majority is required, i.e. the SNB takes decisions by an absolute majority of votes cast by its members, provided such a majority also represents an absolute majority of the employees. Each member has one vote (Art. 16(3)(a) Dir. and Art. 3(4) SE Dir.). This formula inevitably leads to giving more weight to votes cast by SNB members from countries in which the merging companies employ the most employees.

26.   However, this general rule is tempered somewhat when negotiations would result in a reduction of employee participation rights in the company resulting from the cross-border merger, as compared to within the merging companies. For this purpose, a reduction in participation rights shall mean 'a proportion of members of the organs of the [company resulting from the cross-border merger] ... which is lower than the highest proportion existing within the [merging companies]' (Art. 16(3)(a) Dir. and Art. 3(4) SE Dir.).

If such a reduction is envisaged, there are two possibilities (Art. 16(3)(a) Dir. and Art. 3(4) SE Dir.):

   (i)   If employee participation covers at least 25 per cent of the total number of employees of the merging companies, a decision is validly taken by two thirds of the members of the SNB representing at least two thirds of the employees, including the votes of members representing employees from at least two Member States. The purpose of this particular rule is to preserve, insofar as possible, employee participation rights in the merging companies, in accordance with the before-and-after principle.
   (ii) If the above-mentioned 25 per cent threshold is not reached, the general rule remains applicable and a decision can be validly taken by an absolute majority of the SNB members, provided such a majority also represents an absolute majority of the employees.[17]

B   Absence of an agreement within the negotiations period

27.   If no agreement can be reached within the negotiations period, there are two possible options. The competent organs of the merging companies can decide

---

16 See no 30 *et seq.* of this report.
17 In the framework of the SE, see J.-F. Bellis, '*Societas Europaea* – Was it Worth the Waiting?', *Liber Amicorum J.-P. De Bandt*, Bruylant, Brussels, 2004, p. 317.

not to pursue the cross-border merger or they can decide to go ahead with their plans, in which case the standard rules shall apply[18] (Art. 16(3)(e) Dir. and Art. 7(1)(b) SE Dir.).

C   Absence or termination of negotiations

28.   If the SNB decides not to open negotiations or to terminate negotiations already under way, the standard rules shall not apply. In this case, the rules on participation, if any, in force in the Member State where the registered office of the company resulting from the cross-border merger will be situated shall apply (Art. 16(4)(b) Dir.).

A decision not to open or to terminate negotiations must be approved by two thirds of the members of the SNB representing at least two thirds of the employees, including those representing employees in at least two Member States.

29.   Moreover, the Directive also gives the competent organs of the merging companies the right to opt, without prior negotiations, to be subject to the standard participation rules and to abide by these rules as from the date of registration (Art. 16(4)(a) Dir.).

3   Standard rules

30.   Like the SE Directive, the Directive contains standard participation rules.

The purpose of including standard rules was to provide the negotiating parties with an alternative solution in order to avoid an impasse in the cross-border merger process.[19]

These standard rules are examined below.

A   Scope

31.   The standard rules are only applicable in the following cases:

    (i)   if the SNB and the competent organs of the merging companies so decide by way of an agreement (Art. 16(3)(a) and (e) Dir. and Arts. 4(3) and 7(1) SE Dir.); or

    (ii) if no agreement has been reached within the six-month negotiations period (possibly extended to one year) and the competent organs of the merging companies so decide (Art. 16(3)(e) Dir. and Art. 7(1) SE Dir.), provided the SNB has not taken the decision to close the negotiations; or

---

18 See no 30 *et seq.* of this report.
19 Eighth recital to the SE Directive; see also, in the framework of the SE, Bellis, '*Societas Europaea*', pp. 318–19.

(iii)   if, prior to any negotiations, the competent organs of the merging companies decide to be directly subject to the standard rules and to abide by them as from the date of registration (Art. 16(4)(a) Dir.).

Moreover, the standard rules on employee participation shall apply only if:

(i)   prior to registration of the cross-border merger, one or more forms of employee participation applied to one or more of the merging companies and covered at least 33.33 per cent of the total number of their employees; or

(ii)   the SNB so decides and prior to registration of the cross-border merger, one or more forms of employee participation applied to one or more of the merging companies but covered less than 33.33 per cent of the total number of employees in all merging companies (Art. 16(3)(e) Dir. and Art. 7(2)(b) SE Dir.).

32.   In any case, if there is more than one form of employee participation in the various merging companies, the SNB shall decide which forms shall be retained in the company resulting from the cross-border merger. The Member States can determine rules applicable to companies resulting from a cross-border merger which are established on their territory in the absence of a decision by the SNB on the matter (Art. 16(3)(e) Dir. and Art. 7(2) SE Dir.).

The SNB shall also inform the competent organs of the merging companies of the decisions taken (Art. 16(3)(e) Dir. and Art. 7(2) SE Dir.).

33.   Finally, it is important to note that the Directive allows the Member States to provide that the standard rules on employee participation shall not apply (Art. 16(3)(e) Dir. and Art. 7(3) SE Dir.). Curiously, this means that the Member States have the option of not providing for an alternative system of participation.

In such a scenario, it is reasonable to assume that the participation rules, if any, in force in the Member State where the registered office of the company resulting from the cross-border merger will be located shall apply. This could result in a reduction in or disappearance of existing participation rights and does not seem to accord with the before-and-after principle.

B   Content

34.   The employees of the company resulting from the cross-border merger and of its subsidiaries and establishments and/or their representative body shall have the right to elect, appoint, recommend or oppose the appointment of a certain number of members of the administrative or supervisory body of the company resulting from the cross-border merger, equal to the highest number in force in the merging companies.

The SNB shall decide on the allocation of seats on the administrative or supervisory body, from amongst its members representing employees from the various Member States, and on how the employees of the company resulting from the merger can recommend or oppose the appointment of members of these bodies, according to the proportion of employees employed in each Member State. If employees from one or more Member States are not covered by this criterion, the SNB shall appoint a member from one of those Member States, specifically the Member State where the company's registered office is located, where appropriate. Each Member State may determine the allocation of its seats on the administrative or supervisory body (Art. 16(3)(h) Dir. and Part 3(b) Annex SE Dir.).

The Member States may, if the standard rules apply following negotiations, decide to limit the proportion of employee representatives on the administrative organ of the company resulting from the cross-border merger. However, if at least one third of a merging company's administrative or supervisory board consisted of employee representatives, any such limitation may never result in a lower proportion of employee representatives on the administrative organ (Art. 16(4)(c) Dir.).

35.   Every member of the administrative body or, where appropriate, the supervisory body of the company resulting from the cross-border merger who has been elected, appointed or recommended by the SNB or, depending on the circumstances, by the employees directly shall be a full member with the same rights and obligations as members representing shareholders, including the right to vote (Art. 16(3)(h) Dir. and Part 3(b) Annex SE Dir.).

36.   Like SNB members, employee representatives on the supervisory or administrative organ of the company resulting from the cross-border merger who are also employees of this company or of one of its subsidiaries or establishments shall enjoy, in the exercise of their duties, the same protection and guarantees provided for employee representatives by national law and/or practice in their country of employment (Art. 16(3)(f) Dir. and Art. 10 SE Dir.).

VI   National rules on employee involvement

37.   The Member States may, in order to preserve existing employee involvement rights, take the necessary measures to guarantee that the structures of employee representation in merging entities that shall cease to exist as separate legal entities are maintained after registration of a cross-border merger (Art. 16(3)(g) Dir. and Art. 13(4) SE Dir.).

VII   Reservation and confidentiality

38.   Employee participation must not jeopardise the confidentiality of sensitive information.[20]

---

20 Thirteenth recital to the SE Directive.

Therefore, the Member States shall provide that employee representatives on the supervisory or administrative organ of the company resulting from a cross-border merger are not authorised to reveal any information that has been given to them in confidence. This obligation continues in effect after expiry of their term of office (Art. 16(3)(f) Dir. and Art. 8(1) SE Dir.).

Moreover, each Member State shall provide, in specific cases and under certain conditions and within certain limits, that the supervisory or administrative organ of a merging company established in its territory is not obliged to transmit information if the nature of the information is such that, according to objective criteria, disclosure would seriously jeopardise the functioning of the company or of its subsidiaries and establishments or would be prejudicial to any of them (Art. 16(3)(f) Dir. and Art. 8(2) SE Dir.).

In any case, provision must also be made for administrative or judicial appeal procedures which employee representatives may initiate when the supervisory or administrative organ of a merging company demands confidentiality or refuses to provide information (Art. 16(3)(f) Dir. and Art. 8(4) SE Dir.).

VIII   Compliance with Article 16 of the Directive

39.   The Member States must ensure that the management of establishments of a company resulting from a cross-border merger, as well as the supervisory or administrative organs of subsidiaries and of merging companies situated on their territory and the employee representatives or, as the case may be, the employees themselves, abide by the obligations set forth in Article 16 of the Directive, regardless of whether the company resulting from the cross-border merger has its registered office in that Member State (Art. 16(3)(f) Dir. and Art. 12(1) SE Dir.).

The Member States must also provide for appropriate measures in the event of failure to comply with the Directive and ensure enforcement of obligations arising from the Directive by way of administrative or legal procedures (Art. 16(3)(f) Dir. and Art. 12(1) SE Dir.).

IX   Protection of employee representatives

40.   The SNB members and any employee representatives on the supervisory or administrative organ of the company resulting from the cross-border merger who are employees of this company or of any of its subsidiaries or establishments or of a merging company shall, in the exercise of their functions, enjoy the same protection and guarantees provided for by national law and/or practice in force in their country of employment (Art. 16(3)(f) Dir. and Art. 10 SE Dir.).

The foregoing shall apply in particular to attendance at SNB meetings, any other meeting under the participation agreement or any meeting of the administrative or supervisory organ and to the payment of wages for members employed by a merging company, the company resulting from the cross-border merger or any of its subsidiaries or establishments during a period of absence necessary for the performance of their duties (Art. 16(3)(f) Dir. and Art. 10 SE Dir.).

X   Acceptable legal form and subsequent domestic mergers

41.   When at least one of the merging companies is subject to a system of employee participation and the company resulting from the cross-border merger is to be governed by that system, the resulting company is obliged to take a legal form that allows the exercise of employee participation rights (Art. 16(6) Dir.).

The purpose of this rule is obviously to avoid jeopardising the system put in place by the Directive, which would be undermined if the company resulting from the cross-border merger were to adopt a legal form that does not allow the exercise of participation rights.

42.   Moreover, when the company resulting from the cross-border merger is subject to a system of employee participation, it is obliged to take measures to ensure that employee participation rights are protected in the event of subsequent domestic mergers for a period of three years after the cross-border merger takes effect, by applying *mutatis mutandis* the rules set forth in the Directive.

3

Tax rules applicable to cross-border mergers

JAN WERBROUCK
NautaDutilh

I   Introduction

1   Purpose

1.   Cross-border mergers entail a transfer of the assets and liabilities of at least one company ('the transferring company') which ceases to exist as a result of the merger, to a newly created or an existing company established in another State (the 'receiving company'). To the extent that such transfer goes hand in hand with a relocation of business or a physical transfer of assets, the merger will cause the State of the transferring company to lose potential tax revenue. For this reason, most States only allow domestic mergers to be carried out in a tax-neutral way.

    The absence of a tax-neutral regime for cross-border mergers constitutes a clear impediment to international reorganisations and integrations of companies. Already by 1969, a proposal for a directive was drafted by the European Commission, which prohibited taxation in case of intra-community mergers.

It took more than twenty years to enact this proposal as Council Directive 90/434/EEC of 23 July 1990 on the common system of taxation applicable to mergers, divisions, transfers of assets and exchanges of shares concerning companies of different Member States, hereafter 'the Merger Tax Directive' ('Tax Dir.').[1]

The Merger Tax Directive provides for a common tax system applicable throughout the Community. The simple extension at the Community level of the national tax-neutral regimes for domestic mergers was considered to be insufficient because of the risk that differences between these national regimes would continue to produce distortions. The core principle of this common system of taxation is to defer taxation of profits and gains relating to assets and liabilities transferred and to shares allotted in the merger until those assets, liabilities and shares are disposed of by the receiving entities or shareholders. By only deferring the tax charge, the system safeguards the financial interests of the Member States involved.

Only tax levied directly on companies or shareholders is covered by the Merger Tax Directive. Certain indirect tax aspects of cross-border mergers are covered by Council Directive 69/335 EEC on indirect taxes on the raising of capital[2] and by VAT directives. The present chapter only comments on the Merger Tax Directive.

2   History

2.   The Merger Tax Directive has its roots in the 'Programme for the Harmonisation of Direct Taxes' published by the Commission's Fiscal and Finance Committee in 1967. This Programme led to a proposal presented by the European Commission on 15 January 1969.[3] The proposal was based on Article 94 EC, which allows the adoption of harmonising measures on matters which directly affect the functioning of the common market.[4] It was adopted on 23 July 1990. On the same date, the European Council also adopted the so-called 'Parent-Subsidiary Directive', which aims at eliminating double taxation of cross-border dividend payments.[5]

3.   The Merger Tax Directive only applies to the forms of companies included in a list annexed to its text. It was soon concluded that its scope was too narrow. On 26 July 1993, the European Commission submitted a proposal for a

---

1 *Official Journal* L 225 of 20 August 1990, 1–5.
2 *Official Journal* L 249 of 3 October 1969, 25–9.
3 COM (1969) 5 final, *Official Journal* C 39 of 22 March 1969, 4.
4 Formerly Art. 100 of the EC Treaty.
5 Directive 90/435/EEC of 23 July 1990 on the common system of taxation applicable in the case of parent companies and subsidiaries of different Member States, *Official Journal* L 225 of 20 August 1990, 6.

directive amending the Merger Tax Directive by extending it to all companies resident and subject to corporation tax in a Member State.[6] But the diversity of the Member States' legal and tax rules governing companies led to various technical problems about which no agreement could be reached within the Council.

4.   A new attempt to improve the coverage of the Merger Tax Directive was made in 2003, resulting in a proposal of 17 October 2003 for a Council directive amending Directive 90/434/EEC of 23 July 1990,[7] and followed by the withdrawal of the 1993 proposal. The new proposal was adopted on 17 February 2005 and entered into force on 24 March 2005.[8] It extended the list of entities annexed to the Merger Tax Directive to cover new named legal types as well as the European company (SE) and the European cooperative society (SCE).[9] In addition, a broader range of transactions was covered. The Merger Tax Directive was extended to apply to 'partial divisions' as well as to the transfer of the registered office of an SE or SCE between Member States. Finally, the text was clarified to ensure that the tax deferral regime applied to the conversion of a foreign branch into a subsidiary.

5.   In the absence of harmonised company law provisions permitting cross-border mergers, many Member States did not fully implement the Merger Tax Directive by the required date of 1 January 1992. This obstacle was partly eliminated on 15 December 2007 when the Cross-border Merger Directive came into force. With respect to other transactions covered by the Merger Tax Directive, such as divisions, a harmonisation of company law provisions has still to be realised.[10]

6   COM (1993) 293 final, *Official Journal* C 225 of 20 August 1993, 3.

7   COM (2003) 613 final.

8   Council Directive 2005/19/EC of 17 February 2005 amending Directive 90/434/EEC of 23 July 1990 on the common system of taxation applicable to mergers, divisions, transfers of assets and exchanges of shares concerning companies of different Member States, *Official Journal* L 58/79 of 4 March 2005.

9   With respect to the SE, see Council Regulation (EC) 2157/2001 of 8 October 2001 on the Statute for a European company (SE), *Official Journal* L 294 of 10 November 2001, 1, and Council Directive 2001/86/EC of 8 October 2001 supplementing the Statute for a European company with regard to the involvement of employees, *Official Journal* L 294 of 10 November 2001, 22. With respect to the SCE, see Council Regulation (EC) 1435/2003 of 22 July 2003 on the Statute for a European cooperative society (SCE), *Official Journal* L 207 of 18 August 2003, 1 and Council Directive 2003/72/EC of 22 July 2003 supplementing the Statute for a European cooperative society with regard to the involvement of employees, *Official Journal* L 207 of 18 August 2003, 25.

10   With respect to divisions, for instance, the Sixth Company Law Directive of 17 December 1982 only applies to domestic divisions and does not oblige the Member States to introduce company law for division transactions but only requires those States whose company law recognises division transactions to apply the rules set out in the Directive (*Official Journal* L 376 of 31 December 1982, 47).

II   Application

6.   The Merger Tax Directive had to be implemented into national law by the Member States not later than 1 January 1992 (Art. 12).[11] The amendments introduced by the Council Directive of 17 February 2005 entered into force on 24 March 2005 and had to be implemented not later than 1 January 2007.

7.   The Merger Tax Directive applies to all twenty-seven Member States of the European Union.

III   Scope

8.   The Merger Tax Directive applies to a range of transactions, including mergers, divisions, partial divisions, transfers of assets and exchanges of shares involving companies from two or more Member States (Art. 1 Tax Dir.). These concepts are defined in its Articles 2 and 3. In addition, the Merger Tax Directive applies to transfers from one Member State to another Member State of the registered office of an SE or SCE. The present chapter only comments on the common system of taxation applicable to mergers.

9.   In the same way as the Cross-border Merger Directive, the Merger Tax Directive distinguishes three types of mergers: (i) one or more companies are merged into another, existing company; (ii) two or more companies are merged into a new company; or (iii) one or more wholly owned companies are merged into their parent company (Art. 2(a) Tax Dir.).

10.   The first and second types of merger entail a transfer of all assets and liabilities of the merged companies to the merging company, in return for the issuance of shares to the shareholders of the merged companies. The third type of merger also entails a transfer of all assets and liabilities of the merged companies, but logically no shares are issued.

11.   A cash payment may be made by the receiving company to shareholders of the transferring company or companies up to 10 per cent of the nominal value or, absent a nominal value, the accounting par value of the allotted shares (Art. 2(d) Tax Dir.).[12] However, no protection or relief is available under the Merger Tax Directive with respect to such cash payment. Furthermore, if the aggregate cash payments exceed the maximum allowed amount, the entire merger will

---

11   An exception was made only for Portugal, which was allowed to delay implementation of provisions concerning certain transactions (transfers of assets and exchanges of shares) until 1 January 1993 because Portuguese law did not yet offer the necessary legal framework for these transactions.

12   The Merger Tax Directive refers to 'securities or shares representing the capital' of the merging company. For more information about these concepts, see Chapter 1 of this book.

be disallowed under the Merger Tax Directive. By contrast, the Cross-border Merger Directive may still apply, provided that such cash payment in excess of the maximum amount is allowed by at least one of the Member States involved (Art. 3(1) Tax Dir.).

12.   The Merger Tax Directive does not apply to domestic reorganisations but requires that companies from two or more Member States are involved in the merger (Art. 1 Tax Dir.). Contrary to the Cross-border Merger Directive, it does not specify at which level these companies must be involved, but from its provisions with respect to tax relief one can infer that it only concerns mergers whereby assets and liabilities are transferred between companies established in different Member States.

A company of a Member State includes any company which satisfies the following three conditions: (i) it takes one of the forms listed in the Annex to the Merger Tax Directive; (ii) it is considered to be a resident in a Member State for tax purposes according to the tax laws of that Member State and, under the terms of a double taxation agreement concluded with a third State, it is not considered to be resident for tax purposes outside the Community; and (iii) it is subject to corporate income tax in a Member State.

The Annex was amended in 2005 in order to broaden the Merger Tax Directive's scope. It now includes many legal forms, including cooperative companies, mutual funds, SEs and SCEs. Some Member States have added to the list a sentence stating that all relevant legal forms, present and future, are covered.

13.   The requirements that companies must be subject to corporate income tax without the option of being exempt and may not be a resident of a third State outside the Community under the terms of a tax treaty aim to ensure that a Member State, in particular the Member State of the transferring company, may tax future capital gains on the assets and liabilities transferred, i.e. at the moment that the receiving company actually disposes of those assets and liabilities. Such taxation is not possible if the receiving company is not subject to corporate income tax or is, at the time of the disposal, also a resident of a State outside the Community and a treaty with that State exclusively attributes the authority to tax those capital gains to that State.

In view of the above, these conditions should continue to be satisfied as long as protection under the Merger Tax Directive is sought.

IV   Taxation

1   Transfer of assets and liabilities

14.   The first and most important tax relief provided by the Merger Tax Directive is that a merger may not give rise to any taxation of capital gains relating to assets and liabilities transferred (Art. 4(1) Tax Dir.). Capital gains are calculated by

reference to the difference between the real values of the assets and liabilities transferred and their values for tax purposes.[13]

Arguably, the obligation not to tax capital gains implies that the Member State of the transferring company should refrain from any taxation which would lead to the same economic result as a straightforward taxation of the capital gains, e.g. by recapturing depreciation and other allowances in relation to those assets and liabilities. However, this does not imply that the Member State of the transferring company should allow the transfer of the transferring company's losses to (the permanent establishment of) the receiving company. As further explained below, the Merger Tax Directive states that Member States are only obliged to allow such transfer of losses to the extent that a transfer of losses is possible in case of a domestic merger.

15. A company may be treated as a corporate taxpayer in the Member State where it is established while being considered as transparent for tax purposes by other Member States. A fiscally transparent company is not taxed as a separate entity. Its profits are taxed in the hands of the persons holding an interest in that company, i.e. its shareholders or partners, regardless of whether those profits are distributed or not. Typically, another Member State would treat a foreign entity which is a corporate taxpayer in its State of residence as transparent for tax purposes when it does not have, under its law of incorporation, the legal characteristics which are typical for legal entities under the law of that other Member State.

If a transferring company is considered fiscally transparent by another Member State, shareholders of the transferring company who are resident in that other Member State risk being taxed by that other Member State on their share of the capital gains, subject to any relief (exemption or tax credit) provided by a tax treaty. To ensure that the other Member State will refrain from taxing the shareholders, a new Article 4(2) was inserted in the Merger Tax Directive in 2005, stating that, in summary, where a Member State considers a non-resident transferring company as fiscally transparent, that State shall not tax any income, profits or capital gains relating to the transferred assets and liabilities, calculated by reference to the difference between their real values and their values for tax purposes.

16. Article 4(2) of the Merger Tax Directive only deals with the situation where a Member State considers a *non-resident* company as fiscally transparent. A cross-border merger involving a company which is considered as fiscally transparent by the Member State where that company is established will not fall within the scope of the Merger Tax Directive. A fiscally transparent

---

13 'Value for tax purposes' is defined as the value on the basis of which any gain or loss would have been computed for the purposes of tax upon the income, profits or capital gains of the transferring company if such assets or liabilities had been sold at the time of the merger, division or partial division but independently of it.

company is not as such subject to tax while the Merger Tax Directive only applies to mergers involving companies that are subject to corporate income tax. Furthermore, for the same reason, such company will not satisfy the condition that it is a resident of a Member State for tax purposes.

17.   Relief is only available to the extent that the assets and liabilities of the transferring company are, in consequence of the merger, effectively connected with a permanent establishment of the receiving company in the Member State of the transferring company (Art. 4(1)(b) Tax Dir.). Consequently, the transferring company's business may not be relocated and its assets and liabilities may not be physically transferred but must remain in the Member State of the transferring company. It is generally accepted that the concept of permanent establishment may be defined in accordance with the OECD Model Convention.

The absence of such relocation or physical transfer is an essential condition for tax neutrality. In this way, the Member State of the transferring company will be able to continue taxing all income generated by the transferred assets and liabilities as well as the capital gains arising thereon when the receiving company disposes of the assets and liabilities.

18.   Furthermore, relief will only be available if the receiving company does not claim any 'step up' in the tax basis of the assets and liabilities transferred, but computes any new depreciation and any gains or losses in respect of the assets and liabilities transferred on the basis of their pre-merger tax value, i.e. in accordance with the rules that would have applied to the transferring company if the merger had not taken place (Art. 4(3) Tax Dir.). But the mere fact that the Member State of the transferring company allows opting for a step up in the tax basis of the transferred assets and liabilities does not as such exclude the merger from relief. Only if the receiving company actually opts for such step up will the merger no longer qualify (Art. 4(4) Tax Dir.). Whether or not the tax basis of the assets and liabilities transferred is stepped up in the Member State of the receiving company is of no importance.

The absence of a step up in the tax basis of the assets and liabilities transferred is also an essential condition for tax neutrality. It allows the Member State of the transferring company to tax those capital gains later on, when the receiving company actually disposes of the assets and liabilities.

2   Transfer of reserves and provisions

19.   The permanent establishment of the receiving company in the Member State of the transferring company may take over all tax-exempt provisions or reserves properly constituted by the transferring company (Art. 5 Tax Dir.). These provisions or reserves continue to be tax exempt and the receiving company will assume the rights and obligations of the transferring company in this respect.

The merger may consequently not lead to taxation of past profits or capital gains which were exempt in the hands of the transferring company, provided that the receiving company continues to satisfy the conditions on which the tax exemption depends, e.g. a reinvestment of the tax-exempt profit. The continued exemption of provisions and reserves does not imply a loss of revenue to the Member State of the transferring company since it will be able to tax those reserves and provisions in the hands of the permanent establishment when the conditions for the exemption are no longer satisfied.

As an exception to the above principle, the Member State of the transferring company may tax reserves and provisions constituted by the transferring company in relation to its foreign permanent establishments. In consequence of the merger, these permanent establishments will be directly dependent on the receiving company's head office. The Member State of the transferring company will not be able to tax these reserves and provisions in the future and, therefore, would suffer a loss of revenue if it had to refrain from taxing those reserves and provisions at the moment of the merger.

3   Transfer of losses

20.   Unused tax losses of the transferring company are transferred to the permanent establishment of the receiving company, but only to the extent that this Member State would allow such transfer of losses in case of a domestic merger (Art. 6 Tax Dir.). An unconditional transfer of losses, independent from the rules which apply in case of a domestic merger, was considered as potentially creating tax avoidance opportunities and therefore undesirable.

4   Cancellation of shares

21.   In consequence of the merger, a holding of the receiving company in the capital of the transferring company will normally be cancelled. In the case of mergers falling within the scope of the Cross-border Merger Directive, the receiving company may not issue shares to itself in exchange for the shares of the transferring company held by it (Art. 14(5) Cross-border Merger Dir.).

Article 7 of the Merger Tax Directive states that gains accruing to the receiving company on such cancellation of its holding shall not be liable to any taxation. The receiving company may not be taxed on the difference between the tax value of its holding and the corresponding portion of the actual value of the transferred assets and liabilities.

Nevertheless, the Member States may tax such gains if the receiving company has a holding of less than 10 per cent in the capital of the transferring company (holding percentage applicable as of 1 January 2009).[14] These holding percentages and their dates of entry into force correspond to the percentages and dates of the Parent-Subsidiary Directive. This directive states

---

14 Prior to 2007, taxation was allowed in case of a holding of less than 20 per cent in the capital of the transferring company. Until 1 January 2009, taxation of such gain was allowed if the receiving company had a holding of less than 15 per cent.

that cross-border profit distributions to companies having a qualifying holding are in principle not liable to withholding tax at source and are not liable to tax in the hands of the parent company.

Contrary to an earlier draft, the Directive does not cover situations where the transferring company holds own shares or holds shares in another transferring company. These shares will normally have to be cancelled. The Cross-border Merger Directive states that an exchange for shares in such situations is forbidden as well (Art. 14(5) Cross-border Merger Dir.).

5   Exchange of shares

22.   Further to the merger, shareholders in the transferring company receive shares representing the capital of the receiving company in exchange for the shares they previously held in the transferring company, and possibly a cash payment of up to 10 per cent of the value of the new shares issued. This allotment of shares in the receiving company may not lead to taxation of any income, profits or capital gains of the shareholders.

Relief is only temporary. The Member States may tax the shareholders on capital gains arising at the actual disposal of the shares, whereby those capital gains are determined by reference to the pre-merger tax value of the exchanged shares. Relief is therefore conditional upon the absence of a step up in the taxable basis of the shares. The shareholders may not attribute a higher tax value to the shares received than the tax value the exchanged shares had immediately before the merger. The mere existence of an option for the shareholders to attribute a higher tax value, however, does not of itself allow taxation of the gains.

Relief is restricted to the allotment of shares. No relief is provided with respect to a cash element of the consideration. It is unclear, however, to what extent the Member States may tax capital gains in case of a cash payment.

23.   If a Member State considers a shareholder as fiscally transparent, it should refrain from taxing the persons having an interest in the shareholder on their share of that shareholder's income, profit or capital gains.

6   Transfer of a permanent establishment

24.   The Member States should refrain from taxing a permanent establishment of the transferring company on the occasion of the merger if this permanent establishment is part of the assets and liabilities transferred to the receiving company and is situated in a Member State other than the Member State of the transferring company. A permanent establishment situated in the Member State of the transferring company is not covered, but this follows from the fact that relief is then already provided by Article 4 of the Merger Tax Directive.

A company situated in one Member State often sets up a branch in another Member State in order to be able to set off start-up losses of the branch against its worldwide profits. Later on, for example when the branch becomes profitable, the company may decide to convert this branch into a subsidiary. The Merger Tax Directive clarifies that such 'conversion' of a branch into a subsidiary is also covered by the Merger Tax Directive, even if the subsidiary is situated in the same State as the branch. However, the Member State of the transferring company may tax the transferring company on the occasion of the merger on profits and gains relating to the branch, up to the amount of losses of the branch that it previously has set off against its taxable profits. If the Member State of the transferring company so taxes the transferring company, it should at the same time give relief to the transferring company as if the branch were also taxed on those profits and gains in the Member State where it is situated.

The Member State in which the permanent establishment is situated must apply the Merger Tax Directive as if it were the Member State of the transferring company, i.e. as if the permanent establishment were a separate company. The Member State of the permanent establishment should therefore refrain from taxing capital gains on the permanent establishment, provided that the assets and liabilities of the permanent establishment are effectively connected to a permanent establishment of the receiving company. It should furthermore allow the transfer of tax-exempt reserves and provisions and of unused losses in the same way as described above.

7   Exclusions

25.   A Member State may refuse to apply, or may withdraw the benefit of, all or any part of the provisions of the Merger Tax Directive if the merger has tax evasion or avoidance as one of its principal objectives or if, as a result of the merger, a company no longer fulfils the necessary conditions for the representation of employees on company organs.

The fact that the merger is not carried out for valid commercial reasons such as the rationalisation of activities may constitute a presumption that the operation has tax evasion or avoidance as one of its principal objectives.

4

Scope and limitations of the Cross-border Merger Directive

PAUL STORM
NautaDutilh

1.   Now that the Cross-border Merger Directive has been transposed in all Member States, it appears useful to examine the extent of its potential impact and its position in the context of cross-border mobility of companies in the European Union. Given the series of groundbreaking decisions of the Court of Justice of the EC ('the European Court of Justice' or 'the Court') on cross-border operations,[1] such an examination must necessarily be carried out in the light of the fundamental freedoms enshrined in the EC Treaty, in particular the freedom of establishment. These decisions do not always produce the desired certainty. Consequently, this examination cannot yield more than a picture of the situation in October 2009.

2.   Various questions arise. First, which cross-border operations are or are not feasible in the current state of development of Community law, apart from cross-border mergers under the Cross-border Directive? Second, which

---

1 28.01.1986, Case 270/83, *Commission* v. *France*; 10.07.1986, Case 79/85, *Segers*; 27.09.1988, Case 81/87, *Daily Mail*; 09.03.1999, Case C-212/97, *Centros*; 05.11.2002, Case C-208/00, *Überseering*; 30.09.2003, Case C-167/01, *Inspire Art*; 13.12.2005, Case C-411/03, *SEVIC*; and 16.12.2008, Case C-210/06, *Cartesio*.

cross-border operations can companies achieve thanks to the Directive? Third, what are the limitations to which a cross-border merger under the Directive is subjected? These questions will briefly be examined in the next pages. First of all, however, I will make clear what I mean by 'cross-border operations' of companies, in particular in the context of freedom of establishment in the EU. Also, I will make a few introductory remarks on an issue that is vital to cross-border operations: the old controversy between two doctrines concerning the law applicable to companies, the incorporation doctrine and the real seat doctrine.

3.   Freedom of establishment in the EU is based on Articles 43 and 48 of the EC Treaty (also referred to as 'EC'), which read as follows:

> *Article 43*
> *Within the framework of the provisions set out below, restrictions on the freedom of establishment of nationals of a Member State on the territory of another Member State shall be prohibited. Such prohibition shall also apply to restrictions on the setting-up of agencies, branches or subsidiaries by nationals of any Member State in the territory of any Member State.*
>
> *Freedom of establishment shall include the right to take up and pursue activities as self-employed persons and to set up and manage undertakings, in particular companies or firms within the meaning of the second paragraph of Article 48, under the conditions laid down for its own nationals by the law of the country where such establishment is effected, subject to the provisions of the chapter relating to capital.*
>
> *Article 48*
> *Companies or firms formed in accordance with the law of a Member State and having their registered office, central administration or principal place of business within the Community shall, for the purposes of this Chapter, be treated in the same way as natural persons who are nationals of Member States.*
>
> *'Companies or firms' means companies or firms constituted under civil or commercial law, including cooperative societies, and other legal persons governed by public or private law, save for those which are non-profit-making.*

The second paragraph of Article 43 relates to the so-called 'primary right of establishment', the right of an individual or a legal entity, national of a Member State, to set up and manage undertakings in another Member State, resulting in economic activity predominantly in the host Member State. The second sentence of the first paragraph of Article 43 relates to the so-called 'secondary right of establishment', the right of an undertaking already existing in one Member State to set up an agency, branch or subsidiary of that undertaking in another Member State, resulting in economic activity in both Member States, albeit predominantly in the former Member State.[2]

It will be clear that the definition of 'companies or firms' in Article 48 is very broad.

4.   In *SEVIC*,[3] (the European Court of Justice ruled: 'the right of establishment covers all measures which permit or even merely facilitate access to another Member State and the pursuit of an economic activity in that State by allowing the persons concerned to participate in the economic life of the country effectively and under the same conditions as national operators'. It follows from this and other paragraphs of *SEVIC* and from earlier decisions of the Court[4] that the right of establishment covers the formation and management of companies and branch offices in another Member State, the transfer of the registered office and/or the central administration ('real seat') of a company to another Member State as well as cross-border mergers and 'other company transformation operations'.[5] All these operations fall within my concept of 'cross-border operations'. I will examine the above questions with respect to cross-border (i) mergers, (ii) transfers of registered office and/or real seat and (iii) divisions of companies, exclusively within the EU and the EEA. Therefore, where 'country' is mentioned, this should be understood to be a Member State of the EU or a Contracting Party to the EEA.

5.   As to the law applicable to companies, this is determined by private international law ('PIL') on the basis of connecting factors, such as the registered office, the country of incorporation or the 'real seat'.[6] In principle, PIL is national law. Consequently, it differs from country to country, but there are two main doctrines: the incorporation doctrine and the real seat doctrine. According to the former, a company is governed by the company law[7] of the

---

2 This distinction is blurred when it comes to cases like *Centros* and *Inspire Art* (see footnote 1), where the European Court of Justice held that the establishment of a branch in another Member State fell within the exercise of freedom of secondary establishment, even if the company concerned did not have any activity in its home Member State (see *Inspire Art*, paragraphs 95 and 105). One could argue that this is a case of primary establishment.

3 13.12.2005, Case C-411/03, para. 18

4 See footnote 1.

5 In German, the original language of the *SEVIC* proceedings, *Gesellschaftsumwandlungen*, a term which, under the *Umwandlungsgesetz* (Act on Transformation Operations) covers mergers, three different forms of division, some specific forms of transfer of assets and liabilities, and transformation from one form of entity into another.

6 The concept of 'real seat' is not given the same meaning in all Member States. In some Member States (e.g. France and Italy) emphasis is laid upon the location of the centre of administration or decision-making, in others (e.g. Germany) it is rather the activities of the company that determine the 'real seat'.

7 Which includes such matters as incorporation, transformation, dissolution, registration, capacity, share capital, 'organs' and their powers and liability of their members, etc. (*'lex societatis'*).

country where it was incorporated and/or registered or where it has its 'seat' according to its articles of association ('statutes'). In principle, the incorporation doctrine[8] does not attach any meaning to the transfer of the real seat to another country. The company remains subject to the law of the country of incorporation, its home country. The host country, however, may treat the company very differently. Where this country applies the incorporation doctrine (an 'incorporation country'), the company will, according to the law of this country, remain subject to the law of its home country. However, where the host country applies the real seat doctrine (a 'real seat country'),[9] there is still a great variety of possibilities and, in many countries, quite some uncertainty. The company may even become subject to the company laws of both countries.[10] According to the real seat doctrine, the company is governed by the *lex societatis* of the country of its 'real seat', which concept is multiform and vague.[11]

I   Which cross-border operations outside the Cross-border Merger Directive are or are not currently feasible?

1   Cross-border mergers

6.   In the almost total absence of relevant interlocking national laws (apart, of course, from the laws transposing the Cross-border Merger Directive), Articles 43 and 48 EC form the basis for cross-border operations of 'companies or firms'. As to cross-border mergers, the decision of the European Court of Justice in *SEVIC* was widely understood to render these possible on a large scale, until the Court delivered its judgment in *Cartesio*.[12] In this judgment, the Court gave a very narrow interpretation of its own decision in *SEVIC*. It explained that *SEVIC* 'concerned the recognition, in the Member State of incorporation

---

8   Countries applying the incorporation doctrine include: Bulgaria, Cyprus, the Czech Republic, Denmark, Finland, Hungary, Ireland, Italy (for Italian companies), Lithuania, the Netherlands, probably, as between EEA States: Norway, Slovakia, Sweden and the UK (and, outside the EU, Switzerland, Liechtenstein, Russia, Belarus, the USA and many (former) Commonwealth countries).

9   Countries applying the real seat doctrine include: Austria, Belgium, Estonia, France, Germany (changing), Greece, Italy (for foreign companies), Latvia, Luxembourg, Poland, Portugal, Romania, Slovenia and Spain. It should be noted that some countries apply mixed systems and there are great differences in the application of the real seat doctrine. The information in this footnote and the previous one is largely taken from the Commission Staff Working Document, Impact assessment on the Directive on the cross-border transfer of registered office, Part I, 12.12.2007, SEC (2007) 1707, to be found on the Commission's website.

10 For example, a Dutch company having transferred its real seat to Italy will, according to Dutch PIL, still be governed by Dutch company law (Art. 2 Act on Conflicts of Law relating to Corporations), but, according to Italian PIL (Art. 25(1) *Legge* 218/1995), by Italian company law.

11 See footnote 6.

12 16.12.2008, Case C-210/06.

of a company [Germany], of an establishment operation carried out by that company in another Member State [Luxembourg] by means of a cross-border merger'. The Court's reasoning based on *recognition*[13] presupposes a cross-border merger to be possible under Luxembourg law. Luxembourg[14] happens to be one of the very few Member States,[15] together with Italy,[16] where this is the case. The result is that cross-border mergers outside the rather limited scope of the Cross-border Merger Directive (whose scope will be discussed at nos 7 and 27 of this chapter) have been very severely curtailed. This will last until Member States change their legislation so as to permit their companies other than 'limited liability companies' to merge into companies from other Member States, or a Community instrument to that effect is adopted. Cross-border mergers of all 'companies or firms' other than 'limited liability companies' will now be governed by the same regime as SEVIC at the time of its merger.

7.   It is tempting to examine exactly which companies or firms are covered by *SEVIC and* fall outside the scope of the Cross-border Merger Directive. In this respect, it is remarkable that, although the European Court of Justice refers to Article 48 EC in both *SEVIC* and *Cartesio*, it never mentions 'firms' in those decisions. It only spoke of 'companies'. In fact, Cartesio was a limited partnership which qualified as a company under Hungarian law. The European Court of Justice treated it as a company. This raises the question of whether the Court's rulings in *SEVIC* and *Cartesio* apply to firms (non-legal entities). I will not try to answer this question here, the more so since there is little point in considering firms in connection with cross-border mergers because to my knowledge there is only one Member State (Germany) that provides for mergers between non-legal entities. But there are legal entities that are not covered by the Cross-border Merger Directive. First of all, in most Member States cooperative societies either do not fall within the definition of 'limited liability company' in the Directive (see no 27 of this chapter) or fall outside the scope of the Directive because the Member State concerned has decided, in accordance with Article 3(2) of the Directive, not to apply the Directive to cooperative societies. Then there are foundations and associations, both of which may in some Member States be profit-making and therefore fall within Article 48 EC. Some Member States provide for (national) mergers involving foundations, associations and other legal persons (e.g. Germany and the Netherlands). There are countries that do not provide for partnerships limited by shares (e.g. the Netherlands

---

13 It is interesting to note that in effect the European Court of Justice ruled that Germany had to forgo applying several rules of its company law in order to meet its Community law obligation to recognise the Luxembourg merger.

14 Art. 257(3) of the 1915 Companies Act as amended by one of two laws of 23 March 2007.

15 But see Art. 163b of the Swiss *Bundesgesetz über das internationale Privatrecht*.

16 Art. 25(3) *Legge* 218/1995.

and Sweden). There is at least one country (the Netherlands) that does not follow Article 3(3) of the Directive and does apply the Directive regime to cross-border mergers involving open-ended undertakings for collective investment in transferable securities (UCITS). Also, there is a country with a unique legal form: France with the *SAS* (*société par actions simplifiée*). There are probably many more similar oddities.

8. In the context of this study, the question that matters is whether an entity of type A, established in Member State Z and capable under Z's law of merging with an entity of type B, can merge with an entity of type B in Member State X if Member State X does not provide for the possibility of an entity of type B merging at all or merging with an entity of type A. It follows from the interpretation of *SEVIC* given by the European Court of Justice in *Cartesio* that this is a matter of recognition by the Member State where the relevant 'establishment operation' has *not* taken place.[17] In this case, the establishment operation must take place in Z, because X does not provide for such a merger. The preliminary question, then, is whether this *cross-border* merger can take place in Z. This depends on Z's law. Should this possibility exist, then the next question is whether X must recognise the merger. Contrary to *SEVIC* (see paragraph 22), in this case there cannot be a difference in treatment if X does not recognise the merger in Z, because X's own entities of type B cannot merge with an entity of type A. In my view, the conclusion must be that such a merger cannot take place, unless X is prepared to recognise it without being obliged to do so under Articles 43 and 48 EC. The conclusion would be in the opposite direction if X also permitted mergers between entities A and entities B, even if it did not provide for cross-border mergers between such entities. In that event, X would discriminate against the merger in Z if it did not recognise that merger (see paragraph 22 of *SEVIC*).

It is conceivable that the differences between various types of entity are so great that any merger between them, let alone a cross-border merger, would meet insurmountable legal obstacles. This is why Article 4(1)(a) of the Cross-border Merger Directive provides that cross-border mergers shall only be possible between companies of a type which may merge under the national law of the relevant Member States. It should be kept in mind that even legal entities of the same type, e.g. cooperative societies, may differ very substantially as to certain characteristics, such as limitation of members' liability. However, one should not exaggerate such differences. They should not serve as an excuse for refusing recognition of a cross-border operation if it is clear that the interests of none of the parties involved have been prejudiced.

---

17 It could be argued that, in the event of a cross-border merger, an 'establishment operation' takes place in both (or all) Member States involved. If that is the case, the reasoning that follows applies to all Member States involved.

2   Cross-border transfer of real seat

9.   The primary decision in *Cartesio* concerned the transfer of the *real* seat of a Hungarian 'company' to another country (Italy). In fact, Cartesio had transferred its real seat to Italy and applied to its Hungarian ('home') court for registration of that transfer, implying that it wished to remain a Hungarian company. Under Hungarian law as it was at that time, the seat of a company governed by Hungarian law was to be the place where its central administration was situated. The difference from previous cases (except *Daily Mail*) was that the objections were not raised by the country to which the seat was transferred (the host country) but by the country from which the company wished to emigrate (the home country). In *Daily Mail*, the European Court of Justice had upheld the objections of the British government in a similar situation, even though under UK PIL the incorporation doctrine applies. The Court's reasoning in this latter decision has given rise to uncertainty and controversy.[18] In *Cartesio*, the Court has made an effort to improve on its reasoning. I quote five of the most essential paragraphs:

> 109 Consequently, in accordance with Article 43 EC, in the absence of a uniform Community law definition of the companies which may enjoy the right of establishment on the basis of a single connecting factor determining the national law applicable to a company, the question whether Article 43 EC applies to a company which seeks to rely on the fundamental freedom enshrined in that article – like the question whether a natural person is a national of a Member State, hence entitled to enjoy that freedom – is a preliminary matter which, as Community law now stands, can only be resolved by the applicable national law. In consequence, the question whether the company is faced with a restriction on the freedom of establishment, within the meaning of Article 43 EC, can arise only if it has been established, in the light of the conditions laid down in Article 48 EC, that the company actually has a right to that freedom.

> 110 Thus a Member State has the power to define both the connecting factor required of a company if it is to be regarded as incorporated under the law of that Member State and, as such, capable of enjoying the right of establishment, and that required if the company is to be able subsequently to maintain that status. That power includes the possibility for that Member State not to permit a company governed by its law to retain that status if the company intends to reorganise itself in another Member State by moving its seat to the territory of the latter, thereby breaking the connecting factor required under the national law of the Member State of incorporation.

18 The Court itself went out of its way to explain the true meaning of *Daily Mail* in its decision in *Überseering*, but the controversy remained.

111 Nevertheless, the situation where the seat of a company incorporated under the law of one Member State is transferred to another Member State with no change as regards the law which governs that company falls to be distinguished from the situation where a company governed by the law of one Member State moves to another Member State with an attendant change as regards the national law applicable, since in the latter situation the company is converted into a form of company which is governed by the law of the Member State to which it has moved.

112 In fact, in that latter case, the power referred to in paragraph 110 above, far from implying that national legislation on the incorporation and winding-up of companies enjoys any form of immunity from the rules of the EC Treaty on freedom of establishment, cannot, in particular, justify the Member State of incorporation, by requiring the winding-up or liquidation of the company, in preventing that company from converting itself into a company governed by the law of the other Member State, to the extent that it is permitted under that law to do so.

113 Such a barrier to the actual conversion of such a company, without prior winding-up or liquidation, into a company governed by the law of the Member State to which it wishes to relocate constitutes a restriction on the freedom of establishment of the company concerned which, unless it serves overriding requirements in the public interest, is prohibited under Article 43 EC (see, to that effect, inter alia, paragraphs 11 and 17). CaixaBank France.

10.   I have the following comments on *Cartesio*. First of all, the Court emphasises repeatedly (see paragraphs 108 and 114) that the question whether – and, if so, how – a company's registered office or head office (*siège réel*, real seat) may be transferred from one Member State to another cannot be resolved by the rules concerning the right of establishment, but must be dealt with by harmonisation directives and conventions provided for in Article 293 EC. So far, neither the Member States nor the Community institutions have taken decisive action to address this issue. It should be noted that in December 2007, after an impact assessment, the Commissioner for the Internal Market decided that there was no need for further action with respect to the cross-border transfer of registered office. The impact assessment had concluded that it might be more appropriate to wait until the impact of the Cross-border Merger Directive and the expected judgment in *Cartesio* could be fully assessed. *Cartesio* could be regarded as the European Court of Justice's reply to this decision. The Court makes it clear that it considers the ball to be in the court of the Member States and the Commission. See also paragraph 109, where the Court says its ruling applies in the absence of a uniform Community law definition of the connecting factor determining the national law applicable to a company. It is very difficult to reconcile this alleged dependence on directives or conventions with a

number of earlier statements by the Court, precisely in company law matters[19] and most recently in *SEVIC*, where the Court ruled:

> 26 It should be noted in that respect that, whilst Community harmonisation rules are useful for facilitating cross-border mergers, the existence of such harmonisation rules cannot be made a precondition for the implementation of the freedom of establishment laid down by Articles 43 EC and 48 EC (see, to that effect, Case C-204/90 *Bachmann* [1992] ECR I-249, paragraph 11).

11.   It will be noted that in *Cartesio* (paragraphs 108, 109, 110 and 114), as, for that matter, in *Daily Mail* and *Überseering*, the European Court of Justice approaches the subject from the angle of private international law, emphasising the lack of a uniform connecting factor and relying heavily on national connecting factors. Whatever one may think of this approach (my opinion is given below), one would expect consistency in the Court's reasoning based upon this approach. In this respect, it is useful to repeat a few sentences from the above quote:

– in paragraph 109: 'the question whether Article 43 EC applies to a company … is a preliminary matter which, as Community law now stands, *can only be resolved by the applicable national law*'.
– in paragraph 110: '*That power includes the possibility for that Member State not to permit a company governed by its law to retain that status if the company intends to reorganise itself in another Member State …* thereby breaking the connecting factor required under the national law of the Member State of incorporation.'
– in paragraph 113: 'Such a barrier to the actual conversion … *constitutes a restriction on the freedom of establishment ...* which … is prohibited under Article 43 EC'

On the one hand, in paragraphs 109 and 110, the European Court of Justice considers the question of whether a company can enjoy the freedom of establishment to be one that is totally dependent on national law. On the other, in paragraphs 112 and 113, it relies on the freedom of establishment, therefore on Community law, to limit the Member States' power it has just recognised in absolute terms. In these latter paragraphs, it completely ignores the 'preliminary matter' it stated so emphatically in paragraph 109.

12.   In my view, the inconsistency pointed out at no 11 above exposes a fundamental flaw in the argumentation of the European Court of Justice. Contrary to the clear wording and intent of Article 48(1) EC, the Court subjects the application of Article 43 to a condition that is alien to the subject-matter of that provision. By the Court's own settled case law,[20] the three sub-criteria referred to

---

19 See *Centros*, paragraph 28, and *Überseering*, paragraphs 54 and 55.
20 E.g. *Daily Mail*, paragraph 21, and *Cartesio*, paragraph 106.

in Article 48(1) EC have been placed on the same footing, which means that any one of those criteria is sufficient to qualify a company or firm as a beneficiary of the right of establishment. Those criteria cannot, therefore, be made cumulative in any way without repudiating the text and the intent of Article 48 EC. The essential intent of Article 48 is to distinguish 'EC nationals' from 'non-EC nationals', not to make a distinction between various 'EC nationals'. I submit that the fundamental flaw in the Court's argumentation is that it uses concepts of private international law, which is national law, and so undermines the essence of Article 48, a provision of Community law which is of a higher order than, and has priority over, national law. In the context of company law, private international law is about attaching companies to a specific country. Article 48 is about attaching companies to the Community. It does so in a very clear way: in order to benefit from the freedom of establishment, a company must (i) have been formed in accordance with the law of a Member State and (ii) have either its registered office *or* its central administration *or* its principal place of business 'within the Community' (not even necessarily in the Member State of its incorporation).

13.   Following the wording of Article 48, in all decisions under discussion here, the Court parallels companies with, or distinguishes them from, natural persons (*Daily Mail*, paragraph 19, *Überseering*, paragraph 57, and *Cartesio*, paragraph 109). In doing so, it reinforces the impression that it bases its reasoning in those cases on national PIL rather than on substantive national law. Curiously, neither in *Daily Mail* nor in *Cartesio* was the prohibition of the cross-border transfer of the real seat based on rules of PIL. In *Daily Mail* it was a provision of British tax law which prohibited companies resident for tax purposes in the UK from ceasing to be so resident without consent of the Treasury. The legal substratum underlying *Cartesio* is rather difficult to understand. This is partly due to the fact that several different Hungarian laws seem to have been held relevant to this case. The Decree-Law No 13 of 1979 on private international law rules is clearly based on the incorporation doctrine (see paragraph 20 of the Court's decision in *Cartesio*: 'The personal law of a legal person shall be the law of the State in the territory of which it is registered'). In 2005, when Cartesio filed for registration of the transfer of its (real) seat to Italy, the Hungarian Law on the commercial register provided that the seat of a company was the place where its central administration was situated. This was an administrative rule that did not belong to Hungarian PIL proper, but served to set out the scope of application of the Hungarian Law on Commercial Companies by requiring a Hungarian company to have its real seat in Hungary.[21] By implication, this rule

21 It should be noted that in 2007 the Law on the commercial register was amended to provide that the seat of a company is the place where the company is registered and this need not be the real seat. Since 2007, a company registered in Hungary may transfer its 'primary place of activity' to any Member State of the EU.

imposed on Hungarian companies an impediment to transferring their real seat to another country, where Hungarian PIL did not do so.

In spite of the Court's words cited above, therefore, the Court's opinions in both *Daily Mail* and *Cartesio* appear to have very little, if anything, to do with the controversy between the incorporation doctrine and the real seat doctrine, even if this controversy may have been present in the minds of all parties to the proceedings and the Judges. That controversy concerns the connecting of companies to a national legal order based on the requirements (i) and (ii) referred to in 12 above. *Daily Mail* and *Cartesio* have to do with *additional* requirements. To revert to the parallel with, or the distinction from, natural persons: if the law of Member State A provides that a natural person is a *national* of A if he was born on the territory of A, this is sufficient for that person to enjoy the freedom of establishment provided for by the EC Treaty. Articles 43 and 48 EC do not prohibit Member State A from imposing some additional requirement, e.g. that the person must be born to a mother who was at the time a national of Member State A (although such requirement should, of course, not result in persons being deprived of the benefit of freedom of establishment they already enjoyed). No provision of EC law defines the term 'nationals' as used in Articles 43 and 48 EC. By contrast, Article 48 EC does define, precisely but with some latitude, what requirements companies must meet in order to benefit from the freedom of establishment. See (i) and (ii) in 12 above. That definition does not permit Member States to impose any additional requirements.

The foregoing does not mean that the prohibition of (or at least the sanction consisting of loss of legal personality in the event of) a cross-border transfer of the real seat cannot explicitly or implicitly be part of the PIL of a Member State and that such Member State would not be likely to be one that applies the real seat doctrine. However, as submitted above and below, such prohibition (or sanction) would be in violation of the freedom of establishment and must therefore not be applied, unless it could be justified under the rule of reason.

14.   The effect of *Cartesio* (and of *Daily Mail* and a number of paragraphs in *Überseering*) is that companies incorporated under the law of a real seat country are effectively deprived of a very important element of their right of establishment, even though Articles 43 and 48 EC do not permit any exception as to the companies that can benefit from the freedom of establishment, if they meet the conditions of Article 48. The European Court of Justice draws a distinction between companies incorporated in a Member State that permits them to freely transfer their real seat to another Member State, and companies incorporated in a Member State that does not so permit. However, Daily Mail and Cartesio are just as well companies within the meaning of Article 48 as Centros and Inspire Art. In *Daily Mail, Überseering* and *Cartesio*, the reasoning was based on a distinction between restrictions on freedom of establishment imposed by the host Member State and restrictions having exactly the same effect but imposed by the home Member State. This distinction appears to be artificial.

It is at odds with the other freedoms guaranteed by the EC Treaty where no distinction is made between import and export.[22] The distinction also leads to legal inequality and legal insecurity: one Member State will restrict emigration, another will not. It is unclear how far a Member State can go in restricting emigration. The rulings by the European Court of Justice in *Daily Mail* and *Überseering* were without any reservation, rendering this submission to national law quite atypical of the Court's case law. In *SEVIC* the Court did not hesitate to set aside the application of a provision of the law of a Member State which, on the strength of that provision, had refused to recognise an establishment operation carried out in another Member State. Why then should the Court pay so much deference to an equally restrictive rule of a home Member State (the requirement that a company must have both its registered office and its real seat in that State)?

15.   In *Cartesio*, the European Court of Justice has apparently shied away from the ultimate logical consequence of *Daily Mail* and *Überseering* with which the Advocate General[23] had confronted it: in paragraphs 111, 112 and 113 it develops a rather unconvincing argumentation to diminish the matter of 'life and death'. To that end, the Court distinguishes (in paragraph 111), from the point of view of the home country, two situations that I think can be described as follows: (i) cross-border transfer of the real seat only; and (ii) cross-border conversion (without winding-up or liquidation) where the company *wishes* to completely sever the links with the Member State of its incorporation.[24] As to the first situation, the Court confirms its 'licence to kill'. The new element in the Court's argumentation is the second situation, *cross-border conversion*. In principle, this part of the argumentation applies to incorporation countries as well as real seat countries. With respect to this case, the Court says that the power referred to in paragraph 110 is 'far from implying that national legislation on the incorporation and winding-up of companies enjoys any form of immunity from the rules of the EC Treaty on freedom of establishment'. However, national legislation on the incorporation and winding-up of companies is not under discussion here or in any of the other cases on freedom of establishment. The discussion is about an (in some countries unwritten) rule of PIL, which in certain cases, where the company wishes to benefit from the freedom of establishment, implies winding-up. It is precisely this rule that the Court, in *Daily Mail*, *Überseering* and *Cartesio*, takes under its protection

22 See Articles 23, 25, 28, 29 and 56 EC.
23 See paragraph 26 of his Opinion: 'The suggestion, therefore, is that the terms of the "life and death" of a company are determined solely by the State under whose laws that company was created [reference to paragraph 19 of *Daily Mail*]. The State gave; and so we must acquiesce when the State hath taken away.'
24 Apparently, the wish of the company is essential to this distinction, because in the event of cross-border transfer of the real seat, too, the result may be that the host country treats it as its 'own' national, with or without winding-up or liquidation.

at the expense of freedom of establishment. Now the Court decrees, without stating any reason, that there is an exception to this rule where 'the Member State of incorporation, by requiring the winding-up or liquidation of the company, [prevents] that company from converting itself into a company governed by the law of the other Member State'. It is unclear what, theoretically, this exception implies: is it only by requiring the winding-up or liquidation that the home country is prohibited from preventing its companies from converting themselves? Or is it also prohibited from making conversion impossible, or even difficult, by other means, such as putting up tax barriers?[25] One thing is certain: in today's practice this exception offers hardly any comfort. This is because the Court added, to paragraph 112, the ominous words 'to the extent that it is permitted under that law to do so'.

16.   What do these words mean? They relate to the law of the host Member State. It would seem that the European Court of Justice looks upon conversion as a deliberate, formal act. To my knowledge, only the laws of Portugal, Cyprus and Malta[26] provide for such a formal act.[27] If the Court actually refers to conversion as a formal act, it would leave an extremely small window of opportunity for cross-border conversions, at least for the time being. Member States may in due course introduce in their legislation rules on formal conversion of foreign companies into companies governed by their law.

Or does the Court mean by 'conversion' the mere application of the host country's own law? Many Member States that apply the real seat doctrine permit foreign companies to establish their real seat on their territory. Most of them will simply apply to those companies their own company law or certain (mandatory) provisions of that law.[28] It seems unlikely that the Court understood by 'conversion' the mere application of the host country's own company law. First of all, it is not yet clear if and, if so, to what extent freedom of establishment permits the host country to apply its own company law to the

---

25 See the quote from *SEVIC* at no 4 of this chapter, as well as the Commission's Communication on exit taxation (COM (2006) 825 of 19 December 2006), and Cases C-9/02, *De Lasteyrie du Saillant*, and C-470/04, *N*.

26 In Portugal, Art. 3(2) and (3) Código das Sociedades Comerciais, in Cyprus, the Companies (Amendment) Law 186(I)/2007, and in Malta Legal Notice 344 of 2002, Subsidiary Legislation 386.05, Continuation of Companies Regulations, as amended in 2003, 2006 and 2007.

27 However, Art. 161 of the Swiss *Bundesgesetz über das internationale Privatrecht* does provide for such a conversion without liquidation or reincorporation, provided the foreign law so permits, the conditions of that law have been met, and adaptation to a Swiss legal form is possible.

28 France would apply the mandatory rules of French company law; Belgium (and probably Luxembourg) 'at least' the mandatory rules of their company law; Italy would apply all rules of Italian company law; it is uncertain to what extent Portugal and Spain would apply their own company law (see E. Wymeersch, 'The transfer of the company's seat in European company law', 40 CML Rev. 2003, 661–95).

immigrating company. In *Inspire Art* the Court ruled that Articles 43 and 48 EC precluded Dutch legislation which imposed on a British company certain conditions of Dutch company law in respect of minimum capital and directors' liability. This case concerned the exercise of freedom of secondary establishment (the British company was considered to have established a branch in the Netherlands). It is likely, but not yet certain, that the same would apply where the primary right of establishment (transfer of real seat) is exercised. Second, if the Court had understood by 'conversion' the mere application of the host country's own company law, Cartesio could have benefited from the exception laid down in paragraph 112 of *Cartesio* because it had transferred its real seat to Italy and under Article 25(1) of the Italian *Legge* 218/1995 this meant that from then on it was governed by Italian company law. In the event that the Court did refer to such an informal way of conversion, the companies concerned will face serious uncertainty as to whether there is a 'conversion' if, assuming that *Überseering* and *Inspire Art* so permit, the host country applies some, but not all, of its rules of company law. It will be clear that, where the host Member State is an incorporation country, there can be no informal conversion, because, in principle (there are important exceptions, e.g. Italy) such a country will not apply its own company law to a foreign company. In any event, it follows from the above-quoted ominous words that freedom of establishment does not compel Member States to provide for formal conversion.

17.   Could the European Court of Justice not have achieved the same result in *Cartesio* as in *Centros, Inspire Art* and *SEVIC* by putting freedom of establishment first and foremost and then permitting the rule of reason to be applied as a safety valve? This is what Advocate General Poiares Maduro proposed. It looks as if the Court has allowed itself to be led astray by the old and moribund[29] real seat doctrine to take a political decision at the expense of Community law.

18.   This brings me to the *rule of reason*. This is a thirty-year-old rule authorising Member States to make exceptions to provisions of the EC Treaty, in particular those concerning the four fundamental freedoms. In *SEVIC*, the European Court of Justice expressed it, almost reluctantly,[30] as follows: 'it is not possible to exclude the possibility that imperative reasons in the public interest such as protection of the interests of creditors, minority shareholders and employees (see ...*Überseering* ... paragraph 92), and the preservation of the effectiveness of fiscal supervision and the fairness of commercial transactions (see ... *Inspire*

---

29 In Germany, a *Referentenentwurf* of a law to change from the real seat doctrine to the incorporation doctrine has been under discussion since January 2008. From 1 November 2008 German AG and GmbH may have their real seat outside Germany (see Arts. 1(4) and 5(1) *Gesetz zur Modernisierung des GmbH-Rechts und zur Bekämpfung von Missbräuchen (MoMiG)*). An important argument put forward against retention of the real seat doctrine in Germany is that it disadvantages the German economy in the regulatory competition within Europe. That argument is likely to play in other Member States as well.

30 See also *Überseering*, paragraph 92: 'It is not inconceivable ...'

Art ... paragraph 132) may, in certain circumstances and under certain conditions, justify a measure restricting the freedom of establishment'. The rule of reason means that the Court recognises certain 'imperative requirements in the public interest' that may justify a restriction on a fundamental provision of the EC Treaty. According to the Court's settled case law, in order to be justified, such a restriction must meet four conditions: (i) it must be justified by an imperative requirement in the public interest; (ii) it must be appropriate for ensuring the attainment of the objectives pursued with the restriction; (iii) it must not go beyond what is necessary to obtain those objectives (proportionality); and (iv) it must be applied in a non-discriminatory way.[31] It may safely be assumed that these are the conditions alluded to in the last passage cited above. It should be noted that, so far, the Court has not honoured any claim that the rule of reason should be applied in a company law case. In *Inspire Art* (see paragraph 143 and the operative part), the Court ruled that restrictions may only be imposed 'where the existence of an abuse is established on a case-by-case basis'. See also the operative part of *Centros*, in particular the words 'in fact'. In *SEVIC*, the Court specifically objected to the *general nature* of the restriction imposed (a general refusal by Germany to register a merger between a German and a Luxembourg company, 'even if the interests [of creditors etc.] are not threatened'). Such a restriction goes beyond what is necessary to protect those interests and therefore does not meet condition (iii) referred to above. In addition, the Court found that the German law was discriminatory where one of the companies involved in the merger was established in another Member State. In *Cartesio* too, the Court referred to the rule of reason: see paragraph 113. Again, it did not apply that rule.

19.   So far, I have discussed the cross-border transfer of the *real seat* of a company. It follows from *Cartesio* that freedom of establishment as interpreted by the European Court of Justice is of very little help to a company incorporated in a *real seat country* wishing to transfer its real seat to either a real seat country or an incorporation country. Paragraph 112 of *Cartesio* offers one exception to this rather negative conclusion, where the transfer of real seat is accompanied by the explicit or implicit intention to convert into a company of the host country (and the possibility to do so). It should be noted, though, that some real seat countries permit 'their' companies to transfer their real seat to another country. This may occur without winding-up or liquidation, provided certain requirements are met.[32] A company incorporated in an *incorporation country* will have no problem under the PIL of that country when it transfers its real

---

31 See e.g. *Inspire Art*, paragraphs 105 and 133, and *SEVIC*, paragraphs 28 and 29.
32 E. g. Belgium (under Art. 112 of the 2004 Code on Private International Law, provided the law of the host country is observed), Germany (see footnote 28), Luxembourg, Portugal and Spain (for the latter three, see Wymeersch, 'Transfer of the company's seat'). See also Art. 163 of the Swiss *Gesetz über das internationale Privatrecht*, which requires certain conditions of Swiss law to be met. Also, the law of the host country must provide that the company continues to exist.

seat to another country. As we have seen, however, the home country may put up other barriers by way of additional requirements.

As briefly mentioned at nos 5 and 16 of this chapter, a company that can transfer its real seat out of its home country may encounter a variety of problems in its envisaged *host country*, in particular if this is a real seat country. But, in the host country, a company transferring its real seat to another Member State is, in principle, protected by freedom of establishment as interpreted by the European Court of Justice in *Segers*, *Centros*, *Überseering* and *Inspire Art*.

3   Cross-border transfer of registered office

20.   The transfer of the *registered* office is quite a different matter. Here again, emigration and immigration must be distinguished. As to emigration, some Member States permit their companies to transfer their registered office to another country: e.g. Italy,[33] France,[34] Belgium,[35] Cyprus,[36] Luxembourg[37] and Malta.[38] Some Member States provide that a company incorporated under their law must have its registered office on their territory.[39] I would expect the European Court of Justice to be prepared to rule that freedom of establishment overrides the latter kind of provision, as it did in *SEVIC* with respect to paragraph 1(1) *Umwandlungsgesetz* which provides that certain transformation operations can be effected by entities *with their seat in Germany*. However, as set out above, it follows from *Daily Mail*, *Überseering* and *Cartesio* that the home country may restrict 'its' companies' freedom to emigrate. The crucial question after *Cartesio* is how far such restriction may go. I refer to paragraphs 112 and 113 of *Cartesio*, according to which the home country would violate Articles 43 and 48 EC if it prevented 'its' companies from converting themselves into companies governed by the law of another Member State,

---

33 Art. 25(3) *Legge* 218/1995, which requires compliance with the laws of both the home country and the host country.

34 Art. L223–30 as to the *sàrl*, provided the *associés* so decide unanimously; Art. L222–9 as to the *société en commandite simple* (also by unanimous vote); Art. L225–97 as to the SA (*société anonyme*), provided there is a convention with the host country. As there are no such conventions, it is generally assumed that Art. L222–9 can be applied by analogy. There is no similar provision with respect to the SAS (*société par actions simplifiée*; see Art. L227–1).

35 Based on case law, Conseil d'État, 29 June 1987, *Transports internationaux* v. *Vanneste*, No 28.267, *Tijdschrift voor Rechtspersoon en Vennootschap* 1988, p. 110, ann. Lenaerts.

36 See footnote 26.

37 Art. 67(1) of the 1915 Companies Act, which requires a unanimous vote of the shareholders and the bondholders.

38 See footnote 26.

39 E.g. the Netherlands, Art. 2:66(3) Civil Code for the *naamloze vennootschap* (NV) and Art. 2:177(3) for the *besloten vennootschap* (BV). In 1995, the Dutch government was of the opinion that, due to these provisions, Dutch companies could not transfer their registered office to another country (see the Explanatory Memorandum to Art. 4 of the Bill on Conflicts of Laws relating to Corporations).

by requiring their winding-up or liquidation. It is precisely such conversion (whether in the formal or in the informal sense: see no 16 of this chapter) that occurs in the event of a cross-border transfer of registered office. Apparently, therefore, the European Court of Justice permits a cross-border transfer of the registered office. But do not shout victory, because there are still these ominous words 'to the extent that it is permitted under that law to do so'. See no 16 of this chapter.

21.   As mentioned at no 16 of this chapter, there is uncertainty as to what the European Court of Justice means by 'conversion' and the attitude of real seat countries towards companies wishing to establish their real seat on their territories varies widely from one country to the other, but usually implies the requirement that those companies establish their registered office in the host country.

22.   The conclusion from the foregoing on *cross-border transfer of real seat or registered office* could be that companies are largely stuck in their Member State of incorporation. Yet, this is not necessarily so. A limited liability company falling within the definition of Article 1 of the Cross-border Merger Directive may create a (small) subsidiary in another Member State and then enter into a 'downstream merger' with that subsidiary. The result would be a single company with its registered office in the other Member State. The same could be done by creating an SE (*Societas Europaea*) by way of a (downstream) merger with such a subsidiary.[40] In that event, both the company and its subsidiary must be public limited liability companies (Article 2 SE Regulation). One should keep in mind, though, that such mergers may entail quite formidable procedural complications, in particular where there are employees. Of course, an SE can transfer its registered office to another Member State, provided it also transfers its real seat to the same Member State. However, such a transfer is subject to a cumbersome procedure under Article 8 SE Regulation.

4   Cross-border divisions

23.   The last operation to be examined in the context of the question of which cross-border operations are or are not feasible in the current state of development of Community law, apart from cross-border mergers under the Directive, is the division, sometimes called demerger. So far, the European Court of Justice has not explicitly dealt with divisions, but it follows from two paragraphs of *SEVIC* that cross-border divisions can, in principle, benefit from the freedom of establishment. The first of these paragraphs (18) has already been quoted at no 4 of this chapter. The second reads as follows:

---

40 In the realm of cooperatives, the same can be achieved by two or more cooperatives formed under the law of at least two Member States creating a *Societas Cooperativa Europaea* (SCE) by way of a merger (Art. 2(1) SCE Regulation).

19 Cross-border merger operations, *like other company transforma-tion operations*, respond to the needs for cooperation and consolidation between companies established in different Member States. They con-stitute particular methods of exercise of the freedom of establishment, important for the proper functioning of the internal market, and are therefore amongst those economic activities in respect of which Member States are required to comply with the freedom of establishment laid down by Article 43 EC.

24.   Reference is made to no 4 of this chapter (footnote 5) for the meaning of 'other company transformation operations'. They include divisions. Divisions may take various forms. The Sixth Company Law Directive distinguishes division by acquisition, division by the formation of new companies or a combination of these two. In all cases, the companies receiving contributions (in the form of assets and possibly liabilities) as a result of the division will allot shares to the shareholders of the company being divided. The German *Umwandlungsgesetz* distinguishes more forms of division, including *Ausgliederung*, where a com-pany transfers one or more parts of its assets and liabilities to one or more existing or newly formed companies which allot shares in their capital not to the shareholders of the company being divided but to that company itself. In cross-border situations, the company being divided will have its seat in one Member State and the recipient company or companies in one or more other Member States. The most interesting situation is where, in the process of the division of company A in Member State A, recipient company B is formed in Member State B. The division involves, inter alia, the creation, by an operation in country A, of company B in country B; the *ipso jure* transfer of all or part of the assets and liabilities of company A to company B; and, in principle, the shareholders of company A becoming *ipso jure* shareholders of company B. It could be argued that in a cross-border context this is stretching legal pos-sibilities too far. How could a company be created in country B by an opera-tion performed in country A? How can that company B *ipso jure* allot shares to the shareholders of company A in another country and be liable for the debts of company A as a result of an operation of that company A? However, Luxembourg law provides for just this on the sole condition that the law of the other country does not oppose the operation.[41] Denmark[42] and Finland[43] also provide for cross-border divisions. This seems to fit perfectly in the reasoning of the European Court of Justice in *Cartesio*: it is a matter of *recognition* by country B of the operations in country A. It could be argued that establishment operations are carried out in both countries, in which case each country needs

41 Art. 285(3) of the 1915 Companies Act, as amended by a law of 23 March 2007. The same applies under Swiss law (Arts. 163d and 164 of the Swiss *Gesetz über das internationale Privatrecht*).
42 Art. 138 *Lou om aktieselskaber*, provided certain conditions are met.
43 Act of 31 December 2007 for the implementation of the CBM Directive.

to recognise the operations on the other's territory. But the heart of the operations is clearly located in country A, the country of the dividing company. That country must provide for a *cross-border* division in order for country B to recognise it. It is sufficient for country B to permit the *domestic* division: if that is the case, *SEVIC* (as interpreted in *Cartesio*) prohibits country B refusing recognition of the division in country A. If in each country the national law on divisions is complied with (and this law has been harmonised to a great extent as a result of the Sixth Directive), why should the result be different from a cross-border merger? We are only waiting for more Member States to permit cross-border divisions.

25.   As to the question whether cross-border divisions could be achieved by other companies than public limited liability companies, reference is made to nos 6, 7 and 8 of this chapter.

II   Which cross-border operations can companies achieve thanks to the Cross-border Merger Directive?

26.   In several cases, including *Überseering* (paragraphs 55 and 60) and *SEVIC* (paragraph 26), the European Court of Justice has ruled that 'harmonising directives' provided for in Article 44 EC and conventions which may be entered into pursuant to Article 293 EC (e.g. on cross-border transfers of registered office and mergers) may be useful for facilitating such transfers or mergers, but the existence of such directives or conventions cannot be made a precondition for the implementation of the freedom of establishment. Must the answer to the above question therefore be in the negative? After the Court's interpretation (in *Cartesio*) of its judgment in *SEVIC*, I do not think so. As set out at nos 6, 7 and 8 of this chapter, the Court has reduced the chances of cross-border mergers outside the scope of the Directive to a bare minimum. Within the scope of the Directive, chances are very much better.

27.   What, then, is the scope of the Cross-border Merger Directive? To what kind of company does it apply? I refer to Dirk Van Gerven's chapter in this book (Chapter 1), and add the following remarks. As stated by him, the Directive applies to 'limited liability companies',[44] as defined in Article 2(1) of the Directive. This article refers to Article 1 of the First Company Law Directive, which has been amended with each accession of new Member States. For the reader's convenience, the current list has been included in Annex II to this book. Roughly speaking, limited liability companies include public limited

---

44 It should be noted that in the different language versions of the Directive the terms *Kapitalgesellschaft, société de capitaux, società di capitali, sociedad de capital, kapitálovou spoločností*, etc. are used, which do not necessarily have exactly the same meaning in each country. That is why the reference, in Art. 2 of the Cross-border Merger Directive, to Art. 1 of the First Directive is useful.

liability companies (e.g. the British plc, the German AG, the French SA, the Italian SpA, the Dutch NV or the Belgian NV/SA), private limited liability companies (e.g. the British Ltd, the German GmbH, the French SARL, the Belgian SPRL, the Luxembourg sàrl, the Italian sarl or the Dutch BV) and, in the majority of Member States, partnerships limited by shares. See Dirk Van Gerven's chapter for the extension to the scope given in Article 2(1)(b) of the Cross-border Merger Directive, as well as no 6 of this chapter. The scope of the Directive is even broader if one realises that, under Article 10 of the SE Regulation, an SE must be treated in every Member State as if it were a public limited liability company of the country where it has its registered office. This means that an SE can enter into a cross-border merger with any 'limited liability company' within the meaning of Article 1 of the Cross-border Merger Directive which under the law of the Member States involved can merge with a public limited liability company. Article 9 of the SCE Regulation is of similar import to Article 10 of the SE Regulation. Therefore, an SCE can enter into a cross-border merger with any 'limited liability company' that under the law of the Member States involved can merge with a cooperative, provided that in the Member State where it has its registered office a cooperative society falls within the definition of 'limited liability company' and that Member State has not excluded it from the application of the Directive.

28.   The most positive achievement of the Cross-border Merger Directive is that it is now beyond any doubt that cross-border mergers between 'limited liability companies' are possible (within the confines of the Directive), even where the law of Member States (other than the law implementing the Directive) does not permit such cross-border mergers. Another achievement is that for those cross-border mergers there is now a single date on which they take effect. In a number of cross-border mergers to which the Directive did not yet apply there were problems because the date of entry into effect differed under the laws of the Member States involved. There are, however, also limitations to the Directive.

III   What are the limitations under the Cross-border Merger Directive?

29.   First of all, mergers between 'limited liability companies' falling within the scope of the Directive can no longer be effected outside the Directive. This means that all such mergers must comply with all the formalities prescribed by the Directive, including the ones on employee participation. Another limitation applies to the Member States: they are no longer free to enact rules on cross-border mergers of limited liability companies. This is due to the so-called 'Sperrwirkung'[45] of Community law vis-à-vis subsequent national law, to the

---

45 In French, 'Effet privatif', which I would translate into 'blocking effect'. See e.g. Case 106/77, *Simmenthal*, Case 148/78, *Ratti*, and Case C-355/96, *Silhouette*.

extent that such national law is incompatible with final and complete provisions on the relevant subject-matter contained in for example, a directive. It would appear that the Directive contains such final and complete provisions, even though these include references to national law. An expression of a somewhat mitigated form of this blocking effect can be found in the second sentence of the third recital to the Cross-border Merger Directive.[46] Some other limitations have already been mentioned at no 7 of this chapter. As mentioned at no 8 of this chapter, Article 4(1)(a) of the Directive limits cross-border mergers to types of company that may merge under the national law of each of the Member States involved. This rule is understandable if one considers that various types of limited liability company falling within the Directive may differ so much that if they were to merge the problems of a technical legal nature would be insurmountable. However, one could think of situations where no such problems could arise. For example, under English law, a company cannot merge with a cooperative society, whereas a Dutch association, cooperative or foundation may acquire, by way of merger, an NV or BV of which it holds all the shares.[47] Conversely, a Dutch foundation, NV or BV can acquire, by way of merger, an association or cooperative of which it is the only member. In these situations, it is unlikely that technical problems arise that would not arise in a merger between two NVs or an NV and a BV. The same would apply if an English plc, as the acquiring company, merged with a Dutch cooperative of which it was the only member or if a Dutch cooperative, as the acquiring cooperative, merged with an English Ltd of which it held all the shares. However, such mergers do not fall within the scope of the Cross-border Merger Directive and can, therefore, not benefit from its regime. It seems to follow from *Cartesio* that, by analogy with *SEVIC*, such mergers cannot be effected outside the scope of the Directive either (see no 8 of this chapter).

30.   The most impeding limitation in the Directive is, in my view, Article 16, the extremely complicated and far-reaching provision on employee participation. Reference is made to the chapter by Philippe François and Julien Hick in this book (Chapter 2). To avoid any misunderstanding, employee participation is the influence of representatives of employees in the structure of a company, in particular by way of influencing the composition of a company's supervisory board or one-tier board (see Art. 2(k) of the SE Directive[48]). For many decades, the issue of employee participation has been the major stumbling block on the road to realisation of the SE as well as Community instruments on cross-border

---

46 Note that the last part of that sentence reflects the rule of reason (see no 18 of this chapter).
47 Although under Dutch law the main rule is that legal persons can merge with other legal persons of the same type (Art. 2:310 Civil Code).
48 Council Directive 2001/86/EC of 8 October 2001 supplementing the Statute for a European company with regard to the involvement of employees, OJ L 294, 10.11.2001, p. 22. It should be noted that the SE Directive also provides for information and consultation of employees, but the Cross-border Merger Directive does not.

mergers and transfer of registered office. In about fifteen Member States there is some form of employee participation, whereas in about twelve Member States there is no desire to introduce it. Because employee participation takes place within the corporate structure, there is concern in the Member States with participation that their undertakings might 'escape' to company forms governed by the law of Member States without participation. It is difficult to say whether this concern is justified. Since the judgments of the European Court of Justice in *Centros* and *Inspire Art*, companies and individuals are free to incorporate a company governed by the law of any Member State, including Member States without employee participation. Germany has the most severe participation regime, but so far hardly any use appears to have been made of this 'escape route'. After more than thirty years of stalemate, an initial break-through was achieved in 1994 when the EWC Directive[49] was adopted. This directive introduced a mechanism for negotiations between management and employees consisting of the creation of a 'special negotiating body' (SNB) and a set of standard rules that would apply in the event that no agreement was reached in the SNB. Seven years on, the same mechanism was introduced in the SE Directive. Another four years later, Article 16 of the Cross-border Merger Directive declared the regime of the SE Directive applicable with only some minor mitigations. See Chapter 2 of this book.

31.   The creation of, and the negotiations with, the SNB may take a long time and involve considerable expense. The provisions summarised below appear to tip the balance heavily in favour of the SNB:

    (i)   If no agreement is reached between management and the SNB, the latter may force upon the merging companies a regime of employee participation even though only one of those companies was subject to some form of employee participation covering a very small percentage (say, less than 5 per cent) of the total number of employees in all the companies (see Art. 16(3)(e) Cross-border Merger Directive and Art. 7(2)(b)(second indent) SE Directive).

    (ii)   Also, if no agreement is reached, the SNB may decide which form of participation will apply in the acquiring company if different forms of participation are applied in the merging companies (Art. 16(3)(e) Cross-border Merger Directive and Art. 7(2)(second sub-paragraph) SE Directive). Think of a Swedish company with up to 1,000 employees (under Swedish law having a fixed number of two employee representatives on the board) acquiring by way of merger a Danish company with 40 employees (Danish law requires the board to include not less than one

49 Council Directive 94/45/EC of 22 September 1994 on the establishment of a European Works Council or a procedure in Community-scale undertakings and Community-scale groups of undertakings for the purposes of informing and consulting employees, OJ L 254, 30.12.1994, p. 64.

third employee representatives, with a minimum of two). The SNB may decide that the Danish regime will apply to the Swedish company, if no agreement is reached between the SNB and management. It is clear that against this background management may be in a very uncomfortable negotiating position.

(iii)   Under Article 16(4)(b) of the Cross-border Merger Directive, the SNB may, by special majority, decide not to open or to terminate negotiations and to rely on the participation rules of the Member State where the acquiring company will have its registered office. Admittedly, under Article 16(4)(a) the merging companies have the right to choose 'without prior negotiation' to be directly subject to the SE Directive's standard rules for participation, but these rules may be very tough on the acquiring company. Also, on the assumption that the words 'without prior negotiation' mean that, by exercising their right under Article 16(4)(a), the companies can avoid having to create an SNB, they must decide whether or not to make use of that right 'as soon as possible after publishing the draft terms of merger' (see Article 3(1) SE Directive). This means that, unlike the SNB, they cannot test the water in negotiations before deciding.

32.   There are other elements that make the regime of Article 16 very severe on most companies falling within its scope. Where the acquiring merging company is a subsidiary of a company that is already subject to employee participation, neither the Cross-border Merger Directive nor the SE Directive provide for any exemption from employee participation at the level of the acquiring company. This may lead to a duplication of participation rights and thereby to conflicts, delays and a lack of cohesion in decision-making within the group of companies.

Another element is that under Article 13(4) SE Directive (declared applicable in Article 16(3)(g) of the Cross-border Merger Directive), Member States may provide that the structures of employee representation in the merging companies that cease to exist as separate legal entities are maintained after entry into force of the merger.[50] Quite apart from the question how there could be employee representation on a non-existing board of a non-existing company, such a provision could result in the same problems as the ones referred to at the end of the preceding paragraph.

Then there is Article 16(7) of the Cross-border Merger Directive that provides:

> When the company resulting from the cross-border merger is operating under an employee participation system, that company shall be obliged to take measures to ensure that employees' participation rights are protected in the event of subsequent domestic mergers for a period of three

---

50 Several Member States, including Austria, France and Germany, have made use of this option.

years after the cross-border merger has taken effect, by applying *mutatis mutandis* the rules laid down in this article.

This provision takes the place, for cross-border mergers, of Article 11 SE Directive, which is not referred to in Article 16 of the Cross-border Merger Directive. On the one hand, it requires protection of participation rights only in the event of 'domestic *mergers*'. This means that acquisitions of shares or assets (possibly with substantial numbers of employees) do not count, which greatly reduces the impact of this provision. The restriction to *domestic* mergers is not significant because cross-border mergers involving a company that is already subject to participation will in most cases result in the same or similar participation applying.[51] On the other hand, the period of three years seems to be longer than necessary to prevent misuse or abuse. During such a long period there may be many *bona fide* and urgent reasons for restructuring, including domestic mergers.

33.   When one considers the whole of Article 16, one must conclude that the protection of employee participation is rather strong. In many cases, Article 16 is likely to result in the application of the highest level of participation to be found in any of the merging companies. At first sight, there seems to be one possible exception to this rule: where the law applicable to the acquiring company grants employees of establishments in other Member States the same participation rights as the employees of the acquiring company in its own Member State have. Article 16(2)(b) seems to present this situation as an alternative to the 'highest level requirement' of Article 16(2)(a). However, to my knowledge, no provision as referred to in Article 16(2)(b) currently exists in any of the Member States. This exception will therefore be illusory until Member States introduce such a provision.[52]

34.   I revert to the rule of reason, this time in connection with Community instruments, such as directives. In principle, the Treaty provisions are binding on the Community institutions just as much as they are on the Member States. This means that the Directive must comply with the provisions of the EC Treaty, in particular such fundamental ones as those on freedom of establishment (see Articles 249, 230 and 231). However, it is settled case law of the European Court of Justice that Community instruments can also benefit from the rule of reason to escape from too rigid an application of Treaty provisions.[53] In Case

---

51 Application of Art. 16(4)(c) of the Directive could result in a somewhat lower level of participation by reference to the proportion of employee representatives on the board (see Art. 16(2)(a)).

52 It should be noted that the words 'national law applicable to the company resulting from the cross-border merger' in Art. 16(2) leave no room for companies to obtain the same result by voluntarily granting such participation rights to their employees in other Member States.

53 See e.g. Case 379/87, *Groener* (paras. 19 and 24); Case C-168/98, *Luxembourg* v. *European Parliament and Council of the EU* (para. 32); and Case C-299/02, *Commission* v. *the Netherlands* (para. 24).

C-168/98 (*Luxembourg* v. *European Parliament and Council of the EU*), the Court ruled that, when adopting harmonisation measures, 'the Community legislature is to have regard to the public interest pursued by the various Member States and to adopt a level of protection for that interest which seems acceptable in the Community ... It enjoys a measure of discretion for the purposes of its assessment of the acceptable level of protection.'[54]

35.   Given this discretion, one would not expect the European Court of Justice easily to refuse to apply a provision of the Directive on the ground that it infringes the Treaty and does not meet the conditions of the rule of reason. It is only with respect to some provisions of Article 16 of the Cross-border Merger Directive that I would express some doubt. These provisions are the ones referred to at no 31 of this chapter under (i) and (ii). I would submit that these provisions restrict freedom of establishment further than necessary for the protection of the interests of employees, and therefore do not stand the proportionality test. However, given the incompatibility of the (perceived) urgency of any merger and the time needed to obtain a decision of a court, let alone the European Court of Justice, this submission is very unlikely ever to be put to the test.

54 Note that in this Community context the concept of 'imperative requirements in the public interest' of a Member State is restated as public interest of all the Member States.

PART II

Application in each Member State
National reports for the EU Member States

5

Austria

GOTTFRIED GASSNER, ANDREAS HABLE AND HORST LUKANEC
Binder Grösswang Rechtsanwälte

I   Introduction

1.   The Cross-border Merger Directive has been implemented in Austria by the Corporate Law Amendment Act 2007 (*Gesellschaftsrechts-Änderungsgesetz 2007*).[1] This Act has introduced the EU Merger Act (*EU-Verschmelzungsgesetz, short name: EU-VerschG*) – a new Act which supplements the provisions on domestic mergers provided for in the Limited Liability Companies Act (*Gesetz über Gesellschaften mit beschränkter Haftung, short name: GmbH-Gesetz*) and the Stock Corporation Act (*Aktiengesetz*). The EU Merger Act provides that the provisions applicable to domestic mergers shall apply also to cross-border mergers unless provided for otherwise in the EU Merger Act. Therefore, basically the Stock Corporation Act, the Limited Liability Companies Act (in case a limited liability company is involved) and the EU Merger Act form the Austrian statutory framework applicable to cross-border mergers.[2]

The EU Merger Act became effective on 15 December 2007; Austria therefore has met the deadline for transposition provided for in Article 19 of the Cross-border Merger Directive.

II   Scope of the new rules

2.   The EU Merger Act applies expressly to Austrian stock corporations (*Aktiengesellschaften*) and Austrian limited liability companies (*Gesellschaften mit beschränkter Haftung*). Although not expressly provided for by the EU Merger Act, the new rules on cross-border mergers also apply to existing European companies (SEs).[3] The EU Merger Act does not apply to the formation of a (new) SE by means of a merger (see Chapter 1, no 9 of this book).

3.   In line with Article 3(2) of the Cross-border Merger Directive Austria has opted to decide that the EU Merger Act does not apply to cross-border mergers involving an existing cooperative society (*Genossenschaft*). This, of course, does not prevent Austrian cooperatives from participating in mergers to form a European cooperative society (see Chapter 1, no 7 of this book). Further, the EU Merger Act most importantly does not apply to general partnerships (*Offene Gesellschaften*), limited partnerships (*Kommanditgesellschaften*), economic

---

1   *Austrian Federal Law Gazette* I 72/2007, published on 24 October 2007.

2   The Limited Liability Companies Act provides for certain reliefs if a limited liability company is involved in a domestic Austrian merger; apart from that, it mainly refers to the pertinent provisions of the Stock Corporation Act. The material provisions relevant to a cross-border merger are, therefore, basically contained in the Stock Corporation Act and the EU Merger Act. By way of reference such provisions also apply if limited liability companies are involved. For ease of reading, we refrain, however, from citing the relevant provision of the Limited Liability Companies Act establishing such cross-reference each time.

3   See explanations to the government bill (ErlRV 171 BlgNR 23. GP) with respect to Sec. 3 EU Merger Act; see further A. Hable and G. Gassner, 'EU-Verschmelzungsgesetz', *Verlag Österreich*, Vienna, 2007, 72.

interest groupings (*Europäische wirtschaftliche Interessenvereinigung*) and savings banks (*Sparkassen*).

4. The EU Merger Act does not apply to cross-border mergers involving a company the object of which is the collective investment of capital provided by the public, which operates on the principle of risk-spreading and the units of which are, at the holders' request, repurchased or redeemed, directly or indirectly, out of the assets of that company. Section 4 of the EU Merger Act transposes the respective exemption provided for in Article 3(3) of the Cross-border Merger Directive on a word-by-word basis.

III   Cash payment

5. Under Austrian law cash payments granted in addition to the issuance of shares representing the capital of the company resulting from the cross-border merger may not exceed 10 per cent of the proportionate amount of the nominal capital attributable to the shares granted by the company resulting from the cross-border merger (Section 224(5) Stock Corporation Act). This rule applies principally without distinction to both purely domestic mergers and cross-border mergers.

In view of Article 3(1) of the Cross-border Merger Directive, the Austrian legislator argues that Austria is not required to permit cross-border mergers which involve a cash payment exceeding 10 per cent of the nominal capital. The argument provided is basically that an Austrian company taking part in a cross-border merger shall comply with the provisions and formalities of Austrian law (Art. 4(1)(b) and 4(2) Dir.).[4] Therefore, as a first aspect, if a cross-border merger involves an Austrian company resulting from the merger, an additional cash payment in excess of 10 per cent of the nominal capital attributable to the shares granted by the Austrian company is not permitted. As a second aspect, if a cross-border merger involves an Austrian transferring company and if the national law of the non-Austrian company resulting from the merger allows for a cash payment in excess of 10 per cent, this would be permissible from an Austrian legal perspective. The EU Merger Act (and the Austrian legislator's explanations thereto) is, however, not distinct in this second aspect.

IV   Consequences of the merger under national law

6. Under Austrian law the consequences of a cross-border merger are the same as the consequences of a domestic (Austrian) merger. In detail:

    (i)   all assets and liabilities, including rights and obligations, of the transferring companies are transferred to the company resulting from the merger

---

4 See explanations to the government bill (ErlRV 171 BlgNR 23. GP) with respect to Sec. 3 EU Merger Act.

(i.e. surviving or newly established company) by operation of law and by way of universal succession (*Universalsukzession*);

(ii) the transferring companies are dissolved without going into liquidation;

(iii) Austrian transferring companies are de-registered in the Austrian commercial register as a result of the merger; in case of a merger by new incorporation, a new receiving company is established and registered;

(iv) the shareholders of the companies which cease to exist become normally (see no 41 *et seq.* of this chapter) shareholders in the company resulting from the merger.

7.   If the company resulting from the cross-border merger is an Austrian company, the cross-border merger becomes legally effective upon its registration in the Austrian commercial register (see no 39 of this chapter). In this context the company details of the further companies participating in the merger are also mentioned in the Austrian commercial register.

Pursuant to Section 230(2) of the Austrian Stock Corporation Act and in line with Article 17 of the Cross-border Merger Directive, as of the registration of the merger in the Austrian commercial register potential defects of the merger do not have any effect on the merger as outlined above. Further, as of such registration, it is no longer possible to petition either for the avoidance of the merger or for declaring it null and void (see also Chapter 1, no 37 of this book).

If an Austrian transferring company continues to operate a business in Austria after the cross-border merger, this might trigger the obligation to have a branch office registered in the Austrian commercial register.

V   Procedure

1   Introductory remark: two-tier management system

8.   Austrian stock corporations and limited liability companies are subject to a mandatory two-tier management system, consisting of a managing body (managing directors (*Geschäftsführer*) in case of a limited liability company or management board (*Vorstand*) in case of a stock corporation) and of the supervisory board (*Aufsichtsrat*). Whereas all stock corporations are required by law to have a supervisory board, only certain limited liability companies – basically those of a sufficient size determined by financial indicators and number of employees – must have one. If the Austrian company taking part in the merger has a mandatory supervisory board, such supervisory board is required to be involved in the merger procedure (see nos 20 *et seq.* and 52 *et seq.* of this chapter).

2   Common draft terms of cross-border merger *(Verschmelzungsplan)*

9.   Pursuant to Section 5(1) of the EU Merger Act, the management bodies of the companies taking part in the cross-border merger shall prepare common draft

terms of cross-border merger.[5] Under Austrian law, same as the terms of merger in case of a domestic merger, the common draft terms of cross-border merger need to be set up in the form of a notarial deed (Sec. 5(5) EU Merger Act).

Firstly, the common draft terms of cross-border merger are required to include the information discussed in Chapter 1, no 19 of this book.[6] In case a wholly owned subsidiary is merged upstream into its parent company, information on the share-exchange ratio may be omitted (Sec. 5(3) EU Merger Act).

Secondly, the common draft terms of cross-border merger need to include the offer[7] of the transferring company or a third party to grant shareholders of the transferring company opposing the cross-border merger cash compensation and the terms of such cash compensation (see in more detail no 41 *et seq.* of this chapter). This does not apply only if either the transferring company does not have more than one shareholder or the shareholders waive their right to cash compensation (Sec. 5(4) EU Merger Act).

10.   Each transferring company must prepare a final balance sheet (*Schlussbilanz*) as per the effective date of the merger. The final balance sheet must be drawn up as of an effective date no more than nine months prior to the filing of the merger (Sec. 220(3) Stock Corporation Act). In practical terms this means that if, for example, the annual financial statements of a transferring company at 31 December shall serve as the final balance sheet and 31 December as the effective date, the merger must be filed with the commercial register court on 30 September at the latest.

11.   No later than one month before the general meeting to approve the cross-border merger is held,

   (i)   the common draft terms of cross-border merger must be filed with the commercial register court competent for the district where the Austrian participating company's registered office is located; and

   (ii)   a reference to such filing must be published in the respective announcement bulletin(s) of the Austrian company. Such publication needs to

---

5 The equivalent to the expression 'common draft terms of cross-border merger' in the German version of the Directive is '*Verschmelzungsplan*'. Consequently, the EU Merger Act also uses the expression *Verschmelzungsplan*. Interestingly, the relevant provisions applying to purely domestic mergers speak of a merger agreement (*Verschmelzungsvertrag*) rather than of draft terms.

6 This information goes beyond what is required in case of a purely domestic Austrian merger.

7 Sec. 5(4) of the EU Merger Act only mentions that the common draft terms of cross-border merger need to include the terms of the cash compensation offered; according to the explanations to the government bill (ErlRV 171 BlgNR 23. GP) with respect to this Section, however, the common draft terms of cross-border merger also need to include the offer of the cash compensation itself. Nevertheless, we think there are good arguments that it should be permissible to offer the cash compensation – in particular if granted by a third party – in a document separate from the common draft terms of cross-border merger (see also Hable and Gassner, 'EU-Verschmelzungsgesetz', 93).

include the information set forth in Article 6(2) of the Cross-border Merger Directive (see also Chapter 1, no 20 of this book). The announcement bulletin is normally the *Amtsblatt zur Wiener Zeitung*.

12.   In case an Austrian company is participating in a cross-border merger as the transferring company, known creditors of this company need to be informed directly about the intended cross-border merger if the sum of the nominal capital and appropriated reserves of the (non-Austrian) company resulting from the merger does not at least equal the sum of the nominal capital and appropriated reserves of the Austrian transferring company (Sec. 8(2)(3) EU Merger Act).

Failure to include the mandatory required information and provisions in the common draft terms of cross-border merger may – besides leading to potential criminal fines on and liability of the members of the management – lead to the commercial register court refusing the registration and thus completion of the cross-border merger.

The common draft terms of cross-border merger, amongst other documents, need to be made available to the shareholders and upon request to creditors of an Austrian company participating in the merger as the transferring company (see in more detail no 23 *et seq.* of this chapter).

3   Management report

13.   The management body of each company participating in the cross-border merger shall compulsorily[8] render a detailed written report on the cross-border merger. Such report shall legally and economically explain and substantiate the anticipated consequences of the merger, the common draft terms of cross-border merger, in particular the share-exchange ratio, and if applicable the amount of additional cash payments, as well as measures (if any) taken for the protection of positions of holders of bonds and rights to participate in profits. In case any particular difficulties were encountered regarding the valuation of the companies, reference must be made thereto (Sec. 6 EU Merger Act in conjunction with Sec. 220a Stock Corporation Act). In addition, the report shall explain the implications of the cross-border merger for creditors and employees (including their contractual claims) of the companies participating in the cross-border merger (Sec. 6 EU Merger Act).

In case of a merger by absorption of a wholly owned subsidiary, the audit and report in relation to the share-exchange ratio may be omitted (Sec. 5(3) EU Merger Act, Sec. 232(1) Stock Corporation Act).

If the Austrian company participating in the merger is a transferring company, the management report shall also make a statement regarding the amount of the nominal capital and appropriated reserves of all companies participating

---

8 In the case of a domestic Austrian merger, the preparation of the management report may be waived by the shareholders; such waiver is not permissible in the case of a cross-border merger.

in the cross-border merger (see for the background of this rule no 50 *et seq.* of this chapter).

14. No later than one month before the general meeting to vote on the cross-border merger is held, the management report must be provided to the employee representatives or, in the absence thereof, to the employees themselves. In case any of the management bodies of the companies involved in the cross-border merger receives, prior to the shareholders' meeting which is to resolve upon the merger, an opinion of the representatives of its employees on the merger, such opinion needs to be enclosed with the management report (Sec. 6(1) EU Merger Act).

Finally, the management report, amongst other documents, needs to be made available to the shareholders and, upon request, to creditors of an Austrian company participating in the merger as the transferring company (see also nos 23 and 25 of this chapter).

4   Report of the independent expert (auditor's report)

15. The common draft terms of cross-border merger shall be audited by a merger auditor for each of the companies participating in the merger. The merger auditor is appointed by the supervisory board. In the absence of a supervisory board (see no 8 of this chapter), the auditor is appointed by the commercial register court upon request of the management body of the company. The supervisory board and/or the management bodies, as the case may be, of the merging companies may jointly petition to the court to appoint a common auditor for all merging companies together (Sec. 220b Stock Corporation Act).

The merger auditor(s) shall be independent from the merging companies. Therefore, the regular auditor of a company is usually not accepted by Austrian courts to act also as merger auditor.

16. The auditor's report – in contrast to the management report discussed under no 13 *et seq.* of this chapter – need not be prepared if all shareholders of all companies participating in the cross-border merger unanimously waive, either in written form or in the minutes of the shareholders' meeting, the examination and report of the auditor (Sec. 232(2) Stock Corporation Act). Further, the auditor's report is also not required in the event of a merger by absorption of a wholly owned subsidiary (Sec. 3(2) EU Merger Act in conjunction with Sec. 232(4) Stock Corporation Act).[9]

17. The merger auditor(s) shall provide a written report on the results of the audit. If more than one merger auditor is involved, the auditors may nevertheless provide a single and common report (Sec. 220b Stock Corporation Act, see also Chapter 1, no 23 of this book).

---

9 See in this respect also Article 15(1) and (2) of the Cross-border Merger Directive.

In order to prepare its report, the auditor may request from the merging companies any information deemed necessary (see also Chapter 1, no 24 of this book).

18.   As with domestic (Austrian) mergers, the auditor shall in particular make a statement whether or not, in the auditor's opinion, the share-exchange ratio and, if applicable, the additional cash payments are appropriate (Sec. 220b Stock Corporation Act). In the context of a cross-border merger, the auditor shall in addition certify whether the cash compensation offered to shareholders opposing the cross-border merger and the terms thereof (see no 41 *et seq.* of this chapter) are, in the auditor's opinion, appropriate (Sec. 7(3) EU Merger Act). In relation to these respective statements, the auditor should at least (i) indicate by which methods the share-exchange ratio or cash compensation were determined, (ii) indicate for which reasons the application of these methods is appropriate, (iii) indicate which share-exchange ratio or cash compensation would result if different methods were applied, inasmuch as several methods have been applied, and (iv) make a statement as to what weight these methods were given at the determination of the share-exchange ratio or cash compensation. Finally, the report must mention any specific difficulties encountered in the valuation process (Sec. 7(3) EU Merger Act in conjunction with Sec. 220b Stock Corporation Act).

In case of a merger by absorption of a wholly owned subsidiary, the audit and report in relation to the share-exchange ratio may be omitted (Sec. 232(1) Stock Corporation Act).

The audit and report of the cash compensation may be omitted if either the transferring company does not have more than one shareholder or its shareholders waive their right to cash compensation (Sec. 7(3)(4) EU Merger Act).

On the other hand, in case an Austrian company participating in the merger is a transferring company, the audit report shall also include a statement regarding the amount of the nominal capital and appropriated reserves of all companies participating in the cross-border merger (see for the background of this rule no 50 of this chapter).

19.   The auditor's report, amongst other documents, needs to be made available to the shareholders and, upon request, to creditors of an Austrian company participating in the merger as a transferring company (see also nos 23 and 25 of this chapter).

5   Report of the supervisory board

20.   The supervisory boards of Austrian companies involved in the merger shall review the intended merger on the basis of the management report (see no 13 *et seq.* of this chapter) and the auditor's report (see no 15 *et seq.* of this chapter) and shall render a written report thereon (Sec. 220c Stock Corporation Act).

Provided that the Austrian company participating in the merger is mandatorily required to have a supervisory board, the shareholders are not entitled to waive the supervisory board's audit and report. The audit and written report of the supervisory board may, however, be omitted if the book value of the transferring company does not exceed a certain value determined by the supervisory board in connection with acquisitions generally requiring supervisory board approval (Sec. 220c, second sentence, Stock Corporation Act).

21.   From a timing perspective, it is to be noted that the report of the supervisory board must be based on the management report and the auditor's report. This implies that these reports must be readily prepared before the supervisory board is in a position to issue its report. The supervisory board report – same as the other reports – needs to be made available to the shareholders and, upon request, to creditors of an Austrian company participating in the merger as a transferring company (see nos 23 and 25 of this chapter).

6   General meetings of shareholders

A   Information requirements prior to the shareholders' meeting(s)

22.   No later than one month before the general meeting(s) to approve the cross-border merger is/are held pursuant to Section 221a(1) of the Stock Corporation Act:

   (i)   the common draft terms of cross-border merger must be filed with the commercial register court competent for the district where the Austrian company's registered office is located; and

   (ii) a reference to such filing needs to be published in the respective announcements bulletin(s) of the Austrian company. Such publication most importantly needs to include the information set forth in Section 6(2) of the Cross-border Merger Directive (see also Chapter 1, no 19 of this book) and, as the case may be, reference to certain creditor and shareholders' protection rights. The announcement bulletin is normally the *Amtsblatt zur Wiener Zeitung*.

For purposes of the before-mentioned filing, the common draft terms of cross-border merger need to be prepared in the German language or need to be certified translated into the German language.

23.   In case the Austrian company participating in the cross-border merger is a stock corporation or a European company, for at least one month before the shareholders' meeting to resolve upon the merger is scheduled, the following documents – generally for all the merging companies, to the extent that such documents actually exist[10] – shall be made available at the offices

---

10 For example, the preparation of the auditor's report can be waived by the shareholders; a newly established company participating in the merger may not have annual financial statements for the last three years, etc.

of the company for inspection by its shareholders (Sec. 221a(2) Stock Corporation Act):

(i)   common draft terms of cross-border merger;
(ii)   the annual financial statements, including management reports, of the merging companies for the last three years;
(iii) the final balance sheet, if the effective date of the merger deviates from the date of the most recent annual financial statement and if the final balance sheet is available in audited form;
(iv)   a balance sheet which is required to be prepared if the last annual financial statements refer to a fiscal year which ended more than six months before the conclusion of the common draft terms of cross-border merger; the effective date of this so-called interim balance sheet (*Zwischenbilanz*) shall not be before the first day of the third month preceding the month of the conclusion or completion of the common draft terms, and the interim balance sheet shall be drawn up according to the same regulations as applied to the company's last annual balance sheet. A physical stock-taking is not required. The values from the last year's annual balance sheet may be imported. Any write-offs, value adjustment and provisions, as well as any substantial changes in the real values of assets that cannot be perceived from the books up until the effective date of the interim balance sheet shall, however, be taken into account (Sec. 221a(3) Stock Corporation Act);
(v)   the management report(s);
(vi)   the audit report(s);
(vii) the supervisory board report(s).

Each shareholder is entitled to be sent copies of these documents upon request without delay and free of charge (Sec. 221a(1) in conjunction with Sec. 108(5) Stock Corporation Act).

24.   In case the Austrian company participating in the cross-border merger is a limited liability company, the above-mentioned documents shall be sent to each shareholder. Between the day of dispatch of the documents and the day of the shareholders' meeting scheduled to resolve upon the merger there must be a period of at least one month (Sec. 8(1) EU Merger Act).

25.   If an Austrian company is participating in a cross-border merger as a transferring company, known creditors of such company need to be informed no later than one month before the general meeting to resolve upon the cross-border merger is held directly about the intended cross-border merger, provided the sum of the nominal capital and appropriated reserves of the (non-Austrian) company resulting from the merger does not at least equal the sum of the nominal capital and appropriated reserves of the Austrian transferring company (Section 8(2)(3) of the EU Merger Act).

Creditors of an Austrian company which is participating in a cross-border merger as the transferring company are entitled to be sent, upon request, the documents discussed before under no 23 of this chapter without delay and free of charge (Sec. 8(3) EU Merger Act).

26.   In the shareholders' meeting which is voting on the merger, the documents discussed under no 23 of this chapter need to be made available to the shareholders. The management board shall orally explain the common draft terms of cross-border merger. Further, the management board shall inform the shareholders of every substantial change in the company's assets, liabilities or profit or loss that occurred between the preparation of the common draft terms of cross-border merger and the time of passing the resolution on the merger; this particularly applies where such change would justify a different share-exchange ratio (Sec. 221a(5) Stock Corporation Act). Finally, each shareholder, upon request, is entitled to be informed of all matters of significance to the merger pertaining to the other companies participating in the merger (Sec. 221a(6) Stock Corporation Act).[11]

B   Shareholders' approval

27.   Under Austrian law, a merger in general must be approved by the shareholders of the companies taking part in the merger. The common draft terms of cross-border merger shall only become effective if the shareholders of each merging company have approved them (Sec. 221(1) Stock Corporation Act). Further, the content of the common draft terms of cross-border merger shall be recorded in the minutes of the shareholders' meeting; alternatively the common draft terms of cross-border merger may be enclosed with the minutes (Sec. 221(4) Stock Corporation Act).

The shareholders' meeting resolving upon the matter may be held not earlier than one month after the filing of the common draft terms of cross-border merger with the commercial register and the publication of a reference to such filing (see no 22 of this chapter).

28.   The approval of the shareholders' meeting of the surviving company may be omitted if (i) at least 90 per cent of the nominal capital of the transferring company is held by the surviving company (own shares of the transferring company or other shares that belong to another party on account of the transferring company shall be deducted from the nominal capital), or (ii) if shares to be granted due to the merger do not exceed 10 per cent of the nominal capital of the surviving company; in the event the nominal capital of the receiving company shall be increased in the course of the implementation of the merger, the increased amount of the nominal capital shall form the basis of such calculation (Sec. 231(1)(2) Stock Corporation Act).

---

11 There are opinions that to satisfy this information right of the shareholders, representatives of the other companies participating in the merger need to be present in the shareholders' meeting to answer questions.

If the approval of the shareholders' meeting of the receiving company was omitted for any of the aforementioned reasons, shareholders of the receiving company whose shares together add up to at least 5 per cent of the nominal capital of the receiving company are entitled to request within one month as of the day when the shareholders' resolution approving the merger was passed with the transferring company that a shareholders' meeting of the receiving company be called to vote on the merger (Sec. 231(2) Stock Corporation Act). In this connection the articles of association of the receiving company may provide for a threshold lower than 5 per cent. In the notification on the filing of the common draft terms of cross-border merger the shareholders shall be made aware of their right to request the calling of such a shareholders' meeting for the purpose of voting on the merger (Sec. 231(2) Stock Corporation Act).

Further, pursuant to Section 9(2) of the EU Merger Act, the approval of the transferring company may be omitted in case of a cross-border merger by way of absorption of a wholly owned subsidiary.

Provided that the national laws applicable to the non-Austrian companies involved in the cross-border merger are similar to the Austrian rules described above, in case of a cross-border merger by way of absorption of a wholly owned subsidiary, in principle no approval of the shareholders of any of the merging companies would be required.

29.   The resolution of the shareholders' meeting of an Austrian company participating in the cross-border merger shall require both a majority of 50 per cent of the vote cast (*Stimmenmehrheit*) and a majority of 75 per cent of the nominal capital represented in the shareholders' meeting (*Kapitalmehrheit*) at the time of the passing of the resolution.[12] The articles of association may provide for a greater majority and also make the resolution subject to further requirements (Sec. 221(2) Stock Corporation Act).

If a stock corporation has issued shares with different rights, the approval of the merger requires the approval of the shareholders of each class of shares by special resolution. In case of a limited liability company, Section 99 of the Limited Liability Companies Act provides for certain approval rights for shareholders who are granted specific rights. In this context it is also to be noted that the common draft terms of cross-border merger need to address the rights conferred by the company resulting from the merger on shareholders enjoying special rights or on the holders of securities other than shares representing capital or the measures proposed concerning them (Sec. 5(2)(7) EU Merger Act; see also Chapter 1, no 19 of this book).

30.   The shareholders' meeting of a merging company may decide to make the merger subject to its express ratification of the arrangements with respect to

---

12 The majorities of the vote cast and of the capital represented are normally identical; they may, however, deviate if the articles of association of a stock corporation limit the right to vote in accordance with Sec. 12 Stock Corporation Act.

participation of employees in the company resulting from the merger (Sec. 9(2) EU Merger Act).

31.   The minutes of the general meeting resolving upon the merger need to be taken in the form of a notarial protocol.

7   Pre-merger certificate and scrutiny of the legality of the cross-border merger

32.   The authority designated in Austria to supervise the cross-border merger is the commercial register court competent for Austrian companies participating in the cross-border merger.

A   The company resulting from the cross-border merger is not an Austrian company (pre-merger certificate)

33.   The management board of an Austrian company participating in a cross-border merger as the transferring company is required to apply for registration of the intended cross-border merger with the commercial register court competent for the district where the company is domiciled (Sec. 14(1) EU Merger Act). The following documents shall be attached to such application in original, in duplicate or in certified copy:

    (i)   common draft terms of cross-border merger;

    (ii)   the minutes of the general meeting of the (Austrian) transferring company containing the resolution regarding the cross-border merger;

    (iii) in case the merger shall require any official approval,[13] the document(s) certifying such approval;

    (iv)   management report (see no 13 et seq. of this chapter) pertaining to the (Austrian) transferring company;

    (v)   auditor's report (see no 15 et seq. of this chapter) pertaining to the (Austrian) transferring company;

    (vi)   final balance sheet (see no 10 of this chapter) of the (Austrian) transferring company;

    (vii) evidence that the notification regarding the filing of the common draft terms of cross-border merger was published (see no 11 of this chapter);

    (viii) evidence in relation to the security provided with respect to the cash compensation offered to shareholders opposing the merger (see no 40 et seq. of this chapter) and, as the case may be, evidence that the non-Austrian companies participating in the merger have expressly accepted the initiation of proceedings to examine the share-exchange (Art. 10(3) Dir., see also no 49 of this chapter);

    (ix)   evidence that creditors were granted security coupled with a statement that the claims of all creditors who approached the company within the

---

13 This refers basically to approval potentially required if a company is operated in a regulated field of business (e.g. banks, insurance companies, etc.). Normally, therefore, no such approval is required.

period as set out in Section 13(1) EU Merger Act were either settled or that they were granted security.

34.   In addition, a declaration of all the members of the management board (or of all the managing directors in case of a limited liability company) must be presented to the court which states that (i) no action of opposition or for the establishment of nullity of the merger resolution has been asserted within one month following the passing of the resolution, or that such action has been withdrawn or that all shareholders have waived their rights to file such an action by means of a declaration certified by a notary public, and further (ii) whether any shareholders have exercised their right to cash compensation pursuant to Section 10 of the EU Merger Act and, if so, how many (see no 41 *et seq.* of this chapter), and confirmation that the shares of such shareholders may be lawfully taken over (Sec. 14(2) EU Merger Act).

If such declarations are unable to be submitted, the commercial register court may decide to suspend the proceedings until such declarations are presented to it (Sec. 14(2) EU Merger Act in conjunction with Sec. 19 Commercial Register Act). Therefore, there is a risk that shareholders could try to block or delay the merger by filing claims for opposition or establishment of nullity of the merger resolution.

35.   Upon having scrutinised and verified on the basis of the documents filed whether all pre-merger acts and formalities provided for by Austrian law have been properly completed, the commercial register court shall without delay:

(i)   issue a certificate attesting to the proper completion of all pre-merger acts and formalities; and

(ii)   register the intended cross-border merger in the Austrian commercial register; this registration shall mention the public registry and the (intended) corporate seat of the company resulting from the cross-border merger and the fact that the pre-merger certificate was issued (Sec. 14(3) and (4) EU Merger Act).

36.   After the cross-border merger is completed, the management of the Austrian transferring company shall present the notice of completion to the commercial register court and apply for the de-registration of the Austrian company in the Austrian commercial register. The Austrian commercial register does not de-register the company *ex officio*, even if it is provided with the notice of completion directly by the issuing (non-Austrian) authority.

B   The company resulting from the cross-border merger is an Austrian company (effects of the decision)

37.   The management of all companies participating in the merger (i.e. also the management of the non-Austrian company) shall apply for the registration of

the cross-border merger with the commercial register court competent for the district where the Austrian company resulting from the merger is domiciled (Sec. 15(1) EU Merger Act). Pursuant to Section 15(2) of the EU Merger Act, the following documents shall be attached to such application in original, in duplicate or in certified copy:

(i) common draft terms of cross-border merger;
(ii) the minutes of the general meetings;
(iii) in case the merger shall require any official approval,[14] the document certifying such approval;
(iv) management report(s) (see no 13 *et seq.* of this chapter);
(v) auditor's report(s) (see no 15 *et seq* of this chapter);
(vi) final balance sheet (see no 10 of this chapter);
(vii) evidence that the reference in relation to the filing of the common draft terms of cross-border merger was published (see no 11 of this chapter).

In case the Austrian company resulting from the cross-border merger is a company newly established through a cross-border merger by new incorporation, certain further documents need to be enclosed with the application (e.g. articles of association).

In addition to the above-mentioned documents, evidence of the arrangements for employee participation and the pre-merger certificates, not being older than six months, of the non-Austrian companies participating in the cross-border merger need to be enclosed with the application (Sec. 15(2) EU Merger Act).

38. Upon having scrutinised and verified on the basis of the documents filed whether all acts and formalities required for the cross-border merger are completed, the commercial register court shall register the cross-border merger in the Austrian commercial register with the Austrian company resulting from the cross-border merger (Sec. 15(3) EU Merger Act). Further, the Austrian court shall notify, without delay, the public registry in which each of the non-Austrian companies was required to file its documents that the cross-border merger is completed (Sec. 15(4) EU Merger Act).

39. On the day of the registration of the cross-border merger in the Austrian commercial register the cross-border merger enters into effect and has the consequences discussed in no 6 of this chapter. Further, the commercial register court arranges for the publication of a notice on the cross-border merger in the official Austrian gazette, *Amtsblatt zur Wiener Zeitung.*

---

14 This refers basically to approval potentially required if a company is operated in a regulated field of business (e.g. banks, insurance companies, etc.). Normally, therefore, no such approval is required.

VI   Protection of minority shareholders

The EU Merger Act provides for various protection mechanisms regarding minority shareholders of the (Austrian) companies participating in the cross-border merger, in particular if the Austrian company is the transferring company.

1   Right to cash compensation (exit right)

40.   Minority shareholders who together hold more than 25 per cent of the nominal capital and who are present when the shareholders' resolution on the cross-border merger is taken may vote against the cross-border merger and, in doing so, block the transaction. If the decision of the shareholders is, however, taken with a majority vote as discussed above under no 29 of this chapter, such decision is in principle binding also on the minority shareholders.

41.   In case an Austrian company participates in a cross-border merger as the transferring company and the company resulting from the merger is not an Austrian company, each single shareholder of the transferring company is entitled to exit the transferring company in exchange for appropriate cash compensation. For this reason, the draft terms of cross-border merger are required to include an offer of appropriate cash compensation (see no 9 of this chapter).

42.   In order to exercise such right, a minority shareholder is required to object expressly to the approval of the shareholders on the cross-border merger and to have such objection recorded in the minutes of the respective shareholders' meeting. Further, it is required that such shareholder is a shareholder of the Austrian transferring company from the point in time when the shareholders' meeting approved the cross-border merger through to the point in time when the exit right is exercised (Sec. 10(1) EU Merger Act).

43.   The exit right shall be exercised by accepting the offered cash compensation either at the shareholders' meeting (in such case coupled with the above-mentioned statement of objection) or by writing to the party which offered the cash compensation no later than one month after the approval of the shareholders on the cross-border merger was resolved upon (Sec. 10(1) EU Merger Act).

The entitlement to cash compensation is subject to the cross-border merger taking effect; at this point in time, the cash compensation becomes due and three years thereafter it becomes time-barred (Sec. 10(1) EU Merger Act). Further, the shareholders entitled to cash compensation need to be provided security (e.g. a bank guarantee) to ensure payment (including costs of arranging for payment) of the cash compensation (Sec. 10(1) EU Merger Act).

44.   The pre-merger certificate (see no 33 *et seq.* of this chapter) shall be issued only if it is evident that all entitlements to cash compensation have been properly

secured or that all shareholders have waived their right to cash compensation (Sec. 10(1) EU Merger Act).

45.   Under Austrian law, actions of opposition against the shareholders' resolution approving the merger are excluded if they are based on the grounds that the cash compensation has not been properly determined or the explanations of the cash compensation contained in the management report (see no 13 *et seq.* of this chapter), the auditor's report (see no 15 *et seq.* of this chapter) or the supervisory board report (see no 20 *et seq.* of this chapter) were not in accordance with the law (Sec. 11(1) EU Merger Act). The rationale behind this is to avoid delay to the merger coming into effect[15] by shareholders who initiate lawsuits to have the cash compensation scrutinised by the court prior to the merger taking effect.

However, in order to ensure protection of the (minority) shareholders' property rights, shareholders who expressly objected to the decision of the shareholders on the cross-border merger and had such objection recorded in the minutes of the respective shareholders' meeting are entitled, pursuant to Section 11(2) of the EU Merger Act, to petition to the court within one month of the date of the shareholders' approval to have the cash compensation scrutinised by an independent experts committee and – depending on the result – amended by the court. The decision in a procedure so initiated is binding and effective on all shareholders who have opted for the offered cash compensation (this means that if the cash compensation is held to be inappropriate, such shareholders who have not filed their petition to review also benefit from such a decision).

46.   In connection with the cash compensation, please note accompanying rules of the EU Merger Act as discussed under nos 9, 18, 33 and 34 of this chapter.

2   Right to petition for the share-exchange ratio to be scrutinised and amended

47.   Under Austrian law, it is the concept with mergers that shareholders may petition to the court to have the share-exchange ratio scrutinised and amended (only) within one month of the coming into effect of the merger (Sec. 225(c) Stock Corporation Act). The procedure to scrutinise and amend the share-exchange ratio does not therefore prevent the merger becoming effective; in fact, it requires that the merger has taken effect. In terms of Section 10(3) of the Cross-border Merger Directive, Austria therefore provides for a procedure to scrutinise and amend the ratio applicable to the share-exchange of shares without preventing the registration of the cross-border merger.

48.   Shareholders could try to circumvent this concept that the share-exchange ratio be scrutinised and amended only after the merger comes into effect by

---

15 As discussed under no 34 of this chapter, the court may suspend the registration proceedings if such claims were raised.

initiating legal procedures aiming to scrutinise and amend the share-exchange ratio before the merger comes into effect. In order to prevent such behaviour, actions of opposition against the shareholders' resolution approving the merger are excluded if they are based on the grounds that the share-exchange ratio has not been properly determined or the explanations on the share-exchange ratio contained in the management report (see no 13 *et seq.* of this chapter), the auditor's report (see no 15 *et seq.* of this chapter) or the supervisory board report (see no 20 *et seq.* of this chapter) were not in accordance with the law (Sec. 225b Stock Corporation Act).

49.   Pursuant to Section 12(1) of the EU Merger Act, the exclusion of actions of opposition on the grounds discussed above, however, applies in the context of cross-border mergers only if all shareholders of the non-Austrian companies participating in the merger, when approving the common draft terms of cross-border merger, expressly agreed to allow the shareholders of the Austrian company to have recourse to the Austrian courts to initiate such a procedure of having the share-exchange ratio scrutinised and amended without preventing the merger coming into effect.

   If the Austrian company participating in the cross-border merger is the transferring company, only such shareholders are entitled to have recourse to such a procedure as have declared their intention to initiate such a procedure either by express and recorded declaration in the shareholders' meeting approving the merger or within one month after such shareholders' meeting in writing. The pre-merger certificate (see no 33 *et seq.* of this chapter) has to state whether such a declaration was made and, in the affirmative, the name of the respective shareholder(s).

   Non-Austrian transferring companies are entitled to initiate such a procedure in Austria if (i) it becomes apparent from the pre-merger certificate pertaining to this company that its shareholders have waived their right to take action of opposition on the grounds that the share-exchange ratio was not properly determined, and (ii) the national law applying to all transferring companies accepts such procedure.

VII   Creditor protection

50.   If the Austrian company participating in the cross-border merger is a transferring company, the creditors of such company are entitled to request security within two months from the date of publication of the common draft terms of cross-border merger for claims that already existed but which are not yet due as of this date (Sec. 13(1) EU Merger Act). This right, however, only exists if the creditors demonstrate that the settlement of the claim is threatened by the merger.

   There is no obligation to demonstrate that the settlement of the claim is threatened if the sum of the nominal capital and appropriate reserves of the (non-Austrian) company resulting from the merger is lower than the sum of the nominal capital and appropriate reserves of the Austrian transferring company (Sec. 13(1) EU Merger Act). It is to be noted that in such case the known creditors of the Austrian company need to be personally informed about the intended cross-border merger in advance (see no 25 of this chapter).

The company may avoid having to provide security by settling the claims in question. In the event of a dispute, the creditor has to bring the matter to the court.

The pre-merger certificate may only be issued by the commercial register court competent for the Austrian company if it is evident that creditors that approached the company were granted security (see no 33 *et seq.* of this chapter).

51.   If the Austrian company is the company resulting from the merger, the general creditor protection rules for (domestic Austrian) mergers set forth by Section 226 of the Stock Corporation Act apply. Accordingly, creditors of the companies involved in the merger may request security within six months from the date of registration of the merger with the commercial register court for claims that already existed as of the date of registration of the merger but which have not yet become due as of this date.

VIII   Employee participation[16]

52.   With respect to employee participation, the Cross-border Merger Directive has been implemented in Austria by Sections 258 *et seq.*, i.e. Chapter VIII, of the Labour Constitutional Act (*Arbeitsverfassungsgesetz*) which entered into effect on 15 December 2007. Austrian law only provides for employee participation for companies established in Austria resulting from a cross-border merger. If the company resulting from the merger is established abroad, the employee participation rules of the Member State where such company is registered, if any, shall apply.

1   Employee participation in companies established in Austria resulting from a cross-border merger

53.   Austrian law does provide for certain employee participation rights, in particular for the right of employees to appoint one third of the members of the supervisory board of the company, if established (see no 8 of this chapter).[17] In case the company resulting from the cross-border merger has its registered

---

16 This part has been written with the assistance of Angelika Pallwein-Prettner, attorney-at-law at Binder Grösswang.

17 The Corporate Law Amendment Act 2007 introduced the requirement for limited liability companies, which otherwise would not be obliged to have a supervisory board, to establish one in case the negotiations or the application of the standard rules lead to certain employee participation rights in the supervisory board.

office in Austria, the Austrian rules of employee participation generally apply. They will be set aside if:

(i) at least one of the merging companies has employed more than 500 employees on average in the six months leading up to publication of the common draft terms of cross-border merger and this company provides for a system of employee participation; or

(ii) Austrian law does not provide for at least the same level of employee participation as the relevant merging companies; or

(iii) employees of establishments of the company resulting from the merger located in another Member State are under Austrian law not granted the same participation rights as employees of the company employed in Austria.

54.   In these cases, the employee participation regulations in accordance with Chapter VIII of the Labour Constitutional Act apply. In case of merger by absorption where the company resulting from the merger is a European company (SE), the rules regarding employee participation in an SE[18] shall apply.

2   Special negotiation body ('SNB')

55.   In case Chapter VIII of the Labour Constitutional Act applies, an SNB has to be established by the employee representatives which shall negotiate and conclude a written agreement on employee participation with the management of the participating companies. The agreement shall include (i) the number of members of the supervisory board that are appointed by employees or that can be recommended or rejected by employees, (ii) the procedure therefore, and (iii) the determination of the rights of the members.

56.   In order to establish the SNB, employee representatives have to be provided with certain information, such as, for example, the identity and form of each participating company, concerned subsidiaries and establishments, the identity of the employee representatives and the number of employees they represent and the date of the first meeting of the SNB.

The members of the SNB are elected from members of the works council or amongst officials and employees of the responsible union. Austrian SNB members are appointed in accordance with the comparatively detailed and complex provisions of Sections 217 and 218 of the Labour Constitutional Act by the employees' representative bodies only.

The allocation of seats in the SNB is based on the ratio of employees in the participating companies, concerned subsidiaries and establishments and

18 I.e. Council Regulation No 2157/2001 on the Statute for a European company and Council Directive 2001/86 supplementing the Statute for a European company with regard to the involvement of employees, which has been implemented in Austria for the most part by adding Chapter VI to the Labour Constitutional Act.

the total number of employees. If necessary, additional members of the SNB have to be appointed, to ensure that the employees of a transferring company are represented by a member of the SNB.

The duration of the negotiations between the SNB and the employer representatives shall not exceed six months. If both parties agree, the negotiation period may be extended up to one year.

57.   The SNB has the right to reject or abandon negotiations with the management. In such case Austrian rules regarding employee participation apply to the company (see no 53 of this chapter).

58.   In case (i) the parties to the negotiations agree that no agreement can be reached or no agreement is concluded within the six-month period, or (ii) the management decides that it will not enter into negotiations regarding employee participation, the standard rules for employee participation shall apply. According to the standard rules the number of members of the supervisory board that shall be appointed by employees is based on the highest level of employment participation in the participating companies. Furthermore, the SNB shall decide on allocation of seats and election of Austrian members to the supervisory board.

59.   In case (i) described in no 58 above, the standard rules for participation only apply if either:

(i)   at least one participating company has a system of employee participation which applies to at least one third of all employees of all participating companies; or

(ii)   at least one participating company has a system of employee participation and the SNB passes a resolution with regard to the applicability of the standard rules.

60.   In case the management refuses to enter into negotiations regarding employee participation, the standard rules for participation apply in any case. The employee representatives shall be notified of the decision not to enter into negotiations and shall establish a special appointment body ('SAB'), which basically has the same tasks as the SNB, i.e., in particular, to allocate the seats and elect the Austrian members of the supervisory board.

61.   With regard to protection of employee participation rights in the event of subsequent domestic mergers, the Austrian legislation more or less reflects the provisions of the Cross-border Merger Directive. However, the Austrian legislator extended the period of protection from three years to five years.

3   Protection of employee representatives

62.   Employee representatives are afforded special protection according to the Labour Constitutional Act. In particular, they may not be discriminated against and they enjoy special protection against termination of their employment.

IX   Tax treatment

63.   Austria has implemented the Merger Tax Directive, as amended by Council Directive 2005/19,[19] by an amendment of the Austrian Reorganisation Tax Act (*Umgründungssteuergesetz*). The Reorganisation Tax Act generally provides for a tax-neutral regime for mergers and other types of reorganisations.[20]

64.   A basic prerequisite for the Reorganisation Tax Act to apply is that the right of taxation of Austria in respect of hidden reserves of the transferred assets (including good will, if any) is not limited to the level of the receiving company (i.e. the company resulting from the merger). This prerequisite – which is relevant in particular for 'outbound' cross-border mergers – ensures that tax neutrality, i.e. a roll-over of book values upon the merger, only applies in respect of assets that remain within the tax laws of Austria. Therefore, originally domestic assets of the transferring company transferred upon a merger can partially be subject to a book value roll-over and partially not, depending on whether or not Austria loses its right of taxation or not in respect of the assets. Generally, such mergers are referred to as partially or totally tax neutral.

65.   If Austria loses its right of taxation in respect of assets that are transferred to a company resident in the EU or in an EEA country which provides comprehensive administrative and enforcement assistance towards Austria,[21] no immediate taxation is triggered. Rather, the transferring company may opt for the deferral regime. Under the deferral regime, the realised capital gain is only taxed once the respective asset is disposed of by the receiving company. This recapture shall be deemed to have retroactive effect as of the effective date of the merger. Consequent capital gains realised after expiry of the statute of limitations (ten years) shall not be subject to tax.

Losses upon a disposal of assets are only taken into account in Austria (i) up to the tax basis of the respective assets as of the effective date of the merger, and (ii) if not considered abroad. Due to the wording of the law, the tax deferral regime does not apply if the transferring company is a dual resident company. This constitutes a limitation which is likely to be held a violation of the EC freedom of establishment.

66.   In case of 'inbound' mergers, insofar as Austria acquires the right of taxation, the tax basis of the imported assets shall be stepped up to their fair market value. Repatriated assets that have been subject to the deferral regime are to be shown at their original book value.

19 Council Directive 2005/19 of 17 February 2005 amending Directive 90/434 of 23 July 1990.
20 It is to be noted that the present chapter covers only taxes levied directly on companies or shareholders but does not comment on indirect tax and transfer tax aspects of cross-border mergers.
21 Currently only Norway.

67.   The exchange of shares upon a merger is not considered a taxable event according to the Reorganisation Tax Act, thereby ensuring tax neutrality of those dispositions. In case of a merger, however, that is (partially) taxable, the exchange of shares is considered a taxable disposition. In such a context, tax neutrality is only granted if the shareholder is a resident of the EU or an EEA member state that provides comprehensive administrative and enforcement assistance. In respect of third-country residents, full or partial taxation is triggered depending on the proportion of the assets to be taxed at the level of the transferring company.

6

Belgium

DIRK VAN GERVEN
NautaDutilh

I   Introduction

1.   The Cross-border Merger Directive has been implemented in Belgium by the
Omnibus Act of 8 June 2008 (I).[1] This Act amended the Company Code by
introducing a new section on cross-border mergers. It also provides that the provisions applicable to domestic mergers shall apply unless provided otherwise
in the section on cross-border mergers.

---

1 *Belgian State Gazette*, 16 June 2008.

II   Scope of the new rules

2.   The new rules on cross-border mergers apply to all companies governed by the Company Code, i.e. public limited liability companies (*société anonyme/ naamloze vennootschap*) (SAs), partnerships limited by shares (*société en commandite par actions/commanditaire vennootschap op aandelen*) (SCAs) and European companies (SEs), in addition to cooperatives (*société cooperative/coöperatieve vennootschap*), private limited liability companies (*société privée à responsabilité limitée/besloten vennootschap met beperkte aansprakelijkheid*) (SPRLs) and European cooperative societies (SCEs). The rules also apply to companies with unlimited shareholder liability (i.e. general partnerships). However, in this case the company can only benefit from the rule that a merger by operation of law shall be deemed to result from an assignment of all rights and obligations (assets and liabilities) if the national law of the Member States where the other participating companies are located so allows (see Chapter 1, no 5 of this book). Neither agricultural companies nor economic interest groupings can participate in a cross-border merger (Art. 670 Company Code).

     In the event of a merger by absorption by an SPRL or a cooperative, the shareholders of the participating companies must meet the legal and statutory requirements to become shareholders of the surviving company (Art. 698 Company Code).

3.   The Cross-border Merger Directive does not apply to cross-border mergers involving a company whose corporate purpose is the collective investment of capital provided by the public, which operates on the principle of risk-spreading and whose units may be, at the holder's request, purchased or redeemed, directly or indirectly, out of the company's assets (Art. 3(3) Dir.). Under Belgian law, such companies are governed by the Act of 20 July 2004 on certain forms of collective management of investment portfolios. The companies so excluded are open-ended public institutions for collective investment which can take the form of a publicly held limited liability company (*société anonyme/naamloze vennootschap*) and limited partnerships with shares (*société en commandite par actions/commanditaire vennootschap op aandelen*) (Art. 772(1) Company Code).

     Belgian companies in liquidation cannot take part in a cross-border merger (Art. 772(1) Company Code). This follows from the provision in the Cross-border Merger Directive that the assets and liabilities are transferred on the date of dissolution without liquidation of the disappearing companies. Consequently, it is not possible to merge with companies that have already been dissolved and are in liquidation. Under Belgian law, a company in liquidation is entitled to participate in a purely domestic merger in accordance with the provisions of national law implementing the Merger Directive, provided it has yet to distribute its liquidation proceeds (Art. 681 Company Code).

A company which has declared bankruptcy is not considered to be 'in liquidation' under Belgian law as long as the bankruptcy proceedings have not yet been closed. Consequently, it can participate in a cross-border merger.

III   Cash payment

4.   A cross-border merger is possible even if the cash payment exceeds 10 per cent of the nominal value or, in the absence thereof, the accounting par value of the securities or shares representing capital of the surviving company, provided the law of the Member State of one of the participating companies so allows (Art. 772(2) Company Code).

Under Belgian law, mergers involving such a cash payment cannot benefit from the rules applicable to cross-border mergers. Consequently, only if the national law applicable to one of the foreign companies participating in the merger, in which a Belgian company participates as well, so provides will a cash payment in excess of 10 per cent be allowed. In this case, the shareholders of the Belgian company may also benefit from the cash payment. If the national law governing the participating foreign companies does not permit such a payment, the cross-border merger can only benefit from the rules implementing the Cross-border Merger Directive if the cash payment does not exceed 10 per cent of the nominal value or accounting par value of the securities or shares representing capital of the surviving company.

IV   Legal consequences and enforceability of a cross-border merger

5.   A cross-border merger results in all assets and liabilities being transferred to the surviving entity by operation of law, without liquidation of the participating companies. It has the same legal effects as an internal (domestic) merger under the Merger Directive, i.e.:

(i)   the participating companies (with the exception of the surviving company if no new company is established) cease to exist;

(ii)   the shareholders of the companies which cease to exist become shareholders in the surviving company; and

(iii)   all assets and liabilities, including rights and obligations, are transferred to the surviving company (Art. 772(3) Company Code).

As from completion of the cross-border merger (see no 26 of this chapter), it is no longer possible to petition the competent court to avoid the merger (Art. 772(5) Company Code).

6.   A cross-border merger is enforceable against third parties as from the publication date of the cross-border merger instrument in the annexes to the *Belgian State Gazette*, unless the company can prove that the third parties in question

knew of the merger earlier. For fifteen days following publication, third parties can claim that the merger is not enforceable against them if they can prove that it was impossible for them to have known of it. Third parties can, at their own initiative, choose to rely on the merger prior to such publication date (Art. 76 Company Code). Any real property and other rights *in rem* assigned to the surviving company must be recorded with the mortgage registrar (*conservateur des hypothèques/hypotheekbewaarder*). The transfer of intellectual property rights to the surviving company must be registered in accordance with the laws applicable to such rights (Art. 683 Company Code).

Rights and obligations resulting from employment contracts and employment relations existing on the date of completion of the cross-border merger (see no 26 of this chapter) are transferred by operation of law on that date to the surviving company or the new company resulting from the merger (Art. 772(4) Company Code).

The surviving company or the new company resulting from the merger is responsible for fulfilling all formalities required to complete the assignment and the vesting of rights and obligations in it (Art. 772(4) Company Code).

V   Procedure

1   Draft terms of cross-border merger

7. The management organs of the merging companies shall prepare draft terms of cross-border merger. This document need not be in notarised form (Art. 77(6) Company Code).

    The draft terms should include the information described in Chapter 1, no 19 of this book as well as the corporate purpose of each merging company (Art. 772(6)(a) Company Code). In the event of a parent company merging with its wholly owned subsidiary, the information mentioned in Chapter 1, no 39 of this book can be omitted (Art. 772(6) Company Code).

    Failure to include the above-mentioned information can result in the imposition of criminal fines on members of the management organ, i.e. the directors or managers, depending on the type of company (Art. 773 Company Code). Furthermore, the directors or managers can be held liable to third parties for any damage resulting from failure to include required information in the draft terms of merger. However, such an omission cannot constitute a ground to avoid the merger (see no 5 of this chapter).

8. The draft terms of cross-border merger must be filed with the clerk's office of the commercial court of the judicial district where each participating company's registered office is located no later than six weeks before the general meeting called to approve the cross-border merger. In addition, the draft terms must be published by extract, containing the information set forth in Chapter 1, no 19 of this book, in the annexes to the *Belgian State Gazette* (Art. 772(7) Company Code). Each participating company is responsible for fulfilling these

filing and publication requirements in the judicial district where its registered office is located.

2 Management report

9. The management body of each merging company must prepare a written and justified report for the company's shareholders. This report should mention the value of the company's assets and liabilities and provide a legal and economic explanation and justification for (i) the reasons for and terms and conditions of the merger; (ii) the implications of the merger for shareholders, creditors and employees; (iii) the methods used to determine the share-exchange ratio;[2] (iv) the relative importance of each method; (v) the values resulting from each method; (vi) the difficulties encountered; and (vii) the proposed share-exchange ratio (Art. 772(8) Company Code).

    In the event of the trade unions represented on the works council preparing an opinion on the merger in the framework of the information procedure provided for by Collective Bargaining Agreement No 9 of 9 March 1972 and this opinion is submitted to management in a timely manner, it must be attached to the management report.

10. The shareholders and the employee representatives or, in the absence thereof, the employees themselves are entitled to examine at the company's registered office the management report at least one month before the date of the general meeting called to approve the draft terms of cross-border merger (Art. 772(8) Company Code and no 16 of this chapter). The management report must not otherwise be made public.

11. Members of the management organ, i.e. the directors or the managers depending on the type of company (Art. 773 Company Code), can be criminally sanctioned (fined) for failure to prepare and submit a management report on the cross-border merger.

3 Auditor's report

12. The auditor of each participating company should prepare a report on the draft terms of cross-border merger. If a Belgian company does not have an auditor, it must appoint one from amongst the members of the Institute of Certified Auditors (*Institut des réviseurs d'entreprise/Instituut der bedrijfsrevisoren*) or an external accountant who belongs to the Institute of Accountants and Tax Consultants, appointed by the management body of the company (Art. 772(9) (1) Company Code). A separate report on the contribution in kind need not be prepared if the absorbing company is a limited liability company.[3]

---

2 This is not required in the event of a simplified merger of a wholly owned subsidiary (see Chapter 1, no 39 of this book).

3 Arts. 313, 423 and 602 of the Company Code do not apply (Art. 772(9)(1) Company Code).

The management bodies of the merging companies may jointly petition the court to appoint one or more auditors or accountants. To this end, a written petition must be submitted to the president of the competent commercial court (in accordance with Article 588(17) of the Judicial Code). The auditor(s) so appointed shall prepare a report on the draft terms of cross-border merger (Art. 772(9)(2) Company Code).

The above-mentioned report need not be prepared if all shareholders of all companies participating in the cross-border merger unanimously decide that no report need be drafted and the draft terms of cross-border merger need not be examined by an auditor or accountant (Art. 772(9)(3) Company Code).

An auditor's report is also not required in the event of a merger by absorption of a wholly owned subsidiary (Art. 772(9)(4) Company Code). However, an auditor's report is required for a cross-border merger of a subsidiary if the parent company holds 90 per cent or more, but not all, of the subsidiary's shares.[4]

13.   In its report the auditor should certify whether, in its opinion, the share-exchange ratio is relevant and reasonable (Art. 772(9)(1) Company Code). The auditor's report should at least (i) indicate the methods used to determine the share-exchange ratio; (ii) indicate whether these methods are appropriate in the case at hand and mention the resulting value yielded by each method; and (iii) give an opinion on the relative importance of each method in determining the value eventually retained. The report furthermore should indicate the particular difficulties, if any, encountered in the valuation process.

In order to prepare its report, the auditor may request from the merging companies any information deemed necessary.

14.   The auditor's report must be made available to the shareholders of the merging companies at the latest one month before the general meeting called to approve the draft terms of cross-border merger (see no 16 of this chapter for more details). It must not otherwise be made public.

15.   In the event of an auditor's report not being prepared as described above, but is required, the members of the management body may be fined (Art. 773 Company Code).

4   General meeting of shareholders

A   Information for shareholders

16.   The draft terms of cross-border merger, the management report and the auditor's report as well as the shareholders' right to obtain a copy of these documents free of charge shall be mentioned on the agenda of the general meeting

---

4 The Cross-border Merger Directive (Art. 15(2)) allows the Member States not to require an auditor's report in this case (see Chapter 1, no 39 of this book), but Belgium did not enact this option.

called to vote on the draft terms of cross-border merger (Art. 772(10)(1) Company Code). The agenda shall be enclosed with the convocation notice sent to the shareholders or published in accordance with the rules applicable to convocation notices for an SE, SA or SCA whose shares are in bearer or dematerialised form.

17.   The shareholders are entitled to consult the draft terms of a cross-border merger and the reports at the office of each participating company, for one month prior to the date of the general meeting scheduled to vote on the merger (Art. 772(10)(2) of the Company Code). There is no obligation to send these documents to the shareholders, including the holders of registered shares whose names are mentioned in the shareholders' register. The company can of course decide to send these documents on its own initiative.

In addition to these documents, the company should simultaneously make available to shareholders the annual accounts for the last three fiscal years of each merging company and, for limited liability companies, the reports for the last three fiscal years of the company's board of directors, managers, management committee, supervisory board and auditors.

If the draft terms of cross-border merger are dated more than six months after the close of the last fiscal year to which the latest annual accounts relate, an accounting statement (for each merging company) dated no earlier than three months prior to the date of the draft terms of cross-border merger must also be made available at the company's registered office. This statement shall be prepared in accordance with the methods used for, and the presentation of, the latest annual accounts. The company need not, however, take a new inventory. Changes to the balance sheet made further to valuations may be limited to those resulting from bookings. However, the statement must take into account recent amortisations and reserves and important changes in value which do not appear from the books of account.

Each shareholder may request free of charge a complete or partial copy of any of the above-mentioned documents, except for those which are sent to shareholders together with the notice of the general meeting (Art. 772(10)(3) Company Code).

The management of a merging company must inform the general meeting and the management of the other participating companies (which must in turn inform their shareholders) of each material change in the assets and liabilities of the company between the date of the draft terms of cross-border merger and the date of the (last) general meeting called to vote on the merger (Art. 709 Company Code).

B   Shareholder approval

18.   With respect to the Belgian participating companies, the merger and the draft terms of cross-border merger must be approved by the general meeting of shareholders. However, for the absorption of a wholly owned subsidiary by

its parent company, shareholder approval is not required at the level of the subsidiary (Art. 772(11)(1) Company Code).

19. In order to approve the cross-border merger, at least 50 per cent of the capital must be present or represented. If this quorum is not met, a second meeting can be called, which can take decisions regardless of the number of shares present or represented (Art. 772(11)(1)(1) Company Code).

The merger must be approved by a special majority of three quarters of the votes present or represented; the articles may provide for a larger majority (Art. 772(11)(1)(2) Company Code). Non-voting shares are exceptionally entitled to vote on the merger (Art. 481(3) Company Code). In a silent partnership (*société en commandite simple/gewone commanditaire vennootschap*) or a cooperative company (*société cooperative/coöperatieve vennootschap*), including an SCE, votes are allocated in proportion to the shareholder's share in the capital and attendance is calculated based on the company's assets (Art. 772(11)(1) Company Code).

If there are different classes of shares or other securities (which do not represent the capital), i.e. shares or securities with different rights, and if the merger results in a change of their respective rights, the quorum and special majority requirements must be met for each class of shares. Furthermore, securities which do not represent capital are entitled to vote notwithstanding any provision to the contrary in the articles of association, and voting restrictions in the articles do not apply. Finally, each share carries one vote (Art. 772(11)(2) Company Code). The draft terms of cross-border merger must define the rights conferred by the company resulting from the merger on shareholders enjoying special rights or on the holders of securities other than shares representing capital or the measures proposed concerning them (Art. 5 Dir.).

20. In certain cases, the approval of all shareholders (i.e. unanimity) is required in order to proceed with a cross-border merger. This is the case with respect to the following companies participating in a cross-border merger: (i) general partnerships (*société en nom collectif/vennootschap onder firma*) regardless of whether the partnership is the surviving company or the company that ceases to exist; and (ii) Belgian companies which shall cease to exist if the surviving company is a general partnership, a silent partnership or a cooperative with unlimited liability (Art. 772(11)(3) Company Code). The consent of all holders of securities which do not represent the capital is also required.

In a silent partnership or a limited partnership with shares (*société en commandite par actions/commanditaire vennootschap op aandelen*), the approval of the general partners is in any event required (Art. 772(11)(4) Company Code).

21. The general meeting of a merging company may decide to make its decision subject to express ratification of the arrangements with respect to the participation of employees in the company resulting from the merger (Art. 772(11)(5) Company Code).

22.   In the event of a merger with an existing company, the general meeting of the surviving company must vote on the proposed changes to the articles of association of that company, immediately after having approved the cross-border merger. The quorum and majority required to approve these changes are determined by the rules applicable to the relevant corporate form of the surviving or new company. A special majority may be required in the event of a change in the corporate purpose (Art. 772(11)(6) Company Code). Such approval is required for the merger to take effect.

        Any changes to the articles of association shall be included in the draft terms of cross-border merger and will therefore already have been approved by the shareholders of the companies that cease to exist.

        In the event of a newly formed company resulting from the merger, the new company's articles of association will have been approved as part of the terms of cross-border merger.

23.   The general meeting of each Belgian participating company must be held before a notary, and the minutes must be prepared in notarised form. The notarial instrument should contain the conclusion of the auditor's report (Art. 772(11)(7) Company Code).

5   Pre-merger certificate

24.   The notary who prepares the notarial instrument containing the minutes of the meeting approving the cross-border merger must verify and certify the existence and legality, both internally and externally, of all instruments and formalities to be accomplished by the merging company. External legality refers to the formalities and form in which the required actions must be effected. Internal legality refers to the content of the actions, which should be in accordance with the law. If the instruments and formalities are not in accordance with the law, the notary shall refuse to proceed with the general meeting. If not, he can be held liable.

        The notary will, after verification, issue without delay a pre-merger certificate conclusively attesting to completion of the requisite pre-merger acts and formalities discussed above (Art. 772(12) Company Code). This certificate is valid for six months (see Chapter 1, no 29 of this book).

25.   Each participating company must send to the notary responsible for attesting to the completion of the merger for the surviving company the pre-merger certificate mentioned in no 24 of this chapter, within six months from issuance of this certificate by the notary (for a Belgian company) or other authority designated under local law (for a foreign company participating in the merger), together with the approved terms of cross-border merger (Art. 772(13) Company Code).

        The completion of the merger must be scrutinised by the notary of the surviving company or of the new company resulting from the merger. The notary is responsible for ensuring that the merging companies have approved the common terms of cross-border merger and, if required, that arrangements in relation to employee participation have been agreed in accordance with the rules implementing Article 16 of the Cross-border Merger Directive (see Chapter 2, no 6 *et seq.* of this book). Once the notary has verified the foregoing, s/he will issue an attestation confirming completion of the cross-border merger.

6   Effects of the decision

26.   A cross-border merger only enters into effect on the date on which the notary of the company resulting from the merger attests to completion of the merger on the basis of the pre-merger certificates and other documents evidencing this fact. The attestation is enacted by the notary. If the merger is realised through the formation of a new company, it will only take effect as from the formation of this company.

The notary's attestation is filed with the clerk of the commercial court of the place where the surviving or new company's registered office is located. The clerk's office ensures publication of an extract in the annexes to the *Belgian State Gazette*. Any changes to the surviving company's articles of association or the articles of association of the newly formed company must also be published in a similar manner. Publication is required to render the attestation and the amendments to the articles enforceable against third parties (Art. 76 Company Code). The creation of a newly formed company is only enforceable as from the filing of its articles of association with the clerk of the competent commercial court (Art. 2 Company Code).

Notification of the above-mentioned attestation to the registries where the foreign companies participating in the merger are recorded shall be organised by royal decree (Art. 772(14) Company Code).

27.   As from the effective date of the cross-border merger, it cannot be declared void by a court (Art. 772(5) Company Code). This rule applies regardless of whether the decision has been published and thus made enforceable against third parties.

VI   Minority shareholders

28.   A decision to carry out a cross-border merger approved by the majority discussed under no 19 of this chapter is binding on the company's minority shareholders. They have no choice but to go along with the merger and will receive shares in the surviving or new company. Belgian law does not provide for any special remedies for minority shareholders.

Only the shareholders of a cooperative which proposes merging with a company that is not a Belgian cooperative are entitled to exit the company in the fiscal year of the merger as from the date of the notice of the general meeting scheduled to vote on the merger, provided the terms of merger are approved (Arts. 698 and 711 Company Code). This right does not exist if the company resulting from the merger is a cooperative governed by Belgian law.

VII   Protection of creditors

29.   Creditors of the merging companies whose claims existed prior to publication of the certificate attesting to completion of the cross-border merger (see nos 25 and 26 of this chapter) and which are not yet due are entitled to request security within two months from the publication date of this certificate (Art. 684 Company Code). The company can avoid having to provide security by settling the claim at a discount for early repayment. In the event of a dispute, the matter shall be referred to the president of the commercial court in the judicial district where the debtor company's registered office is located.

Creditors of financial institutions, such as credit institutions and insurance companies, which are subject to supervision by the Belgian Banking, Finance and Insurance Commission (the 'CBFA') do not benefit from this protection. Oversight by the CBFA is considered sufficient to ensure the protection of their interests.

VIII   Employee participation

30.   With respect to employee participation, the Cross-border Merger Directive has been implemented in Belgian law by Collective Bargaining Agreement No 94, entered into within the National Labour Council on 29 April 2008 ('CBA No 94'). CBA No 94 entered into force on 29 April 2008.

1   Employee participation in companies established in Belgium resulting from a cross-border merger

31.   Belgian law currently does not provide for employee participation rights or the right for employees to sit on the management bodies of limited liability companies. Consequently, for companies resulting from a cross-border merger that are established in Belgium, the Belgian rules will be set aside and participation will be possible if such rights existed within other participating companies (Art. 16(2) Dir. and Art. 2 CBA No 94).

2   Special negotiating body ('SNB')

32.   Where the rules in force concerning employee participation, if any, in the Member State where the company resulting from the cross-border merger has its registered office are set aside, a special negotiating body ('SNB') must be set up with a view to negotiating arrangements on employee participation, in the company resulting from the cross-border merger, with the management organs of the participating companies (Art. 16(3) Dir.).

33.   CBA No 94 provides specific rules for the appointment of the Belgian member(s) of the SNB (Art. 10(2) CBA No 94).

In general, such member(s) are appointed by and from amongst the members of the works council(s) of the Belgian participating companies. In the absence of a works council, appointment will occur from amongst the members of the committee(s) for prevention and protection at work.

In the absence of a works council and a committee for prevention and protection at work, the competent joint committee may authorise the trade union delegation to appoint the SNB members. In the absence of such authorisation or in the absence of a trade union delegation, the employees have the right to elect their representative(s) to the SNB directly. However, in this case, practical problems could arise as CBA No 94 does not provide for an election procedure.

In the event of appointment by the trade union delegation or election by the employees directly, the employee representative(s) chosen need not necessarily be employed by one of the participating companies or by a concerned subsidiary or establishment (Art. 10(3) CBA No 94).

3   Protection of employee representatives

34.   Members of the SNB and of the representative body employed in Belgium, as well as employee representatives sitting on the administrative or supervisory board of a company resulting from a cross-border merger that are employed in Belgium, enjoy same rights and protection as employee representatives on a Belgian works council, in particular as concerns participation in meetings and preparatory meetings, the payment of salaries and the length of absences necessary to exercise their functions (Art. 34 CBA No 94).

Changes must still be made to national law in order to reinforce this provision, with a view to ensuring effective protection of the above-mentioned employee representatives against dismissal.

IX   Tax treatment[5]

35.   The Act of 11 December 2008 (the 'Belgian Merger Taxation Act') brought the Belgian Income Tax Code in line with Council Directive 90/434/EEC of 23 July 1990 on the common system of taxation applicable to mergers, divisions, transfers of assets and exchanges of shares concerning companies of different Member States, as amended by Council Directive 2005/19/EC of 17 February 2005 (hereinafter the 'Merger Tax Directive').[6] The Act entered into force on

5 This part has been written by Jan Werbrouck, a tax partner with NautaDutilh in Brussels.
6 Law of 11 December 2008 modifying the Belgian Income Tax Code 1992 in order to align it with Directive 90/434/EEC of the Council of 23 July 1990 on the common system of taxation applicable to mergers, divisions, partial divisions, transfers of assets and exchanges of shares concerning companies of different Member States and to the transfer of the registered office,

12 January 2009, i.e. the date of its publication in the *Belgian State Gazette*, and applies in principle to transactions and transfers carried out as from this date. Under specific conditions, Belgian tax resident entities and/or permanent establishments can now be part of pan-European tax neutral reorganisations. Previously, for most cross-border reorganisations, a tax-neutral regime was not available. The European Court of Justice criticised Belgium on 8 May 2008 for failing to implement the Merger Tax Directive (Case C-392/07). The Act not only regulates the corporate tax consequences of both inbound and outbound cross-border mergers but also changes existing tax rules on domestic reorganisations, in order to bring those provisions into line with the Merger Tax Directive and to implement certain other improvements, e.g. the mergers between parent companies and subsidiaries can now benefit from complete tax neutrality.

36.   The Act allows reorganisations involving two or more Belgian-resident companies (or permanent establishments) or between a Belgian-resident company (or permanent establishment) and an 'intra-European company' to be carried out in a tax-neutral way. Tax neutrality is achieved by exempting from tax the capital gains on the transferred assets and liabilities and is contingent on those assets and liabilities being effectively connected with a Belgian permanent establishment of the acquiring company. Capital gains and depreciation are calculated as if the transaction had not taken place, meaning there is no step-up, and the transfer of tax losses is allowed also in cross-border situations.

37.   The following conditions must be met in order to be eligible for tax neutrality:

   (i)   the absorbing or receiving company must be a resident or an intra-European company;
   (ii)   the transaction must be carried out in accordance with Belgian and foreign company law;
   (iii) after the reorganisation, the exempt reserves must form part of the equity (own funds) of the Belgian permanent establishment. This is made possible through a capital endowment (*toevoeging aan het kapitaal/dotation en capital*) to the Belgian establishment by its headquarters;
   (iv)   the assets acquired pursuant to the reorganisation must be held by a Belgian company or an establishment and must contribute to its taxable profit. In this way, the Belgian tax authorities do not lose their power to tax the assets, which retain the same value for tax purposes. The Act provides that the reduction of tax-exempt reserves as well as any capital gain realised on the occasion of the withdrawal of assets by a foreign head office must be added to the taxable basis of the Belgian establishment;

of an SE or SCE, between Member States, modified by Directive2005/19/EC of the Council of 17 February 2005, *Belgian State Gazette* of 12 January2009.

(v)   the transaction may not have as its principal objective, or as one of its principal objectives, tax evasion or tax avoidance.

38.   The 'intra-European company' is defined as any company of an EU Member State which is not a resident company, takes one of the forms listed in the Annex to the Directive, has no dual tax residence (in the sense that the company, according to the laws of an EU Member State, is considered to be resident in that Member State without being considered under a tax treaty concluded with a third state to be resident outside the EU), and, without the possibility of an option of being exempt, is subject to a tax similar to the Belgian corporate income tax as listed in the Directive.

39.   Reorganisations include cross-border (inbound/outbound) mergers and demergers and cross-border (inbound/outbound) contributions of assets (lines of business/permanent establishment) and exchange of shares. The new rules also apply to the transfer of the seat of a foreign company to Belgium. The transfer of the seat of a resident company to another State continues to be considered for tax purposes as a liquidation of the company, except if it concerns the transfer of a European company or a European cooperative company.

40.   Domestic reorganisations and qualifying cross-border reorganisations are now subject to the same rules. Previously, in the case of a cross-border reorganisation (contrary to a domestic one), Belgian-source losses of a Belgian company could not be taken into account when determining the taxable profit of the Belgian establishment that remains after a reorganisation involving a foreign company. Under the Belgian Merger Taxation Act, the carry-forward of losses is also possible in cross-border situations. The assumption of losses is only allowed on a proportionate basis, with reference to the net asset value for tax purposes of the companies participating in the merger.

At the same time, the rules concerning the deduction of losses of foreign establishments of Belgian companies were tightened. Furthermore, with respect to losses of establishments in countries with which Belgium has concluded a tax treaty, the principle of 'recapture' has now been inserted into Belgian domestic law.

7

Bulgaria

ANELIA TATAROVA, RAINA DIMITROVA AND YORDAN NAYDENOV
Borislav Boyanov & Co.

I   Introduction

1.   The Cross-border Merger Directive (including the employee participation rules) has been implemented in Bulgaria through amendments to the Commerce Act[1] approved in December 2007, introducing a new section on cross-border mergers with companies from other EU Member States or companies from Member

---

1 Bulgarian Commerce Act promulgated in State Gazette No 48 of 1991, as amended from time to time.

States of the European Economic Area. The provisions applicable to domestic mergers shall apply only when this is explicitly provided for in the cross-border mergers section.

II   Scope of the new rules

2.   The new rules on cross-border mergers apply to the following types of companies governed by the Commerce Act: public limited liability companies (*акционерни дружества*) (EAD/AD), partnerships limited by shares (*командитни дружества с акции*) (KDA), private limited liability companies (*дружества с ограничена отговорност*) (EOOD/OOD) and European companies (SE).

3.   The Cross-border Merger Directive shall not apply to cross-border mergers involving a company whose corporate purpose is the collective investment of capital provided by the public, which operates on the principle of risk-spreading and whose units may be, at the holder's request, purchased or redeemed, directly or indirectly, out of the company's assets (Art. 3(3) Dir.). Under Bulgarian law such companies are governed by the Public Offering of Securities Act.[2] The companies so excluded are open-ended public entities for collective investment, which can be in the form of public limited liability companies (*акционерно дружество*) (Art. 164(1) Public Offering of Securities Act).

The Cross-border Merger Directive rules shall not apply in cases where a merging company with a registered office in Bulgaria owns land and at the same time the new or surviving company's registered office is located outside the country.

The Commerce Act does not explicitly provide for rules related to a cross-border merger in case a liquidation or insolvency procedure is initiated for a local participating company. As mentioned above, there is no general provision stipulating the common applicability of the national law (which includes the above two cases when a domestic merger occurs within its scope) to cross-border mergers. The possibility for a cross-border merger with a local company in liquidation or insolvency shall be further decided by court practice as it is possible that the domestic rules can be considered to be applicable *by analogy*.

III   Cash payment

4.   The local legislation does not allow cash payments in favour of the shareholders to exceed 10 per cent of the whole nominal value of the securities

---

2 Public Offering of Securities Act promulgated in State Gazette No 114 of 1999, as amended from time to time.

or shares acquired in the share capital of the new/surviving company (Art. 261b(2) Commerce Act) in case of a cross-border merger.

IV   Legal consequences and enforceability of a cross-border merger

5.   A cross-border merger shall have the same legal consequences as an internal (domestic) merger, i.e.:

(i)   the participating entities (with the exception of the surviving company if no new company is established) shall cease to exist;

(ii)   the shareholders of the companies which cease to exist shall become shareholders in the new/surviving entity; and

(iii)   all rights and obligations of the merging companies which cease to exist shall be transferred to the new/surviving company by operation of law without liquidation of the participating companies.

6.   A cross-border merger (and any related issues subject to registration in the Commercial Register) shall be considered effective, including being enforceable against third parties, as from the date of registration in the Commercial Register. Third parties can claim, within fifteen days of the registration date, that the merger is not enforceable against them if they can prove that it was impossible for them to have had knowledge thereof. Third parties are not entitled to rely on the merger itself prior to such registration date (Art. 7(2) Commercial Register Act[3] in connection with Article 265n [265o[4]] Commerce Act).

When there are any rights *in rem* related to real estates, movables or any other rights (property of a local merging entity) subject to entry in a specific Bulgarian register,[5] the certificate for the registration of the merger, or the notification from the surviving company's Member State's register for the merger registration, should be submitted for entry into the respective local register.

Any permits, licences or concessions granted to a merging company shall be considered transferred to the new/surviving entity as of the registration date, unless a law or the granting document provides otherwise.

According to an explicit provision of the Labour Code[6] approved in December 2007, the employment relationship with the employee shall not be terminated in the event of mergers, including cross-border mergers, i.e. a change of employer as a result of: (i) a merger of companies by the formation of a new company; (ii) a merger by acquisition of one (or more) company by another; (iii) a distribution of the operations of one company among two or

---

3 The Commercial Register Act promulgated in State Gazette issue No 34 of 2006, as amended from time to time.

4 The number of the Article according to the Cyrillic alphabet.

5 For example, the Land Register where all immovable properties have to be registered.

6 Labour Code promulgated in State Gazette No 26 of 1986, as amended from time to time.

more companies; and (iv) a passing of a self-contained part of one enterprise to another; etc.

In the above cases the rights and obligations of the merging employer arising from the employment relationships existing on the date of the change (registration date) shall be transferred to the new or surviving employer.

Liability in respect of the obligations to the employee which arose before the change or merger of employer shall be incurred by the new/surviving employer upon merger of companies.

It should be noted, however, that without the above explicit rules the general rule for automatic transfer from the merging companies which cease to exist to the new or surviving company of all rights and obligations (including those which are employment related) shall apply.

V   Procedure

1   Draft terms of cross-border merger

7.   The management organs of the merging companies shall prepare common draft terms of cross-border merger. This document should be in simple written form and should be signed by the representatives of the local merging companies (Art. 265e [265д] (2) Commerce Act). The draft terms should include the information described in Chapter 1, no 19 of this book as well as information on the term within which the cash payments (if such) should be made, description of the securities and shares to be received in the resulting entity and the planned increase (if needed) of the surviving company's share capital (Art. 265e [265д] (3) Commerce Act). In the event a parent company merges with its wholly owned subsidiary, the information mentioned in Chapter 1, no 39 of this book as well as the additional information indicated in the immediate preceding sentence can be omitted (Art. 265p [265p] (6) Commerce Act).

Generally, the directors or managers (if acting intentionally) may be held jointly liable for any damages to the respective local merging entity during the merger process.

8.   The common draft terms of cross-border merger together with the management report of each local participating entity (see no 9 of this chapter) should be filed with the Commercial Register not later than one month prior to the local general meeting(s) convened to adopt the cross-border merger resolution. Together with the above documents, there should be submitted a list containing information on the name, registered office and register in which each merging company is entered,[7] as well as information on the rules for protection

---

7 It is not explicitly provided for the type of each merging company and its number of entry in the respective register to be indicated in the list, although it is required as per Art. 6(2) of the Cross-border Merger Directive.

of the creditors and minority shareholders of each company and the place from which complete data on these issues can be obtained.

2   Management report

9.   The management body of each merging company should prepare a written report on the cross-border merger. The report should contain a detailed legal and economic explanation of the common draft terms and in particular (i) the methods used to determine the share-exchange ratio and (ii) the implications of the merger for shareholders, creditors and employees (Art. 265f [265e] Commerce Act).

The management report of each participating Bulgarian entity should be made public (see no 8 of this chapter) as well as available to the shareholders of the participating companies at the registered office of the respective company not later than one month prior to its general meeting. Upon request a copy or an excerpt from the management report should be provided to each shareholder free of charge.

Each local merging entity should provide its management report to its employees' representatives or, in the absence thereof, to the employees not later than one month prior to its general meeting which will take a decision on the merger. Any opinions of the employees or their representatives should be enclosed with the management report.

3   Auditor's report

10.   Each Bulgarian participating company should choose an auditor to audit (and subsequently to prepare a report to the shareholders on) the common draft terms of the cross-border merger. The auditor should be appointed by the management body of the respective company and should be a certified (registered) auditor. The auditor may not, over the past two years, have been an auditor of the company which is appointing it or which has produced an evaluation of an in-kind contribution. The appointed auditor may not be elected auditor of the new/surviving company for two years following the effective merger date (see no 19 of this chapter).

An auditor's report is not required in the event of a simplified merger of a wholly owned subsidiary (see Chapter 1, no 39 of this book).

All merging companies may jointly require that the Registry Agency[8] appoint an auditor for all participating companies, including those with a seat in another Member State. The auditor so appointed shall prepare a report on the common draft terms of cross-border merger.

The auditor's report shall not be prepared if all shareholders of all companies (the merging companies and the surviving company) participating in

---

8 The Agency keeping the Commercial Register.

the cross-border merger unanimously decide in writing that no audit of the common draft terms shall be made (Art. 265h [265з] (5) Commerce Act).

11.   In its report the auditor appointed as per the local legislation should certify whether, in its opinion, the share-exchange ratio is adequate and reasonable (Art. 262m [262м] (2) Commerce Act). The auditor's report should indicate at least (i) the methods used to determine the share-exchange ratio; (ii) whether these methods are appropriate and correct in the case at hand; (iii) the value as per each of the methods and the relative importance of each method in determining the shares and securities value; and (iv) the particular difficulties (if any) encountered in the valuation process.

If the new company shall have a registered office in Bulgaria or there shall be an increase in the share capital of the local surviving entity, the auditor shall prepare also a report on the share capital audit[9] which should check if the following statutory requirements are met:

(i)   the share capital of the new company shall not exceed the net property[10] transferred to it upon merger;

(ii)   the share capital of the surviving entity may be increased as long as new shares are to be issued for the shareholders of the participating companies. The capital increase shall not exceed the net property transferred to the surviving company upon merger;

(iii) no share capital increase of the surviving entity shall be allowed in case:

- the latter owns shares in a merging company;
- a merging company has its own shares; or
- a merging company has shares in the acquiring company which have not been paid in full.

The auditor (irrespective of whether it was appointed as per the local legislation or that of another Member State) shall be entitled to request from any merging company any information and documentation related to the auditor's report preparation.

12.   The auditor's report for each merging entity (or the common one) should be made available to the shareholders of the merging companies at the registered office of the respective local entity (see no 8 of this chapter). It should not be made public otherwise.

13.   The auditor (irrespective of whether it was appointed as per the local legislation or that of another Member State) shall be liable to all participating entities

---

9 The Cross-border Merger Directive does not provide for such a report.
10 The net property is equal to the difference between the market (fair) price of the rights and that of the obligations which are transferred to the new/surviving entity upon merger.

and their shareholders for any damages resulting from non-fulfilment of its obligations (Art. 262m [262м] (3) Commerce Act).

4   General meeting of shareholders

A   Information for shareholders

14.   The following documents shall be made available to the shareholders at the registered offices of each participating company and/or of the surviving company with its seat in Bulgaria at least one month prior to the respective general meeting:

    (i)   common draft terms;
    (ii) management report;
    (iii) auditor's report;
    (iv) drafts of the new/amended articles of association/statutes of the new, respectively the surviving, company.

Each shareholder may request free of charge a complete or partial copy of any of the above-mentioned documents.

B   Shareholder approval

15.   With respect to the Bulgarian participating companies, the merger and the draft terms of cross-border merger must be approved as follows:

    (i)   by the general meeting of shareholders – for the public and private limited liability companies; and
    (ii) by the general meeting of shareholders and with a resolution of shareholders with unlimited liability – for a partnership limited by shares.

The absorption of a wholly owned subsidiary by its parent company shall be approved through a resolution of the sole owner (Art. 265p [265p] Commerce Act).

The Bulgarian legislation does not provide for the simplified merger procedure where a company is acquired by another one holding 90 per cent of the shares/securities of the first one.

16.   In order for a general meeting of a public limited liability company and a partnership limited by shares to approve the cross-border merger, at least 50 per cent of the capital should be represented. If this quorum is not met, a second meeting may be called not earlier than fourteen days after the date of the initial meeting and this second meeting may resolve on the respective issues on the agenda regardless of the number of shares represented.

The merger should be approved by a special majority as follows:

    (i)   three quarters of the share capital for a private limited liability company;
    (ii) three quarters of the voting shares represented for a public limited liability company;

(iii)   three quarters of the voting shares represented for a partnership limited by shares as well as unanimously by resolution of the shareholders with unlimited liability, in written form and certified by a notary, as the articles may provide for a larger majority. If there are different classes of shares, special majority requirements should be met for each class of shares.

The draft terms of cross-border merger shall define the rights conferred by the company resulting from the merger on shareholders enjoying special rights or on the holders of securities other than shares representing capital.

17.   Any resolutions related to the merger and within the competence of the general meetings shall be adopted together with the voting on the merger and the common draft terms and thus no further general meeting shall be needed in relation to the merger process.

18.   Once the cross-border merger resolution is adopted by the general meeting[11] of a participating local entity none of its shareholders shall be entitled to file a claim with the court for deletion of this resolution on the grounds that it contradicts the law or the articles of association/statute of the merging company.

5   Pre-merger certificate

19.   In case the new/surviving company is not located in Bulgaria, the management body of each participating local company requires from the Commercial Register the issuance of a pre-merger certificate stating the legality of the merger in relation to the respective entity. There is no time limit to how long the certificate is valid.

In order for a certificate to be issued, each local company involved should provide the following documents to the Commercial Register:

(i)   the cross-border resolution taken;
(ii)   the auditor's report;
(iii) a declaration that the participating local company does not own any land in Bulgaria (see no 3 of this chapter);
(iv)   any other evidence that the merger resolution has been taken in compliance with all statutory requirements.

6   Effects of the decision

20.   A cross-border merger where the new/surviving company is located in Bulgaria enters into effect on the date of the merger registration with the Commercial Register. The management body of the new or surviving company should

---

11 Please refer to no 15 of this chapter regarding the specifics related to the body/persons entitled to take a cross-border merger resolution in case of a partnership limited by shares.

submit an application for registration of the merger accompanied by the following documents:

(i) the common merger terms;

(ii) the merger resolutions and the pre-merger certificates of the other participating companies;

(iii) a copy of the new/amended articles of association/statutes of the new, respectively the surviving company;

(iv) the auditor's report;

(v) a list of the persons acquiring shares in the new/surviving company and data for any attachments or pledges on the shares;

(vi) other documents specified in the law, depending on the specific case, e.g. the consent of a shareholder who, as a result of the merger, becomes a shareholder with unlimited liability, etc.

The registration of the merger shall be completed on the files of the local new or surviving company not earlier than fourteen days as from the application submission, providing that:

(i) the non-local participating companies have provided pre-merger certificates;

(ii) the local companies have met all local cross-border merger requirements and, in particular, the merger resolution has been taken with the majority needed;

(iii) the merging companies have approved the common terms of cross-border merger; and

(iv) all local requirements regarding the new/surviving Bulgarian company have been fulfilled.

Changes in the articles of association, share capital and management bodies of the surviving company (if any) shall be registered together with the merger registration.

The new Bulgarian entity should be considered as established and the other participating local companies (if the new/surviving company is a local one) respectively terminated as of the date of registration of the merger in the Commercial Register.

In case the resulting company is not located in Bulgaria the deletion (and respectively the termination) of the local companies involved from the Commercial Register shall take place only after receipt of a notification from the Register of the Member State that the new/surviving company has been entered in, confirming that the merger has been duly registered.

21. As from the effective date (date of registration) of the cross-border merger, it cannot be declared null and void by the court. In addition, it is forbidden to file with the court a claim to declare the new company (resulting from the cross-border merger) null and void.

However, Article 265p [265п] (2) of the Commerce Act provides for an opportunity for the merger to be challenged in case the legal requirements of the chapter of the Commerce Act regulating cross-border mergers have not been met for any of the companies involved. Each shareholder of the participating companies or the latter themselves are entitled to make such a claim as the competent court is the one where the registered office of the new/surviving company is located. The non-equivalent share-exchange ratio cannot be a ground for filing of such a claim.

In case the resulting company – new or surviving – is located

(i)   in Bulgaria, the claim should be filed not later than the date of merger registration in the Commercial Register. Filing of the claim shall result in stoppage of the registration. On the grounds of an effective (entered into force) court ruling, which awards the claim, the Commercial Register shall refuse registration of the cross-border merger;

(ii) in another Member State, the claim should be submitted not later than the issuance of the pre-merger certificate for the resulting company. Although that this option (and the respective consequences) is given in the local legislation, its practical enforcement is disputable as its implementation should be regulated by the legislation of the Member State where the resulting company is located. However, an effective court ruling, awarding the claim against the merger, can result in the refusal of the Bulgarian Registration Agency to issue a pre-merger certificate and respective blocking of the registration of the cross-border merger in the other Member State.

VI   Minority shareholders

22.   Bulgarian law does not provide for any special rights for minority shareholders in the case of cross-border mergers.

VII   Protection of creditors

23.   Although not explicitly regulated in the cross-border mergers section of the Commerce Act, we assume that the creditor protection rules would be applicable as indicated in the general merger section accordingly, as follows:

(i)   the creditors are considered to be informed of their rights as of the effective merger date without any further notification being needed;

(ii) the new/surviving local company should manage separately the property acquired by each participating entity for six months as of the merger registration date. Members of the management body of the resulting company shall be jointly responsible for the separate management of the property;

(iii)   each creditor holding a receivable which has not been secured and has arisen prior to the effective date shall be entitled to require either security or receipt of its receivable. In case the respective request is not fulfilled, this creditor shall be entitled to preferable performance of the rights which have been the property of its debtor (i.e. the respective former participating company).

VIII   Employee participation

24.   The Commerce Act sets out the general rules of employees' protection in case of cross-border merger depending on the seat of the new/surviving company and the existence of rights of employees in the legislation of the accepting country. As for the constitution of the special negotiating body ('SNB') and its functions in case of cross-border mergers, the Commerce Act refers directly to the regulatory framework set out by the Information and Consultation with Employees in Multinational Undertakings, Groups of Undertakings and European Companies Act[12] ('LICE') – implementing Directive 2001/86[13] of 8 October 2001 supplementing the Statute for a European company (SE) with regard to the involvement of employees in the management of an SE.

1   Employee participation in companies established in Bulgaria resulting from a cross-border merger

25.   Currently Bulgarian law does not provide for a wide range of rights of employees to participate in the management of limited liability companies. The Commerce Act provides for the right of representatives of the employees to participate in the general meeting of the shareholders of a company with a consultative vote, provided that the company has more than fifty employees. Thus, the Commerce Act explicitly states that when the seat of the new/surviving company is in Bulgaria and one of the merging companies has applied rules for participation of the employees in the management, the new/surviving company has to procure the exercise of the rights resulting from the said rules. This rule shall be applied even in case of subsequent transformation of the company under the Commerce Act of Bulgaria or under Council Regulation No 2157/2001 of 8 October 2001 on the Statute for a European company (SE), but in any case no longer than three years after the registration of the transformation with the competent authority where the seat of the new/surviving company is.

12 The Information and Consultation with Employees in Multinational Undertakings, Groups of Undertakings and European Companies Act promulgated in State Gazette No 57 of 2006.
13 Council Directive 2001/86 supplementing the Statute for a European company with regard to the involvement of employees.

2   Special negotiating body ('SNB')

26.   With regard to the method to be used for appointment of members of the SNB, the LICE provides that such election may be made by the general meeting of employees under the Labour Code.[14] The latter provides that the general meeting of employees comprises all employees in an enterprise and it may be convened by the employer, the management of the trade union as well as on an initiative of one tenth of the employees in the enterprise. The quorum required for the meeting to be conducted is more than half of the employees. The resolutions for election of members of the SNB are approved by a simple majority. The meeting may choose to delegate the election of members of the SNB to representatives designated by the management of the trade union(s) at the enterprise or to representatives of the employees as determined by the Labour Code.[15] Candidates for representatives in the SNB may be nominated by any employee, by groups of employees as well as by the trade unions at the enterprise. The central management/the management of the enterprise participating in the incorporation of the SE (respectively in the case of a cross-border merger – the management of the new/surviving company) determines the number of members of the SNB in such a manner that each Member State in which a multinational enterprise has one or more establishments or one or more controlled enterprises or a controlling enterprise is represented by at least one member.

As to the possibility for trade union representatives to become members of the SNB (employed or not employed by the participating company/concerned subsidiary/establishment – Article 3(2)(b) paragraph 2 of Directive 2001/86), the LICE provides that the candidates for election of employees' representatives in the SNB may be nominated by an individual or group of employees as well as by the trade unions existing within the undertaking.

As mentioned above, the employees are entitled to form freely, by their own choice, trade union organisations, to join and leave them. Neither the LICE as *lex specialis* nor the Labour Code expressly prohibits the election of trade union representatives in the SNB.

Therefore, interpretation of the existing legal provisions of the LICE leads to the conclusion that candidates for the SNB election may be employees as well as trade union representatives who work within the undertaking participating in the creation of the SE. *A contrario*, trade union representatives who are not employed by such an undertaking cannot be candidates for the SNB election.

---

14 The Labour Code promulgated in State Gazette Nos 26 and 27 of 1986, as amended from to time.

15 According to the Labour Code, the general meeting of employees may choose representatives to participate in the decision-making process with consultation votes on issues relevant to the management of the company, if such participation is provided by the law.

The LICE does not provide for any rules in a situation where the SNB fails to take any decision on the form of participation to be chosen within the various participating companies in order to be applied to the newly established SE (i.e. there are no subsidiary rules to be applied in the absence of a particular decision of the SNB).

Similarly, the Bulgarian legislator did not use in the LICE the options granted:

(i)   under Article 7(3) of Directive 2001/86, i.e. the possibility to provide for non-application of the Standard Rules of Participation included in Part III of the Annex to Directive 2001/86 to an SE established by merger; or

(ii) under Article 8(3) of Directive 2001/86, i.e. the possibility to adopt particular provisions on an SE pursuing directly and essentially the aim of ideological guidance with respect to information and expression of opinions; or

(iii) under Article 13(4) of Directive 2001/86, i.e. the opportunity to guarantee that structures of employees' representation existing within Bulgarian participating companies which will cease to exist as separate legal entities remain even after the SE's registration. In the case of cross-border mergers, however, the Commerce Act provides explicitly that where the new or surviving company has its registered office in Bulgaria and one of the merging companies has applied rules for participation of the employees within the terms given by section 1, item 20 of the Supplementary Provisions of the LICE, the new or surviving company shall be obliged to ensure the exercise of the rights arising from the said rules. This rule shall furthermore apply upon a subsequent transformation (merger) according to the procedure established in the cross-border mergers section of the Commerce Act or by Council Regulation (EC) No 2157/2001 on the Statute for a European company (SE), but for not more than three years after the date of registration of the merger in the Commercial Register.

Section 1, item 20 of the Supplementary Provisions of the LICE stipulates the following: 'participation' shall be the ability of the representative body and/or the employees' representatives to participate in the affairs of the company by way of exercise of the right:

(i)   to elect or appoint some of the members of the company's supervisory or administrative body, or

(ii) to recommend and/or oppose the appointment of some or all of the members of the company's supervisory or administrative body.

In conformity with Article 8(2) of Directive 2001/86, which grants to a Member State the possibility to release the participating companies' supervisory or administrative organ from the obligation to disclose information to the

SNB/representative body/assistants if the nature of the information, according to objective criteria, is such that any disclosure may seriously harm the functioning of the companies or would be prejudicial to them, the LICE grants to the management the right to withhold any sensitive information. Upon refusal of disclosure the parties may seek assistance for settlement of the dispute through mediation and/or voluntary arbitration of the National Institute of Conciliation and Arbitration.

3   Protection of employee representatives

27.   Members of the SNB and of the representative body of the employees enjoy additional rights under the Labour Code, namely additional leave (if they have to be absent from work due to commitments related to their membership of the SNB/representative functions) as well as a defence mechanism with respect to the termination of their labour agreements. As a general rule, the company has to obtain the prior approval of the Bulgarian Labour Inspectorate in case of dismissal of such employees.

IX   Tax treatment

28.   The Merger Tax Directive[16] has been implemented in Bulgaria by State Gazette No 105 of 22 December 2006 through the new Corporate Income Tax Act.[17]

29.   The rules provided in the Corporate Income Tax Act are related only to companies and their places of permanent establishment located in the European Union in contrast to the Merger Tax Directive which covers all European Economic Area states.

   The legislation provides for a tax-neutral regime for outbound reorganisations covered by the Merger Tax Directive, including the merger of a Bulgarian resident corporate taxpayer with a receiving company, resident of a Member State, and the transfer of a local establishment to such receiving company in consequence of a merger covered by the Merger Tax Directive.

   Tax neutrality is achieved by way of an exemption of capital gains on assets and liabilities transferred. It is conditional on those assets and liabilities being effectively connected with a Bulgarian establishment of the acquiring company, and on the absence of a principal objective of tax evasion or tax avoidance. If the operation is not effected for 'valid commercial reasons' or disguises asset disposal, there is a rebuttable presumption of tax evasion.

16 Council Directive 90/434 of 23 July 1990 on the common system of taxation applicable to mergers, divisions, transfers of assets and exchanges of shares concerning companies of different Member States.
17 The Corporate Income Tax Act promulgated in State Gazette No 105 of 2006, as amended from time to time.

In general, the acquiring (new/surviving) company is not allowed to:

(i)   transfer tax losses accumulated by the participating (transferring) company(ies); and

(ii) recognise for tax purposes interest costs booked with the transferring entities but not recognised under the thin capitalisation rules,

with the exception of a merger as a result of which a local permanent establishment of a Member State company occurs and this company has not had such establishment before the merger.

Latent non-taxed gains with the Bulgarian transferring company may not be recognised for tax purposes and shall be considered as initially arising with the acquiring company.

30.   Any accounting losses/profit accumulated by the receiving company as a result of cancellation of shares owned in the transferring entity shall not be recognised for tax purposes irrespective of the holding share. Any related income shall not be subject to local withholding taxation.

31.   Any profit/losses of the shareholders of the transferring companies resulting from the acquisition of shares/securities of the receiving entity shall not be recognised for tax purposes in the respective year and shall be treated as a temporary tax difference (related to the new shares) recognisable upon further disposal.

The taxation of any further disposal of shall be regulated as per the general rules.

8

Cyprus

ALEXANDROS TSADIRAS

LLPO Law Firm

I   Introduction

1.   The Cross-border Merger Directive has been transposed into the Cypriot legal order by Law 186(I)/2007, which was published on 31 December 2007.[1] That

---

1   Law 186(I)/2007 amending the Cypriot Companies Law, Chapter 113, *Official Gazette of the Republic of Cyprus* 2007, Issue no 4154, Appendix 1, Part I of 31 December 2007. That Law is referred to as 'the Companies (Amendment) (No 4) Law of 2007' and should be read in conjunction with the (basic) Cypriot Companies Law, Chapter 113. It will be recalled that the deadline for the transposition of the Cross-border Merger Directive was 15 December 2007.

piece of legislation amended the Cypriot Companies Law, Chapter 113 (the 'CCL') by inserting a new section on cross-border mergers (Arts. 201I–201X CCL).

II   Scope of the new rules

2. The new section applies to cross-border mergers of limited liability companies under the conditions that (i) at least one of the merging limited liability companies is a Cypriot company or the limited liability company resulting from the cross-border merger is a Cypriot company (Art. 201J(1) CCL), and (ii) at least one of the rest of the participating companies is subject to the jurisdiction of another European Economic Area Member State (Art. 201I CCL).

Cross-border mergers are only possible between types of limited liability companies which may merge under the national law of the relevant Member States. Every Cypriot company may take part in a cross-border merger except (i) the limited liability companies by guarantee, and (ii) the companies subject to liquidation.[2] A Cypriot company participating in such a merger must comply with the provisions and formalities of the CCL (Art. 201K CCL).

It is worth noting that the Cyprus legislature chose not to exercise the option given by Article 3(2) of the Cross-border Merger Directive and therefore the new rules are applicable to cooperative societies falling within the definition of 'limited liability company' as laid down in Article 201I of the CCL.

3. The amended section of the CCL does not apply to cross-border mergers involving a limited liability company the object of which is the collective investment of capital provided by the public, which operates on the principle of risk-spreading and the units of which are, at the holders' request, repurchased or redeemed, directly or indirectly, out of the assets of that company. Action taken by such a company to ensure that the stock exchange value of its units does not vary significantly from its net asset value will be regarded as equivalent to such repurchase or redemption (Art. 201J(3) CCL).

III   Cash payment

4. Notwithstanding the definition given to the term 'merger' in Article 201I of the CCL, the newly introduced rules also apply to cross-border mergers where the relevant cash payment exceeds 10 per cent of the nominal value, or, in the absence thereof, of the accounting par value of the securities or shares representing the capital of the company resulting from the cross-border merger provided that such a possibility is permitted by the legislation of a Member State regulating at least one of the merging limited liability companies (Art. 201J(2) CCL).

2 A similar restriction applies to domestic mergers (Art. 201A(3) CCL).

Under Cyprus law, mergers involving such a cash payment are not permitted (Art. 201B CCL). It follows that the shareholders of a Cypriot company involved in a cross-border merger will only benefit from the cash payment in excess of 10 per cent if the domestic rules applicable to at least one of the participating foreign companies so allow. If that is not the case, the cross-border merger can only be brought under the material scope of application of the Cross-border Merger Directive if the cash payment does not exceed 10 per cent of the nominal value, or, in the absence thereof, of the accounting par value of the securities or shares representing the capital of the company resulting from the cross-border merger.

IV   Legal consequences and enforceability of a cross-border merger

5.   Article 201U(1) of the CCL mirrors Article 14 of the Cross-border Merger Directive, spelling out the legal consequences of cross-border mergers (see also Chapter 1, no 16 of this book). Those are similar to the effects of a domestic merger (Art. 201F CCL).

In the event of a cross-border merger by acquisition, the legal effects are the following (Art. 201U(1) CCL):

   (i)   all the assets and liabilities of the acquired company are transferred to the acquiring company;
  (ii)   the shareholders of the acquired company become shareholders of the acquiring company;
 (iii)   the acquired company ceases to exist.

In case of a cross-border merger by formation of a new company the consequences are as follows (Art. 201U(2) CCL):

   (i)   all the assets and liabilities of the merging companies are transferred to the new company;
  (ii)   the shareholders of the merging companies become shareholders of the new company;
 (iii)   the merging companies cease to exist.

The rights and obligations of the merging companies arising from contracts of employment or from employment relationships and existing at the date on which the cross-border merger takes effect will, by reason of that cross-border merger taking effect, be transferred to the company resulting from the cross-border merger on the date on which the cross-border merger takes effect (Art. 201U(4) CCL).

No shares in the acquiring company may be exchanged for shares in the company being acquired held by either (i) the acquiring company itself or through a person acting in his or her own name but on its behalf, or (ii) the company being acquired itself or through a person acting in his or her own name but on its behalf (Art. 201U(5) CCL).

6.   The company resulting from the cross-border merger must comply with the formalities that are imposed by the CCL or the legislation governing any of the merging non-Cypriot companies with respect to the right to enforce against third parties the transfer by the merging companies of certain assets, rights and obligations (Art. 201U(3) CCL).

Under Cyprus law a cross-border merger is enforceable by the resulting company against third parties as from the date on which a copy of the Court Order approving completion of the merger is published in the *Official Gazette of the Republic of Cyprus* pursuant to Article 365A of the CCL (see no 21 of this chapter). That is so unless the resulting company can prove that the third parties in question knew of the completion of the merger earlier. For fifteen days following publication, the merger may not be enforced against third parties if they are in the position to prove that it had been impossible for them to have known of it.

Third parties may invoke the cross-border merger even before the publication formalities have been complied with (Art. 365A(6) CCL).

V   Procedure

1   Draft terms of cross-border merger

7.   Article 201L of the CCL faithfully replicates Article 5 of the Cross-border Merger Directive, imposing upon the directors of each of the merging Cypriot companies the obligation to draw up the common draft terms of the cross-border merger. There is no need for this document to be in notarised form.

The information that the draft terms must include is clearly set out in Chapter 1, no 19 of this book and includes:

(i)   the form, name and registered office of the merging companies and those proposed for the company resulting from the cross-border merger;
(ii)   the ratio applicable to the exchange of securities or shares representing the company capital and the amount of any cash payment;
(iii) the terms for the allotment of securities or shares representing the capital of the company resulting from the cross-border merger;
(iv)   the likely repercussions of the cross-border merger on employment;
(v)   information on the evaluation of the assets and liabilities which are transferred to the company resulting from the cross-border merger.

Certain information, which is described in Chapter 1, no 39, of this book, can be omitted from the relevant document if either of the following scenarios apply: (i) a cross-border merger by acquisition is carried out by a Cypriot company which holds all the shares and other securities granting a voting right at the general meeting of the company being acquired;[3] or (ii) a cross-border

---

3 Similar provisions apply to domestic mergers: see Art. 201C CCL.

merger by acquisition is carried out by a non-Cypriot company of another Member State which holds all the shares and the other securities granting a voting right at the general meeting of the company being acquired (Art. 201V CCL).

8. The draft terms of the cross-border merger along with a number of further particulars, set out in Chapter 1, no 20 of this book, must be filed with the Registrar of Companies in Cyprus and published in the *Official Gazette of the Republic of Cyprus* pursuant to Article 365A of the CCL at least one month before the date of the general meeting which is to decide whether to proceed with the merger (Art. 201M CCL).

2 Management report

9. The directors of each of the merging Cypriot companies must draw up a report intended for the members thereof, explaining and justifying the legal and economic aspects of the cross-border merger for members, creditors and employees (Art. 201N(1) CCL). Such a report is required even in the case of a merger by absorption of a wholly owned subsidiary.

   The report must be made available to the members of the merging Cypriot companies and to the representatives of the employees or, where there are no such representatives, to the employees themselves, at least one month before the date of the general meeting which is to decide whether to proceed with the merger (Art. 201N(2) CCL).

   In case the directors receive, in good time, an opinion from the representatives of their employees, that opinion must be appended to the report (Art. 201N(3) CCL).

10. Save in cases of merger by acquisition by a Cypriot company which holds all the shares of the acquired company, the directors signing the draft terms of cross-border merger and the relevant report are liable for every loss their negligent behaviour caused to the shareholders of the merging companies in accordance with Article 43 of the CCL (Art. 201G(1) CCL).

    In addition, if the draft terms of cross-border merger and/or the directors' report include any untrue statement of facts, any person who signs the aforementioned documents commits a criminal offence and, if convicted, he/she will be punished with imprisonment for a period of time which may not exceed two years or with a fine which may not exceed €2,562 or with both penalties, except if he/she proves that he/she had reasonable cause to believe and indeed believed at the time of the submission of the above documents that the statement was true (Art. 201G(3) CCL).

3 Auditor's report

11. It is in principle mandatory that an independent expert report is drawn up for each of the merging Cypriot companies. That report is intended for the

members of the companies and must be made available to them not less than one month before the date of the general meeting of the shareholders which is to decide whether to proceed with the merger. The experts are appointed by the competent Court following an application filed by the merging Cypriot company and may be natural or legal persons (Art. 201O(1) CCL).

As an alternative to experts operating on behalf of each of the merging limited liability companies, one or more independent experts, appointed for that purpose at the joint request of the merging limited liability companies by the competent judicial or administrative authority in the Member State of one of the merging companies or of the limited liability company resulting from the cross-border merger or approved by such an authority, may examine the common draft terms of cross-border merger and draw up a single written report to all the members of the merging limited liability companies (Art. 201O(2) CCL).

12.   The expert is expected to comment on the fair and reasonable character of the share-exchange ratio and his report must at least indicate (Art. 201O(3) CCL):

    (i)   the method or methods used to arrive at the share-exchange ratio proposed;

   (ii)   whether such method or methods are adequate in the case in question, mentioning the values arrived at using each such method and giving at the same time an opinion on the relative importance attributed to such methods in arriving at the value decided on;

   (iii)   any special valuation difficulties.

The independent experts are entitled to secure from each of the merging companies all information they consider necessary for the discharge of their duties (Art. 201O(4) CCL).

13.   The requirement for drafting an expert report can be waived if any of the following three cases occurs:

    (i)   all the members of each of the companies involved in the cross-border merger agree that neither an examination of the common draft terms of cross-border merger by independent experts nor an expert report is required (Art. 201O(5) CCL);

   (ii)   a cross-border merger by acquisition is carried out by a Cypriot company which holds all the shares and other securities granting a voting right at the general meeting of the company being acquired (201V(1) CCL);[4]

   (iii)   a cross-border merger by acquisition is carried out by a non-Cypriot company of another Member State which holds all the shares and other securities granting a voting right at the general meeting of the company being acquired (Art. 201V(2) CCL).

---

4 A similar provision exists in the context of domestic mergers: see Art. 201C(3)(d) CCL.

14.   As is the case with the directors of the merging companies, the experts signing the report on the proposed cross-border merger are liable for any loss their negligent behaviour caused to the shareholders of the merging companies in accordance with Article 43 of the CCL (Art. 201G(1) CCL). That is so, except if the merger in question is one by acquisition and the acquiring company holds all the shares of the acquired company (Art. 201G(2) CCL).

Moreover, if an expert report includes any untrue statement of facts, the person who signs it commits a criminal offence and, if convicted, he/she will be punished with imprisonment for a period of time which may not exceed two years or with a fine which may not exceed €2,562 or with both penalties, except if he/she proves that he/she had reasonable cause to believe and indeed believed at the time of the submission of the report that the statement was true (Art. 201G(3) CCL).

4   General meeting of shareholders

A   Information for shareholders

15.   At least one month before the date fixed for the general meeting which is to decide on the draft terms of merger, all shareholders of the participating companies are entitled to inspect at the registered office of their company and obtain, on request and free of charge, full or, if so desired, partial copies of the following documents (Art. 201C(4) CCL):

(i)   the draft terms of cross-border merger;
(ii)   the annual accounts and management reports of the merging companies for the preceding three financial years;
(iii) interim accounts drawn up as at a date which must not be earlier than the first day of the third month preceding the date of the draft terms of merger, if the latest annual accounts relate to a financial year which ended more than six months before that date. The interim accounts must be drawn up using the same methods and the same layout as the last annual accounts. It is not necessary to take a fresh physical inventory. The valuations shown in the last balance sheet can only be altered to reflect entries in the books of account. Interim depreciation and provisions as well as material changes in actual value not shown in the books will nevertheless be taken into account;
(iv)   the directors' reports for each merging company;
(v)   the expert report for each merging company.

B   Shareholder approval

16.   The general meeting of each of the merging Cypriot companies will decide on the approval of the common draft terms of the cross-border merger after taking note of the directors' and expert reports. In the event of the absorption of a wholly owned subsidiary by its parent company, be it Cypriot or non-Cypriot of

another Member State, the approval of shareholders is required for the parent company but not for the subsidiary (Art. 201V CCL).

Article 201K(2) of the CCL contemplates that a Cypriot company participating in a cross-border merger must comply with the provisions of the CCL, including those concerning the decision-making process in relation to the merger. Pursuant to Article 201C(5) of the CCL, the merger must be decided by the general meeting of the shareholders and the voting requirements are those prescribed in (i) Article 198(2) of the CCL, and (ii) the CCL provisions on the amendment of the articles of association (e.g. Art. 12 of the CCL). It follows that the merger resolution is treated as a special resolution, with the consequential implication being that its approval requires a majority of at least three quarters of the members or class of members present and voting either in person or by proxy at the general meeting.

17.   Similar to what applies in the case of formation of an SE, the general meeting of each of the merging companies may reserve the right to make implementation of the cross-border merger conditional upon express ratification by it of the arrangements decided on with respect to the participation of employees in the company resulting from the cross-border merger (Art. 201P(2) CCL).

With the approval of the cross-border merger the general meeting of shareholders must also state expressly whether it accepts the possibility for the members of any other merging non-Cypriot company to make use of the procedure contemplated by the national legislation of such other merging company, which allows the examination and amendment of the share-exchange ratio or compensation to minority shareholders, without preventing the filing of the cross-border merger. Any such decision is binding on the company resulting from the cross-border merger and all its members (Art. 201P(3) CCL).

5   Pre-merger certificate

18.   Provided that the general meeting of shareholders approves the cross-border merger, the merging Cypriot company must make an application to the competent Court and request the issuing of a certificate conclusively attesting to the proper completion of the pre-merger acts and formalities (Art. 201Q(2) CCL). The competent Court is that of the district where the registered office of each merging Cypriot company is located and it is required to scrutinise the legality of the cross-border merger as regards that part of the procedure which concerns each merging Cypriot company (Art. 201Q(1) CCL).

The District Court, on becoming satisfied that the pre-merger procedure has been complied with, must issue without delay the requested certificate to each merging Cypriot company (Art. 201Q(3) CCL). The validity of the certificate is six months. The Court is empowered to issue such a certificate irrespective of whether the procedure is under way pursuant to the domestic legislation of a participating non-Cypriot company for the examination and amendment of the share-exchange ratio or compensation to minority shareholders, provided that the aforementioned procedure has been approved by the general meeting of the shareholders of the participating Cypriot company. If that is the case, the Court must clearly indicate it in the pre-merger certificate (Art. 201Q(4) CCL).

Each merging non-Cypriot company is expected to obtain a similar pre-merger certificate in its own jurisdiction.

19.   If the registered office of the company which results from the cross-border merger is located in Cyprus, the District Court where the company's registered office is situated has jurisdiction to scrutinise the legality of the cross-border merger as regards its completion and, where appropriate, the incorporation of a new company as a result of the cross-border merger (Art. 201R(1) CCL).

Within six months of the issue of the pre-merger certificate, a second application must be filed with the District Court accompanied by the following particulars (Art. 201R(3) CCL):

(i)   the local pre-merger certificate for each merging Cypriot company;
(ii)   the foreign pre-merger certificate for each merging non-Cypriot company;
(iii) the common draft terms of the cross-border merger as approved by the general meetings of shareholders of each of the participating companies.

On the basis of the aforementioned documents, the District Court is called to examine in particular whether (i) the merging companies have approved the common draft terms of cross-border merger under the same conditions, and (ii) where appropriate, the arrangements for employee participation are in line with Article 201W of the CCL for the merging Cypriot companies and with the domestic legislation implementing Article 16 of the Cross-border Merger Directive for the participating non-Cypriot companies (Art. 201R(2) CCL).

If the District Court is satisfied as to the legality of the procedures followed for the completion of the cross-border merger, it must issue an Order approving completion of the merger and setting the exact date on which the cross-border merger is deemed to take effect (Art. 201R(4) CCL).

6   Effects of the decision

20.   The cross-border merger produces legal effects as from the date on which it takes effect according to the Order issued by the District Court on the basis of Article 201R of the CCL or, where the authority competent to approve the completion of the cross-border merger is that of another Member State, from the date determined by the relevant national legislation (Art. 201S CCL). A cross-border merger which has already taken effect along the above lines may not be declared null and void (Art. 210X CCL).

21.   Each merging Cypriot company must submit an official copy of the Court Order approving completion of the merger to the Registrar of Companies for registration and publication in the Official Gazette of the Republic of Cyprus

pursuant to Article 365A of the CCL. A copy of that Order must be attached to every copy of the memorandum of the new company which is incorporated with the completion of the cross-border merger (Art. 201T(1) CCL).

Upon receipt of the aforementioned copy of the Court Order, the Registrar is required to publish it in the *Official Gazette of the Republic of Cyprus* and notify without delay the registry of the Member State in which the non-Cypriot participating company was required to file documents proving that the cross-border merger has taken effect (Art. 201T(2) CCL).

Conversely, in the event of the approval of completion of the cross-border merger being issued by the competent authority of another Member State, the Registrar of Companies upon receipt of the relevant notification is obliged to register and publish it without delay in the *Official Gazette of the Republic of Cyprus* pursuant to Article 365A of the CCL (Art. 201T(3) CCL).

Upon registration in the Companies Register of the Court Order approving completion of the merger, the Registrar must remove from the Register the Cypriot companies which have been absorbed in the merger and indicate the exact date on which the cross-border merger took effect (Art. 201T(4) CCL).

VI   Minority shareholders

22.   Once the general meeting of the merging Cypriot company has approved the common draft terms of the cross-border merger through the procedure laid down in no 16 of this chapter, the minority shareholders are bound by that decision. The interests of the minority shareholders can be protected in either of the following two ways.

On the one hand, Article 201 of the CCL, reflecting Article 209 of the UK Companies Act of 1948, regulates the power to acquire shares of shareholders dissenting from schemes approved by majority. In brief, where a plan involving the transfer of shares or any class of shares in a company to another company has been approved by the holders of not less than nine tenths in value of the shares whose transfer is involved, the transferee company may give notice to any dissenting shareholder that it desires to acquire his shares. Further to such a notice, the transferee company is entitled and bound to acquire those shares on the terms on which, under the approved plan, the shares of the approving shareholders are to be transferred to the transferee company.

On the other hand, Article 202 of the CCL, replicating Article 210 of the UK Companies Act of 1948, provides an alternative remedy to winding up in cases of minority oppression. More precisely, any member of a company who complains that the affairs of the company are being conducted in a manner oppressive to some part of the members, including himself, may petition the competent Cyprus Court for an Order. If it transpires that the company's affairs are indeed being conducted in the aforementioned manner and to wind up the company would unfairly prejudice the oppressed members, but otherwise the facts would justify the making of a winding-up order on the ground that it was just and equitable that the company should be wound up, the Court may, with a view to bringing to an end the matters complained of, make such Order as it thinks fit, whether for regulating the conduct of the company's affairs in future, or for the purchase of the shares of any members of the company by other members of the company or by the company and, in the case of a purchase by the company, for the reduction accordingly of the company's capital, or otherwise.

VII   Protection of creditors

23.   Pursuant to Article 201K(2) of the CCL, a Cypriot company taking part in a cross-border merger is required to comply with the provisions of the CCL, including those pertaining to the protection of creditors of the merging companies. Article 201D(1) in conjunction with Article 200(1)(e) of the CCL contemplates the possibility that the creditors of the merging companies make an application to the competent Court with a view to obtaining protection for their claims which antedate the publication of the draft terms of merger and have not fallen due at the time of such publication.

The Court Order is required to make provision for the obligation of the participating companies to offer adequate safeguards to the creditors where the financial situation of the merging companies makes such protection necessary and where those creditors do not already have such safeguards (Art. 201D(1)(b) CCL).

VIII   Employee participation

24.   According to Article 201W of the CCL, the norms regulating employee participation in the resulting company are those of the Member State where its registered office is located.

1   Employee participation in companies established in Cyprus resulting from a cross-border merger

25.   Cyprus law, as it currently stands, provides for the information and consultation of the employees by their employer, but not for their participation in the affairs of a company as that term is defined in Article 2(k) of Council Directive 2001/86/EC of 8 October 2001[5] supplementing the Statute for a European company with regard to the involvement of employees. Employees do not therefore possess the right to elect or appoint members of the company's management bodies or recommend and/or oppose the appointment of such members. If the company resulting from the cross-border merger is established in Cyprus, participation rights for the employees will only arise if such rights existed in any

5 *Official Journal* L 294/22 of 10 November 2001.

of the merged companies under the conditions prescribed in Article 201W of the CCL, which faithfully mirrors Article 16(2) of the Cross-border Merger Directive.

2   Special negotiating body ('SNB')

26.   In the event that any of the scenarios envisaged in Article 201W(2) of the CCL occurs, the employee participation rules of the Member State where the company resulting from the cross-border merger resides will disapply and a special negotiating body ('SNB') must be formed with a view to negotiating the participation of employees in the resulting company and their involvement in the definition of such rights.

Pursuant to Article 201W(3) of the CCL, the manner in which the SNB is composed in case of a cross-border merger is identical to that which applies in the event of an incorporation of a European company ('SE'). Employee participation in the latter scenario is regulated by Law No 277(I)/2004,[6] which transposed into the Cyprus legal order Council Directive 2001/86/EC of 8 October 2001 supplementing the Statute for a European company with regard to the involvement of employees. Article 7 of the aforementioned Cyprus law contemplates that the employee representatives in the SNB as well as the alternative members of that body will be elected by the existing trade unions representing the employees or, in the absence thereof, by the employees themselves through direct election. Further details on the composition of the SNB are provided in Article 6 of the implementing Cyprus law (see also Chapter 2, no 10 *et seq.* of this book).

3   Protection of employee representatives

27.   In Cyprus, employee representatives performing their duties in the context of a cross-border merger enjoy the same level of protection as that applicable in the event of the establishment of an SE. Article 201W(3) of the CCL extends the application of Article 18 of Law No 277(I)/2004 to cross-border mergers. More precisely, the latter provision contemplates that the members of the SNB, the members of the representative body, any employees' representatives exercising functions under the information and consultation procedure and any employees' representatives in the management body of a Cypriot company must be protected in the exercise of their functions in accordance with the provisions of Law 30(III)/1995 as amended,[7] which ratified the International Labour Organisation Convention on Employee Participation of 1971.

---

6 *Official Gazette of the Republic of Cyprus* 2004, Issue no 3940, Appendix 1, Part I of 31 December 2004.
7 *Official Gazette of the Republic of Cyprus* 1995, Issue no 3022, Appendix 1, Part III of 8 December 1995.

The aforementioned protection for employee representatives includes (i) attendance at meetings of the SNB and the management body of the Cypriot company, (ii) the payment of wages, (iii) the length of absence necessary for the performance of their duties, and (iv) their dismissal.

IX   Tax treatment

28.   Cross-border mergers are treated by Cyprus law in a privileged manner. That claim is substantiated by taking a close look at the Income Tax Law, the Capital Gains Tax Law, the Department of Lands and Surveys (Charges and Fees) Law and the Stamp Law. It is worth noting that all of above legislative instruments include mergers within the definitional scope of the term 'reorganisation' and approach the concept of 'merger' identically in line with the definition given in Article 2(2) of the Cross-border Merger Directive.

29.   The Income Tax Law, No 118(I)/2002 as amended,[8] transposes into Cyprus law Council Directive 90/434/EEC of 23 July 1990[9] on the common system of taxation applicable to mergers, divisions, transfers of assets and exchanges of shares concerning companies of different Member States, as amended by Council Directive 2005/19/EC of 17 February 2005.[10] The Income Tax Law dedicates a special part to the rules pertaining to reorganisations. Part VI (Arts. 26–30) provides exemptions from income tax as follows (see also Chapter 3, no 14 *et seq.* of this book):

  (i)   assets and liabilities, including provisions and reserves, which are transferred under reorganisation do not give rise to any gains or profits liable to tax for the transferring company (Art. 26(1) of the Income Tax Law);

  (ii)   the receiving company will claim any profits or losses with respect to the transferred assets, liabilities, provisions and reserves under the rules that would have applied to the transferring company if the reorganisation had not taken place (Art. 26(2) of the Income Tax Law);

  (iii)   any accumulated losses of a transferring company are transferred to the resulting company to be set off against the income of the latter under the condition that both the transferring and the resulting company either reside in Cyprus or have a permanent establishment in Cyprus (Art. 27 of the Income Tax Law);

  (iv)   any gains accruing to the receiving company by reason of the cancellation of the holding in the capital of the transferring company are not liable to tax under the condition that both the transferring and the resulting

---

8 *Official Gazette of the Republic of Cyprus* 2002, Issue no 3622, Appendix 1, Part I of 15 July 2002.

9 *Official Journal* L 225/1 of 20 August 1990.

10 *Official Journal* L 58/19 of 4 March 2005.

company either reside in Cyprus or have a permanent establishment in Cyprus (Art. 28 of the Income Tax Law);

(v)   the new shares of the receiving or acquiring company received by a shareholder in exchange for the shares of the transferring or acquired company will not *per se* give rise to any gains or profits liable to tax. The new shares received will have the same value for tax purposes as the shares exchanged had immediately before the reorganisation. The taxing of the profit arising out of the subsequent transfer of shares received is not however excluded (Art. 29 of the Income Tax Law).

30.   In addition, the Capital Gains Tax Law, No 52/80,[11] has been amended by Law No 119(I)/2002 to the effect that the following two types of transaction fall outside the definition of 'transfer of property' and are not therefore taxable:

(i)   the transfer of property in the event of reorganisation (Art. 10(h) of the Capital Gains Tax Law);

(ii) the transfer of shares under a reorganisation scheme, representing the capital of the receiving or acquiring company, to or by a shareholder of the transferring or acquired company in exchange for shares representing the capital of the latter company (Art. 10(i) of the Capital Gains Tax Law).

31.   Furthermore, Law No 236(I)/2002 has introduced Article 7(1)(d) in the Department of Lands and Surveys (Charges and Fees) Law, Chapter 219, providing that no transfer fees are imposed on any transfer of immovable property taking place in the course of a reorganisation.

32.   Finally, Law No 121(I)/2002 has amended the Stamp Law, No 19/1963,[12] by inserting a new provision, Article 4A, which contemplates that transactions involved in a reorganisation scheme are exempted from the stamp duty.

---

11 *Official Gazette of the Republic of Cyprus* 1980, Issue no 1620, Appendix 1 of 1 August 1980.

12 *Official Gazette of the Republic of Cyprus* 1963, Issue no 240, Appendix 1, Part I of 28 March 1963.

9

Czech Republic

ADAM JIROUSEK AND JAN LASÁK
Kocián Šolc Balaštík

I   Introduction

1.   The Cross-border Merger Directive has been implemented in the Czech Republic by the Act on Transformation of Commercial Companies and Cooperatives which the Czech Parliament adopted on 19 March 2008 (the 'Transformation Act').[1] The Transformation Act is a broad regulation, however, that sets forth the rules governing all types of transformations of companies

---

1 Act no 125/2008 Coll.

and cooperatives (e.g. merger, split-off, transfer of assets of shareholders and change of legal form of a company) carried out at both the national and the cross-border level that replace the older relevant provisions of the Czech Commercial Code.[2] These provisions applied only to domestic transactions and were abolished with the enactment of the Transformation Act.[3] The second part of the Transformation Act contains the rules on mergers and section IX of this part lays down special provisions on cross-border merger in accordance with the Cross-border Merger Directive.

The realisation of a cross-border merger is subject to the provisions of the Transformation Act on domestic mergers unless section IX stipulates otherwise (Art. 180 Transformation Act). The Transformation Act and other special Czech laws and regulations govern Czech entities participating in a cross-border merger (Art. 187 Transformation Act).

II   Scope of the new rules

2.   The Transformation Act's rules apply to cross-border merger, which is defined as a merger of one or more (Czech) commercial companies or cooperatives with one or more foreign corporations (Art. 68 Transformation Act). Regarding Czech companies allowed to participate in cross-border mergers, these are all types of Czech companies deemed to be limited liability companies within the meaning of Article 2(1) of the Cross-border Merger Directive, i.e. the Czech public limited liability company (*akciová společnost*) (AS), private limited liability company (*společnost s ručením omezeným*) (SRO) or cooperative (*družstvo*). Moreover, the Czech legislators took the opportunity to extend the application of rules to corporate forms with unlimited liability (see Chapter 1, no 5 of this book), i.e. general commercial partnerships (*veřejná obchodní společnost*) (VOS) and limited partnerships (*komanditní společnost*) (KS). In accordance with this approach, a broader definition of foreign corporations encompassing forms of unlimited companies has been included, as long as the Shareholder State whose legal rules govern the foreign corporation in question permits this type of company to participate in a cross-border merger (Art. 181(b) Transformation Act). A Shareholder State is understood to be any country forming part of the European Economic Area (see Chapter 1, no 3 of this book). The Transformation Act also explicitly refers to a merger of a Czech company with a foreign limited partnership with capital divided in shares that is of a corporate form unknown to Czech corporate law (as opposed to, for example, German corporate law), stipulating that such merger shall be subject to terms and conditions applying to cross-border mergers with foreign limited partnerships (Art. 190(2) Transformation Act).

---

2   Act no 513/1991 Coll.

3   By Act no 126/2008 Coll., amending certain other Acts in connection with the adoption of the Act on transformation of commercial companies and cooperatives.

3.   A cross-border merger that involves a company the business object of which is the collective investment of capital provided by the public and that operates on the principle of risk-spreading, and the units of which are, at the holders' request, repurchased or redeemed, directly or indirectly, out of the assets of that company, does not benefit from the provisions of the Cross-border Merger Directive (Art. 3(3) Dir.). Czech corporations that engage in collective investment are investment funds and investment companies pursuant to the Act on Collective Investment.[4] Both the investment funds and investment companies may only have the form of public limited liability companies. In accordance with Article 96(5) of the Act on Collective Investment, an investment fund that collects capital from the public and ensures the stock exchange value of the securities issued by it on the regulated market does not vary significantly from their actual value must not participate in a cross-border merger. However, investment funds other than those defined in the said provision are not precluded from a cross-border merger. Pursuant to the Act on Collective Investment, the investment funds exist only as closed-end funds that do not repurchase or redeem the securities issued by them so that they principally fall outside the definition of Article 3(3) of the Cross-border Merger Directive. Similarly, the investment companies do not seem to be caught by this provision since they administer the capital collected in investment funds whose ownership structure is separated from the corporate structure of the company. Therefore, the changes in the corporate structure of investment companies do not directly affect the capital concentrated in their funds. In any event, the Czech legislators did not explicitly rule out investment companies from the application of the Cross-border Merger Directive. A cross-border merger of an investment fund or an investment company shall require the consent of the Czech National Bank.

The cross-border merger of a non-profit organisation is explicitly not allowed.[5]

4.   A cross-border merger may be carried out regardless of the fact that the company or cooperative in question has entered into liquidation. The liquidation terminates on the day when the company shareholders or the competent body of the company or cooperative approves the merger. Further, pending insolvency proceedings in respect of a company or cooperative, as well as a court decision declaring a company or cooperative insolvent, shall pose no obstacle for them to participate in a cross-border merger. During the realisation of a cross-border merger involving an insolvent company or pending insolvency proceedings, however, special provisions of the Czech Insolvency Act[6] have to be observed, in particular with regard to persons authorised to act on behalf

4 Act no 189/2004 Coll.
5 Art. 7(3) of Act no 248/1995 Coll., on non-profit organisations and amendment of certain acts.
6 Act no 182/2006 Coll.

of the company (that depends, *inter alia*, on the phase of the proceedings) and requisite approvals to the draft terms of cross-border merger according to the Insolvency Act (e.g. by the committee of creditors of the insolvent company).

5.   The Transformation Act permits, in addition to the provisions of the Cross-border Merger Directive, a cross-border dissolution of a commercial company without liquidation and transfer of its business assets to a shareholder of the company. This transaction should not be confused with the type of merger described in Article 2(2)(c) of the Cross-border Merger Directive pursuant to which the assets and liabilities of the company ceasing to exist are transferred to its sole shareholder. The transfer of business assets and liabilities regulated in Article 337 ff. of the Transformation Act (or the so-called 'improper squeeze-out') applies in particular to limited liability companies where a majority shareholder holds shares representing at least 90 per cent of the registered capital of the company. Pursuant to Article 3(2) of the Transformation Act, the shareholder taking over may have its company seat or domicile in any of the Shareholder States. On the other hand, this is all that the Transformation Act says on this issue and therefore many substantive questions remain unresolved, *inter alia*, what evidence is necessary to demonstrate to the Czech registration court the fulfilment of obligations required by the law of the other Shareholder State, the relation between the foreign and Czech registration proceedings, etc. Therefore, it seems doubtful whether the provisions on the cross-border 'improper squeeze-out' may be successfully invoked.

III   Cash payment

6.   The Transformation Act stipulates in respect of a domestic merger of public limited liability companies that if shareholders of any of the companies participating in a merger receive a cash payment as compensation for their loss resulting from the exchange of shares in the company or companies ceasing to exist for the shares in the successor company, such cash payment must not exceed 10 per cent of the nominal value of the shares to be exchanged for the shares of the company or companies ceasing to exist (Art. 106(3) Transformation Act). A similar rule applies to mergers of private limited liability companies (Art. 88 Transformation Act) and to mergers of public limited liability companies with private limited liability companies (Art. 155(1) Transformation Act). Cross-border mergers of limited liability companies are subject to the same restriction (Art. 180 Transformation Act). Therefore, in accordance with Article 3(1) of the Cross-border Merger Directive, the rules of the Directive may be applied to cross-border mergers involving cash payment in excess of the indicated amount only if the law of at least one of the Shareholder States where the other participating company or companies have their corporate seat so allows (see Chapter 1, no 8 of this book).

IV   Legal consequences and enforceability of a cross-border merger

7.   The completion of a cross-border merger of a commercial company or cooperative has *ipso iure* the same effects as the completion of a domestic merger. This means, in the case of merger by acquisition, that (i) the acquired company or cooperative ceases to exist, (ii) all their assets and liabilities, including rights and obligations arising from labour relations, are transferred to another company or cooperative, and (iii) shareholders of the company or cooperative ceasing to exist become shareholders of the successor company or cooperative (except for cases where the Act stipulates otherwise) (Arts. 61(1) and 64(1) Transformation Act). The legal consequences of merger by formation of a new company are similar, only the assets and liabilities of at least two companies or cooperatives participating in the merger and ceasing to exist shall be transferred to a newly created successor company or cooperative (Arts. 62 and 64(2) Transformation Act).

8.   The cross-border merger takes effect on the date of registration of the merger in the Czech or foreign commercial register (Art. 213 Transformation Act), i.e. in the commercial register of the Shareholder State where the successor company has its corporate seat. Upon registration, the cross-border merger is completed and the subsequent deletion of the company or cooperative ceasing to exist from the relevant commercial register shall have only declaratory significance. Czech law did not implement Article 13(2) of the Cross-border Merger Directive, stipulating that deletion of the old registration shall be effected only on receipt of the notification of the registry of the company resulting from the cross-border merger. Nevertheless, considering the legal quality of the said provision as directly applicable, this provision is binding for the Czech courts without further need for implementation.

          The completion of a cross-border merger has to be published in the Czech commercial bulletin in accordance with Article 3 of the First Company Law Directive as implemented in the Czech Commercial Code. The cross-border merger is enforceable against third parties as from the date of the publication unless the successor company demonstrates that a third party was informed of the registration prior to the publication. Furthermore, if a third party demonstrates that it could not learn about the cross-border merger earlier, the successor company may not rely on it until the sixteenth day following the publication (Art. 29 Commercial Code).

9.   Only a court may decide on the nullity of the resolution of the company's general meeting or cooperative's shareholders' meeting by which the cross-border merger was approved or on the nullity of the common draft terms of cross-border merger. Such decision has to be made before the registration of the cross-border merger in the commercial register. Following the registration, it is not allowed (i) to annul this registration, (ii) to challenge the validity of the common draft terms of cross-border merger or the validity of the resolution of

the company's general meeting or the cooperative's shareholders' meeting, and (iii) to amend or annul the draft terms of merger. The claim of a shareholder that the share-exchange ratio or cash payment was inadequate (see no 6 of this chapter) does not constitute grounds for the general (shareholders') meeting resolution or draft terms of merger to be invalidated. The shareholders can, however, lodge an action for compensation in separate court proceedings (see no 11 of this chapter). If proceedings where the plaintiff claims nullity of a cross-border merger are initiated prior to registration in the commercial register, these proceedings may continue after the merger has been registered only if the subject matter of the proceedings is changed to a compensation claim pursuant to Article 45 ff. or action for damages pursuant to Article 50 of the Transformation Act (see no 38 of this chapter).

V   Procedure

1   Draft terms of cross-border merger

10.   The draft terms of cross-border merger are prepared by the management bodies of merging entities and approved in the same wording by the general meeting of all participating entities. The document is only required to be in writing and is not required to be in notarised form (Art. 15(1) Transformation Act). If the draft terms are prepared in several language versions, the Czech version shall be decisive for the Czech authorities even if the notary should not issue the pre-merger certificate required to proceed with a cross-border merger due to the failure of participating entities to approve the draft terms of the cross-border merger in the same wording (Arts. 192 and 210 Transformation Act). However, this provision cannot regulate situations where a merging entity does not have its registered seat in the Czech Republic.

11.   The draft terms of cross-border merger should include the information described in Chapter 1, no 18 of this book as well as other information. Should a new entity result from the merger, the draft terms shall contain the names, corporate forms, registered offices and identity numbers of shareholders of the management body or supervisory board of the entity resulting from the merger and terms for situations when shareholders of Czech merging entities have the right to sell their shares in the company resulting from the merger to the new or surviving company (see no 37 of this chapter), particularly the name of the newspapers where the proposal to buy these shares shall be published.

Pursuant to Articles 208 and 209 of the Transformation Act, failure to include the above-mentioned information may constitute grounds for the notary to decline issuing the pre-merger certificate attesting that the Czech merging entity fulfilled all the requirements necessary to proceed with a cross-border merger (see no 33 of this chapter). Furthermore, the directors or managers can be held liable to third parties for damages resulting from failure to include required information in the draft terms of merger under Article 50 of the Transformation Act.

12.   The draft terms of cross-border merger must be filed with the commercial register of the judicial district where each participating entity's registered office is located by no later than one month before a general meeting is called to approve the cross-border merger.

In addition, the common draft terms must be announced to the public at least one month before the general meeting is convened to approve the cross-border merger by a notice in the commercial bulletin that the draft terms are available at the collection of documents at the commercial register. Each participating entity is responsible for fulfilling their respective filing and publication requirements in the judicial district where their registered office is located.

2   Management report

13.   The management body of each merging entity must prepare a written report for entity shareholders that justifies the economic reasons for the cross-border merger. In contrast with national mergers, the management bodies of all merging entities cannot prepare a single management report for all participating entities in the case of a cross-border merger. In the case of a merger where the surviving entity is the sole shareholder of the entity ceasing to exist, the management report is not required to be prepared (Art. 211 Transformation Act).

This report should provide a legal and economic explanation and justification for: (i) the implications of the merger for shareholders and creditors; (ii) the difficulties encountered; (iii) reasoning on the ratio applicable to the exchange of securities or shares representing the entity capital with potential cash payments; (iv) possible consequences for the employees of the merging entity; (v) reasoning on the shareholders' deposit to the basic capital of the entity resulting from the merger and the amount of any cash payment as well as the reasoning on the measures proposed to holders of shares or securities of the merging entities. If the inclusion of certain information might cause serious harm to the participating entity, its parent entity or subsidiary, or the information is a part of their trade secret or restricted information pursuant to Act no 148/1998 Coll., *o ochraně utajovaných skutečností*, the management body shall not include such information in the management report. However, the management body shall explain in the management report why such information was not included (Art. 26 Transformation Act).

14.   Should the trade unions operating with a merging entity prepare an opinion on the merger and this opinion be submitted to the management in a timely manner, it must be attached to the management report and made available for shareholders at the general meeting called to approve the cross-border merger before voting. Also employees are entitled to examine the management report (as well as the independent expert's report – see no 16 ff. of this chapter) and submit their opinion. Merging entities shall inform the trade unions and employees (by no later than publication of the notice in the commercial bulletin announcing

that the draft terms of the cross-border merger are available at the collection of documents at the commercial register) of their right to examine the management report and independent expert's report and submit their opinion.

Before the general meeting, the shareholders are entitled to examine the management report at the entity's registered office at least one month before the date of the general meeting called to approve the draft terms of the cross-border merger (Art. 194(3) Transformation Act). The management report must not be otherwise made public.

15. Shareholders of the management body are liable to third parties for damages resulting from failure to prepare and submit a management report on the cross-border merger (Art. 50(1) Transformation Act). Such failure can also constitute grounds for the notary to decline issuing the pre-merger certificate (Arts. 208 and 209 Transformation Act) (see no 33 of this chapter).

3   Independent expert

16. The independent expert(s) should prepare a written report on the draft terms of cross-border merger for each entity participating in the cross-border merger. In case of a merger where the surviving entity is the sole shareholder of the entity ceasing to exist, the independent expert's report is not required to be prepared (Art. 211 Transformation Act). This rule applies only to public and private limited liability companies.

17. The court must appoint the independent expert within fifteen days after a merging entity submits the petition to appoint the expert. The independent expert may be appointed for each merging entity, for some of them or for all participating entities. In such a case, the management bodies of the merging entities may jointly petition the court to appoint the expert. The Czech court shall appoint the independent expert for all merging entities or for some of them if the registered seat of the participating entities or of the entity resulting from the merger is in the Czech Republic (Art. 195(3) Transformation Act). The merging entity to which the independent expert has been appointed shall cover all expenses and remuneration of the expert. The remuneration is set based on mutual agreement of the independent expert and the merging entity. In the absence of agreement the court will determine the expert's remuneration *ad hoc*.

18. The above-mentioned expert's report is not required if all shareholders of all entities participating in the cross-border merger unanimously decide that no report need be drafted and the draft terms of cross-border merger need not be examined by an expert (Art. 196(2) Transformation Act). In this case, shareholders of the Czech participating entity may express their approval that the independent expert's report need not be drafted at the general meeting convened prior to the general meeting called to approve the cross-border merger. Shareholders of Czech participating entities may also express their decision in written form if their signature is verified.

The independent expert's report is also not required in the event of a merger by absorption of a wholly owned subsidiary if the merging entities are private limited liability companies or public limited liability companies (Art. 211 Transformation Act). However, an expert's report is required for a cross-border merger of a subsidiary if the parent entity holds 90 per cent or more, but not 100 per cent, of the subsidiary's shares.[7]

19. To prepare its report, the expert may request the merging entities, their subsidiaries and parent entities for any information deemed necessary.

20. In its report the expert should certify whether, in their opinion, the share-exchange ratio of the cross-border merger with potential cash payments is appropriate and reasonable (Arts. 114, 180 and 196(1) Transformation Act). The expert's report should at least indicate (i) the method(s) used to determine the share-exchange ratio; (ii) whether this method (or these methods) is appropriate in the case at hand; (iii) the share-exchange ratio if one method is used for each and an opinion on the relative importance of each method in determining the value eventually reached; (iv) particular difficulties, if any, encountered in the valuation process.

The expert's report shall not include any information that might cause serious harm to any of the participating entities, their parent entities or subsidiaries, or information deemed to be a trade secret or restricted information pursuant to Act no 148/1998 Coll., *o ochraně utajovaných skutečností*. In such cases, the independent expert shall explain why the information was omitted in the report (Art. 115(2) and (3) Transformation Act).

21. The expert's report must be made available to the shareholders of the merging entities at the general meeting called to approve the draft terms of cross-border merger (Arts. 116(2) and 180 Transformation Act). Before the general meeting, the shareholders of the Czech public limited liability company participating in the cross-border merger are entitled to examine the expert's report at the entity's registered office at least one month before the date of the general meeting called to approve the draft terms of cross-border merger (Art. 119(1) Transformation Act). Moreover, shareholders have a right to obtain a copy or an abstract of the expert's report. Employees and trade unions are entitled to examine the expert's report as well and submit their opinion (Arts. 199 and 200 Transformation Act). The expert's report must not be otherwise made public.

22. Should an expert's report be required but it has not been prepared, this fact shall constitute grounds for the notary to decline to issue the pre-merger certificate (Arts. 208 and 209 Transformation Act) (see no 33 of this chapter).

---

7 Even though Art. 15(2) Cross-border Merger Directive allows Member States not to have an expert's report in this case. The Czech Republic did not enact this option.

4   General meeting of shareholders

A   Information for shareholders

23.   The draft terms of cross-border merger, management report, independent expert's report and shareholders' right to obtain a copy of these documents free of charge shall all be mentioned on the agenda of the general meeting called to vote on the draft terms of cross-border merger of a public limited liability company (Arts. 121(1) and 180 Transformation Act). The agenda, including these notices, shall be enclosed in the convocation notices sent to shareholders of the merging company in accordance with the rules applicable to convocation notices for public limited liability companies.

Furthermore, the shareholders are entitled to consult the draft terms of cross-border merger, management report, independent expert's report and expert's opinion evaluating assets at the office of each participating entity, for one month prior to the date of the general meeting scheduled to vote on the merger (Arts. 119(2) and 180 Transformation Act). There is no obligation of the merging public limited liability company to send these documents to the shareholders, including the holders of registered shares whose names are mentioned in the shareholders' register. The company can, of course, decide to send these documents on its own initiative.

In addition to these documents, the public limited liability company should simultaneously make available to shareholders the annual accounts for the last three fiscal years of each merging company if the company has existed for at least three years, and the reports of auditors if they are necessary under Czech law.

24.   If the draft terms of cross-border merger are dated more than six months after the close of the last fiscal year to which the last annual account relates, an accounting statement dated no later than three months before the date of the draft terms of cross-border merger must be prepared and be made available at the entity's registered office. This statement shall be prepared in accordance with the methods used for, and the presentation of, the latest annual accounts.

25.   Alongside the information duties of the participating entities, each shareholder of the public limited liability company may request free of charge a complete or partial copy of any of the above-mentioned documents, except the expert's opinion evaluating the assets of the merging entities. However, if the expert's opinion evaluating the assets is included in the independent expert's report under Art. 74(1) of the Transformation Act, the shareholders can demand a copy or abstract of the expert's opinion as well (Art. 119(1)(f) and (2) Transformation Act).

26.   The management body of a merging entity must inform the general meeting of the public limited liability company called to approve the cross-border merger of the expert's report conclusions and of each material change in the assets and liabilities of the participating entity between the date from which the transactions

of the merging entities shall be treated for accounting purposes as those of the entity resulting from the cross-border merger and the date of the general meeting called to vote on the merger (Arts. 180 and 122(3) Transformation Act).

27.   If the merging entity is a private limited liability company or an unlimited liability company (i.e. a general commercial partnership or a limited partnership), the company must send the documents mentioned above to the shareholders. These documents must be delivered two weeks prior to the shareholders' meeting called to vote on the merger (Art. 180 in conjunction with Arts. 78, 81 and 93(1) Transformation Act). Along with the documents, a Czech private limited liability company shall send to the shareholders a notification of their right to consult the expert's opinion evaluating the assets at the registered office of the company. If the private limited liability company decides that the shareholders shall approve the cross-border merger outside the general meeting, the company shall send to the shareholders a draft of the decision on the cross-border merger (Arts. 93(4) and 180 Transformation Act). Shareholders of Czech private limited liability companies or unlimited liability companies participating in the cross-border merger may waive their right to receive the aforementioned documents.

Further, each Czech participating entity shall provide free of charge to any shareholder or creditor of any of the merging entities information on the rights that the Transformation Act grants to the shareholders or creditors of Czech merging entities participating in a cross-border merger (Art. 198 Transformation Act).

B   Shareholders' approval

28.   Regarding public limited liability companies, private limited liability companies and cooperatives being the merging entity, the cross-border merger and the draft terms of cross-border merger must be approved by the general meeting or shareholders' meeting. For the absorption of a wholly owned subsidiary by its parent entity, shareholder approval at the general meeting is not required when the draft terms of cross-border merger can be approved by the managing bodies of the merging entities. However, shareholders may call a general meeting to approve the cross-border merger even though Article 211 of the Transformation Act does not require them to do so.

To approve a public limited liability company's participation in a cross-border merger at least 30 per cent of the capital must be present or represented at the general meeting unless the articles of association require a higher quorum (Art. 185(1) Commercial Code). If this quorum is not met, a second meeting of the general meeting may be called and this second meeting shall decide on the cross-border merger regardless of the number of shares present or represented. In the private company, at least 50 per cent of the votes must be present or represented unless the articles of association require a higher quorum (Art. 127(1) Commercial Code). In a cooperative, at least 50 per cent of the votes must be present or represented (Art. 238(3) Commercial Code).

The cross-border merger must be approved by a special majority of three quarters of the votes present or represented in a public limited liability company, a private limited liability company or a cooperative. If there are different classes of shares or other securities in the public limited liability company, i.e. shares or securities with different rights, the special majority requirements of three quarters of the votes present or represented must be met for each class of shares. The draft terms of cross-border merger must define the rights conferred by the entity resulting from the merger on shareholders enjoying special rights or on the holders of securities other than shares representing capital or the measures proposed concerning them (Art. 5 Dir.).

29.   If a shareholder of a private limited liability company is not present at the general meeting called to vote on the cross-border merger, they may express their vote afterwards provided the vote is delivered to the registered seat of the company within one month after the general meeting. This decision must be in notarised form with the draft terms of the cross-border merger as an attachment to the notarial record (Art. 18(1) Transformation Act).

Shareholders of a private limited liability company may also approve the cross-border merger outside the general meeting in accordance with the Commercial Code. In such instances, shareholders shall have at least two weeks to express their approval or disapproval (Art. 19(1) Transformation Act). The voting majority remains the same as in the event of approving the cross-border merger at the general meeting.

30.   In certain cases, the approval of all shareholders is required to proceed with a cross-border merger. This is the case with respect to the following entities participating in the cross-border merger: (i) limited partnerships, regardless of whether the general commercial partnership is the surviving company or the company that ceases to exist; (ii) general commercial partnerships, regardless of whether the general commercial partnership is the surviving company or the company that ceases to exist (Art. 16(1) Transformation Act). The approval of all shareholders of all participating companies is necessary when the full repayment of basic capital is not registered for all merging companies in the commercial register (Art. 20(4) Transformation Act). In specific instances, the approval of a certain group of shareholders is required: (i) if a cross-border merger results in a material change that affects shareholders (or some of them) of a merging private limited liability company, approval of all of the affected shareholders is necessary (Art. 20(1) Transformation Act); (ii) if shareholders of a merging private limited liability company receive shares with limited transferability of the company resulting from the cross-border merger, approval of all affected shareholders is necessary (Art. 20(3) Transformation Act).

Furthermore, the general meeting of a merging entity may decide to make its decision subject to express ratification of the arrangements with respect to the participation of employees in the entity resulting from the merger if the merging entity is a public limited liability company, a private limited liability company or a cooperative. Ratification of the arrangements must be approved in the same manner and by the same special majority as the cross-border merger itself (Art. 202 Transformation Act).

31.   In the event of a merger with an existing entity, the draft terms of cross-border merger must contain any proposed changes to the articles of association of that entity and be approved by the shareholders at the general meeting of all merging entities. Any changes to the articles of association shall be included in the draft terms of cross-border merger. If the draft terms of cross-border merger contain no proposed changes to the entity's articles of association, the articles of association shall be deemed to be unchanged. Should a new entity result from the merger, the new entity's articles of association will have to be approved as part of the terms of the cross-border merger.

32.   The general meeting of each Czech participating entity must be held before a notary, and the minutes must be prepared in notarised form regardless of the type of entity (Arts. 16(2), 17(3), 21(4) and 23(3) Transformation Act).

5   Pre-merger certificate

33.   A notary must verify and certify the existence and legality of all instruments and formalities carried out by the Czech merging entity by issuing the pre-merger certificate. The notary who issues the pre-merger certificate need not be the notary who prepares the notarial instrument of the general meeting approving the cross-border merger under Arts. 17(3), 21(4) and 23(3) Transformation Act.

When a Czech entity participates in the merger, the notary will, after verification, issue a pre-merger certificate attesting to completion of the requisite pre-merger acts and formalities (Arts. 208 and 209 Transformation Act) in order to proceed with the cross-border merger. This certificate is valid for six months (Art. 210(4) Transformation Act). If the instruments and formalities are not in accordance with Czech law, the notary shall refuse to issue the pre-merger certificate to the Czech merging entity.

34.   Each participating entity must send the pre-merger certificate to the notary responsible for attesting the completion of the merger for the surviving entity or the entity resulting from the merger within six months from issuance of this certificate by the notary (for a Czech entity) or other authority designated under local law of other EU Shareholder States for a foreign entity participating in the cross-border merger. When the entity resulting from the merger is supposed to have its registered office in the Czech Republic, the failure to send the pre-merger certificate to the Czech notary constitutes grounds to refuse to issue the final pre-merger certificate attesting to the lawful completion of the cross-border merger.

If the entity resulting from the cross-border merger is supposed to have its registered office in the Czech Republic, the notary attesting the completion of the cross-border merger shall be provided with the draft terms of cross-border merger in the official languages of all Shareholder States in question, the pre-merger certificates in respect of all merging companies and documentation regarding arrangements with respect to the participation of employees in the company resulting from the merger (Art. 1 of Ministry Regulation no 207/2008 Coll.). This notary attestation must be filed together with the pre-merger certificates for each merging entity and other required documentation[8] with the Czech registration court in order to enter the cross-border merger in the commercial register.

6   Effects of the decision

35. A cross-border merger where the successor entity is a Czech entity enters into effect upon registration in the Czech commercial register. The registration court shall publicise the entry of the cross-border merger in the commercial register as well as the filing of the necessary documents with the collection of documents at the commercial register without undue delay in the commercial bulletin (Art. 27(4) Commercial Code). The cross-border merger takes effect vis-à-vis third parties in principle only upon publication (see no 8 of this chapter). The registration court shall also notify, within three days following the registration of the cross-border merger in the commercial register, the body administering the foreign commercial register of the merging entity located in another Shareholder State of this registration (Art. 200db(4) Code of Civil Procedure).[9]

After a cross-border merger takes effect, it cannot be declared void by a court regardless of whether the cross-border merger has been challenged or not (Art. 56 Transformation Act). This rule applies irrespective of whether the decision has been published and thus made enforceable against third parties (see no 9 of this chapter).

VI   Minority shareholders

36. The rights of shareholders of participating entities, including minority shareholders, are protected during the merger process by statutory provisions granting their right to early and correct information and to transparency and fairness of the process. The relevant rules, as laid down in the Cross-border Merger Directive and in the Merger Directive (as far as the general rules for domestic mergers of public limited liability companies apply), have been implemented in the Transformation Act and include, *inter alia*, the obligation of the statutory organ of the Czech merging company to file the common draft terms of cross-border merger with the collection of documents at the commercial register, to provide for the publication of the envisaged merger in the Czech commercial

8 As laid down in the Commercial Code and in the implementing Ministry Regulation no 250/2005 Coll.
9 Act no 99/1963 Coll.

bulletin and to make the crucial merger documentation, including the report of the statutory body on the cross-border merger, available to shareholders (for more details, see no 23 of this chapter).

37.   As for the protection of the rights of the minority shareholders who have opposed the cross-border merger, the Shareholder States themselves have the power to lay down the relevant rules (Art. 4(2) *in fine* Dir.). Therefore, the level of 'appropriate protection' (as mentioned in the aforementioned provision) differs between the Shareholder States (see Chapter 1, no 27 of this book).

Czech law provides, in respect of domestic mergers, for the sell-out right of the shareholders of a public limited liability company if the merger results in a worsening of their legal position compared to the situation preceding the merger. To make use of this right, the shareholders must participate in the general meeting deciding on the merger and vote against it. In such a case, the draft terms of merger must set out the obligation of the successor company to purchase the shares of the shareholders opposing the merger (Art. 145 ff. Transformation Act). Similarly, a shareholder who opposed a domestic merger between a public limited liability company and a private limited liability company as the successor company may exit the public limited liability company ceasing to exist. The leaving shareholder has the right to payment of a settlement share (Art. 159 Transformation Act). A shareholder disagreeing with a domestic merger of a cooperative may exit the cooperative provided that either they did not participate in the shareholders' meeting or, if they did, they did not vote for the approval of the merger (Art. 175 Transformation Act).

The shareholders of a Czech public limited liability company merging with a private limited liability company seated in another Shareholder State, as well as the shareholders of a Czech cooperative participating in a cross-border merger, may exit the company or cooperative in accordance with the above rules governing domestic mergers (Arts. 180 and 187 Transformation Act, see no 1 of this chapter). As regards the sell-out right of the shareholders of a Czech public limited liability company merging with a public limited liability company with its corporate seat in another Shareholder State, it is necessary that the competent body of the foreign entity, when approving the common draft terms of cross-border merger, explicitly accepts that the shareholders of the Czech participating entity enjoy the right to sell their shares to the successor company. The pre-merger certificate issued by the Czech notary pursuant to Article 10 of the Cross-border Merger Directive (see no 33 of this chapter) must indicate that the draft terms of merger contain the sell-out right of the Czech shareholders (Art. 209(1) Transformation Act).

38.   Under Czech law on domestic mergers, the shareholders who are not satisfied with the ratio applicable to the exchange of shares in the company or cooperative ceasing to exist for the shares in the successor company or cooperative or deem the cash payment related to the share exchange to be inadequate, may file a lawsuit against the successor company or cooperative for compensation.

This right must be invoked within one year following the date when the cross-border merger became effective vis-à-vis third parties, otherwise the right shall expire. A judicial ruling granting a shareholder the right to compensation is binding on the successor company or cooperative as the basis for the according of such right to other shareholders (Art. 45 ff. Transformation Act). In the case of a cross-border merger, however, Czech shareholders may have recourse to the aforementioned right only if either the law of the Shareholder States where all the other merging entities are situated provides for such scrutiny procedure or all the foreign participating entities situated in Shareholder States that do not provide for such procedure explicitly accept, when approving the cross-border merger, that the shareholders of the Czech merging entity may have such right subject to the provisions of the Transformation Act (Art. 206 Transformation Act). Czech courts have jurisdiction over compensation claims of Czech shareholders, even after the registration of the cross-border merger in the Czech commercial register or commercial register of another Shareholder State (Art. 207 Transformation Act). The Czech notary may issue the pre-merger certificate pursuant to Article 10 of the Cross-border Merger Directive even if the action for compensation is lodged, but the certificate must state this fact.

The Transformation Act also provides the shareholders of Czech merging entities, as well as their creditors, with the right to claim damages against the shareholders of statutory organs of merging entities or against the experts who deliver mandatory reports in relation to the merger in case they cause damage by breaching their relevant obligations. Also judicial rulings in these matters that award the right to damages are binding on the responsible persons as the basis for the according of such right to other entitled persons. The right to damages lapses after five years following the date when the cross-border merger became effective vis-à-vis third parties (Art. 50 Transformation Act). Since the Cross-border Merger Directive is silent on this question and the Transformation Act lacks special provisions for cross-border mergers, the above rules equally apply to the managements' and experts' liability for damages resulting from cross-border mergers. The laws and regulations of the Shareholder States should be harmonised in respect of the civil liability of management bodies and experts at least to a certain extent in accordance with Articles 20 and 21 of the Merger Directive, although these provisions relate only to public limited liability companies and protect rights of the shareholders of companies being acquired as opposed to Czech regulation that favours shareholders of all merging entities.

VII   Protection of creditors

39.   The rights of creditors in the course of the merger process are, on the one hand, secured by a set of obligations of the merging entities and their competent bodies that are very similar, and sometimes identical, to those securing the rights of

shareholders of entities. Their purpose is to ensure the transparency and fairness of the cross-border merger (see no 36 of this chapter). The notice of publication of the cross-border merger to be announced in the Czech commercial bulletin must, *inter alia*, indicate the address at which the creditors of merging entities can obtain, free of charge, complete information about their rights, and must inform on rights that the creditors of each of the foreign merging entities have according to the laws and regulations of the Shareholder State where the foreign entity has its corporate seat (Art. 197(2)(c) Transformation Act).

40.   It is up to the national law to put in place safeguards granted to creditors of the merging entities and to the debenture holders, taking into account the cross-border nature of the merger (Art. 4(2) Dir.). The relevant national rules are harmonised to a certain extent through the Merger Directive with regard to public limited liability companies (see Chapter 1, no 44 of this book).

The creditors of the merging entity, including the debenture holders, who satisfy the following conditions may request sufficient security from the merging company: (i) the creditors must notify their claim within six months following the date when the entry of the cross-border merger into the (Czech or foreign) commercial register became effective vis-à-vis third parties (upon passage of this time the right lapses); (ii) at the time of notification, the creditors cannot demand satisfaction of their claims (the receivables are not due and payable); (iii) the recoverability of such claims deteriorates; (iv) the creditors do not benefit from preferential or separate treatment in the sense of the Insolvency Act; (v) their receivables did not arise only after the entry of the cross-border merger in the commercial register (Arts. 35(1) and 36 Transformation Act). The security shall not be granted to the debenture holders if a meeting of debenture holders approves the cross-border merger. A creditor is entitled to demand security even before entry of the merger in the commercial register if they demonstrate that, due to the merger, the recoverability of their receivables deteriorates substantially. Should the creditor and the merging company or cooperative not come to an agreement on the manner of securing the claim, the competent court shall decide.

Holders of convertible bonds and priority bonds and holders of securities bearing special rights (other than shares) shall acquire in the successor entity at least the same legal position that they enjoyed in the merging entity. This shall not apply if a meeting of such securities holders or all holders of such securities expressed agreement with their rights being changed or if they are entitled to have their securities repurchased by the successor company (Art. 37 Transformation Act).

41.   The creditors of merging entities have the same right as their shareholders to file a lawsuit against the shareholders of statutory organs of the participating entities and the responsible experts for damages caused by breach of their obligations in respect of the cross-border merger (see no 38 of this chapter).

VIII   Employee participation

42.   Pursuant to the Cross-border Merger Directive, the general meeting or share-holders' meeting of the Czech merging entity shall approve the manner and extent of employee participation in the Czech or foreign successor entity. This approval by the aforementioned bodies constitutes an integral part of the approval process of the cross-border merger (Art. 202 Transformation Act). If employee participation is not approved in the prescribed manner, the cross-border merger may not be completed (Art. 203 Transformation Act).

1   **Employee participation in companies resulting from the cross-border merger established in the Czech Republic**

43.   Should the successor company or cooperative have its corporate seat in the Czech Republic, the special provisions of the Commercial Code shall apply to employee participation, unless the Transformation Act implementing the relevant provisions of the Cross-border Merger Directive[10] stipulates otherwise (Art. 215(2) Transformation Act).

   Pursuant to Article 200 of the Commercial Code, one third of the share-holders of the supervisory board of a public limited liability company shall be elected by company employees provided that the company employs more than fifty employees for working hours exceeding one half of weekly working hours according to the Labour Code[11] on the first day of the financial year for which the shareholders of the supervisory board are to be elected by the general meeting of the company. The articles of association of the company may determine a higher number of shareholders of the supervisory board to be elected by employees; however, this number must not be higher than the number of shareholders elected by the general meeting. The articles of association may also stipulate that the employees shall elect all or part of the shareholders of the supervisory board even if the company employs fewer than fifty employees. If the negotiations on employee participation in a public limited liability company emerging as successor entity from a cross-border merger are initiated pursuant to the Transformation Act (see no 44 of this chapter), reducing the participation right below the limits set in the Commercial Code is prohibited and shall be deemed null and void (Art. 236(2) Transformation Act).

   As for the other types of limited liability companies within the meaning of the Cross-border Merger Directive, i.e. the private limited liability company and the cooperative, the Commercial Code does not, as a general rule, foresee any participation of employees within the meaning of Article 2(k) of Directive 2001/86 of 8 October 2001 supplementing the Statute for a European company with regard to the involvement of employees (the 'SE Directive'). Article 215(2)

---

10 Art. 16(2) Dir. or Art. 215(3) Transformation Act.
11 Act no 262/2006 Coll., Labour Code. Pursuant to Art. 79(1) Labour Code, the determined weekly working hours may not exceed forty hours per week.

of the Transformation Act basically excludes employee participation rights in these types of Czech successor entities save for situations when Czech rules on participation are set aside. With regard to these situations, the Commercial Code has been amended accordingly.

2   Special negotiating body ('SNB')

44.   Should the successor entity have its corporate seat in the Czech Republic and the national rules on employee participation be set aside by virtue of Article 215(3) of the Transformation Act (i.e. on grounds laid down in Art. 16(2) Dir., see Chapter 1, no 41 of this book), the statutory or other management bodies of the merging entities shall, in accordance with the provisions of the Transformation Act, initiate negotiations with the employees with a view to making arrangements on employee participation in the successor entity. Should the successor entity have its corporate seat in another Shareholder State, the relevant laws and regulations of that Shareholder State shall apply as regards employee participation rights and the proceedings leading to their determination (Art. 216 Transformation Act).

The special negotiating body shall represent the employees of the merging entities, the concerned subsidiaries and establishments during the negotiations on the extent of employee participation rights. The allocation of seats in the SNB between the representatives of employees from different Shareholder States is laid down in Articles 221 and 222 of the Transformation Act in accordance with the applicable European Union rules (Art. 16(3)(a) Cross-border Merger Directive in conjunction with Art. 3(2)(a) Merger Directive, see Chapter 3 of this book). The Czech representatives on the SNB shall be elected at the joint meeting of Czech employees' representatives, i.e. trade unions, works council(s) or representative for safety of work and health protection (Art. 220(2) Transformation Act in conjunction with Art. 290(4) Labour Code). An employee of a merging entity, concerned subsidiary or establishment, or a trade union representative, even if they are not employed in the merging or concerned entity, may be elected as an SNB representative. In principle, the employees of each Czech merging or concerned entity shall be represented by at least one representative in the SNB. If this is not possible, the employees of each Czech entity ceasing to exist must be represented first and the remaining seats in the SNB, if any, shall be distributed among the other entities according to the number of employees of each entity (Art. 222 Transformation Act).

The SNB negotiates with statutory or managing bodies of the merging entities with the aim of concluding an agreement on the extent of participation rights of employees of the successor entity. However, the SNB may also decide not to open negotiations or to terminate negotiations already opened and to rely on the participation rules set out in the Commercial Code (see no 43 of this chapter). A qualified majority of votes in the SNB is required for such a decision to be made (Art. 232 in conjunction with Art. 231(2) Transformation Act).

Merging entities have similar options to avoid the negotiations if they accept that the employees of the successor entity will have the participation rights in accordance with the provisions of the Transformation Act. In such a case, the SNB shall be replaced by the so-called employees' committee. Seats in the employees' committee shall be distributed according to the same rules as in the SNB. Provided employee participation rights differ substantially between the merging entities, the employees' committee shall decide which manner of employee participation should apply in the successor entity. If the employees' committee fails to make this decision within the given deadline, the employees of the successor entity shall be granted the same participation rights as in the merging entity with the highest level of participation. The employees' committee shall also decide on distribution of seats in the supervisory board of the successor entity among the employees from different Shareholder States and on the manner of exercising their participation rights. Upon making the aforesaid decisions or lapse of the above-mentioned deadline, the employees' committee shall be dissolved (Arts. 238 and 239 Transformation Act).

3   Protection of employee representatives

45.   Article 229 of the Transformation Act prohibits any form of direct or indirect benefit or direct or indirect discrimination of an SNB representative in relation to the exercise of their functions. Legal acts performed in breach of this rule shall be deemed null and void. This provision corresponds to the protection given to the representatives of Czech employees pursuant to Article 276(2) of the Labour Code.[12] According to Article 16(2) of the Labour Code, the terms direct and indirect discrimination shall be defined in the Antidiscrimination Act.[13] Since the Antidiscrimination Act has not yet been passed in the Czech Parliament,[14] interpretation and application problems could arise given the broad language of the Transformation Act.

The Czech merging companies shall bear all reasonable costs related to the activity of the SNB and its representatives, irrespective of which Shareholder State the corporate seat of the successor company is to be situated in (Art. 228(2) Transformation Act). However, the Transformation Act does not provide, in contrast to the SE Act,[15] for mandatory days off and refund of wages for representatives on the SNB in relation to exercise of their duties. This is probably nothing more than a legislator's omission. There are no grounds to

---

12 Art. 50(4) of Act no 627/2004, on the European company ('SE Act'), which implements similar rules to the SE Directive, refers explicitly to Art. 276(2) Labour Code contrary to Art. 229(2) Transformation Act.

13 The Antidiscrimination Act shall implement, *inter alia*, Directive 2000/78 of 27 November 2000 establishing a general framework for equal treatment in employment and occupation.

14 This contribution was written at the end of October 2008.

15 See footnote 12.

prevent the shareholders of the SNB in accordance with the Transformation Act from enjoying these rights that are enjoyed by both the employees' representatives pursuant to the Labour Code and SNB shareholders pursuant to the SE Act and it would also constitute a violation of Article 16(3)(f) of the Cross-border Merger Directive in conjunction with Article 10 second subparagraph of the SE Directive.

IX   Tax treatment

46.   The Czech Act on Income Tax[16] ('Income Tax Act') has regulated cross-border merger taxation since 2003 when the relevant Directive on the common system of taxation applicable to EU-wide mergers[17] was transposed into Czech law.[18] Until the enactment of the Transformation Act, the application of this regulation was limited only to the incorporation of the *Societas Europaea* (SEs) by cross-border merger in accordance with the SE Regulation.[19] Following the adoption of the Transformation Act, the merger regulation of the Income Tax Act was once again amended by Act no 126/2008 Coll.[20] The basic regulation is laid down in Article 23c(4)–(9) of the Income Tax Act.

The tax-neutral regime applies to cross-border mergers where (i) the company ceasing to exist and the successor company are Czech tax payers that have the form of a public or private limited liability company or a European Cooperative Society (SCE),[21] (ii) the company ceasing to exist is a tax payer in another Shareholder State and the successor company is a Czech tax payer that has the form of a public or private limited liability company or an SCE, provided the assets and liabilities passing to it do not constitute a part of a permanent establishment located outside the Czech Republic, or (iii) the company ceasing to exist is a Czech tax payer that has the form of a public or private limited liability company or an SCE or is a tax payer of another Shareholder State and the successor company is a tax payer in another Shareholder State, provided the assets and liabilities passing to it constitute a part of a permanent establishment of the successor company located in the Czech Republic.

The income (proceeds) of the successor company ensuing from re-evaluation of the assets and liabilities for the purpose of the cross-border merger shall not be included in the tax base. Also the income (proceeds) of a shareholder of the company ceasing to exist ensuing from such re-evaluation of this company shall

16 Act no 586/1992 Coll.
17 Council Directive 90/434/EEC of 23 July 1990 on the common system of taxation applicable to mergers, divisions, transfers of assets and exchanges of shares concerning companies of different Member States.
18 By Act no 438/2003 Coll.
19 Council Regulation 2157/2001 of 8 October 2001 on the Statute for a European Company (SE).
20 See footnote 3.
21 Council Regulation 1435/2003 of 22 July 2003 on the Statute for a European Cooperative Society (SCE).

be exempted from taxation if this shareholder is a Czech tax payer or holds a share in the successor company; this exemption however does not apply to the cash payment given to the shareholder in relation to the share-exchange ratio (see no 6 of this chapter).

The value of the assets and liabilities acquired by a Czech tax payer from a foreign tax payer as a result of cross-border merger shall be calculated on the basis of the exchange rate published by the Czech National Bank on the decisive date of the merger unless the foreign tax payer has a permanent establishment in the Czech Republic. For this purpose, the valuation differences resulting from the re-valuation of the assets and liabilities in accordance with the legal provisions of the relevant Shareholder State shall be disregarded (Art. 23(17) Income Tax Act).

The successor company in the Czech Republic shall continue to amortise tangible and intangible assets that were not a part of a permanent establishment in the Czech Republic and passed to it from the foreign company ceasing to exist. The value of these assets shall be determined in accordance with Art. 23(17) of the Income Tax Act. The successor company may amortise the assets in the aggregate up to the amount corresponding to the difference between the determined foreign depreciable value and the amortisations (or similar amounts) applied under laws of the relevant Shareholder State. Furthermore, the successor company may, subject to certain limitations, take over the reserves and provisions created by the foreign company ceasing to exist pursuant to the applicable laws of the other Shareholder State and continue in their creation. Given that it is necessary for reserves and provisions to be created in a manner that satisfies the requirements of Czech law for their successful application, it is material that the relevant provisions of the other Shareholder State lay down conditions sufficiently similar to those set out in the Income Tax Act and Act on Reserves.[22] The successor company may also take over tax losses and other amounts deductible from the tax base of the merged foreign company subject to conditions stipulated in the Income Tax Act. In particular, the acquired assets and liabilities that are related to the tax losses and were situated in another Shareholder State before the merger have to be transferred to the Czech Republic; also it is permissible to apply only such tax losses and other amounts deductible from the tax base that have not been applied in the other Shareholder State.

22 Act no 593/1992 Coll., on reserves for income-tax-base determination.

10

Denmark

VAGN THORUP AND JEPPE BUSKOV
Kromann Reumert

I   Introduction

1.   The Cross-border Merger Directive has been implemented in Denmark in Chapter 15a of the Danish Public Limited Companies Act (the 'Companies Act') which entered into force on 1 July 2007. The basic rule in Chapter 15a of the Companies Act is that the rules on domestic mergers also apply to cross-border mergers unless otherwise indicated in that chapter.

2.   A cross-border merger is defined as a merger where the merging companies are governed by the laws of at least two different Member States of the European Union or the European Economic Area (Norway, Iceland and Liechtenstein).

II   Scope of the new rules

3.   Chapter 15a of the Companies Act only applies to public limited companies (*aktieselskaber*). However, in connection with the introduction of Chapter 15a in the Companies Act, identical rules were introduced in the Private Limited Companies Act governing private limited companies (*anpartsselskaber*).

4.   In addition, rules on cross-border mergers have been introduced in the Danish Act on Undertakings Carrying on Business for Profit. These rules are similar to Chapter 15a of the Companies Act and allow limited liability companies covered by the said Act to complete a cross-border merger with similar EU or EEA companies, provided the laws of the other company's home country permit such a merger. The rules only apply to limited companies. Finally, the Danish Minister of Commerce has been authorised in the Danish Act on Trusts Carrying on Business for Profit to lay down rules on cross-border mergers of trusts covered by the Act. The minister has not yet utilised this authorisation.

5.   The Companies Act, the Private Limited Companies Act and the Act on Undertakings Carrying on Business for Profit also provide for cross-border demergers.

6.   Unless otherwise indicated, the description of the Danish rules on cross-border mergers only applies to public limited companies and private limited companies.

III   Cash payment

7.   Danish law does not include any restrictions on cash payment to shareholders in the merging companies. Shareholders will be taxed on any cash consideration as discussed below.

IV   Legal consequences and enforceability of a cross-border merger

8.   A cross-border merger will, under Danish law, result in all assets and liabilities of the discontinuing company or companies being transferred to the

surviving entity by operation of law, without liquidation of the participating companies.

9.   A cross-border merger has the same legal effects as an internal (domestic) merger under the Domestic Merger Directive, i.e.:

   (i)   the discontinuing companies cease to exist;

   (ii) all assets and liabilities, including rights and obligations, are transferred to a surviving company or a new company.

10.   The shareholders of the discontinuing company or companies will often receive consideration in the form of shares in the surviving entity, but it is not a requirement and cash payment may, for example, also be an option.

11.   Although the transfer of assets and liabilities is automatic, it may be necessary or advisable to perfect the transfer of certain assets, including real estate and securities. The rules on automatic transfer of all assets and liabilities are not mandatory and contracting parties, including lenders, may therefore obtain special contractual rights in case of a merger.

V   Procedure

1   Draft terms of cross-border merger

12.   The board of directors of the merging companies shall prepare a joint merger plan setting out the proposed terms of the cross-border merger. The merger plan must include the following information:

   (i)   the names and secondary names, if any, of the merging companies, including whether the name or secondary name of a discontinuing company shall be entered as a secondary name of the continuing company;

   (ii) the registered offices of the merging companies;

   (iii) the consideration for the shares in a discontinuing company;

   (iv) the date from which the shares that may be granted in consideration become eligible for dividend;

   (v) the rights in the continuing company to be conferred on holders, if any, of shares and debt instruments with special rights in a discontinuing company;

   (vi) any other measures for the benefit of holders of shares and debt instruments mentioned in paragraph (v) above;

   (vii) the surrender of share certificates for shares granted as consideration;

  (viii) the date from which a discontinuing company's rights and obligations shall be considered to have been transferred for accounting purposes;

   (ix) any special advantages given to the members of the boards of directors, committees of shareholders and management boards of the companies;

(x)   draft articles of association if a new company is formed by the merger; and

(xi)   likely consequences for the employment in the merging companies as a result of the cross-border merger.

13.   As it appears, the list is not identical to Article 5 of the Cross-border Merger Directive the reason being that the list of information to be included is defined by reference to the section of the Companies Act listing information requirements for a merger plan in connection with a domestic merger. This is problematic as the laws of other EU or EEA Member States are likely to mirror the wording of Article 5 of the Cross-border Merger Directive and it is therefore possible that the Companies Act will be amended to better reflect the wording of Article 5 of the Cross-border Merger Directive. Also, it appears from the Companies Act that only the articles of association of a new company established in connection with the merger must be included in the merger plan, whereas the articles of association of any surviving entity must be included pursuant to Article 5 of the Cross-border Merger Directive.

14.   Pursuant to the practice of the Danish Commerce and Companies Agency, the merger plan must be signed by all directors of the merging companies.

15.   It is a requirement that the merger plan be available in Danish (and the Danish text will be governing in respect of Danish law), but it may also be available in other languages.

16.   If a parent company merges with its fully owned subsidiary and the parent company is the surviving entity, only the information set out in nos 1, 2, 5, 6 and 8–11 of this chapter needs to be included.

17.   The merger plan must be filed with the Danish Commerce and Companies Agency no later than four weeks after its signing. The Commerce and Companies Agency announces in its on-line information system that it has received a merger plan and identifies the merging companies, but the plan is not made public as such. The general meeting resolving on the merger cannot be held earlier than four weeks after the announcement of the receipt of the merger plan by the Commerce and Companies Agency, and only the merger described in the merger plan can be adopted at such general meeting. If changes are made to the merger plan, including to the articles of association attached to the merger plan, a new merger plan will have to be prepared and a new filing will have to be made. However, the Danish Commerce and Companies Agency will accept a change of the surviving entity's name if it is subsequently discovered that the proposed name is not available.

18.   In addition, the merger plan must be made available for inspection at the merging companies' registered offices at least four weeks prior to the holding of the general meeting resolving on the cross-border merger and sent free of charge

to any shareholder requesting it, unless all shareholders consent to the merger plan not being available for inspection.

19.   Finally, the merger plan must be signed before the expiry of the financial year of the merging companies within which the merger shall have effect for accounting purposes. If the merging companies do not have the same financial year, the financial year first expiring will be decisive.

2   Management report

20.   The board of directors of each merging company must prepare a written report for the company's shareholders explaining and giving reasons for the plan to merge. The report must explain the fixing of the consideration for the shares, including specific difficulties in connection with such fixing, and include information on the consequences of the cross-border merger for the shareholders, creditors and employees. If a parent company merges with its fully owned subsidiary and the parent company is the surviving entity, the report is not required to include information on the fixing of the consideration for the shares. It is the Danish Commerce and Companies Agency's practice to accept a joint report from the boards of directors of all merging companies. Furthermore, the Danish Commerce and Companies Agency accepts the consolidated into one document of the merger plan and the report from the board of directors if this is clearly stated on the front page.

21.   The report from the board of directors must be made available for inspection at the merging companies' registered offices at least four weeks prior to the holding of the general meeting resolving on the cross-border merger and sent free of charge to any shareholder requesting it, unless all shareholders consent to the merger plan not being available for inspection.

3   Auditor's report

22.   In each of the merging companies one or more impartial valuation experts must prepare a written opinion on the merger plan.

23.   The opinion must include a statement as to whether the consideration for the shares in a discontinuing company is reasonable and factually based. The opinion must include information about the valuation method or methods used to fix the consideration as well as an evaluation of the expediency thereof. The opinion must include the values resulting from each method and the relative importance to be attached to the methods of valuation. If any special difficulties have been experienced in connection with the valuation, such difficulties must be mentioned in the statement.

24.   In addition, the valuation experts must submit a statement as to whether the claims of the creditors in each merging company are expected to be sufficiently

secured after the merger. This statement is often incorporated in the opinion on the merger plan, which the Danish Commerce and Companies Agency accepts.

25.   If the merging companies wish to make use of one or more joint valuation experts, such experts must, at the request of the merging companies, be appointed by the insolvency court of the jurisdiction where the continuing company has its registered office.

26.   If all shareholders in a cross-border merger consent to it, the valuation experts' opinion can be limited to a statement as to whether the claims of the creditors in each merging company are expected to be sufficiently secured after the merger.

27.   The statement as to whether the claims of the creditors in each merging company are expected to be sufficiently secured after the merger must be filed with the Commerce and Companies Agency, which will announce the receipt thereof in its on-line information system. The general meeting resolving on the merger cannot be held earlier than four weeks after the publication of the receipt of the statement from the valuation experts.

28.   The valuation experts' report as mentioned above (as well as the annual reports of the merging companies for the last three financial years or such shorter time as they have been in existence) must be made available for inspection at the merging companies' registered offices at least four weeks prior to the holding of the general meeting resolving on the cross-border merger and sent free of charge to any shareholder requesting it, unless all shareholders consent to the merger plan not being available for inspection.

29.   If a parent company merges with its fully owned subsidiary and the parent company is the surviving entity, the valuation experts' opinion only needs to include a statement as to whether the claims of the creditors in each merging company are expected to be sufficiently secured after the merger.

30.   If the surviving company is a Danish public limited company and all the discontinuing companies are not public limited companies, and if the nominal share capital of the Danish public limited company is increased in connection with the merger or if a new Danish public limited company is established in connection with the merger, valuation experts must be appointed to prepare a report with the following information:

   (i)   a description of the assets being contributed;
   (ii) information on the valuation method used;
   (iii) information on the agreed consideration; and
   (iv) a statement that the value is at least equal to the agreed consideration, including the nominal value of the shares being issued and any share premium.

31.   The valuation report may not be drawn up more than three months prior to the adoption of the merger.

32.   If a parent company merges with its fully owned subsidiary and the parent company is the surviving entity, such a report on the assets contributed is not required.

4   General meeting of shareholders

A   Information for shareholders

33.   The general meeting resolving on the merger must be convened with between eight days' and four weeks' notice and in accordance with the articles of association of each merging company. A written notice convening the general meeting must be sent to all of the shareholders entered in the register of shareholders who have so requested. If the shares of a merging company may be issued to bearer, the notice convening the general meeting must be made public through the Commerce and Companies Agency's on-line information system.

34.   The business to be transacted at the general meeting must be indicated in the notice. If proposals for the passing of resolutions to alter the articles of association are to be considered at the general meeting, all essential aspects of such proposed resolutions must be included in the notice.

35.   With regard to the display of the merger plan, the report from the board of directors and the valuation experts' opinion, we refer to the sub-sections above.

36.   If the merger plan is dated more than six months after the expiry of the last financial year to which the latest annual report relates, an interim balance sheet for each Danish merging company (exceeding the six months' deadline) dated no earlier than three months prior to the date of the merger plan must be prepared. The interim balance sheet must be audited if the company is subject to audit. It has previously been a requirement to prepare merger accounts of the merging companies with a pro forma balance sheet, but this is no longer a requirement.

37.   At the general meeting, the board of directors of each merging company must inform the shareholders of material changes, including in the assets and liabilities of the company, between the date of the merger plan and the general meeting.

B   Shareholder approval

38.   Where a Danish merging company is a discontinuing entity, a resolution to effect a cross-border merger must be adopted by at least two thirds of the votes cast as well as of the voting share capital represented at the general meeting, except where the discontinuing company is owned 100 per cent by the continuing entity, in which case the board of directors may resolve on the merger.

39.   Where a Danish merging company is the continuing entity, a resolution to effect a cross-border merge-may be adopted by the board of directors of the continuing company, save where

     (i)   the articles of association are to be altered, including, for example, an increase of the share capital (other than to include a discontinuing company's name or secondary name as the secondary name of the continuing company); or

     (ii)   shareholders holding 5 per cent or more of the share capital request a general meeting in writing within two weeks from the date on which the receipt of the merger plan was announced by the Danish Commerce and Companies Agency in accordance with the Companies Act.

40.   If the general meeting is to approve the merger, the resolution must be adopted by at least two thirds of the votes cast as well as of the voting share capital represented at the general meeting.

41.   There are no quorum requirements, but the articles of association may lay down quorum requirements as well as stricter majority requirements.

42.   If a new company is formed as a result of a merger, the board of directors and the auditor may be appointed by the general meetings of the merging companies immediately after the companies in general meeting have passed the resolution to merge. However, if the election of the board of directors and the auditor does not take place, a general meeting must be held in the new company within two weeks after the general meeting for the purpose of electing a board of directors and an auditor.

43.   The general meetings of the merging company may approve the merger conditional upon its subsequent approval of the arrangement regarding employee representation.

5   Pre-merger certificate

44.   The Commerce and Companies Agency is responsible for issuing a pre-merger certificate once all actions and formalities to be complied with prior to the merger have been completed.

45.   It should be noted that a merger cannot be registered, and thereby legally perfected, before an arrangement for employee representation in the merged company has been resolved according to the rules governing employee representation.

6   Filing of decision to merge

46.   The Danish Commerce and Companies Agency must receive a filing on the decision to merge no later than two weeks after the decision was made.

47.   In addition, the filing must be made no later than at the time of expiry of the deadline for filing the annual reports of the merging companies for the financial year in which the merger shall have effect for accounting purposes, however no later than one year after the Danish Commerce and Companies Agency's announcement of the receipt of the merger plan. If this latter deadline is not complied with, the Danish Commerce and Companies Agency will not register the merger.

7   Effects of the decision

48.   Where the continuing company is subject to Danish law, a cross-border merger takes effect from the time when the Commerce and Companies Agency registers the merger. The registration is made public via the Commerce and Companies Agency's on-line information system.

49.   In order for the Commerce and Companies Agency to register a cross-border merger, it must receive pre-merger certificates in respect of all non-Danish participating companies as final proof of the fulfilment of all actions and formalities required in the jurisdictions in question in order to effect the merger. As soon as possible after the registration of the merger, the Commerce and Companies Agency will inform the competent authorities in the jurisdictions of the discontinuing companies.

50.   Where the continuing company is subject to the laws of a country other than Denmark, the laws of such country will determine when a cross-border merger takes effect.

VI   Minority shareholders

51.   Shareholders of a discontinuing company in a cross-border merger who have objected to the merger at the general meeting may demand that the company redeems their shares. If an objecting shareholder wishes to exercise this right, notice must be delivered to the company within four weeks after the general meeting.

52.   If the shareholders have been asked to declare before the voting any wish that they may have to avail themselves of their right of redemption, this right is conditional upon the shareholders in question having made this declaration of their wish known at the general meeting.

53.   On the redemption the company must purchase the shares at a price which corresponds to the value of the shares and which, in the absence of an agreement, is fixed by valuation experts appointed by the court in whose jurisdiction the registered office of the company is located. The decision made by the valuation experts may be brought before the court by either party. Proceedings to this effect must be instituted no later than three months after the receipt of the expert opinion.

54.   The Danish Commerce and Companies Agency cannot issue its certificate on completion of the cross-border merger until sufficient security has been posted for the value of the shares to be redeemed. Valuation experts appointed by the court in whose jurisdiction the registered office of the company is located decide whether the security is sufficient. If the decision by the experts is brought before the court, the Commerce and Companies Agency cannot issue the certificate until the matter has been resolved, unless the court decides otherwise.

VII   Protection of creditors

55.   In connection with a cross-border merger, creditors of the Danish merging companies enjoy the same protection as in connection with domestic mergers. The rules in the Companies Act will not apply to any non-Danish participating companies, as the protection of creditors is not harmonised within the EU/EEA.

56.   If it is presumed in the valuation experts' statement that the creditors' claims will not be sufficiently secured following the merger, creditors whose claims have occurred prior to the announcement of the merger plan and for whom no separate security has been provided may prove their claims within four weeks from when the decision to merge was made by all the merging companies. A creditor may not with binding effect, through the agreement on which the claim is based, renounce his right to demand security.

57.   Redemption may be demanded of claims which are proved and due whilst good and valid security may be demanded for claims which are proved but not due.

58.   In case of a dispute as to whether security must be provided or as to whether any security offered is adequate, either party may within two weeks from the lodging of proof of the claim institute proceedings before the insolvency court of the jurisdiction in which the company has its registered office for the purpose of having the matter settled.

VIII   Employee participation[1]

59.   With regard to employee participation, the Cross-border Merger Directive has been implemented in Danish law by virtue of Sections 139–139f in Chapter 15a of the Companies Act.

1   Existing rules on employee participation

60.   In Danish companies which have had a staff of at least thirty-five employees on average over the last three years, the employees of the company are entitled to

---

1 This section was prepared by Claus Juel Hansen, Kromann Reumert.

elect from among themselves a number of members of the board of directors together with alternates to act in their place (company representation). The number of directors so elected may equal up to half the number of members of the board of directors elected by the general meeting or appointed by others pursuant to the articles of association of the company in question. However, the employees can as a minimum appoint two members. If the number of members to be elected to the board of directors does not constitute a whole number, the number is rounded up.

61.   In addition, rules on group representation apply in Denmark but these are not relevant in the context of a cross-border merger.

2   Employee representation in companies established in Denmark resulting from a cross-border merger

62.   In connection with a cross-border merger where the surviving entity is registered in Denmark, the above-mentioned rules on company representation do not apply since the application of these rules does not result in the employees in other Member States having the same right of representation as the employees employed in Denmark. Accordingly, the rules of the Cross-border Merger Directive will apply instead, as implemented in Danish law.

A   Choice of procedures when applying rules implementing the Cross-border Merger Directive

63.   In accordance with the Cross-border Merger Directive, there are two different procedures for deciding on the form of employee representation in the surviving company: (i) the 'short-cut procedure' (no negotiations involved, the 'Standard Rules' apply); or (ii) the negotiation procedure.

B   The 'short-cut procedure'

64.   The competent bodies of the merging companies may decide without prior negotiations to apply the 'Standard Rules' for employee representation.

65.   A decision by the competent bodies of the merging companies to apply the short-cut procedure must be made prior to the establishment of the Special Negotiation Body (SNB), since recourse to the 'short-cut procedure' is no longer an option for the competent bodies once the SNB has been established.

66.   However, by choosing this procedure the competent bodies of the merging companies signal that they do not wish to open the envisaged and desired negotiations with the employees, which may be perceived negatively by the employees. Moreover, application of the Standard Rules means that the wide autonomy of the parties to agree arrangements for employee representation is lost and leaves the parties to deal with the sometimes illogical results that the Standard Rules may lead to, especially when applying the inherent principle of proportionality in distributing the seats among the Member States involved.

67.   The 'short-cut procedure' would in particular be relevant where the risk of extended negotiations should be avoided and/or where it is envisaged that the negotiations eventually will result in the application of the Standard Rules anyway.

C   The negotiation procedure

68.   If the competent bodies do not decide to apply the short-cut procedure, they must establish an SNB 'as soon as possible' after publishing the merger plan and open negotiations on the establishment of employee representation in the surviving company.

69.   In appointing members to the SNB, the seats must be allocated in proportion to the number of employees employed in each Member State by the merging companies and concerned subsidiaries or establishments, by allocating in respect of a Member State one seat per portion of employees employed in that Member State which equals 10 per cent, or a fraction thereof, of the number of employees employed by the participating companies and concerned subsidiaries or establishments in all the Member States taken together. Further seats may be allocated if necessary in order to ensure that the SNB includes at least one member representing each participating company which will cease to exist as a separate legal entity following the registration of the cross-border merger, in so far as the number of such additional members does not exceed 20 per cent of the number of members already designated, and the composition of the SNB does not entail a double representation of the employees concerned.

70.   The negotiation procedure with the SNB can lead to one of the following results:

(i)   the SNB decides not to open negotiations or to terminate negotiations already opened;
(ii)   the right to employee participation is settled by written agreement;
(iii) the SNB and the competent bodies agree to apply the Standard Rules; or
(iv)   the SNB and the competent bodies fail to reach an agreement within six months from the publication of the merger plan (or an agreed extended period of up to an additional six months).

Re (i) the SNB decides not to open negotiations or to terminate negotiations already opened

71.   The SNB may decide – by a majority of two thirds of its members representing at least two thirds of the employees, including the votes of members representing employees in at least two different Member States – not to open negotiations with the competent bodies or to terminate negotiations already opened. In this case the national Danish legislation on employee participation will apply.

Re (ii) the right to employee participation is settled by written agreement

72. The parties have a large degree of freedom to agree on employee participation, subject to very few limitations which are of a formal rather than of a content-based nature. For example, the parties may agree on a lower number of employee representatives than the existing number in the participating companies, but such agreement would have to be passed by a qualified majority of votes within the SNB.

73. If the parties fail to reach an agreement within six months from the publication of the merger plan (with an option for an agreed extended period of an extra six months), and the competent bodies decide to go ahead with the merger, the Standard Rules will apply. This timeframe does not include the actual election of the employee representatives, which may be completed after the execution of the merger.

74. The benefit of the written agreement compared to the application of Standard Rules lies in the wide autonomy of the parties and the possibility to escape the sometimes illogical results that the Standard Rules may lead to, especially when applying the inherent principle of proportionality in distributing the seats among the Member States involved.

Re (iii) the SNB and the competent bodies agree to apply the 'Standard Rules'

75. The SNB and the competent bodies may agree to apply the Standard Rules. The application of the Standard Rules will lead to a result which is known as 'best form, greatest number' in the Danish preparatory works, since it implies that the SNB may decide which of the models for employee representation in the merging companies they find most favourable and that those elements shall apply to the surviving company. However, Denmark has made use of the possibility to limit the number of employee representatives on the board of a company to a maximum of one third of the total number of board members (this does not apply if the short-cut procedure is followed).

Re (iv) the SNB and the competent bodies fail to reach an agreement within six months (or an agreed extended period of an additional six months)

76. If the SNB and the competent bodies of the merging companies fail to reach a mutual agreement for employee representation within six months from the publication of the merger plan (or within a mutually agreed extended period of up to an additional six months) and if the competent bodies of the merging companies wish to move on to registration of the merger they must decide to apply the Standard Rules without the consent of the SNB. The result of applying the Standard Rules will be as described under Re (iii) above.

D   The distribution of seats on the board of the surviving entity when applying
     the Standard Rules

77.   The Standard Rules imply that the SNB decides the allocation of seats for
       the employee representatives on the board of the surviving entity or the way
       in which the employees of the merged company may recommend or oppose
       the appointment of members of these bodies according to the proportion of
       employees in each Member State.

78.   When the SNB has decided on the distribution of seats among the Member
       States involved, the actual election of the members in the Member States con-
       cerned shall follow the national procedures given under their jurisdiction. In
       Denmark this entails that an election committee must be established to super-
       vise the election, and that the actual elections are held as a direct election among
       Danish employees of the surviving company similar to the procedures for the
       election of employee representatives under otherwise applicable Danish law.

IX   Tax[2]

79.   Under Danish tax law a cross-border merger may either be carried out as a
       taxable merger or – provided that certain conditions are met – as a tax-exempt
       merger.

1   Taxable mergers

80.   From a tax point of view, a taxable cross-border merger implies that the discon-
       tinuing company is considered dissolved with the effect that the discontinuing
       company is deemed to have disposed of all its assets and liabilities and that
       the shareholders of the discontinuing company are deemed to have disposed
       of their shares in the discontinuing company. Consequently, a cross-border
       merger may trigger taxation of any capital gains on the assets and liabilities of
       the discontinuing company provided that the discontinuing company is subject
       to Danish taxation. Likewise, a cross-border merger may trigger taxation of
       any capital gains on the shares in the discontinuing company to the extent the
       shareholders of the discontinuing company are subject to Danish taxation.

2   Tax-exempt mergers

81.   Since the implementation of the Merger Tax Directive, the Danish Merger Tax
       Act has contained tax rules governing cross-border mergers.

A   Covered cross-border mergers

82.   The Danish Merger Tax Act deals with five different types of cross-border
       mergers:

2 This section was prepared by Michael Nørremark, Kromann Reumert.

(i)   mergers between a Danish company and a foreign company covered by the Merger Tax Directive, where the foreign company is the discontinuing company;

(ii)   mergers between a Danish company and a foreign company covered by the Mergers Tax Directive, where the Danish company is the discontinuing company;

(iii) mergers between foreign companies covered by the Merger Tax Directive;

(iv)   mergers between a Danish company and a foreign company, which is not covered by the Mergers Tax Directive, where the Danish company is the discontinuing company; and

(v)   mergers between foreign companies which are not covered by the Merger Tax Directive.

83.   In relation to all five scenarios it is a requirement that the foreign companies in question qualify as 'companies' from a Danish tax perspective.

B   Tax treatment of the merged companies

84.   If the Danish Merger Tax Act applies and the foreign company is covered by the Merger Tax Directive, the merger will not give rise to any taxation of capital gains on the assets and liabilities transferred as a consequence of the merger, provided, however, that such assets and liabilities following the merger effectively are connected to a Danish company or a permanent establishment in Denmark. The receiving company's computing of depreciations and any gains or losses in respect of the assets and liabilities transferred without taxation will have to be made as if the merger had not taken place.

85.   Generally, any tax losses carried forward will lapse as a consequence of a tax-exempt merger.

C   Tax treatment of the shareholders of the merged companies

86.   A tax-exempt merger will not trigger taxation of the shareholders of the discontinuing company to the extent such shareholders in exchange for their shares in the discontinuing company receive shares in the continuing company. Any shares in the continuing company received by the shareholders of the discontinuing company in exchange for their shares in the discontinuing company will for tax purposes be deemed acquired at the same time and for the same price as the shares in the discontinuing company.

11

Estonia

AHTO NIRGI AND SVEN PAPP
Raidla Lejins & Norcous

I   Introduction

1.   In Estonia, cross-border mergers are regulated mainly by Part IX, Chapter 6
      of the Commercial Code (*Äriseadustik*). The Act on Amendment of the
      Commercial Code and Related Acts (*Äriseadustiku ja sellega seonduvate
      seaduste muutmise seadus*), implementing the provisions of the Cross-border
      Merger Directive, was passed by the Estonian parliament on 21 November
      2007 and came into force on 15 December 2007, i.e. by the deadline

prescribed by the Directive. In addition to the Commercial Code, the act introduced amendments to the Community-scale Involvement of Employees Act (*Töötajate üleühenduselise kaasamise seadus*) and legislation regulating mergers of financial institutions.

II   Scope of the new rules

2.   The rules on cross-border mergers apply to public limited companies (*aktsiaselts* or *AS*) and private limited companies (*osaühing* or *OÜ*) registered with the Estonian Commercial Register (Art. 433¹(1) Commercial Code). As such, the relevant provisions potentially also apply to European Companies (SEs) registered in Estonia since SEs are, to the extent not regulated by rules specifically applicable to SEs, governed by rules applicable to public limited companies.

3.   In addition to limiting the scope to these two types of companies, the Commercial Code explicitly excludes applicability of the relevant section of the Commercial Code to commercial cooperative societies (*tulundusühistu*)[1] as permitted under Article 3(2) of the Cross-border Merger Directive (Art. 433¹(3) Commercial Code). The main argument for this limitation is the fact that Estonian law currently allows commercial cooperative societies to merge only with other commercial cooperative societies and prohibits mergers with other types of corporate entities. As a result, European Cooperative Societies (SCEs) registered in Estonia also are not allowed to benefit from the new rules on cross-border mergers.

As evident from the explanatory memorandum to the Act on Amendment of the Commercial Code and Related Acts, the legislator did not see any significant reasons for eliminating this restriction applicable to commercial cooperative societies, but referred to the possibility of reviewing this approach in the future if this should be required by practical considerations.

4.   Article 3(3) of the Cross-border Merger Directive provides that companies the object of which is the collective investment of capital provided by the public are excluded from the scope of the Directive. However, pursuant to the amendments introduced to the Investment Funds Act (*Investeerimisfondide seadus*), investment funds established as public limited companies (*aktsiaseltsina asutatud fond*) that correspond to the definition under Article 3(3) of the Cross-border Merger Directive are allowed to benefit from the Estonian cross-border merger regime.[2]

---

1 Under Estonian law, a commercial cooperative society is a company the purpose of which is to support and promote the economic interests of its members through joint economic activity.
2 Article 211(2) of the Investment Funds Act currently provides that funds registered with the Commercial Register may merge with funds established pursuant to the laws of an EEA Member State.

III   Cash payment

5.   As a general rule under Estonian law, cash payments to shareholders of the companies being acquired may not exceed 10 per cent of the sum of the nominal values of their exchanged shares. This rule is aimed at preventing disproportionate dilution of the shareholdings of the shareholders of the companies being acquired. However, in the case of a cross-border merger, this threshold may be exceeded provided that payments in excess of 10 per cent are allowed under the law of the Member State[3] of the company resulting from the merger (Art. $433^2(4)$ Commercial Code). In such case the shareholders of the Estonian company participating in the merger may also benefit from such a higher cash payment.

IV   Legal consequences of the merger and enforceability of a cross-border merger

6.   As a result of a cross-border merger, the assets of the company being acquired, including its obligations, shall transfer to the company resulting from the merger, the shareholders of the company being acquired shall become shareholders of the surviving company and the company or companies being acquired are dissolved without liquidation (Art. 391 Commercial Code). As such, a cross-border merger has the same legal consequences as a domestic merger in Estonia.

   Together with the transfer of assets and obligations of the company or companies being acquired, all the employment contracts valid at the date of the merger shall transfer to the surviving company by virtue of law.

7.   The cross-border merger takes effect and is enforceable against third parties as from entry of the merger in the Commercial Register of the seat of the acquiring company. As from this moment the validity of the merger cannot be contested. The rights of third persons with regard to the exchanged shares shall remain valid with regard to the shares of the surviving company. Entries regarding the transfer of assets shall be made in registers (e.g. the Land Register) upon the application of the acquiring company (Art. 403(1), (3) and (5) Commercial Code).

   The members of the management board and supervisory board[4] of a merging company shall be jointly and severally liable to the company, shareholders and/or creditors of the company for any damage wrongfully caused by the merger. Such claims may be presented for up to five years from entry of the

---

3 Please note that since the Cross-border Merger Directive is applicable throughout the EEA (see Chapter 1, no 4 of this book) reference to Member States in this chapter is to contracting parties to the EEA Agreement.

4 Please note that Estonian law provides for a mandatory two-tier management structure for public limited companies (*aktsiaselts* or *AS*) and an optional two-tier structure for private limited companies (*osaühing* or *OÜ*), comprising the management board which manages and represents the company and the supervisory board which is responsible for planning the company's activities and supervising the management board.

merger in the Commercial Register of the seat of the acquiring company (Art. 403(6) and (7) Commercial Code).

V   Procedure

1   Draft terms of cross-border merger

8.   The management boards of the merging companies are required to prepare and sign the draft terms of the merger.[5] The draft terms must be in notarised form and shall become effective only after approval by the shareholders (see nos 18–20 of this chapter). The articles of association of the company resulting from the merger must be appended to the draft terms of cross-border merger (Arts. 433²(3) and 392(1) and (4) Commercial Code).

The draft terms must include the information set out in Chapter 1, no 18 of this book. In addition, the Commercial Code specifically requires insertion of a clause regarding transfer of all the assets of the merging company to the company resulting from the merger in return for shares in the resulting company (Art. 392(1) Commercial Code). In case of merger of a parent company with its fully owned subsidiary, the information requirements are more limited and specific information indicated under Article 433²(2) of the Commercial Code may be omitted from the draft terms.

Failure to include the required information in the draft terms of cross-border merger may result in the notary declining to notarise the document, which brings about failure to complete the merger process and possibly also liability of the management board members.

9.   At least one month before the general meeting convenes to decide on the merger, the draft terms of cross-border merger must be made available to the shareholders. Further, the management board of each of the merging companies is required to submit the draft terms of cross-border merger to the registrar of the Commercial Register and shall publish a notice concerning the signing of the draft terms in the official publication *Ametlikud Teadaanded*. In addition to the information referred to in Chapter 1, no 19 of this book, the notice must set out that the draft terms of cross-border merger are available for examination in the registration department of the registrar of the Commercial Register and in a place designated by the management board (Arts. 419(4) and 433²(5) Commercial Code).

2   Management report

10.   The management boards of the merging companies are required to prepare a written report[6] to explain and justify legally and economically the merger

---

5 Estonian law actually refers to the document as the 'merger agreement'.
6 Please note that the Commercial Code uses the term 'merger report' when referring to the management report.

and merger agreement, including the share-exchange ratio and amount of additional payments if additional payments are to be made. In case there have been difficulties relating to valuation, this must be referred to separately in the report. Further, if the acquiring company belongs to a group, the merger report must also set out relevant information concerning the other companies of the group. In addition to the general requirements, the management report of a cross-border merger must also set out the implications of the merger for the employees and creditors of the company. The merging companies may also prepare a joint management report.

As an exception to the general information requirements, the management report need not set out information the publication of which may result in significant damage to any of the merging companies or a company belonging to the same group as such company. In such a case, the reason for not disclosing the information must be set out in the report (Arts. 393 and 433^3 Commercial Code).

11. At least one month before the general meeting deciding on the merger is convened, the management report must be made available to the shareholders of the merging companies as well as to the employees' representative or trade union's representative or, in the absence thereof, to the employees. In the event that an opinion of the employees' representative or trade union's representative on the management report is submitted at least one month before the general meeting, this opinion must be appended to the management report (Art. $433^3(1)$ and Art. $433^5(1)$ Commercial Code).

3   Auditor's report

12. As a general rule, the draft terms of cross-border merger are required to be audited. For this purpose, the management boards of each of the merging companies may appoint a separate auditor or some or all of them may appoint a joint auditor or auditors. A joint auditor or auditors may only be appointed on the prior approval of a judicial or administrative authority in the Member State of one of the merging companies. In Estonia, such approval would be granted by a court, which would also determine the remuneration of such an auditor or auditors. In addition to the general requirements applicable to auditors, the auditors of the cross-border merger are required to have knowledge and experience relevant for auditing the draft terms of cross-border merger (Arts. 395 and 433^4 Commercial Code).

The auditor's report must be in writing and must indicate whether the share-exchange ratio and additional payments set out in the draft terms of cross-border merger are appropriate consideration for the shareholders of the company being acquired, and whether the merger may bring about damage to the interests of the creditors of the company. In addition, the auditor's report is required to set out the method which was used to determine the exchange ratio of shares of the companies, possible difficulties relating to determination of the exchange ratio, whether the method used is appropriate for determination of the exchange ratio and other methods for determination of the exchange ratio. If different methods are used to determine the exchange ratio, the exchange ratio in each method and the importance of results obtained on the basis of each method to determine the exchange ratio must be indicated (Art. 396(1)–(2)[1] Commercial Code).

Similarly to the management report, the auditor's report need not set out information the publication of which may result in significant damage to a merging company or a company belonging to the same group as such company. In such case, the reason for not submitting the information shall be set out in the report (Art. 396(2[2]) Commercial Code).

13. Somewhat controversially, the specific provisions of the Commercial Code applicable to cross-border mergers provide that auditing of the draft terms of cross-border merger is mandatory and, contrary to the provisions applicable to domestic mergers, do not provide for any exceptions in this regard. However, as stated in the explanatory memorandum to the Act on Amendment of the Commercial Code and Related Acts implementing the provisions of the Cross-border Merger Directive, the intention of the Estonian legislator has not been to exclude the exceptions to the auditing requirement set forth in the Cross-border Merger Directive (see Chapter 1, no 21 of this book). Therefore, it may be argued that the general exceptions under Article 394(2) of the Commercial Code pursuant to which the auditing of the draft terms is not required in the case of absorption of a fully owned subsidiary or on the unanimous decision of all shareholders of the merging companies to that effect are also applicable to cross-border mergers.

14. When auditing the draft terms of cross-border merger, the auditor has the same rights, obligations and liability as when auditing an annual report. In order to prepare the report, the auditor is entitled to obtain information necessary for auditing from other companies which belong to the same group as the merging company (Art. 396(4) Commercial Code).

15. The auditor's report must be made available to the shareholders of the merging companies at least one month before the general meeting deciding on the merger takes place (Art. 433[5](1) Commercial Code).

4   General meeting of shareholders

A   Information for shareholders

16. At least one month prior to the general meeting deciding on the merger, the shareholders of a merging company must have access to the draft terms of cross-border merger, management report, auditor's report and, in the case of public limited companies, also annual reports of the merging companies for the preceding three financial years. If the last annual report of a merging

public limited company has been prepared earlier than six months before the signing of the merger agreement, an interim balance sheet as at the last quarter must be submitted to the shareholders. The interim balance sheet shall be prepared pursuant to the requirements for an annual report (Arts. 419(1) and (3) and 433⁵(1) Commercial Code).

The documents must be available at the seat of the company and shareholders have the right to receive copies of the documents referred to upon request. In addition, at least one month before the general meeting, the management report must also be made available to the employees' representative or the representative of the trade union or in the absence thereof, to the employees (Arts. 419(2) and 433⁵(1) Commercial Code).

17.   At the general meeting, the shareholders of the merging public limited company have the right to receive information regarding the legal and economic consequences of the merger, including the exchange of shares. At the request of shareholders, the management is also required to provide information concerning circumstances related to other merging companies (Art. 420 Commercial Code). Estonian law does not stipulate respective procedural requirements for private limited companies.

B   Shareholder approval

18.   In respect of Estonian companies participating in a cross-border merger, the Commercial Code prescribes that the draft terms of cross-border merger must be approved by shareholders. Such approval is, however, not required at the level of the subsidiary in the event of acquisition of a fully owned subsidiary by a parent company (Arts. 397(1) and 433⁵(2) Commercial Code).

19.   Further, approval of the shareholders is not required at the level of the surviving company if at least 90 per cent of the share capital of the company being acquired is held by the surviving company and the management board of the acquiring company has (i) at least one month before deciding on approval of the merger agreement by the company being acquired, published a notice concerning the draft terms of cross-border merger and (ii) presented the draft terms of cross-border merger, management report and annual reports of the merging companies for the previous three financial years to the shareholders for examination at the seat of the company. A shareholder vote is, however, mandatory if it is requested by shareholders whose shares represent at least 5 per cent of the share capital (Arts. 421(4) and 433⁵(3) Commercial Code).

20.   In order to approve the cross-border merger, a qualified majority of at least two thirds of the votes represented at the general meeting must be cast in favour, provided that the articles of association do not prescribe a higher requirement. If the company has different classes of shares, the additional approval of at least two thirds of the holders of each class of shares is required. As a prerequisite for passing the resolution, at least 50 per cent of the total share capital of

the company must be represented at the meeting. If this quorum is not met, a new meeting can be called which can take decisions regardless of the number of votes present (Arts. 297(1) and (2) and 421(1) and (2) Commercial Code).

The general meeting of the company being acquired may make the approval of the draft terms of cross-border merger conditional upon the company resulting from the merger having approved an employee participation system (Art. 433^5(4) Commercial Code).

21.   In the event that a newly formed company results from the merger, the shareholders must also decide on the business name and seat of the new company. The articles of association of the new company, required to be approved together with the approval of the draft terms, shall be appended to the draft terms of cross-border merger (Art. 405(4) Commercial Code).

22.   Unlike the draft terms of cross-border merger, the resolution of the shareholders regarding approval of the draft terms of cross-border merger is not subject to a generally applicable notarisation requirement. As a general rule, the minutes of the shareholders' meeting containing the adopted resolutions must be produced in writing and signed by the chairman and secretary of the meeting. A list of participating shareholders or their representatives must be appended to the resolution.

However, the Commercial Code sets out certain specific circumstances when notarisation is mandatory (e.g. in case the increase of share capital of the surviving company is being decided upon in connection with the merger). Further, notarisation may also be requested by the management board, supervisory board or shareholders representing at least 10 per cent of the share capital of the company.

5   Pre-merger certificate

23.   No earlier than one month after the approval of the draft terms of cross-border merger, the management board of a merging company is required to submit a petition for entry of the merger in the Commercial Register of the seat of the company. If the Estonian company participating in the merger is a company being acquired, the registrar of the Commercial Register, which is the competent authority in Estonia designated to scrutinise the legality of a cross-border merger, shall issue a certificate attesting that the company has carried out all the pre-merger formalities and that the merger has been entered in the Commercial Register. The certificate is required to set out the date of entry and reference to the procedure scrutinising the ratio applicable to the exchange of shares, if applicable (Arts. 400(1) and 433^9(1) and (2) Commercial Code).[7]

7 The Commercial Code also states that the detailed procedure for issuing the certificate shall be adopted by a decree of the Minister of Justice. However, such a procedure has not yet been adopted.

In addition to the procedures required by the Cross-border Merger Directive, the Commercial Code also sets out the obligation of the registrar of the Commercial Register to forward electronically to the court, notary or other authority of the Member State of the surviving company all documents submitted to it in respect of the company being acquired (Art. 433⁹(5) Commercial Code).

24.   If the Estonian company participating in the merger is a company resulting from the cross-border merger, the registrar of the Member State of the company being acquired shall submit to the registrar of the Commercial Register a certificate of a court, notary or other authority of the Member State attesting to the proper completion of the pre-merger acts and formalities by the company being acquired, together with the approved terms of the cross-border merger. The certificate must be submitted within six months from its issuance (Art. 433⁹(6) Commercial Code). Estonian companies participating in the merger as companies being acquired must submit applications for entry of the merger in the Commercial Register of the seat of the company similarly to a domestic merger.

6   Effect of the decision

25.   The merger enters into force only after entry in the Commercial Register of the seat of the acquiring company. From that moment, the assets of the company being acquired are transferred to the acquiring company and the shareholders of the company being acquired become shareholders of the acquiring company and their shares are exchanged for shares of the acquiring company. After entry of the merger in the Commercial Register of the seat of the acquiring company, entries regarding the transfer of assets shall be made in registers on the petition of the acquiring company (Art. 403(1)–(3) Commercial Code).

The registrar of the Commercial Register where the seat of the acquiring company is located is required to notify the court, notary or other authority of the Member State of each of the companies being acquired as well as the registrar of the Estonian Central Registry of Securities (*Eesti väärtpaberite keskregister*) of the completion of the cross-border merger (Art. 433⁹(7) Commercial Code).

26.   The validity of the merger cannot be contested after its entry in the Commercial Register of the seat of the acquiring company (Art. 403(5) Commercial Code).

VI   Minority shareholders

27.   As discussed under no 20 of this chapter, the qualified majority of two thirds of the votes represented at the general meeting is required for the merger to take effect and dissenting minority shareholders are bound by this decision. However, due to the fact that in the case of a cross-border merger, the position

of the minority shareholders changes significantly, the Estonian legislator has deemed it necessary to stipulate the right of dissenting minority shareholders to exit the merging company.

Consequently, the Commercial Code provides that in the event of a cross-border merger, a shareholder of the company being acquired who opposes the merger decision may within two months after the coming into effect of the merger demand that the acquiring company acquires the exchanged shares of the shareholder for monetary compensation. The monetary compensation must be equal[8] to the sum of money which the shareholder would have received from the distribution of remaining assets upon liquidation of the company if the company had been liquidated at the time the merger decision was made. Alternatively, the opposing shareholders may exit the company by disposing of the shares within two months, regardless of the restrictions on disposal provided by law or contained in the articles of association (Arts. 433[7]and 404(1) Commercial Code).

In order to be eligible for the exit procedure, the dissenting shareholders have to express their opposition to the merger at the general meeting deciding on the merger and confirm it with their signature (Art. 404(3) Commercial Code).

28.   In addition to the right to exit the merging company, minority shareholders have certain other specific rights under Estonian law. Above all, minority shareholders representing at least 10 per cent of the voting capital have the right to request the inclusion of additional items on the agenda of a general meeting, require the notarisation of the minutes of the general meeting, call a supervisory board meeting and request the conducting of a special audit.

VII   Protection of creditors

29.   In the event that an Estonian company participates in a cross-border merger as a company being acquired and the company resulting from the merger is subject to the laws of another Member State, the creditors of the Estonian company may submit a claim for obtaining security within two months from publication of the notice regarding signing of the draft terms in the official publication *Ametlikud Teadaanded* (see no 9 of this chapter for details).

However, the Commercial Code provides for two qualifications to this general rule. First, only creditors who are not able to claim the satisfaction of their claims and who are able to show that the merger may jeopardise the performance of the claim have the right to apply for security. Second, creditors may claim security with regard to claims that have arisen before or up to fifteen days after the publication of the merger notice in *Ametlikud Teadaanded* (Art. 433[8] Commercial Code).

---

8 Despite the strict wording, the amount of compensation may presumably also be higher.

VIII   Employee participation

30.   Issues relating to employee participation are regulated by the Commercial Code and Community-scale Involvement of Employees Act, which among others provides for the principles of determining the involvement of employees in the case of a cross-border merger.

1   Employee participation in companies established in Estonia resulting from a cross-border merger

31.   Apart from specific rules applicable to the European Company (SE) and the European Cooperative Society (SCE), Estonian law does not provide for any requirements concerning employee participation in the management of companies. Therefore, employee participation in the acquiring company located in Estonia will only be applicable if such rights existed in other participating companies and the additional conditions of Art. 16(2) of the Cross-border Merger Directive are met.

Consequently, the Commercial Code and Community-scale Involvement of Employees Act stipulate that employee participation rights will be determined in accordance with the rules applicable to the European Company and the accompanying directive on employee involvement (see Chapter 1, nos 40–43 of this book for details), where (i) at least one of the merging companies has, in the six months before the publication of the draft terms of cross-border merger, an average number of employees that exceeds 500 and that company is operating under an employee participation system or (ii) all companies of other Member States participating in the cross-border merger are operating under an employee participation system. The management boards of the merging companies may, however, decide to apply, as from entry of the resulting company in the Commercial Register, the standard employee participation rules in effect in Estonia (Art. 41²(1), (2) and (4) Community-scale Involvement of Employees Act).

2   Special negotiating body ('SNB')

32.   Where the involvement of employees is mandatory and the management bodies of the merging companies have not decided to apply the rules regulating the right of the employees to elect, appoint or recall members of management bodies in force in the Members State of the acquiring company, the law requires the starting of negotiations and formation of an SNB with the objective of negotiating arrangements on employee participation.

Members of an SNB are elected or appointed in proportion to the number of employees employed in each Member State where the merging companies are located, by allocating in respect of a Member State one seat per portion of employees employed in that Member State which equals 10 per cent of the number of employees employed by the participating companies in all the

Member States taken together. Members shall be elected in each Member State pursuant to the procedure for election or appointment prescribed in the Member State. A member or members of the SNB of an Estonian company are elected by the general meeting of employees. The procedure for the election of a member or members of the SNB must be approved by the general meeting of employees (Arts. 51(2) and 17(1) Community-scale Involvement of Employees Act).

33.   As an exception to the general procedure, the elected SNB may decide, by a majority of two thirds of its members representing at least two thirds of the employees of the merging companies, including the votes of members representing employees in at least two different Member States, not to open negotiations or to terminate already ongoing negotiations and to apply the rules on participation in force in Estonia (Art. 41²(5) Community-scale Involvement of Employees Act).

3   Protection of employee representatives

34.   Members of the SNB and employees' representatives belonging to the supervisory, administrative or management board enjoy the same guarantees as the employees' representatives under the Estonian Employment Contracts Act (*Eesti Vabariigi töölepingu seadus*). In addition, employees' representatives must be granted a period of absence to represent employees to the extent necessary for the performance of their duties and average wages shall be maintained for the representatives for the period of absence (Arts. 80 and 40 Community-scale Involvement of Employees Act).

IX   Tax treatment

35.   Estonia has generally implemented the Merger Tax Directive by way of amending the Income Tax Act (*Tulumaksuseadus*). Some of the implementing provisions came into force on 1 January 2007 and further provisions entered into force on 1 January 2009.

36.   In Estonia, resident corporate taxpayers are not subject to the traditional corporate income tax. Instead, they are subject to a distribution tax on distributed profits, including transactions that are considered as hidden profit distributions (e.g. fringe benefits, gifts and donations, non-business expenses). As of 2009, distribution tax is also levied on liquidation proceeds and payments upon the reduction of share capital or redemption of shares to the extent that these payments exceed the contributions (monetary and non-monetary) made to the equity capital of the company. No tax is levied on any retained earnings.

The distribution tax rate is 21/79 (approximately 26.6 per cent) on the net amount of the distribution, corresponding to 21 per cent on the gross amount (distribution + distribution tax).

As there is no tax on retained earnings and the distribution tax is applied only to actual profit distributions, valuations of assets and losses have no significance for tax purposes. Due to the absence of annual net taxation of corporate profits, legal entities are not subject to tax depreciation and amortisation rules. No reserves and provisions are applicable and it is not possible to make any deductions from the tax. Profit distributions are subject to distribution tax even if the company has an accounting loss.

37.   If a resident company is deleted from the Commercial Register without liquidation, distribution tax is levied on the part of equity capital which exceeds the contributions made to equity capital. However, if the economic activities of the company are continued in Estonia through a permanent establishment, distribution tax will be imposed on the value of assets taken out of the permanent establishment to the extent that the value exceeds the contributions made to the liquidated company's equity capital and the value of assets brought to Estonia for the permanent establishment after the deletion of the company from the register.

In case a non-resident company in the course of a merger transfers its Estonian permanent establishment to either an Estonian or a non-resident company and economic activities are continued through the permanent establishment, no tax is imposed on the transferring company. The value of assets brought to Estonia for the permanent establishment by the transferring company is later not taken into account when calculating the taxable value of assets that the receiving company decides to take out of its permanent establishment.

38.   Capital gains derived from the exchange of shares in the course of mergers, divisions or other reorganisations are exempt for non-resident shareholders.

12

Germany

ANDREAS WUESTHOFF

SJ Berwin LLP

I   Introduction

1.   The Cross-border Merger Directive has been implemented in Germany by virtue of the Second Act on the Amendment of the German Reorganisation Act of 19 April 2007.[1] The Second Act on the Amendment of the German Reorganisation Act came into force on 25 April 2007. It added a special section

---

1 Zweites Gesetz zur Änderung des Umwandlungsgesetztes, Bundesgesetzblatt Teil I, 24 April 2007, p. 542.

on cross-border mergers to the German Reorganisation Act. The general rules on domestic mergers apply to cross-border mergers, unless stipulated otherwise in the special section on cross-border mergers.

The rules on employee participation in cross-border mergers are regulated in a separate act, namely, the Act on Employee Participation in Cross-border Mergers, which came into force on 29 December 2006.[2] Tax issues of cross-border mergers were implemented by the Act on Tax Measures regarding the Introduction of the European Company, which came into force on 13 December 2006.[3]

II   Scope of the new rules

2.   With respect to the companies that can benefit from the new rules on cross-border mergers, the Reorganisation Act refers to Art. 2(1) of the Cross-border Merger Directive. For Germany, these companies are the German stock corporation (AG), the partnership limited by shares (KGaA), the limited liability company (GmbH) and the European company (SE) which has its seat in Germany. Said companies must have been formed in accordance with the laws of a Member State and must have their registered office, central administration or principal place of business in a Member State (§ 122b(1) Reorganisation Act).

3.   The new rules are applicable neither to partnerships nor to cooperatives. They are also not applicable to cross-border mergers involving a company whose corporate purpose is the collective investment of capital provided by the public, which operates on the principle of risk-diversification and whose units may be, at the holder's request, purchased or redeemed, directly or indirectly, out of the company's assets (§ 122b(2) Reorganisation Act).

III   Cash payment

4.   The Cross-border Merger Directive only regulates mergers whereby the cash payment, which the members of the transferring company may receive in addition to shares in the receiving company, does not exceed 10 per cent of the nominal value of the shares or, in the absence of a nominal value, of the accounting par value of the shares (Art. 2(2)(a) and (b) Dir.). If the cash payment exceeds 10 per cent, the rules on cross-border merger shall apply if at least one of the Member States concerned allows the cash payment to exceed

---

2 Gesetz zur Umsetzung der Regelungen über die Mitbestimmung der Arbeitnehmer bei einer Verschmelzung von Kapitalgesellschaften aus verschiedenen Mitgliedstaaten, Bundesgesetzblatt Teil I, 28 December 2006, p. 3332.

3 Gesetz über steuerliche Begleitmaßnahmen zur Einführung der Europäischen Gesellschaft und zur Änderung weiterer steuerlicher Maßnahmen (SEStEG), Bundesgesetzblatt Teil I, 12 December 2006, p. 2782.

such threshold (Art. 3(1) Dir.). The provisions of the Reorganisation Act on cross-border mergers are not limited to cash payments exceeding 10 per cent. But if a German company is the receiving company, according to the general rules on mergers, any cash compensation cannot exceed 10 per cent of the nominal or accounting value, as applicable, of the shares issued by the receiving company in the course of the merger.

IV   Legal consequences and enforceability of a cross-border merger

5.   A cross-border merger which has been completed has the following consequences (§ 20 Reorganisation Act):

    (i)   the assets as well as the liabilities of the transferring companies are transferred to the acquiring company;
    (ii)   the transferring companies cease to exist;
    (iii) the shareholders of the transferring companies become shareholders of the acquiring company, except to the extent the acquiring company is a shareholder of the transferring company;
    (iv)   the lack of a notarised common merger plan and the lack of specific consent or waiver declarations by individual shareholders is deemed to be corrected.

V   Procedure

1   Draft terms of cross-border merger

6.   The management organs of each of the merging companies must prepare common merger terms. Such terms are referred to as a 'merger plan' in the Reorganisation Act (§ 122c Reorganisation Act). The merger terms can be prepared as draft terms, in which case the final merger terms will be executed following their approval by the shareholders' meeting. Alternatively, the merger terms can be executed prior to the shareholders' meeting, but subject to shareholder approval. The merger terms must be notarised, i.e. the terms must be agreed between the parties in the presence of a notary public.

The merger terms must include the information described in Chapter 1, no 19 of this book. The respective provision of the Reorganisation Act (§ 122c(2)) corresponds to Article 5 of the Cross-border Merger Directive. The information to be included in the merger terms for a cross-border merger is by and large the same as for a domestic merger. Additional information requirements relate to the procedure for employee participation and the valuation of the assets and liabilities being transferred. Unlike a domestic merger, the statute of the receiving company must be included in the merger terms. In the event of a cross-border merger of a wholly owned subsidiary into its parent company, the information with regard to the ratio applicable to the exchange of shares and the details of the share exchange can be omitted, as the cross-border merger will be completed without the issuance of new shares.

7.   The merger terms must be made available to the shareholders (see no 13 of this chapter). It is disputed whether the merger terms must also be submitted to the works council, if a works council has been created for a German company participating in the merger. For a domestic merger, the Reorganisation Act stipulates a respective information requirement. Based on the fact that a respective provision has not been included in the section on the merger terms for cross-border mergers (§ 122c Reorganisation Act), most German legal scholars conclude that no such information requirement applies to a cross-border merger. There are special rules on employee participation applying to a cross-border merger (see no 30 *et seq.* of this chapter) which make this information requirement obsolete.

8.   The merger terms must be filed with the competent trade register at least one month before the shareholders' meeting convened to approve the merger (§ 122d Reorganisation Act). The trade register must publish the filing without undue delay and the publication must contain information on (i) the legal form, name and registered office of the companies participating in the merger; (ii) the public registers in which the participating companies are registered, including the register number; and (iii) modalities for the exercise of the rights of creditors and minority shareholders of the companies involved. Such information must be provided to the trade register together with the filing of the merger terms. If more than one German company participates in the merger, each company must file the merger terms with its competent trade register. In contrast to Article 6(1) of the Cross-border Merger Directive, which requires that the merger terms are published at least one month before the date of the shareholders' meeting, the German rules require the filing with the trade register to be made at least one month before the date of the shareholders' meeting. This can result in a period of less than one month between publication of the merger terms and the shareholders' meeting if the merger terms are filed with the trade register at the end of the one-month period, because usually a couple of days lapse between filing with the trade register and publication.

2   Management report

9.   The management of each of the merging companies is obliged to prepare a written merger report (§ 122e Reorganisation Act). In the report, the merger, the merger terms, and in particular the exchange ratio and the amount of the cash compensation must be explained and justified legally and economically. If one of the merging companies is part of a corporate group, material information for the merger on affiliated companies must be included in the report. In addition to these information requirements, which also apply to domestic mergers, additional information on the implications of the merger for the

creditors and employees of the merging company must be included in the report in the case of cross-border mergers. The implications for the creditors are of particular relevance if a German company is the transferring company, because the creditors will, as a result of the merger, lose their current debtor, who will be replaced by a debtor in another jurisdiction. The management report must therefore provide sufficient information on the creditors' ability to enforce their claims in the foreign jurisdiction, in order to enable the creditors to make an informed decision with respect to their right to demand a security as a precondition for the merger (with respect to such right see no 29 of this chapter).

10.   The merger report must be made available to the shareholders and works council, or, if no works council exists, to the employees of the companies involved in the merger, no later than one month prior to the shareholders' meeting convened to approve the merger. In contrast to domestic mergers, the merger report must be prepared in any event and cannot be waived by the shareholders. A report is also required if a wholly owned subsidiary is merged into its parent company.

3   Expert's report

11.   The merger terms must be reviewed by one or several independent experts (§ 122f Reorganisation Act). This requirement also applies to a German limited liability company participating in a cross-border merger, although in the case of a domestic merger involving a limited liability company, an audit is only necessary if a shareholder demands the audit. The expert will be appointed by the court upon a respective request by the management. Certified auditors and audit firms are eligible to act as experts under the Reorganisation Act. The expert must prepare a written report on the review, which must be available no later than one month prior to the shareholders' meeting approving the merger. In contrast to the management report on the merger, the requirement of a merger audit can be waived by the shareholders (the waiver must be notarised if it relates to a German company) and it is not required if a wholly owned subsidiary is merged into its parent company.

12.   In the report, the expert must confirm the adequacy of the proposed share-exchange ratio and (if applicable) cash compensation, and must also state (i) the methods used to determine the share-exchange ratio; (ii) the reasons for the application of these methods; and (iii) if more than one method was applied, the exchange ratios resulting from the application of the different methods.

4   General meeting of shareholders

A   Information of shareholders

13.   If a German stock corporation participates in a cross-border merger, the following information must be made available at the company's premises for

inspection by the shareholders during the notice period for the shareholders' meeting convened to approve the merger: (i) the (draft) merger terms; (ii) the annual accounts of the participating companies for the last three fiscal years; (iii) the management merger report; and (iv) the expert's report on the merger. If the latest annual accounts contain a balance sheet dated six months prior to the merger terms, additional interim accounts no older than three months must be provided. Each shareholder is entitled to receive, free of charge, a copy of the above documents upon request.

14.   The documents referred to above must also be made available during the shareholders' meeting. At the beginning of the shareholders' meeting, the management board must explain the merger terms. Each shareholder may request in the shareholders' meeting information on the other companies involved in the merger, to the extent such information is material for the merger.

15.   For German limited liability companies the information requirements are slightly different. The merger terms and the management report must not only be made available, but must also be sent to the shareholders together with the agenda of the shareholders' meeting. Shareholders of a German limited liability company can demand further information on the merger from the managing directors at any time, not only in the shareholders' meeting.

B   Shareholder approval

16.   For German companies participating in a cross-border merger, it is required that the shareholders of such companies approve the merger terms and thereby the merger by virtue of a shareholders resolution. If a wholly owned subsidiary is merged into its parent company, no shareholder resolution is required on the subsidiary level.

17.   In the case of a German stock corporation, the merger resolution requires a majority of three quarters of the share capital represented at the shareholders' meeting. The articles may provide for a larger majority or additional requirements, such as a quorum requirement. In the event that different classes of shares exist, each class of shares must approve the merger by a special resolution, to which the preceding majority requirement applies (§ 65 Reorganisation Act).

18.   In the case of a German limited liability company, the merger resolution requires a majority of three quarters of the votes cast in the shareholders' meeting. The articles may provide for a larger majority or additional requirements, such as a quorum requirement (§ 50(1) Reorganisation Act). If, according to the articles, individual shareholders are entitled to minority rights or have been granted the right to conduct the business of the company or to appoint the managing directors of the company, and such rights are impaired as a result of the merger, such shareholders must grant their individual consent to the merger (§ 50(2) Reorganisation Act).

19.   The shareholders' meeting may decide to take its decision on the merger subject to confirmation of the arrangements with respect to the participation of employees in the acquiring company (§ 122g(1) Reorganisation Act).

20.   The shareholder resolution of a German company participating in the merger, which approves the merger, as well as any individual consents by shareholders, if required, must be notarised by a notary public.

5   Pre-merger certificate

21.   If a German company is the transferring company, its management must file the merger with the competent trade register in Germany. The management must confirm that all creditors who are entitled to demand a security pursuant to § 122j Reorganisation Act have received adequate security. A wrong statement regarding creditor security is a criminal offence. The management must also confirm that no actions by shareholders against the merger resolution are pending. Without such confirmation, the merger cannot be registered with the trade register. If an action is pending before a court, the company can ask the court to issue a court release order stating that the action by the shareholder does not prevent the registration of the merger (§ 16(3) Reorganisation Act). The court will issue such an order if the shareholder action is inadmissible or unfounded, or if in the court's opinion the merging companies' interest in completing the merger prevails, taking into account the severity of the alleged violation of the law.

22.   The trade register court reviews the fulfilment of the requirements for a cross-border merger pursuant to German law and confirms this with a merger certificate. The notification of the entry of the merger in the trade register is deemed to be a merger certificate (§ 122k(2) Reorganisation Act). The entry will be made with the note that the cross-border merger will take effect according to the requirements set forth by the laws applying to the acquiring company. The management of the transferring entity must, within six months of its issuance, present the merger certificate together with the merger terms to the competent authority according to the laws applicable to the acquiring company.

        The German approach of considering the notification of the entry of the merger in the trade register to constitute a merger certificate is not without problems. The notification is a simple computer print-out and may not be accepted by all foreign authorities as a merger certificate. A German transferring company is therefore well advised to obtain an additional order from the trade register court confirming the fulfilment of the requirements for a cross-border merger pursuant to German law.

23.   Upon receipt of a notification from the register of the acquiring company confirming that the merger took effect, the trade register of the transferring company enters the date of the merger effectiveness in its register and forwards the electronic files to the acquiring company's register.

6   Effects of the decision

24.   If a German company is the acquiring company, the merger filing registration, which must be made by the management, must also include the pre-merger certificates of each of the transferring companies and, if applicable, the agreement on employee participation (see below). The trade register court reviews in particular whether the shareholders of all transferring companies have approved common and identical merger terms and, if applicable, the agreement on employee participation.

25.   The merger becomes effective upon registration in the trade register of the German acquiring company. The trade register must inform the other registers of the registration date. The trade register court will publish the registration of the merger, but the publication is not a requirement for the merger to take effect. Once registered in the trade register, the merger can no longer be declared void by a court (§ 20(2) Reorganisation Act).

VI   Minority shareholders

26.   The Reorganisation Act offers three remedies to minority shareholders opposing the merger. First, minority shareholders of the transferring company can demand an additional cash payment through a special award proceeding. In a domestic merger, such an award proceeding is the only remedy available to the shareholders of the transferring company if the merger is challenged on the grounds that the share-exchange ratio is too low, that becoming a shareholder of the acquiring company is not an adequate consideration for the shares in the transferring company, or that the offered cash compensation is not adequate.

If in the case of a cross-border merger, the merging companies are from jurisdictions that do not offer legal proceedings comparable to the German award proceeding, the German award proceeding will only be available to shareholders if the shareholders explicitly declare their consent to the award proceeding (§ 122h(1) Reorganisation Act). If the award proceeding is not available, the exchange ratio and the adequacy of a cash compensation can be challenged by general voidance actions against the shareholder resolution on the merger. In this case the merger cannot be effected until all voidance actions have been finally dismissed or a release order has been obtained (see below).

27.   Second, if the acquiring entity is not subject to German law, the German transferring company must, in the merger terms, offer to acquire the shares of its shareholders who object to the merger resolution in exchange for an adequate cash compensation (§ 122i(1) Reorganisation Act). Upon the merger becoming effective, the obligation to pay the cash compensation is assumed by the receiving company by operation of law. The adequacy of the cash compensation can be reviewed in a special award proceeding, if either all jurisdictions

that are involved provide for such a proceeding, or the shareholders of the merging companies, which are subject to jurisdictions that do not offer an award proceeding, explicitly declare their consent to the award proceeding (§ 122i(2) Reorganisation Act).

28.   Finally, shareholders of a German company that participates in a merger may challenge the resolution to approve the merger terms in accordance with general rules on shareholder resolutions. According to such general rules, shareholder resolutions can, for example, be challenged if the shareholders' meeting was not duly convened or if information requirements have not been observed. Until all such actions have been finally dismissed, the merger cannot take effect, unless the company obtains a court release order. The court will issue such a release order if the shareholder action is inadmissible or unfounded, or if in the court's opinion the merging companies' interest in completing the merger prevails, taking into account the severity of the alleged violation of the law.

VII   Protection of creditors

29.   The creditors of the merging companies are entitled to demand security for claims that are not yet due, if creditors notify the company of their claims and demonstrate that the fulfilment of their claims is jeopardised by the merger. Such creditors' right is not specific to cross-border mergers, it also applies to domestic mergers (§ 22 Reorganisation Act). But with respect to cross-border mergers, if the acquiring company is not subject to German law, the obligation to provide security could be triggered earlier. In contrast to domestic mergers, where the security is not due prior to the merger taking effect, in a cross-border case the creditors of a transferring German company can demand security at an earlier point in time. The demand can be made during a period of two months following the publication of the merger terms (§ 122j(1) Reorganisation Act). Creditors are only entitled to security for claims that came into existence prior to or within fifteen days following the publication of the merger terms (§ 122j(2) Reorganisation Act).

VIII   Employee participation

30.   The rules on employee participation in cross-border mergers are laid down in a separate act, the Act on Employee Participation in Cross-border Mergers (the Employee Participation Act), which came into force on 29 December 2006[4] and which fully implements Article 16 of the Cross-border Merger Directive.

---

4 Gesetz zur Umsetzung der Regelungen über die Mitbestimmung der Arbeitnehmer bei einer Verschmelzung von Kapitalgesellschaften aus verschiedenen Mitgliedstaaten, Bundesgesetzblatt Teil I, 28 December 2006, p. 3332.

1   Employee participation in companies established in Germany resulting from a cross-border merger

31.   In accordance with Article 16(1) of the Cross-border Merger Directive, § 4 of the Employee Participation Act stipulates that the company resulting from the cross-border merger shall be subject to the rules in force regarding employee participation in the Member State where the company has its registered office. Therefore, for companies resulting from a cross-border merger that are established in Germany and that have their registered office in Germany, as a general principle the German rules on employee participation will apply, unless one of the exemptions stipulated in Article 16(2) of the Cross-border Merger Directive (implemented into German law by § 5 of the Employee Participation Act) applies. In the latter case a special negotiating body ('SNB'), which represents employees from all affected Member States, must be established to negotiate the co-determination.

In Germany, which has a two-tier board system, employee participation is implemented at the supervisory board level. If the number of employees exceeds 500, the one-third co-determination applies and employee representatives take one third of the supervisory board seats. So called equal co-determination applies to companies with more than 2,000 employees. In this case, there are equal numbers of employees' and shareholders' representatives on the supervisory board. The chairman, who is normally appointed by the shareholders' representatives, has a casting vote. For German stock corporations a supervisory board is mandatory. For German limited liability companies the establishment of a supervisory board becomes mandatory if the number of employees exceeds the above thresholds and the company is subject to the co-determination rules. Different, more employee-friendly co-determination rules apply to the coal and steel industry.

2   Special negotiating body ('SNB')

32.   If the German co-determination rules are set aside because one of the exemptions stipulated in Article 16(2) of the Cross-border Merger Directive (implemented into German law by § 5 of the Employee Participation Act) applies, a special negotiating body ('SNB') must be established to negotiate the co-determination. The German members of the SNB are appointed by an election committee, which may not have more than forty members. The election committee consists of members of the works council(s) of the German participating companies. In the absence of a works council, the employees directly elect the members of the election committee in an employee assembly.

33.   The Employee Participation Act stipulates in § 8 specific requirements applying to the members of the SNB representing the employees of the German companies participating in the merger. Such members of the SNB can be employees of

the German companies and branches as well as trade union representatives. Men and women shall be elected in proportion to the number of male and female employees. If the SNB has more than two members from German companies participating in the merger, every third of such members shall be a representative of the trade union which is represented in one of the companies participating in the merger or in an affected subsidiary or branch. If the SNB has more than six members from German companies participating in the merger, at least every seventh of such members shall be a senior executive (*leitender Angestellter*).

3   Protection of employee representatives

34.   Members of the SNB and employee representatives in the supervisory board of the company resulting from the cross-border merger who are employees of the company resulting from the cross-border merger, its subsidiaries or branches, or of another participating company, its subsidiaries or branches, enjoy the same protection as employee representatives pursuant to the laws and conventions of the Member State in which they are employed (§ 32 of the Employee Participation Act). This shall particularly apply with respect to protection against dismissal, participation in meetings of the SNB and the supervisory board and continuing payment of salary.

IX   Tax treatment

35.   The tax consequences of mergers, including cross-border mergers, are governed by the German Reorganisation Tax Act (*Umwandlungssteuergesetz*). Initially, the Reorganisation Tax Act was limited to domestic reorganisations. The Act was completely restated by virtue of the Act on Tax Measures regarding the Introduction of the European Company, which came into force on 13 December 2006 and which, among other changes, implemented the Merger Tax Directive.[5] The Reorganisation Tax Act now applies to both domestic and cross-border mergers and allows for these mergers to be conducted tax neutrally. Instead of accounting for the assets transferred by virtue of the merger at market value, which is the general principle applying to mergers (§ 11(1) Reorganisation Tax Act), the German transferring company can request that in the final transfer balance sheet, which is relevant for tax purposes, the book value is used for the transferred assets (§ 11(2) Reorganisation Tax Act). Book value accounting is possible if and to the extent that (i) no consideration other than shares is paid, (ii) it is ensured that the assets are subject to corporate income tax at the receiving company, and (iii) Germany's right to levy a tax on the profits from a sale of the transferred assets is neither excluded nor limited. A transfer at book value

---

5 Gesetz über steuerliche Begleitmaßnahmen zur Einführung der Europäischen Gesellschaft und zur Änderung weiterer steuerlicher Maßnahmen (SEStEG), Bundesgesetzblatt Teil I, 12 December 2006, p. 2782.

is therefore not possible if the receiving company is tax exempt. It is important to note that the book value accounting, which results in the tax neutrality of the merger, must be approved by the tax authorities. In this way the tax authorities shall be enabled to assess whether Germany's taxation right is excluded or limited.

36.   At the level of the shareholders, the shares in the transferring company are, as a general principle, deemed sold at market value, i.e. at a price that includes hidden reserves, and the shares in the receiving entity are deemed acquired at such value (§ 13(1) Reorganisation Tax Act). Upon request, the exchange can be made at book value, if (i) Germany's right to levy a tax on the profits from a sale of the shares in the receiving entity is neither excluded nor limited, or (ii) the merger is subject to Article 8 of the Merger Tax Directive (§ 13(2) Reorganisation Tax Act). Again, the application of the book value must be approved by the German tax authorities.

13

Hungary

JACQUES DE SERVIGNY, DR ZSÓFIA FEKETE
AND SZABOLCS ERDŐS
Gide Loyrette Nouel

I   Introduction

1. Cross-border mergers of companies are believed to facilitate the mobility and thus improve the general business position of small and medium-sized companies.

2. The Cross-border Merger Directive was implemented in the Hungarian legislation by a single act, namely Act CXL of 2007 on Cross-border Merger of Limited Liability Companies (the 'CXL Act'). The Act, which entered into force on 15 December 2007, does not extend the scope of the Cross-border Merger Directive and sets only the rules of cross-border mergers.

    Matters not covered by the CXL Act are subject to Act IV of 2006 on Business Companies (the 'Companies Act') and Act V of 2006 on Public Company Information, Company Registration and Winding-up Proceedings (the 'Corporate Procedure Act').

    The CXL Act avails itself of the provision of Article 3(2) of the Cross-border Merger Directive and ensures the participation in cross-border mergers of cooperatives and European cooperative societies having a domestic corporate seat (Section 13 CXL Act). These companies, however, must take into account domestic rules on their mergers and may, thus, merge only with certain kinds of corporate companies in accordance with Hungarian law.

II   Scope of the new rules

3. The CXL Act governs the cross-border mergers of limited liability companies with a registered office in Hungary, and the foundation of companies with a registered office in Hungary by way of the cross-border mergers of such companies. Furthermore, the Act establishes the related company registration proceedings in Hungary (Section 1(1) CXL Act).

    Only companies that are entitled to merge under Hungarian law can participate in a cross-border merger (see Chapter 1, no 13 of this book). These are the (i) limited liability company (*korlátolt felelősségű társaság, 'kft.'*); (ii) limited company (*nyilvános részvénytársaság, 'rt.'*) and (iii) private limited company (*zártkörű részvénytársaság, 'zrt.'*). The common feature of these types of companies is limited liability.

    In accordance with the Act, cross-border mergers may involve a cooperative or a European cooperative society that has its registered office in Hungary. However, special regulations apply to cross-border mergers of cooperatives (Section 13 CXL Act).

4. Definitions are set as follows: 'limited liability companies' means private limited liability companies, public limited companies, European public limited liability companies and, subject to the exceptions set out in this Act, cooperatives; 'cross-border merger' means the merger of limited liability companies in accordance with the Companies Act, where each company taking part in the merger has been formed in accordance with the law of a Member State

of the European Union and has their registered office, central administration or principal place of business within a Member State of the European Union, provided that at least one of them is governed by the law of another Member State of the European Union (Section 1(2) CXL Act).

In general the Companies Act recognises two types of 'merger': (i) fusion, where two companies join in such a way that both cease to exist and a third one is established; and (ii) acquisition, where the companies join and the result is the cessation of one company and the survival of the other (i.e. absorption of a legal entity by another legal entity).

Subject to the exceptions set out in the Act, the provisions of the Companies Act and Corporate Procedure Act governing mergers shall apply to the merger of limited liability companies carried out in accordance with the Act (Section 2(1) CXL Act).

In accordance with the general legal rule of *lex specialis derogat legi generali*, the limited liability companies taking part in a merger operation shall comply with the relevant provisions set out in other specific legislation in connection with mergers (Section 2(2) CXL Act).

III   Cash payment

5.   The Cross-border Merger Directive mentions cash payment when stipulating the definition of the merger (Art. 2).

By contrast, the Act does not mention cash payment. The Act defines merger as merger of limited liability companies in accordance with the Companies Act, where each company taking part in the merger has been formed in accordance with the law of a Member State of the European Union and has their registered office, central administration or principal place of business within a Member State of the European Union, provided that at least one of them is governed by the law of another Member State of the European Union (Section 1(2)(b) CXL Act).

IV   Legal consequences and enforceability of a cross-border merger under national law

6.   Consequences are not expressly mentioned in the CXL Act, therefore in this regard provisions of the Companies Act shall be taken into account.

In general, the business association established by way of transformation is the universal successor of the business association transformed (see Chapter 1, no 16 of this book). The rights of the predecessor business association shall be transferred to the successor business association, as well as the obligations, including the commitments contained in the collective agreement concluded with the employees (Section 70(1) Companies Act).

7.   The cross-border merger becomes effective in respect of third parties when the fact of the merger is published in the Company Gazette (*Cégközlöny*). In

accordance with the Companies Act procedure in respect of third parties, the company may rely on the data on record in the companies register or on documents supporting such data included in the registers of official company records after such data has been published in the Company Gazette, unless it is able to prove that the third party in question had previous knowledge of the data or document. Despite this provision, the third party has actually until the sixteenth day following publication to prove that it did not have the opportunity to gain knowledge of the data or document (Section 22(3) Corporate Procedure Act).

8. As for labour relations, the cross-border merger means a change of employer by legal succession rules of the Hungarian Labour Code (Act XXII of 1992). In connection with legal succession, (i) the rights and obligations of the predecessor concerning employment relations existing at the time of succession, and (ii) if the predecessor is terminated upon the transaction, the rights and obligations of the predecessor in connection with current employment relations and those employment relations already terminated, shall be transferred to the successor at the time of succession (Section 85/A(2) Hungarian Labour Code).

V   Procedure

1   Draft terms of cross-border merger

9. The management of each of the merging companies shall draw up the common draft terms of cross-border merger and, in addition to the requirements laid down in the Companies Act (Section 79(1) Companies Act), it shall include at least the following particulars:

  (i)   the ratio applicable to the exchange of securities or shares representing the capital of the merging companies, and the amount of any cash payment from the funds not comprising part of the subscribed capital, where applicable;
  (ii) the terms for the allotment of securities or shares representing the capital of the company resulting from the cross-border merger;
  (iii) the likely repercussions of the cross-border merger on employment of the workers of companies taking part in the merger;
  (iv) the date from which the holding of such securities or shares representing the company capital will entitle the holders to share in profits and any special conditions affecting that entitlement;
  (v)   the date from which the legal aspects of the merger will take effect;
  (vi) the rights conferred by the company resulting from the cross-border merger on members (shareholders) enjoying special rights or on holders of securities other than shares representing the company capital, or the measures proposed concerning them;

(vii)   any special advantages granted to the auditors or other similar experts who examine the draft terms of the cross-border merger or to the executive officers, executive employees and supervisory board members of the merging companies;

(viii) an indication that the participation of employees in the decision-making mechanism of the company resulting from the cross-border merger is ensured; information on the procedures by which arrangements for the involvement of employees in the definition of their rights to participation in the company resulting from the cross-border merger are determined; or an indication of arrangements made under which the rules for participation apply;

(ix)   where appropriate, information on the fact the members of each of the companies involved in the cross-border merger have so agreed by unanimous decision (Section 3(1) CXL Act).

10.   The supreme body of each of the merging companies may reserve the right to make implementation of the cross-border merger conditional on express ratification by it of the arrangements decided on with respect to the participation of employees in the company resulting from the cross-border merger (Section 3(2) CXL Act).

11.   The merging companies may include in the common draft terms of cross-border merger a clause providing that the registered offices, establishments and branches of the companies which are absorbed constitute branches of the resulting company (Section 3(3) CXL Act).

2   Management report

12.   The executive officers of each of the merging companies shall draw up – together with the common draft terms of the cross-border merger – a report intended for the members (shareholders) explaining and justifying the legal and economic aspects of the cross-border merger and explaining the implications of the cross-border merger for members (shareholders), creditors and employees (for the purposes of this chapter, hereinafter referred to as the 'report'). The executive officers of the merging companies shall be subject to liability for damages resulting from their negligent conduct during the preparation and execution of the cross-border merger according to the provisions of the Companies Act (Section 26(2) Companies Act) (Section 4(1) CXL Act).

3   Auditor's report

13.   The independent expert referred to by Article 8 of the Cross-border Merger Directive is an auditor according to the CXL Act. The auditor shall examine the draft statement of assets and liabilities and shall draw up the report thirty days before the scheduled date of the general meeting convened to adopt a decision concerning the approval of the common draft terms of

the cross-border merger to demonstrate the methods the company used for establishing the exchange ratio and the value each of these methods resulted in, and shall declare whether the exchange ratio is correct in his opinion. If the assessment faces particular difficulties, this shall also be indicated (Section 4(2) CXL Act).

14.   As an alternative to auditors and experts operating on behalf of each of the merging companies mentioned in no 13 of this chapter, one or more independent auditors, appointed for that purpose at the joint request of the companies by the court of registry of competence with respect to one of the merging companies or approved by such an authority, may examine the common draft terms of cross-border merger and draw up a single written report to all the members (shareholders) (Section 4(3) of the Act).

15.   The auditors referred to in nos 13 and 14 of this chapter shall be vested with the same rights as the companies' regular auditors to the extent necessary for drawing up the aforesaid report (Section 4(4) CXL Act).

16.   In accordance with the Cross-border Merger Directive (Art. 8(4)), the conditions set out in nos 13–15 of this chapter shall not apply if all the members of each of the companies involved in the cross-border merger have so agreed by unanimous decision (Section 4(5) CXL Act).

4   General meeting of shareholders

17.   The company taking part in a cross-border merger operation shall ensure that the common draft terms of the merger are published in the form of a notice in the Company Gazette at least thirty days before the common draft terms of the cross-border merger are approved by the supreme body (Section 5(1) CXL Act).

This notice shall contain an indication of the arrangements made for the exercise of the rights of creditors in connection with the proposed merger, and the address at which complete information on those arrangements may be obtained free of charge (Section 5(2) CXL Act).

The company taking part in a cross-border merger operation shall submit to the competent court of registry the report of the management thirty days before the common draft terms of the cross-border merger are approved by the supreme body together with the opinion of the auditor or the independent expert concerning the common draft terms of the cross-border merger, if available, and shall make them available to the members (shareholders) and to the representatives of the employees or, where there are no such representatives, to the employees themselves. If an opinion from the representatives of the employees is made available within the time limit for the submission and conveyance of the above-specified report, that opinion shall be appended to the report (Section 5(3) CXL Act).

5   Pre-merger certificate

18. The court of registry of jurisdiction by reference to the company taking part in a cross-border merger operation shall check – upon request – within fifteen days the company's compliance with the statutory requirements pertaining to mergers, and shall issue a certificate accordingly (Section 6(1) CXL Act).

19. The application for a pre-merger certificate shall have attached all documents prescribed by the relevant provisions of the Corporate Procedure Act concerning mergers, with the exception of the draft statement of assets and liabilities and the draft of the inventory of assets of the company resulting from the cross-border merger (Section 6(2) CXL Act).

Additionally, the following documents shall be enclosed with the application:

(i)   the company's statement to the effect that its role in the cross-border merger operation is in full compliance with the provisions and formalities of its national law;

(ii) the management report and the report of the auditor who examined the draft statement of assets and liabilities of the merging company, or failing this the unanimous decision on the merger and a statement to the effect that the company has made these available to its members and employees;

(iii) copies of the volumes in proof of the publication of the notice concerning the common draft of the cross-border merger;

(iv) in the event that the merger results in concentrations with a Community dimension, the Commission decisions declaring it compatible with the common market, or the company's statement declaring that the notification prescribed in Council Regulation No 139/2004 of 20 January 2004 on the control of concentrations between undertakings is not necessary (Section 6(2) CXL Act);

(v)   the agreement on the participation of employees in the decision-making mechanism of the company resulting from the cross-border merger; or

(vi) the decision of the special negotiating body referred to in Paragraph (b) of Subsection (3) of Section 11 not to open negotiations or to terminate negotiations already opened on the participation of employees in the decision-making mechanism of the company resulting from the cross-border merger; or

(vii) a joint statement by the management of the companies participating in the cross-border merger operation stating that no agreement had been reached with the special negotiating body on arrangements for employee involvement in the decision-making mechanism of the company resulting from the cross-border merger within the time limit set out in Act XLV of 2004 on European Public Limited Companies (the 'Act on European Public Limited Companies') (Section 12(3) CXL Act).

215

If the documents mentioned above are prepared in a language other than Hungarian, an official Hungarian translation shall also be attached (Section 6(3) CXL Act).

Other aspects of the proceedings of the courts of registry regarding the issue of pre-merger certificates shall be governed by the Corporate Procedure Act (Sections 46–7 Corporate Procedure Act), with the exception that on the next working day following the expiry of the deadline prescribed in the Corporate Procedure Act (Section 47(2) Corporate Procedure Act) the pre-merger certificate shall be considered issued as requested (Section 6(4) CXL Act).

20.   The pre-merger certificate shall contain the name, registered office and registration number of the applicant, the corporate form, name and registered office of the company resulting from the cross-border merger, and a clause attesting to the proper completion of the pre-merger acts and formalities prescribed by law. If in connection with a corporate resolution a judicial review is pending, it shall be so indicated in the pre-merger certificate (Section 7(1) CXL Act).

If according to the findings of the court of registry the applicant did not comply with the relevant requirements in full, the court of registry shall adopt a ruling to refuse the issue of the certificate, with the discrepancies indicated (Section 7(2) CXL Act).

The court of registry shall send the pre-merger certificate or the resolution on its rejection to the applicant. The resolution of approval shall require no separate justification (Section 7(3) CXL Act).

Remedy in connection with the court of registry's ruling on the issue of the pre-merger certificate, or in connection with the resolution for rejection, is available in accordance with the relevant provisions of the Corporate Procedure Act (Section 7(4) CXL Act).

21.   The following shall be enclosed with an application for the certificate, or for the registration of the company resulting from the cross-border merger that has its registered office in Hungary:

(i)   the agreement on the participation of employees in the decision-making mechanism of the company resulting from the cross-border merger; or

(ii)   the decision of the special negotiating body referred to in no 31 of this chapter not to open negotiations or to terminate negotiations already opened on the participation of employees in the decision-making mechanism of the company resulting from the cross-border merger; or

(iii)   a joint statement by the management of the companies participating in the cross-border merger operation stating that no agreement had been reached with the special negotiating body on arrangements for employee involvement in the decision-making mechanism of the company resulting from the cross-border merger within the time limit set out in the European Companies Act.

6   Effects of the decision

22.   An application for the registration of a company resulting from the cross-border merger shall be submitted within six months from the date of issue of the pre-merger certificate – or one issued according to the national law of each company – to the court of registry of jurisdiction by reference to the registered office of the merging company (Section 8(1) CXL Act).

23.   In the process of evaluation of the aforementioned application, the court of registry shall scrutinise the legality of the merger for compliance with the relevant statutory requirements, such as the regulations pertaining to the common draft terms of the cross-border merger and to the agreement concerning employee participation. Other aspects of the registration procedures relating to mergers shall be governed by the provisions of the Corporate Procedure Act concerning the transformation of companies, with the exception that the records of the company resulting from the cross-border merger shall also indicate the foreign branch (Section 8(2) CXL Act).

The competent court of registry shall forthwith notify the company registers affected concerning the registration of merger, the date of transformation, on the termination of the proceedings and the rejection of the application for registration (amendment notification) (Section 8(3) CXL Act).

The court of registry of jurisdiction for the merging company shall take the action (Section 87(1) Companies Act) at the request of the competent authority of another Member State effective as of the date of transformation (Section 8(4) CXL Act).

The charter document of a merging company may not be declared null and void following the date of transformation (Section 8(5) CXL Act).

VI   Minority shareholders

24.   The CXL Act does not detail any special protection for minority shareholders, thus, if the majority of the shareholders vote for the merger, the minority shareholders may not be able to prevent the cross-border merger.

As the Act does not contain rights of minority shareholders, the Companies Act and contractual arrangements should be examined.

In general, protection of minority shareholders includes the right to initiate:

(i)   the convocation of the general meeting of the company;
(ii)   the examination of the company's books;
(iii) claims against the company's manager, board of managers or supervisory board that have obligations to the company, but the general meeting failed to adopt a resolution in this regard (Section 49 Companies Act).

VII   Protection of creditors

25.   In accordance with the provisions of the Cross-border Merger Directive, the simplified procedure is carried out in the case where a cross-border merger by acquisition is carried out by a company which holds all the shares and other securities conferring the right to vote at meetings of the supreme body of the company or companies being acquired. A simplified procedure means that the terms of the cross-border merger need not contain (i) the ratio applicable to the exchange of securities or shares representing the capital of the merging companies, and the amount of any cash payment from the funds not comprising part of the subscribed capital, where applicable; (ii) the terms for the allotment of securities or shares representing the capital of the company resulting from the cross-border merger; (iii) the date from which the holding of such securities or shares representing the company capital will entitle the holders to share in profits and any special conditions affecting that entitlement.

Furthermore, the supreme body of the company or companies being acquired is not required to vote concerning the ratification of the common draft terms of the cross-border merger (Section 9 CXL Act).

VIII   Employee participation

26.   The company resulting from the cross-border merger will be subject to rules of employee participation, if any, in the Member State where its registered office is located (Chapter 1, no 41 of this book). In the case that the company seat is in Hungary, various rules are stipulated in the Act concerning employee participation.

27.   If a merger takes place in accordance with the Companies Act within three years following the date of transformation, any deviation from the participation rights of employees in the company resulting from the cross-border merger shall be permitted only if it is to the benefit of the employees (Section 12(2) CXL Act).

1   Employee participation in companies established in Hungary resulting from a cross-border merger

28.   The company resulting from the cross-border merger must comply with the provisions of the Companies Act (Section 38–9 Companies Act) concerning employee participation in the decision-making mechanism (Section 10(1) CXL Act). Thus, the Companies Act gives the general rules on the participation of the employees in the cross-border merger.

If the annual average of the number of full-time employees employed by the company exceeds 200, the employees are entitled to participate in the supervision of the company's activity, unless there is an agreement between the works council and the management of the company to the contrary. In the latter case, the representatives of the employees shall comprise one third of the members of the supervisory board. If one third of the number of members is a fraction, the number of supervisory board members shall be determined in favour of the employees (Section 38(1) Companies Act).

In the case of public limited companies controlled by the board of directors, the procedures for exercising the right of employees – in accordance with the articles of association – in supervising the company's management shall be laid down in agreement between the board of directors and the works council.[1]

Where a company is created by way of transformation from an organisation where the employees had no seat on a supervisory board, however, the criteria above are met. The articles of association must be amended to contain facilities for the employees to participate in the work of the supervisory board (Section 38(3) Companies Act).

The employees' representatives taking part in the supervisory board shall, with the exception of business secrets, inform the company's employees by way of the works council concerning the activities of the supervisory board (Section 38(4) Companies Act).

Upon hearing the opinion of the trade unions operating in the company, the employees' representatives on the supervisory board shall be nominated by the works council from among the employees (Section 39(1) Companies Act).

Persons nominated by the works council shall be elected as members of the supervisory board by the business association's supreme body at its first meeting following such nomination, unless statutory grounds for disqualification exist in respect of the nominees. In this case, a new nomination shall be requested (Section 39(2) Companies Act).

On the supervisory board, employees' representatives shall have the same rights and the same obligations as all other members. If the opinion of the employees' representatives unanimously differs from the majority standpoint of the supervisory board, the minority standpoint of the employees shall be stated at the meeting of the business association's supreme body (Section 39(3) Companies Act).

Employees' representatives shall be entitled to the same protection as members of the works council in accordance with the Labour Code (Section 39(4) Companies Act) (Act XXII of 1992 on the Labour Code).

In the event of the termination of employment of an employees' representative, this shall also bring about the termination of his membership on the supervisory board (Section 39(5) Companies Act).

---

1 Section 38(2) of the Companies Act: the articles of association of public limited companies may also contain provisions to impose management and supervisory functions upon the board of directors (public or private limited companies operated by the one-tier system). Such a (public or private) limited company shall have no supervisory board, and the members of the board of directors shall be treated as executive officers.

The supreme body of the business association may remove an employees' representative only if recommended by the works council, except if the works council failed to comply with the obligation to recall a representative subject to statutory grounds for disqualification within the time limit specified in the memorandum of association or to nominate a new representative (Section 39(6) Companies Act).

29.   Where the general rules apply for a company resulting from the cross-border merger concerning the participation rights of employees, the company must set up a supervisory board.

2   Special negotiating body ('SNB')

30.   In some cases, detailed below, provisions on employee participation of the Act on European Public Limited Companies shall apply.

Employee participation shall be determined in accordance with the rules set out below:

(i)   where at least one of the merging companies has, in the six months before the publication of the draft terms of the cross-border merger, an average number of employees that exceeds 500 and is operating under an employee participation system;

(ii)   where the level of employee participation as operated in the relevant merging companies, measured by reference to the proportion of employee representatives amongst the members of the administrative or supervisory organ or their committees, is higher than is prescribed in no 28 of this chapter; or

(iii)   where the company resulting from the cross-border merger does not provide for employees of its establishments that are situated in other Member States the same entitlement to exercise participation rights as is enjoyed by those employees employed in the Member State where the company resulting from the cross-border merger has its registered office (Section 10(2) CXL Act).

The Act on European Public Limited Companies is the act implementing Directive 2001/86 of 8 October 2001 on the Statute supplementing the Statute for a European Company with regard to the involvement of employees (the 'SE Directive'). More details on this subject can be found in Chapter 2 of this book.

31.   It is possible to differ from the special rules in that (i) the companies taking part in the cross-border merger operation may confer in the common draft terms of the cross-border merger the right to apply directly without any prior negotiation the provisions (Sections 48–50 European Companies Act); (ii) the special negotiating body shall have the right to decide, by a majority of two thirds of its members representing at least two thirds of the employees, including the votes of members representing employees in at least two different

Member States, not to open negotiations or to terminate negotiations already opened and to rely on the general rules on participation in the company resulting from the cross-border merger (Section 11(3) CXL Act).

IX   Tax treatment

32.   The Merger Tax Directive was implemented to the Hungarian tax legislation as of 1 January 2004. As a result, the Hungarian taxation rules relevant to cross-border mergers are largely in line with corresponding European Union legislation. The new Hungarian legislation caters for a minimised tax exposure in paper-to-paper mergers, allowing for the deferral of taxation in certain cases.[2]

33.   The Hungarian corporate taxation[3] aspects of both domestic and cross-border mergers are governed by Act LXXXI of 1996 on Corporate Income Tax (hereinafter 'Corporate Income Tax Act') and Act LIX of 2006 on Solidarity Surtax (hereinafter 'Solidarity Surtax Act').[4] In addition, Act CXXVII of 2007 on Value Added Tax, as well as Act XCIII of 1990 on Duties, should be observed.

1   Introductory thoughts on mergers

34.   There is no definition of 'merger' under the Corporate Income Tax Act and Solidarity Surtax Act. Therefore, the definition construed under corporate law remains to be addressed for taxation purposes as well. The Hungarian corporate law recognises two types of 'merger':

    (i)   fusion: where two companies join in a way in which both cease to exist and a third one is established;

    (ii) acquisition: where the companies join resulting in the cessation of one company and the survival of the other.

    While these two phenomena are greatly similar in various respects, there are some important differences in terms of accounting and taxation. The most important is the possibility to revalue assets to market value and liabilities to their accepted or expected value, as follows:

    (i)   fusion: the assets and liabilities can be revalued at both companies (it is, however, also possible to choose revaluation only at one of the companies);

    (ii) acquisition: only the assets and liabilities of the company being acquired can be revalued, no revaluation is allowed for the acquirer.

---

2 Please note that a preferential exchange of shares as well as a preferential transfer of assets have also been introduced so as to result in a deferral of corporate income taxation. These, however, fall outside the scope of the present chapter.

3 Obviously, the Hungarian taxation rules described below are only applicable to those parties that fall within the personal scope of these acts.

4 The general corporate income tax rate is 16 per cent, while that of solidarity surtax is 4 per cent. Please note that the corporate income tax rate will be increased from the current 16 per cent to 19 per cent, while the solidarity surtax applicable to corporations will cease as of 1 January 2010.

The revaluation can be upward or downward, depending on the specific case. In the event of a revaluation, a so-called *revaluation difference* is generated in the accounting records, comprising the difference between the total revaluation of assets and the total revaluation of liabilities. This revaluation difference should be shown in the equity capital by virtue of Hungarian accounting standards. It is important to note that revaluation is only a possibility and never an obligation. To decide whether or not to opt for a revaluation, various factors should be observed, such as business reasons, accounting aspects and naturally the ultimate tax exposure.

For both a fusion and an acquisition, the Corporate Income Tax Act and Solidarity Surtax Act provide for another differentiation, as follows:

(i)   non-preferential merger
(ii) preferential merger

Since this distinction is more important from a taxation perspective, we continue our tax summary below with a non-preferential merger and will then proceed to describe a preferential merger.

2   Non-preferential merger

35.   Regardless of whether or not a revaluation takes place, the taxation value of the assets has to be amended – upwards or downwards, as the case may be – to book value at the predecessor, due to the merger. In practice, this means the following. The Corporate Income Tax Act does not always fully recognise the depreciation accounted for, i.e. in certain cases a tax base adjustment is required. This results in a difference between the book value of the assets and their 'taxation value', i.e. their value recognised for corporate income taxation purposes. If, however, a merger takes place, the book value will eventually be recognised, i.e. the taxation value will have to be adjusted to book value, resulting in a certain increase or decrease in the actual corporate income tax base at the predecessor.

A   No revaluation

36.   If the assets and liabilities of the merging entities are not revalued in the course of the merger, there should be no direct corporate income tax effects for the predecessor, other than that described above.

B   Revaluation

37.   If the assets and liabilities of the predecessor are revalued, the *revaluation difference* modifies the corporate income tax base[5] upwards or downwards, respectively. In addition, the *positive* revaluation difference increases the solidarity surtax base as well (in this case, no downward modification is allowed).

---

5 Excluding the revaluation of receivables and provisions.

38.   An advantage of the revaluation of assets may be that the successor should be entitled in the future to calculate the depreciation, impairment and any gains or losses on the revalued assets, meaning that more costs and deductions could be allowed to decrease its corporate income tax and solidarity surtax bases.

C   Tax mplications for shareholders

39.   The capital gains accrued by the shareholders as a result of the cancellation of their shares in the predecessor and the receipt of new shares in the successor are subject to both corporate income tax and solidarity surtax.

3   Preferential merger

40.   Under Hungarian tax law, a merger can be a preferential merger if both the predecessor and the successor are *companies*, and (i) the shareholders of the predecessor acquire shares or participation in the successor, and receive cash of at most 10 per cent of the total nominal value of the newly issued shares or participation; or (ii) a single-person company merges into its sole owner.

The Corporate Income Tax Act provides a definition of *company*, which basically constitutes the personal scope of a preferential merger. A company is the following:

(i)   a Hungarian business association (including, e.g., Kft., Nyrt., Zrt., etc.), grouping and cooperative;
(ii)   a company tax resident in a Member State according to the relevant domestic tax law, providing that

- it is not a tax resident in any third country based on any double taxation agreement with a third country, and
- it operates in a corporate form defined under the Merger Tax Directive or the Parent–Subsidiary Directive,[6] and
- it is subject to tax determined in these two directives without the possibility of having an option of being exempt.

As can be seen from the above, the Corporate Income Tax Act fundamentally caters for the possibility of cross-border mergers, in addition to domestic mergers. Qualifying for a preferential merger entails a number of advantageous tax benefits, as detailed below.

First of all, the taxation value of the assets does not have to be amended to book value when the merger takes place, as opposed to a non-preferential merger, provided that all relevant conditions are met (see below under *Revaluation*). This provision is irrespective of whether or not the assets and liabilities are revalued at the predecessor.

6 Council Directive 90/435/EEC.

A   No revaluation

41.   If the assets and liabilities of the predecessor are not revalued in the course of the preferential merger, i.e. the merger takes place at book value, the merger itself is tax neutral, i.e. it leads to no tax payment obligation.

B   Revaluation

42.   If the assets and liabilities of the predecessor are revalued, the consequent revaluation difference does not have to modify the corporate income tax and the solidarity surtax bases, as opposed to a non-preferential merger. So as to benefit from this optional tax treatment, all of the following conditions have to be met:

(i)   the successor has to determine its tax base as if the merger had not taken place. This means that the successor will have to calculate, for example, the depreciation or impairment of the assets transferred upon the merger by taking into account their book value historically shown in the books of the predecessor, instead of using a revalued – potentially higher – value;

(ii) the successor keeps separate accounting records for all the assets and liabilities concerned;

(iii) the articles of association of the successor expressly assume the obligation to fulfil the above;

(iv) the predecessor reports this option to the Tax Authority.

The above option is not a tax exemption but rather constitutes a deferral of taxes, because of the following:

(i)   due to the fact that the historic book values of the assets have to be used to determine, for example, depreciation instead of a higher revalued value, the smaller amount of future depreciation will accordingly result in higher corporate income tax and solidarity surtax bases, i.e. more tax liabilities;

(ii) in the event of a future sale of these assets, the compulsory use of historic book values will result in higher capital gains, thus triggering the payment obligation of the taxes deferred upon the merger.

As indicated above, the tax deferral available for preferential mergers is only an option, which will have an effect on the successor in the future. While tax deferral is in most cases a significant advantage, it always depends on the specific circumstances whether or not a preferential merger should be opted for. This is especially true when there would be no tax base increase but a tax base decrease as a result of the balance of the revaluation reserve. In certain cases, it might be more favourable to opt out of the tax deferral, whereby the above set of extensive administrative conditions will not have to be met.

C   Tax implications for shareholders

43.   The tax deferral system also applies to the capital gains generated at shareholder level due to the cancellation of shares in the predecessor and the consequent

issue of new shares in the successor. This means that the capital gains shown in the books of the shareholders decrease both their corporate income tax and solidarity surtax bases, i.e. they are exempt from both of these taxes.

If, however, later on these shares are alienated by the shareholder, the earlier tax exemption will become due, i.e. the amount of the above decrease will have to be used to increase the tax base, both for corporate income tax and for solidarity surtax purposes.

4   Other tax implications

44.   In general, mergers are subject to *value added tax* (hereinafter 'VAT').[7] Nevertheless, the transaction becomes exempt from VAT if all conditions below are met:

(i)   the merger takes place between business associations, as defined by the Companies Act (general partnership – *Közkereseti társaság*, '*Kkt.*', limited partnership – *Betéti társaság*, '*Bt.*', limited liability company – *Korlátolt felelősségű társaság*, '*Kft.*', limited company – *Nyilvános részvénytársaság*, '*Nyrt.*' and private limited company – *Zártkörű részvénytársaság*, '*Zrt.*');

(ii)   the successor is a taxpayer registered in Hungary at the time of acquisition;

(iii)   the successor undertakes the obligation to act as a successor in respect of rights and liabilities relating to the property acquired;

(iv)   the successor is a taxable person for VAT purposes.

In all other cases, the supplies of goods and/or services in the course of the transaction become subject to VAT, whose general rate is 25 per cent. Nevertheless, in the case of cross-border mergers where the consequent transfer of assets constitutes an intra-Community supply of goods, there should be no VAT effectively payable by the predecessor if the relevant conditions are fully met.

There should be no *transfer tax* triggered on the side of the successor due to a merger, as long as it takes place between *economic operators*.[8] Among others, an economic operator is any business association, European cooperative, European public limited company, etc. This notion, however, excludes business associations incorporated outside Hungary. Therefore, a cross-border merger can trigger Hungarian transfer tax at a general rate of 10 per cent, providing that the successor falls within the scope of Hungarian transfer tax rules.[9]

---

7 Act CXXVII of 2007 on Value Added Tax.

8 As of 1 January 2010, the exemption of mergers from transfer tax will cease in general, and only preferential mergers will be exempted from transfer tax.

9 Act XCIII of 1990 on Duties. From 1 January 2010, the general real estate transfer tax will drop to 4 per cent up to HUF 1 billion while the rate for the excess will be 2 per cent. The tax will be capped at HUF 200 million per real estate.

14

The Netherlands

PAUL VAN DER BIJL AND FRITS OLDENBURG
NautaDutilh

I   Introduction

1   Implementation

1.   The Cross-border Merger Directive was implemented in the Dutch Civil Code ('DCC') with effect from 15 July 2008 by means of an implementing act[1] (the 'Implementation Act'). Pursuant to the Implementation Act a new chapter 3A, containing provisions which apply specifically to cross-border mergers, was added to Book 2 DCC. In addition, the scope of Art. 2:308 DCC, which lists the Dutch entities that are allowed to enter into a domestic merger, was expanded to allow cross-border mergers between certain entities (see no 3 of this chapter). Thirdly, certain technical amendments were made to two provisions of the DCC on domestic mergers.

---

1 Act of 27 June 2008 amending Book 2 of the Civil Code in connection with the implementation of Directive No 2005/56/EC of the European Parliament and of the Council of the European Union on cross-border mergers of limited liability companies (PbEU L 310) (*Wet van 27 juni 2008 tot wijziging van boek 2 van het Burgerlijk Wetboek in verband met de implementatie van richtlijn nr. 2005/56/EG van het Europese Parlement en de Raad van de Europese Unie betreffende grensoverschrijdende fusies van kapitaalvennootschappen (PbEU L 310)*), published in the *Staatsblad* (Bulletin of Acts) of 27 June 2008, no 260. The date of the entry into effect of the Implementation Act was set by means of a subsequent decree dated 3 July 2008 (*Besluit van 3 juli 2008 tot vaststelling van het tijdstip van inwerkingtreding van de wet van 27 juni 2008 houdende wijziging van boek 2 van het Burgerlijk Wetboek in verband met de implementatie van richtlijn nr. 2005/56/EG van het Europese Parlement en de Raad van de Europese Unie betreffende grensoverschrijdende fusies van kapitaalvennootschappen*), published in the *Staatsblad* of 10 July 2008, no 261.

2   Statutory relationship between cross-border mergers and domestic mergers

2.   The provisions of the DCC on domestic mergers apply, *mutatis mutandis*, to cross-border mergers. Although a new chapter on cross-border mergers has been added to Book 2 DCC, a cross-border merger is not considered to be distinct from a domestic merger.

II   Scope of the new rules

1   Dutch entities that are allowed to enter into a cross-border merger

3.   Cross-border mergers can be entered into by any of the following Dutch entities (Art. 2:308(3) DCC):[2]

    (i)   a public limited liability company (*naamloze vennootschap*) ('NV');

    (ii)   a European company (*Europese naamloze vennootschap*) that has its corporate seat in the Netherlands ('SE');[3]

    (iii)   a private company with limited liability (*besloten vennootschap met beperkte aansprakelijkheid*) ('BV'); and

    (iv)   a European cooperative society (*Europése coöperatieve vennootschap*) that has its corporate seat in the Netherlands ('SCE').

4.   NVs, SEs and BVs are allowed to merge with limited liability companies incorporated under the laws of another Member State of the European Union ('EU') or the European Economic Area ('EEA') (Art. 2:333c(1) DCC). SCEs are allowed to merge with cooperative societies incorporated under the laws of another EU or EEA Member State (Art. 2:333c(2) DCC). Mergers between foreign entities[4] as disappearing entities and in which the surviving entity is a newly incorporated NV, SE, BV or SCE have also been facilitated (Art. 2:333c(1)–(2) DCC).[5]

---

2 According to the Explanatory Memorandum (*Memorie van Toelichting*) ('MvT') to the Implementation Act, the extension of the scope of Art. 2:308(3) DCC to other Dutch entities was considered, but it was decided that this would have given rise to practical and legal objections (*MvT*, p. 3). However, in the light of the judgment of the European Court of Justice in the *SEVIC* case (Case C-411/03, 13 December 2005, *SEVIC Systems AG*), which underlined the overriding importance of the freedom of establishment, it has been argued – not without contest – that cross-border mergers involving Dutch entities not referred to in Art. 2:308(3) DCC are allowed.

3 With regard to matters not regulated under Council Regulation (EC) No 2157/2001 of 8 October 2001 on the Statute for a European company (SE) (the 'SE Regulation'), e.g. cross-border mergers involving an SE as a merging entity, SEs are subject to the provisions of Dutch law applicable to NVs (Arts. 9(1)(c)(ii) and 10 SE Regulation).

4 Where reference is made in this chapter to a 'foreign entity' without further specification, this should be understood to mean an entity incorporated under the laws of another EU or EEA Member State.

5 This facility has voluntarily been included in the DCC; it does not follow from the Cross-border Merger Directive.

With the exception of the provisions on triangular mergers (see nos 7 and 8 of this chapter), the provisions which specifically relate to mergers involving NVs or BVs (Arts. 2:324 through 2:333 DCC) apply, *mutatis mutandis*, to cross-border mergers involving an SCE (Art. 2:333c(2) DCC).

2   Mergers involving a cooperative society

5.   Cooperative societies (*coöperaties*) governed by Dutch law do not meet the definition laid down in Art. 2(1) Dir. Therefore, it was not deemed necessary specifically to exclude cooperative societies from the scope of Art. 2:308(3) DCC; they are excluded by virtue of their nature.

3   Mergers involving an open-ended investment institution

6.   An NV that constitutes an open-ended investment institution[6] may merge with a legal entity which meets each of the following requirements (Art. 2:333c(4) DCC):

(i)   the entity's legal form is equivalent to that of an NV;

(ii)   the entity is incorporated under the laws of another EU or EEA Member State;

(iii)   the object of the entity is the collective investment of publicly raised funds under the principle of spreading risk; and

(iv)   the entity is an open-ended investment institution; any acts performed in preventing the deviation of the stock exchange price of the participants in that entity from their intrinsic value are deemed to be equivalent to acts of repurchase or redemption.

Apart from the above-mentioned requirements, the provisions on mergers which apply to 'ordinary' NVs are equally applicable to NVs that constitute open-ended investment institutions (Art. 2:333b(2) DCC).

4   Triangular mergers

7.   In respect of mergers involving an NV or a BV, the notarial deed of merger (see no 52 of this chapter) may stipulate that the shareholders of a disappearing entity will become shareholders of a group company of the surviving entity[7] instead of becoming shareholders of the surviving entity itself (Art. 2:333a(1) DCC). This type of merger is known as a triangular merger (*driehoeksfusie*). The group company involved in a triangular merger is also deemed to be a merging entity.

---

6 An investment institution (*beleggingsinstelling*) within the meaning of the Financial Supervision Act (*Wet op het financieel toezicht*) ('FSA') is open-ended if its participations can be repurchased or redeemed, directly or indirectly, against the institution's assets at any time at the request of its participants.

7 A group company is defined as a legal entity (*rechtspersoon*) or a company (*vennootschap*) which is organisationally connected to the relevant entity in an economic unit (Art. 2:24b DCC).

8.   Triangular cross-border mergers may be entered into by NVs, SEs and BVs,[8] provided that the surviving entity and the relevant group company are both Dutch entities (Art. 2:333c(3) DCC)[9] and the laws governing each disappearing entity do not prohibit the latter's participation in such a merger.

III   Cash payment

9.   If the surviving entity in a cross-border merger is a Dutch entity and cash payments as referred to in Art. 2(2)(a)–(b) Dir. are made, such payments may not be in excess of 10 per cent of the aggregate nominal value of the shares allotted in the surviving entity's capital (Art. 2:325(2) DCC). However, this does not imply that this threshold applies where a Dutch entity is a disappearing entity in a cross-border merger, provided that the national law governing the surviving entity facilitates this (Art. 3(1) Dir.).

The provisions regarding the protection of minority shareholders (see nos 58 to 61 of this chapter) can, in practice, result in an aggregate cash payment in excess of the above-mentioned threshold. However, any cash compensation (*schadeloosstelling*) to be awarded pursuant to these provisions is to be disregarded with respect to the 10 per cent threshold set by Art. 2:325(2) DCC.[10]

IV   Legal consequences and enforceability of a cross-border merger

1   Same legal form for all merging entities

10.   Dutch entities may only merge with entities which have the same legal form (Art. 2:310(1) DCC). The same applies, *mutatis mutandis*, to a Dutch entity being incorporated pursuant to the merger (Art. 2:310(2) DCC). In this respect NVs are considered to have the same legal form as BVs (Art. 2:310(3) DCC). Although this provision is of limited importance for cross-border mergers in view of the derogating effect of Art. 2:333c(1)–(2) DCC (see no 4 of this chapter), the requirements of Art. 2:310(1–2) DCC will apply in the event of multiple Dutch entities entering into a cross-border merger.

---

8   SCEs are excluded from participating in a triangular merger.
9   Since the triangular merger is a purely domestic legal form which does not follow from the Third Company Law Directive (78/855/EEC) (*MvT*, p. 5), it is possible that other EU or EEA Member States do not have the same concept. Consequently, a foreign surviving entity or a foreign group company as referred to in Art. 2:333a(1) DCC may not be able to comply with the obligations arising from the Dutch provisions on triangular mergers (*Kamerstukken II*, 2006–7, 30,929, no 7, p. 11).
10   *MvT*, p. 20; the advice from the advisory corporate law committee on cross-border mergers, no 14; and *Kamerstukken II*, 2006–7, 30,929, no 6, pp. 6–7.

2   Dissolution, bankruptcy and moratorium on payments

11.   A Dutch entity is prohibited from entering into a merger if a resolution to dissolve the entity has been adopted and a distribution has been made in the course of the liquidation procedure (Art. 2:310(5) DCC). Dutch entities are also prohibited from entering into a merger during bankruptcy (*faillissement*) or a suspension of payments (*surseance van betaling*) (Art. 2:310(6) DCC).

3   General legal effects

12.   A cross-border merger will have the following general consequences by operation of law:

(i)   the surviving entity acquires all of the assets and liabilities of each disappearing entity by universal succession (*onder algemene titel*) (Art. 2:309 DCC);[11]

(ii)   each merging entity, except for the surviving entity and, in the case of a triangular merger, the relevant group company (see no 7 of this chapter), ceases to exist (Art. 2:311(1) DCC);

(iii) the members or shareholders of each disappearing entity become members or shareholders, as the case may be, of the surviving entity (Art. 2:311(2) DCC), except in the following situations:

● if shares in the relevant disappearing entity's capital are held by or for the account of any of the merging entities (Art. 2:325(4) DCC);
● in the event of a triangular cross-border merger (Art. 2:333a DCC) (see nos 7 and 8 of this chapter);
● in the case of a minority shareholder of a disappearing entity, if that shareholder has exercised its rights under the provisions regarding minority shareholder protection (Art. 2:333h DCC) (see nos 58 to 61 of this chapter); or
● in the case of a minority shareholder of a disappearing entity being entitled only to a cash payment as a result of the exchange ratio (Art. 2:311(2) DCC) (see no 58 of this chapter);

(iv)   the shares in the capital of each disappearing entity lapse.

11 In deviation from the general principle of universal succession, certain assets are non-transferable either because the law so provides, or by virtue of the 'person-related' nature of the asset or, in the case of a receivable, pursuant to a contractual arrangement (Art. 3:83 DCC). It is held that the 'person-related' nature of certain legal relationships, such as rights and obligations arising from permits or shareholder agreements, can also lead to incompatibility with the principle of universal succession (M. J. G. C. Raaijmakers and G. J. H. van der Sangen, *Rechtspersonen*, Art. 2:309, annotation 7, pp. 43–62). Where certain formalities need to be observed in order to effect the transfer of certain assets, rights or obligations of a disappearing entity to the surviving entity, these must be carried out by the surviving entity following the merger (Art. 14(3) Dir.).

4   Cancellation of shares in the surviving entity's capital

13.   A Dutch surviving entity may cancel (*intrekken*) shares in its own capital which are held by the entity itself or by another merging entity up to the aggregate nominal amount of the shares which the surviving entity allots to the shareholders of a disappearing entity pursuant to the merger. The relevant provisions of the DCC regarding capital reduction by means of the cancellation of shares do not apply to such a cancellation (Art. 2:325(3) DCC).

5   Pledges and rights of usufruct

14.   Pledges (*pandrechten*) and rights of usufruct (*rechten van vruchtgebruik*) in respect of a membership or shares in a disappearing entity will attach, by operation of law, to:

(i)   the membership or shares, as the case may be, in the surviving entity; and

(ii)   the cash payments, if any, which will be made in accordance with the exchange ratio (see no 28 of this chapter) to replace the relevant membership or shares in the disappearing entity (Art. 2:319(1) DCC).[12]

15.   If there is a pledge or right of usufruct in respect of a membership or shares in a disappearing entity and the relevant member or shareholder will not receive a replacing interest in the surviving entity pursuant to the merger, the surviving entity must grant a replacement of equal merit for the pledge or right of usufruct (Art. 2:319(2) DCC).

16.   The provisions of Art. 2:319 DCC apply equally to pledges or rights of usufruct in respect of special rights vis-à-vis a disappearing entity (Art. 2:320(3) DCC) (see no 17 of this chapter).

6   Special rights vis-à-vis a disappearing entity

17.   If a party, other than as a member or shareholder of a disappearing entity, has a special right vis-à-vis that entity, such as an entitlement to profits or a right to subscribe for shares, that party will be entitled to a right of equal merit vis-à-vis the surviving entity or compensation for the loss of its special right (Art. 2:320(1) DCC). In the event that compensation is to be granted and no agreement can be reached on the amount, the compensation will be determined by one or more independent experts to be designated by the district court (*rechtbank*) for the area where the surviving entity has its corporate seat

---

12   Art. 2:319 DCC is a purely domestic provision (P. J. Dortmond and M. J. G. C. Raaijmakers, *De juridische fusie naar wordend recht*, W. E. J. Tjeenk Willink, Zwolle, 1980, p. 55). However, we are of the view that Art. 2:319(1) DCC must also be applied in the event of a cross-border merger involving a foreign surviving entity (see the Explanatory Memorandum to the Cross-border Merger Directive, p. 3).

at the request of the most interested party (*meest gerede partij*) (Art. 2:320(2) in conjunction with Art. 1:10(2) DCC).

7   Agreements with a merging entity

18.   If an agreement to which a merging entity is party should not reasonably remain unaltered as a result of the merger, any of the parties to the agreement may request the court to amend or rescind the agreement; the amendment or rescision may have retroactive effect (Art. 2:322(1) DCC). A request for amendment or rescision can only be filed during a period of six months following the registration of the merger at the public registry at which the surviving entity is registered (Art. 2:322(2) DCC).

19.   If any damage (*schade*) is incurred by a counterparty of the party requesting amendment or rescision of an agreement as described above, the relevant entity must provide compensation to the counterparty (Art. 2:322(3) DCC).

8   Accounting effects

20.   The financial year of a disappearing entity will end on the day prior to the date from which the financial information pertaining to that entity will be accounted for in the annual accounts or other financial reports of the surviving entity (Art. 2:321(1) DCC). The legislative history of Art. 2:321 DCC indicates that the surviving entity may account for the financial information pertaining to a disappearing entity with effect from a date prior to the date of the merger becoming effective, provided that the general regulations applicable to the annual accounts permit this.[13]

However, most accounting regulations, such as the International Financial Reporting Standards (IFRS), currently stipulate that the financial information pertaining to a disappearing entity may not be retroactively accounted for in the surviving entity's financial reports to the extent that this information relates to a period prior to the acquisition by the surviving entity of control over the disappearing entity's assets and liabilities (IFRS 3 *Business Combinations*). Therefore, the facility granted by Art. 2:321(1) DCC is, in practice, restricted by most applicable accounting regulations.

21.   The obligations of a disappearing entity with regard to the annual accounts or other financial reports will be imposed on the surviving entity following the merger (Art. 2:321(2) DCC).[14]

---

13 *Kamerstukken II*, 1980–1, 16,453, nos. 3–4, p. 7.
14 If the laws governing a foreign surviving entity do not contain a provision similar to Art. 2:321(2) DCC, this could lead to a gap in the financial reporting of the relevant disappearing entity. In our view Art. 2:321(2) DCC should also be applicable to foreign surviving entities. A gap in the financial reporting would be inconsistent with the general accounting principles laid down in the Fourth Company Law Directive (78/660/EEC). Furthermore, it can be

22.   If there are differences between the valuation of a disappearing entity's assets and liabilities as included in that entity's most recent annual accounts or other financial reports and the valuation of those assets and liabilities in the first annual accounts or other financial reports drawn up by the surviving entity following the merger, these differences must be explained by the surviving entity in its annual accounts (Art. 2:321(3) DCC).

23.   Following the merger, a surviving entity must form statutory reserves in the same manner as formed by each disappearing entity prior to the merger, unless the statutory basis for maintaining such reserves has lapsed (Art. 2:321(4) DCC).

9   Validity and nullity of the merger

24.   A cross-border merger cannot be nullified (*vernietigen*) or be declared null and void (*nietig*) (Art. 2:333l DCC). The application of this provision extends beyond the scope of Book 2 DCC; any grounds for nullification of a cross-border merger, or for declaring such a merger null and void, that are laid down in provisions outside Book 2 DCC cannot be invoked.

V   Procedure

1   Merger proposal

25.   The merger procedure commences by the administrative organs of the merging entities drawing up a joint merger proposal – the Dutch equivalent of the common draft terms of merger referred to in the Cross-border Merger Directive. The merger proposal must – pursuant to Arts. 2:312(2)(4), 2:326 and 2:333d DCC – include the information set forth in Art. 5 Dir., as adapted to the Dutch legal framework, as well as the following particulars:

(i)   the intentions regarding the composition of the administrative and supervisory organs of the surviving entity after the merger has become effective;

(ii)   the intentions regarding the continuation or termination of the activities of each disappearing entity;

(iii) for each merging entity, the corporate body (or, if applicable, any other party) whose approval is required for the merger pursuant to the relevant entity's articles of association;[15]

argued that the obligations imposed on a disappearing entity pursuant to Art. 2:321(2) DCC are transferred by universal succession to the foreign surviving entity.

15 Although Art. 2:312(2)(i) DCC refers to approval rights in general, it can be derived from the legislative history of Art. 2:312 DCC that this provision refers to approval rights which have been granted pursuant to the articles of association of a merging entity (*Kamerstukken II*, 1983–4, 1, 285, no 3, pp. 6 and 15).

    (iv)   the impact of the merger on the amount of the surviving entity's distributable reserves and the value of its goodwill;

    (v)   if applicable, the number of shares in the surviving entity's capital held by the entity itself or by another merging entity which will be cancelled by the surviving entity (see no 13 of this chapter); and

    (vi)   if a disappearing entity has one or more minority shareholders, the proposed amount of compensation per share to be granted to such shareholders that choose to exercise their rights under the provisions on the protection of minority shareholders (Art. 2:333h DCC).[16]

26.   The merger proposal must be signed by all members of the administrative and supervisory organs of the merging entities; if one of their signatures is missing, the merger proposal must indicate the reasons therefor (Art. 2:312(3)–(4) DCC).

2   Explanatory memorandum

27.   In addition to the merger proposal, an explanatory memorandum – the Dutch equivalent of the management report referred to in Art. 7 Dir. – must be drawn up by the administrative organs of the merging entities.[17] This explanatory memorandum must include an explanation of the expected implications of the merger for the activities of the merging entities from a legal, economic and employment-related point of view, as well as the following particulars (Arts. 2:313(1) and 2:327 DCC):

    (i)   the method(s) used for determining the exchange ratio;

    (ii)   the suitability of the method(s);

    (iii)   the valuation resulting from the method(s);

    (iv)   if more than one method has been used, whether the relative weight assigned to the methods used can be deemed to be generally acceptable; and

    (v)   if applicable, any specific difficulties that have arisen with the valuation or with the determination of the exchange ratio.

---

16 See nos 58 to 61 of this chapter. At the time the merger proposal is drawn up, it may not be possible to establish whether any minority shareholders and, if any, how many will exercise the rights under Art. 2:333h DCC. This can only be determined when the resolution to enter into the merger is adopted, which in turn can only occur after the passage of at least one month following the announcement of the depositing of the relevant merger documents (Art. 2:317(2) DCC). If a disappearing entity has one or more minority shareholders, the merger proposal should indicate the proposed amount of compensation to be awarded in the event that such a shareholder exercises its rights under Art. 2:333h DCC.

17 Art. 2:313(3) DCC states that, under certain circumstances, the disappearing entity's administrative organ is not required to draw up an explanatory memorandum. However, in the case of cross-border mergers, this (national) provision is superseded by Art. 7 Dir., which states – without exception – that an explanatory memorandum must be drawn up by the administrative organs of each merging entity.

3   Exchange ratio

28.   The administrative organs of the merging entities must set an exchange ratio (Art. 2:325(2) DCC), which will establish the number of shares in the surviving entity to be allotted – as well as the amount of the cash sums to be paid, if any – for each share in the relevant disappearing entity.

If shares or depositary receipts for shares (*certificaten van aandelen*) in a merging entity are admitted on a market in financial instruments within the meaning of the FSA, the exchange ratio may be dependent on the stock exchange price for the shares or depositary receipts at one or more points in time, as specified in the merger proposal, prior to the day on which the merger will become effective (Art. 2:325(1) DCC).

4   Auditor's statements and report

29.   Pursuant to Art. 2:328(1) DCC, an auditor as referred to in Art. 2:393 DCC must be designated by the administrative organ of each merging entity to examine the merger proposal and to:

(i)   declare whether he finds the proposed exchange ratio to be reasonable; and

(ii)   certify that the aggregate equity of the disappearing entities is at least equal to the aggregate nominal value of the shares in the surviving entity's capital that are to be allotted to the shareholders of the disappearing entities, plus:

- the aggregate cash payment to which shareholders of the disappearing entities are entitled pursuant to the exchange ratio; and
- the aggregate compensation to which shareholders exercising the right laid down in Art. 2:333h DCC will be entitled (Art. 2:333g(1) DCC).[18]

---

18 See footnote 16. According to the legislative history of the Implementation Act, the auditor must assume a situation in which the maximum number of minority shareholders exercise their rights pursuant to Art. 2:333h DCC (*Kamerstukken I*, 2007–8, 30,929, C, pp. 4–5). This maximum number is the number of shareholders representing one third of the issued share capital if less than half of the issued share capital is represented at the general meeting at which the merger is resolved upon; otherwise, this maximum number is the number of shareholders representing half of the issued share capital (Art. 2:330(1) DCC). However, even when operating under this assumption, the auditor will not be in a position to determine decisively the resulting aggregate amount of the cash compensation, since the merger proposal will only include a proposal for the amount (Art. 2:333d(e) DCC); this proposal can only become definitive after the minority shareholders, if any, have exercised their rights pursuant to Art. 2:333h DCC (*Kamerstukken I*, 2007–8, 30,929, D, pp. 3–4, and W. J. M. van Veen, 'Het wetsvoorstel grensoverschrijdende fusies', *Tijdschrift voor Ondernemingsbestuur*, 2007-3, p. 82). The auditor will need to make his statement in this respect subject to the assumption that the proposal for the amount of the cash compensation as included in the merger proposal will be followed in the event that the rights under Art. 2:333h DCC are exercised.

The aggregate equity of the disappearing entities must be determined as at the balance sheet date of their most recent annual accounts or, if these have been drawn up in the course of the merger procedure, the interim accounts,[19] on the basis of valuation methods that are deemed to be generally acceptable (Art. 2:328(1) DCC).

30.   The auditor must also draw up a report giving his opinion on the particulars that are to be included in the explanatory memorandum as set out in (i) to (v) in no 27 of this chapter (Art. 2:328(2) DCC).

31.   No statement regarding the reasonableness of the exchange ratio and no auditor's report as referred to above are required if all shareholders or members,[20] as the case may be, of the merging entities consent thereto (Art. 2:333g(2) DCC). However, the statement with respect to the aggregate equity of the disappearing entities will still be required, except in the event of a merger under the simplified procedure (see nos 43 and 44 of this chapter).

32.   In order to be able to perform his services, each auditor has the right to request and examine information and documents from any of the merging entities, regardless of which entity designated him (Art. 2:328(4) DCC).

33.   If two or more merging entities are NVs or SEs, the administrative organs of these entities may only designate the same auditor if this has been approved by the president of the Enterprise Division of the Amsterdam Court of Appeal based on a joint request by the relevant entities (Art. 2:328(3) DCC).

5   Annual accounts and interim accounts

34.   If the financial year of a merging entity in respect of which annual accounts have been adopted, or other financial reports drawn up, ended more than six months prior to the depositing of the merger proposal with the trade registry (*handelsregister*), the administrative organ of that entity must draw up annual accounts or interim accounts (Art. 2:313(2) DCC). These accounts must relate to the composition of the assets and liabilities of the relevant entity on a date which is no earlier than the first day of the third month prior to the month in which the accounts are deposited with the trade registry.

35.   If interim accounts rather than annual accounts are drawn up, this must be done with due observance of the layout and valuation methods applied in the relevant entity's last adopted annual accounts or other financial reports, unless the interim accounts contain a justification for deviating from that

---

19 See nos 34 and 35 of this chapter.
20 Although Art. 2:333g(2) DCC only refers to shareholders, this provision should be interpreted also to refer to members (Art. 8(4) Dir.) and to usufructuaries or pledgees that have voting rights in the general meeting of shareholders (*Kamerstukken I*, 2007–8, 30,929, C, p. 7).

layout or those valuation methods on the grounds that the actual value of the entity's assets and liabilities significantly differs from their book value. In addition, the interim accounts must include the amount of the reserves that the entity is required to maintain by law or pursuant to its articles of association.

6   Depositing of merger documents

36.   After the merger proposal has been prepared and signed, it must be deposited with the trade registry by each merging entity, together with the following documents (Art. 2:314(1) DCC):

   (i)   the last three adopted annual accounts or other financial reports of each merging entity, together with, if applicable, the auditor's statement(s) with respect to such accounts or reports, to the extent that these documents have been made or must be made publicly available pursuant to applicable law;
   (ii)   the annual reports over the previous three financial years of each merging entity, to the extent that these documents have been made or must be made publicly available pursuant to applicable law;
   (iii) the annual accounts or interim accounts as referred to in Art. 2:313(2) DCC (see nos 34 and 35 of this chapter) of each merging entity, unless the relevant entity is exempt from making its annual accounts publicly available or Art. 2:313(2) DCC does not apply; and
   (iv)   if applicable, the auditor's statement(s) referred to in Art. 2:328(1) DCC (see no 29 of this chapter).

37.   It should be noted that, unless Dutch law provides otherwise, a document which has been drawn up in any language other than Dutch cannot be deposited with the trade registry, unless it is accompanied by a certified translation into Dutch drawn up by a sworn translator. For the purposes of the merger procedure, the main exception to this rule is that the trade registry will accept annual accounts of a Dutch entity which have been drawn up in French, German or English (Art. 2:394(1) DCC).

38.   After the explanatory memorandum has been prepared and signed, this document must be deposited by each merging entity at its respective office address, together with the following documents (Art. 2:314(2) and (4) DCC):

   (i)   the above-mentioned documents which must be deposited with the trade registry pursuant to Art. 2:314(1) DCC;
   (ii)   the annual accounts and annual reports over the previous three financial years of each of the merging entities which have not been made publicly available; and
   (iii) if applicable, the auditor's report(s) referred to in Art. 2:328(2) DCC (see no 30 of this chapter).

If a merging entity does not have an office address, the above-mentioned documents must be deposited at the residence of a member of the entity's administrative organ.

39. If the works council (*ondernemingsraad*) or co-determination council (*medezeggenschapsraad*) of a merging entity or a trade union which has employees of a merging entity or a subsidiary thereof among its members submits advice or comments in writing with respect to the merger, such advice or comments must be deposited at the entity's office together with the other relevant documents as referred to above. If the administrative organ of the relevant entity receives such advice or comments after the explanatory memorandum has already been deposited at the entity's office, the advice or comments must be deposited immediately upon receipt (Art. 2:314(4) DCC).

40. The documents deposited at the offices of the merging entities must remain available for inspection there until the merger becomes effective and, following the merger, for a further six months at the surviving entity's office (Art. 2:314(2) DCC). The following parties are entitled to inspect such documents and to request a copy thereof free of charge during this period (Art. 2:314(2) DCC):

   (i)   members or shareholders, as the case may be, of the merging entities;
   (ii) parties having special rights vis-à-vis a disappearing entity as referred to in Art. 2:320 DCC (Art. 2:313(3) DCC) (see no 17 of this chapter); and
   (iii) holders of depositary receipts for shares in the capital of a merging entity which are issued with the cooperation of that entity (Art. 2:329 DCC).

The works council, or, if no works council has been established, the employees of a merging entity, are allowed to inspect the explanatory memorandum at the relevant entity's office until the merger becomes effective (Art. 2:333f DCC).

41. If the administrative organs of the merging entities amend the merger proposal, the procedural formalities referred to in nos 36 to 40 and the last paragraph of no 42 of this chapter, must be complied with again in respect of the amended merger proposal (Art. 2:314(5) DCC).

7   Announcement of the merger

42. The Dutch merging entity must announce the merger, on behalf of all merging entities, by publishing the following information in the State Gazette (*Staatscourant*) (Art. 2:333e(1) DCC):

   (i)   the legal form, name and corporate seat of the merging entities;
   (ii) the registry where the relevant information regarding the merging entities is filed, as well as the registration numbers of the merging entities;
   (iii) the provisions pursuant to which the rights of minority shareholders and creditors of the merging entities can be exercised, as well as the

address where they can receive information regarding such rights free of charge.

If there is more than one Dutch merging entity, a joint announcement is sufficient (Art. 2:333e(2) DCC).

In addition to this publication in the State Gazette, the merging entities must announce in a Dutch daily newspaper with national distribution that the various merger documents have been deposited, as well as where these documents have been made available (Art. 2:314(3) DCC).[21] It is debatable whether the State Gazette can be considered to be a daily newspaper with national distribution within the meaning of Art. 2:314(3) DCC.[22]

8   Simplified procedure

43.   If (i) a surviving entity holds all the shares in each disappearing entity's capital (Art. 2:333(1) DCC), or (ii) all of the shares in the merging entities' capital are held by or on behalf of a third party and the surviving entity will not allot any shares in its capital pursuant to the merger to shareholders of a disappearing entity (Art. 2:333(2) DCC),[23] the following apply:

(i)   certain particulars required by Art. 2:326 DCC, such as the exchange ratio, do not need to be included in the merger proposal;

(ii)   the particulars referred to in (i) to (v) in no 27 of this chapter do not need to be included in the explanatory memorandum; and

(iii)   no auditor's statement(s) or report(s) as referred to in Art. 2:327 DCC are required (see nos 29 and 30 of this chapter).

44.   No facility has been implemented allowing a simplified procedure for mergers in which, prior to the merger, the surviving entity holds 90 per cent or more but not all of the shares of a disappearing entity (Art. 15(2) Dir.).

9   Resolution to enter into the merger

45.   For each Dutch merging entity, a resolution to enter into the merger must be adopted by the entity's general meeting of shareholders or general meeting

---

21 Although Art. 2:333e(3) DCC states that Art. 2:314(3) DCC does not apply in the event of a cross-border merger, the legislative history of Art. 2:333e DCC shows that this should be understood to mean that the information to be published in the State Gazette pursuant to Art. 2:333e(1) DCC does not need to be repeated in the announcement required pursuant to Art. 2:314(3) DCC, but that the requirement to announce the various deposits in a Dutch newspaper still applies: see *Kamerstukken II*, 2006–7, 30,929, no 6, p. 13; and *Kamerstukken I*, 2007–8, 30,929, C, pp. 3–4.

22 See the criteria stipulated by the Enterprise Division (*Ondernemingskamer*) of the Amsterdam Court of Appeal, judgment of 26 July 1993, NJ 1994, 132.

23 Art 2:333(2) DCC is a purely domestic provision; the facilities provided thereby are in addition to those provided by the Third Company Law Directive (78/855/EEC) and by Art. 15 Dir.

of members, as the case may be. The general meeting can only resolve to enter into the merger on the terms set out in the merger proposal (Art. 2:317(1) DCC). The resolution can only be adopted after the opposition period referred to in nos 62 to 65 of this chapter has lapsed (Art. 2:317(2) DCC).

46.   A resolution to enter into a merger must be adopted by the general meeting in the same manner as a resolution to amend the relevant entity's articles of association. If, with respect to their amendment, the articles of association stipulate that the approval of a particular corporate body or third party is required or that a certain majority vote or quorum requirement applies, these requirements will apply, *mutatis mutandis*, to a resolution to enter into a merger. If the articles of association exclude the amendment of certain provisions of the articles of association, a resolution to enter into the merger will require the affirmative vote of all shareholders or members, as the case may be, that are entitled to vote, unless the same provisions excluding certain amendments to the articles of association are to be included in the surviving entity's articles of association following the merger (Art. 2:317(3) DCC). Art. 2:317(3) DCC does not apply if the merging entity's articles of association contain any specific or deviating provisions regarding mergers (Art. 2:317(4) DCC).

Without prejudice to the provisions of Art. 2:317(3)–(4) DCC, if less than half of the entity's issued share capital is present or represented at the meeting, the resolution to enter into the merger can only be adopted with a majority of at least two thirds of the valid votes cast (Art. 2:330(1) DCC).

If the issued share capital of a merging NV, SE or BV is divided into separate classes of shares, a prior or simultaneous resolution to approve the merger is required from each group of holders of shares of a class whose rights will be adversely affected by the merger. Such a resolution can only be adopted after the opposition period has lapsed (Art. 2:330(2) DCC).

47.   The minutes of the proceedings at the general meeting evidencing the resolution to enter into the merger must be laid down in an official report (*proces-verbaal-akte*) executed before a civil law notary (*notaris*) officiating in the Netherlands. This requirement applies, *mutatis mutandis*, to the proceedings evidencing a resolution by the holders of a particular class of shares, as described in no 46 of this chapter, to approve the merger (Art. 2:330(4) DCC).

48.   Unless its articles of association provide otherwise, the administrative organ of a Dutch surviving entity may resolve on the merger (Art. 2:331(1) DCC), provided that the intention to do so has been stated in the announcement in the State Gazette (Art. 2:331(2) DCC) (see no 42 of this chapter). The administrative organ cannot resolve on the merger if, within one month after the announcement in the State Gazette, one or more shareholders representing at least 5 per cent of the entity's issued share capital have requested the convening of a general meeting to resolve on the merger. The articles of association may provide for a lower threshold than 5 per cent (Art. 2:331(3) DCC). A

resolution by the entity's administrative organ as described above does not need to be laid down in an official report.

49.   In the event of a triangular merger (see nos 7 and 8 of this chapter), the above-mentioned provisions apply, *mutatis mutandis*, to the resolution by the shareholders or members, as the case may be, of the relevant group company to enter into the merger (Art. 2:333a(2) DCC).

10   Pre-merger scrutiny of the legality of the merger

50.   Prior to the merger becoming effective and, in case of a merger involving a Dutch surviving entity, prior to the execution of the notarial deed of merger, a notary must issue a certificate to the effect that he has found the following with respect to each merging entity (Art. 2:333i(3) DCC):

> (i)   that the procedural requirements have been observed in respect of all resolutions required in order for each such entity to participate in the merger pursuant to:
>
> - the statutory provisions relating to mergers in general;
> - the statutory provisions relating specifically to cross-border mergers; and
> - the articles of association of each such entity; and
>
> (ii)   that all other requirements stipulated by (a) the statutory provisions relating to mergers in general, and (b) the statutory provisions relating specifically to cross-border mergers, have been complied with.[24]

51.   If the surviving entity is not a Dutch entity, the notary can only issue the above certificate if no request for compensation as referred to in Art. 2:333h DCC (see nos 58 to 61 of this chapter) has been submitted in a timely manner or if such compensation has been paid (Art. 2:333i(4) DCC).[25] If a request for compensation has been submitted in a timely manner but no payment has yet been made, the notary can only issue the certificate after having received copies of all of the relevant resolutions evidencing that the merging entities have decided that the surviving entity must pay such compensation (see no 60 of this chapter). In such a case, the certificate must state that the relevant request for compensation has been submitted.

11   Effectiveness of the merger

52.   A merger involving a Dutch surviving entity will become effective on the day after the execution of the notarial deed of merger. The deed must be executed

---

24 With respect to a cross-border merger, the certificate must be laid down in a notarial deed (*MvT*, pp. 21–2) in the form of an official report containing the notary's observations.

25 As there is no way for the notary to establish objectively whether any requests for compensation have been submitted, he may rely on the certificates of the relevant disappearing entity in this regard (*MvT*, pp. 21–2).

within six months after the announcement in the State Gazette (see no 42 of this chapter) or, if this is not possible due to the initiation of opposition proceedings by a creditor of a merging entity (see nos 62 to 65 of this chapter), within one month after the opposition has been withdrawn or after a court judgment dismissing the opposition has become enforceable (Art. 2:318(1) DCC). In the event that the negotiation period in respect of an employee participation system is prolonged pursuant to Art. 1:17(2) of the European Legal Entities Employee Involvement Act (*Wet rol werknemers bij Europese rechtspersonen*) ('EIA'), the period during which the notarial deed of merger must be executed will be extended to three months after the end of the prolonged negotiation period as referred to in Art. 1:17(2) EIA, subject to the condition that the deed must be executed within a period of one year and three months after the announcement in the State Gazette (Art. 2:333k(8) DCC).

53. If the surviving entity is a Dutch entity whose articles of association are amended pursuant to the merger, or a new Dutch entity is incorporated pursuant to the merger, the relevant formalities required to effectuate the amendment or incorporation, as the case may be, must have been complied with prior to the execution of the notarial deed of merger.[26]

54. At the end of the notarial deed of merger, the notary must include a certificate[27] to the effect that he has found the following (Art. 2:333i(5) DCC):[28]

(i) that the merger has been laid down in a notarial deed which has been executed within the period stipulated by Art. 2:318(1) DCC and, if applicable, prolonged pursuant to Art. 2:333k(8) DCC;

(ii) that the procedural requirements have been observed in respect of all resolutions required in order for each entity to participate in the merger pursuant to:

- the statutory provisions relating to mergers in general;
- the statutory provisions relating specifically to cross-border mergers; and

---

26 It would fall outside the scope of this report to describe these formalities in detail.
27 In including this certificate, the notary must rely on the pre-merger certificates issued in respect of each merging entity (*MvT*, p. 22, and Art. 11(2) Dir.). The notary executing the notarial deed of merger may be the same individual as the notary who has issued the pre-merger certificate in relation to the surviving entity, in which case he will rely on, *inter alia*, his own certificate.
28 Although Art. 2:333i(5) DCC stipulates that the certificate must state, *inter alia*, that all procedural requirements as referred to in Art. 2:318(1) DCC have been complied with, the relevant procedural requirements are in fact referred to in Art. 2:318(2) DCC. We are of the view that Art. 2:333i(5) DCC should be read as though it refers to Art. 2:318(2) DCC (see also W. J. M. van Veen, 'Het wetsvoorstel grensoverschrijdende fusies', *op. cit.*, p. 78). However, a notary would be ill-advised to ignore the literal text of Art. 2:333i(5) DCC; accordingly, the notary should also confirm the matters referred to in Art. 2:318(1) DCC, namely that the merger has been laid down in a notarial deed and that the deed has been executed within the period prescribed by law.

- the articles of association of each such entity;

(iii) that all other requirements stipulated by (a) the statutory provisions relating to mergers in general, and (b) the statutory provisions relating specifically to cross-border mergers, have been complied with;

(iv) that the same merger proposal has been decided on by each disappearing entity:[29]

(v) that the arrangements with respect to employee participation, if any, have been determined in accordance with Art. 2:333k DCC (see nos 66 to 84 of this chapter); and

(vi) if applicable, that the formalities regarding the incorporation of the surviving entity have been fulfilled.[30]

55. A merger involving a foreign surviving entity will become effective in the manner and on the date stipulated by the laws of the Member State where the surviving entity has its corporate seat (Art. 2:333i(1) DCC).[31]

12   Registration of the merger

56. If the surviving entity is a Dutch entity, it must register the merger with the trade registry within eight days after the execution of the notarial deed of merger (Art. 2:318(3) DCC). Immediately after the registration, the trade registry must notify the registries where the relevant information regarding the foreign merging entities is filed that it has registered the merger (Art. 2:333j DCC).

If the surviving entity is a foreign entity, the trade registry will register the merger and delete the registration of any Dutch disappearing entity upon receipt of the notification, as referred to in Art. 13 Dir., from the registry where the relevant information regarding the surviving entity is filed.

57. Pursuant to Art. 2:318(4) DCC,[32] within one month after the merger has become effective the surviving entity must send a notification of the merger to the registrars of all other public registries in the Netherlands where transfers of rights

---

29 For this purpose, each disappearing entity must provide the notary with the merger proposal that has been resolved upon by the entity's general meeting (Art. 11(2) Dir.).

30 This requirement follows from Art. 11 Dir.

31 Complications may arise when determining which jurisdiction governs the surviving entity, especially where the latter has been incorporated under the laws of a Member State which applies the doctrine of the actual seat but has its actual seat in another Member State which applies the doctrine of incorporation. In such a case, each of the Member States will designate the other as having jurisdiction over the surviving entity. Unless the tenet of redirection (*renvoi*) is applied, this will give rise to a stalemate (*Kamerstukken I*, 2007–8, 30,929, B, pp. 5–6, and *Kamerstukken I*, 2007–8, 30,929, C, p. 9). Another possible scenario is a situation in which more than one jurisdiction governs the surviving entity. It would fall outside the scope of this chapter to address these complexities in detail.

32 In respect of a foreign surviving entity this obligation will not arise from Art. 2:318(4) DCC, but from Art. 14(3) Dir. (*MvT*, p. 23). It should be noted that, due to a poor selection

or mergers can be registered. In the event of a transfer of Dutch property or rights to property (e.g. real estate or mortgages) which can only be created or transferred by means of an entry in the relevant public registry (Art. 3:10 DCC) pursuant to a merger, the surviving entity must provide the Land Registry and Public Registry Agency (*Dienst voor het kadaster en de openbare registers*) with the documents which are required by the Agency to register the merger.

VI   Minority shareholders

58. Art. 2:333h DCC provides for the protection of minority shareholders. The reason for implementing Art. 4(2) Dir. is that a shareholder exchanging its shares in a Dutch disappearing entity for shares in a foreign surviving entity loses the protection afforded by certain provisions of the DCC providing for specific shareholders' rights[33] and should therefore be entitled to compensation.[34]

A shareholder[35] of a Dutch disappearing entity can only benefit from the provisions on the protection of minority shareholders if the surviving entity in the merger is a foreign entity and provided that the shareholder:

(i)   explicitly opposes the merger by voting against entering into the merger at the general meeting (see nos 45 to 49 of this chapter); and

(ii) submits a request for compensation with the Dutch disappearing entity within one month following the date of the adoption of the resolution to enter into the merger.

The request for compensation does not need to be justified.

59. In the event that one or more dissenting shareholders exercise their rights under Art. 2:333h(1) DCC in a timely manner, the merger cannot be implemented until the relevant disappearing entity has reached agreement with the

of words, the English version of Art. 14(3) Dir. does not entirely match, for instance, the Dutch and French versions. The English version refers to the completion of formalities required for the transfer of assets, rights and obligations to become effective vis-à-vis third parties, while the Dutch and French versions refer to the invocability (*tegenwerpen* or *opposabilité*) of such transfers against third parties. The latter is more accurate and is consistent with Art. 2:318(4) DCC.

33 Examples given in this regard in the legislative history of the Implementation Act are the dispute settlement procedure (*geschillenregeling*), the right of inquiry (*recht van enquête*), the requirement of a qualified majority for the adoption of certain resolutions, the ability to exercise influence on the decisions or appointment of members of the administrative and supervisory organs and the right to receive information (*MvT*, pp. 16–17).

34 Such minority shareholder protection does not apply in the event of a merger by which an SE (*Kamerstukken II*, 2003–4, 29,309, no 3, p. 9) or SCE (*Kamerstukken II*, 2005–6, 30,382, no 3, p. 3) is formed.

35 Holders of depositary receipts for shares in the capital of an NV which are listed on a regulated market (*gereglementeerde markt*) or multilateral trading facility (*multilaterale handelsfaciliteit*) as referred to in Art. 1:1 FSA have the same rights as a shareholder in this respect (Art. 2:333h(4) DCC).

dissenting shareholders on the amount of compensation to be paid.[36] If no agreement can be reached,[37] the amount of compensation will be determined by one or more independent experts, to be designated by the president of the Enterprise Division of the Amsterdam Court of Appeal[38] at the request of the most interested party (Art. 2:333h(2) DCC).[39]

60.   The merging entities may agree that the compensation due to dissenting shareholders will be paid by the surviving entity. In such a case, starting from the date on which the merger becomes effective, the dissenting shareholders will have a claim on the surviving entity as the legal successor of the relevant Dutch disappearing entity (Art. 2:333i(4) DCC).

61.   The shares held by a dissenting shareholder in the relevant disappearing entity will lapse by operation of law when the merger becomes effective (Art. 2:333h(3) DCC).

VII   Protection of creditors

62.   During a period of one month after the announcement of the merger in the State Gazette,[40] any creditor[41] of a merging entity may file a petition with the competent district court stating its opposition to the merger proposal and specifying the form of security desired for the purpose of safeguarding its claim(s)

---

36 A proposal for this compensation is included in the merger proposal. See no 25 of this chapter.

37 Art. 2:333h DCC does not specify any method for determining the amount of compensation. According to the legislative history of the Implementation Act, it is expected that the amount of compensation will, in practice, be set at the value of the shares held by the dissenting shareholder as it stood at the time the merger proposal was deposited (*MvT*, p. 18).

38 It is apparently expected that the involvement of the president of the Enterprise Division will ensure that the procedure is expedited.

39 Certain writers (e.g. M. Zilinsky, 'Grensoverschrijdende juridische fusie van rechtspersonen, enkele problemen van IPR', *WPNR*, 2007-6721, pp. 685–7) are doubtful whether Art. 2:333h(2) DCC is consistent with the jurisdiction provisions of Council Regulation (EC) No 44/2001 of 22 December 2000 on jurisdiction and the recognition and enforcement of judgments in civil and commercial matters in the event that shareholders of a Dutch disappearing entity are not domiciled in the Netherlands or if a Dutch disappearing entity has its registered office in the Netherlands and its central administration in another Member State.

40 The district court of Amsterdam has ruled that the opposition period starts on the day after the date of the announcement of the depositing of the relevant merger documents and ends one month and one day later (Amsterdam District Court, 4 April 2003, *JOR* 2003/105). If the last day of the opposition period falls on a Saturday, Sunday or national official holiday, the period will be extended up to and including the first subsequent day that is not a Saturday, Sunday or national official holiday (Art. 2(1) of the General Act on Terms (*Algemene termijnenwet*)).

41 Dutch national authorities do not have the right to oppose a merger on the grounds of public interest as referred to in Art. 4(1)(b) Dir.

(Art. 2:316(2) DCC). Unless at least one of the merging entities provides security for, or otherwise guarantees, the satisfaction of the creditor's claim(s), the district court will rule that the objection is well founded (Art. 2:316(1) DCC). However, this does not apply if the satisfaction of a claim has already been sufficiently safeguarded or if the surviving entity's financial position will provide at least the same level of security for the satisfaction of the claim compared to the security provided prior to the merger.

63. Before ruling on the creditor's petition, the district court may give the merging entities the opportunity to provide security as specified by the court within a period determined by it (Art. 2:316(3) DCC).

64. If an opposition to the merger proposal has been filed by a creditor, the notarial deed of merger (see no 52 of this chapter) cannot be executed prior to the opposition having been withdrawn or a court judgment dismissing the opposition having become enforceable (*uitvoerbaar*) (Art. 2:316(4) DCC). If the deed is executed in violation of this provision, the district court may, upon a remedy being sought against the violation, order security as specified by the district court to be provided by the surviving entity, subject to a penalty payment (*dwangsom*) for non-compliance (Art. 2:316(5) DCC).

65. Where the opposition period lapses without an opposition having been filed by a creditor, it is common practice in the Netherlands for the Dutch notary involved in the merger procedure to apply to the district court for, and the district court to issue, a declaration evidencing that no opposition to the merger proposal has been filed by any creditor within the period permitted for that purpose.

VIII Employee participation

1 General

66. The principal rule laid down in Art. 16(1) Dir. – namely, that a surviving entity shall be subject to the employee participation system ('EPS') which is in force in the Member State where it has its corporate seat – has not been transposed into Dutch legislation. This was considered to be superfluous since, if the surviving entity is Dutch, the provisions on what is known as the structure regime[42] will apply and, if the surviving entity is foreign, the EPS in the relevant Member State will apply, in both cases without the enactment of an additional provision in the DCC being required.

---

42 See nos 67 and 68 of this chapter. Where reference is made in this chapter to the 'structure regime' without further specification, this should be understood to mean the structure regime as provided for in Arts. 2:152 *et seq.* and Arts. 2:262 *et seq.* DCC in relation to NVs and BVs, respectively.

The concept of employee participation as set out in Art. 16 Dir. has been codified in the EIA[43] in the context of the implementation in the Netherlands of the SE Regulation and the SE Directive. By referencing Art. 1:1(1) EIA, Art. 2:333k(1) DCC clarifies that an EPS as referred to in Art. 16 Dir. should be understood to mean a system of employee participation pursuant to which the works council or other employee representatives can influence the course of events of an entity by:

(i)   having the right to elect or appoint a certain number of members of the entity's administrative or supervisory organ; or

(ii) having the right to make recommendations with respect to, or to raise objections against, the appointment of a certain number or all of the members of the entity's administrative or supervisory organ.

2   Structure regime

67. The only EPS provided for under Dutch law is known as the structure regime. The principal feature[44] of the structure regime is that entities subject to the regime must establish a supervisory organ whose members are appointed by the general meeting on the basis of a nomination by the supervisory organ, in which respect the works council and the general meeting can recommend candidates to the supervisory organ to be nominated for appointment. In addition, the works council has an enhanced right of recommendation in respect of one third of the members of the supervisory organ (Arts. 2:158 and 2:268 DCC).

68. Unless an exemption applies, the application of the structure regime is mandatory for, *inter alia*,[45] an NV or a BV which has met the following requirements for at least three consecutive years (Arts. 2:153(2) and 2:263(2) DCC):[46]

(i)   according to its balance sheet and the explanatory notes thereto, the entity's issued share capital plus reserves equal at least €16 million;

(ii) the entity or a 'dependent entity' (*afhankelijke maatschappij*)[47] has established a works council pursuant to a statutory requirement to do so; and

(iii) the entity together with its dependent entities normally employs at least 100 employees in the Netherlands.

---

43 Art. 1:1(1) EIA contains, adapted to the Dutch legal system, the definition of 'participation' as set out in Art. 2(k) of Council Directive 2001/86/EC of 8 October 2001 supplementing the Statute for a European company with regard to the involvement of employees (the 'SE Directive').

44 It would fall outside the scope of this report to describe the structure regime in detail.

45 With regard to employee participation rights in SEs and SCEs, Arts. 1:6(2) and 2:6(2) EIA provide that the works councils of such entities do not have the rights as provided for under the DCC provisions on the structure regime; the structure regime can therefore only be applicable to SEs and SCEs on a voluntary basis.

46 There are certain full and partial exemptions from the mandatory application of the structure regime.

47 The definition of 'dependent entity' is laid down in Arts. 2:152 and 2:262 DCC.

The structure regime may also be applied voluntarily if an NV or BV or any of its dependent entities has voluntarily established a works council (Arts. 2:157 and 2:267 DCC).

3   Obligation to negotiate on an EPS

69.   In the event that either of the following criteria is met, the main rule laid down in Art. 16(1) Dir. will not apply and negotiations must be initiated on the EPS that is to apply to the surviving entity following the merger (Art. 2:333k(2) DCC):

(i)   any of the merging entities is operating under an EPS and employed, in the six months prior to the date on which the merger proposal is deposited (see no 36 of this chapter), more than 500 employees on average; or

(ii) any of the merging entities is operating under an EPS and the surviving entity is not subject to the structure regime.[48]

Criterion (i) implies that even if one of the merging entities is subject to the structure regime, negotiations must be initiated if that entity employed, on average, more than 500 employees during the relevant period. The negotiations may result in a regime different from the structure regime.

Criterion (ii) implies that if the surviving entity is subject to Dutch law and the structure regime applies to it, no negotiations (see nos 76 to 79 of this chapter) need be initiated. The rationale for this is that if a merger is entered into between entities which operate under different EPSs, the structure regime – in view of the fact that it gives the works council the power to influence the appointment of all members of the supervisory organ – will always provide for a level of employee participation that is higher than, or at least equal to, that under an EPS of another Member State, even if the structure regime is applied voluntarily. Therefore, an undesired loss of employee participation rights will not materialise if the surviving entity applies the structure regime.[49] Consequently, negotiations on the EPS can be evaded if the structure regime is applied by a Dutch surviving entity (whether mandatorily or voluntarily).

---

48 Although neither the Cross-border Merger Directive nor the DCC explicitly provides this, it is generally held that the second criterion only applies if the first criterion is not applicable (J. Roest, 'Grensoverschrijdende fusie en vennootschappelijke medezeggenschap', *WPNR*, 2007-6721, p. 711; J. D. M. Schoonbrood and R. Bosveld, 'Richtlijn betreffende grensoverschrijdende fusies van kapitaalvennootschappen definitief en in werking getreden', *Ondernemingsrecht*, 2006–1, p. 24; and *MvT*, p. 24).

49 *MvT*, pp. 23–4. It is debatable whether this reasoning is correct. Under the structure regime, the works council has specific rights with a view to the appointment of members of the supervisory organ. Employees of establishments of the surviving entity located in other Member States are, by virtue of the law, not represented in such a council and therefore cannot exercise any direct or indirect participation rights.

70.   Art. 16(2)(b) Dir., which lays down an exception to the main rule of Art. 16(1) Dir., has not been implemented in Dutch law, the rationale being that where the structure regime is applicable to a surviving entity, employee participation rights are secured at the highest level.

4   Applicable provisions on negotiation procedure

71.   If the surviving entity will have its corporate seat in the Netherlands and, pursuant to Art. 2:333k(2) DCC, the initiation of negotiations on the EPS that is to apply is required, these negotiations will be governed by Dutch law and the negotiation procedure will be subject to the following provisions (Art. 1:7 EIA in conjunction with Art. 2:333k(2) DCC):

> (i)   Art. 12(2)–(4) SE Regulation;
> (ii) the relevant provisions of the SE Directive[50] as implemented in the EIA;[51] and
> (iii) Arts. 7:670(4)(11) and 7:670a(1)(a) DCC.

Although it would fall outside the scope of this chapter to provide a full overview of the matters governed by the above-mentioned provisions, a general outline of the negotiation procedure will be given below.

5   The special negotiating body

72.   The EPS should be negotiated between the merging entities and a special negotiating body ('SNB') formed for this purpose (Art. 1:1 EIA).[52] The SNB must be representative of the employees of the merging entities and their relevant subsidiaries and establishments (Art. 1:8(1) EIA) and must be established as soon as possible after the depositing of the merger proposal (Art. 1:8(3) EIA) (see no 36 of this chapter).

73.   The SNB must consist of such number of employee representatives that, for each Member State in which a merging entity or a relevant subsidiary or establishment thereof has employees, one seat is allocated per portion of employees employed in that Member State which equals 10 per cent, or a fraction thereof, of the aggregate number of employees employed by all merging entities and their relevant subsidiaries and establishments in all Member States (Art. 1:9(1) EIA). Furthermore, in the event that the members elected as described above do not include, for each Member State in which a disappearing entity is registered and has employees, at least one member representing each such disappearing

---

50 Referred to in Art. 16(3)(a)–(h) Dir.

51 Arts. 1:4 to 1:12; Art. 1:14(1)–(3(a))(4); Arts. 1:16 and 1:17; Art. 1:18(1)(a)(h)–(j); Art. 1:18(3) (6); Art.1:20; Art. 1:21(2)(a) – with the proviso that the percentage referred to therein is increased to 33.33 per cent – Art. 1:21(4)–(5); Art. 1:26(3) and Art. 1:31(2) EIA.

52 Where reference is made in this chapter to 'negotiating parties' without further specification, this should be understood to mean the merging entities and the SNB, collectively.

entity, the SNB must consist of such number of additional members as to satisfy this requirement (Art. 1:9(2)(4) EIA). The number of these additional members may not exceed 20 per cent of the aggregate number of members elected pursuant to Art. 1:9(1) EIA (Art. 1:9(3) EIA).

74.   Each member of the SNB is elected or appointed pursuant to the governing laws or practice in the Member State where the entity that employs the member is registered (Art. 1:10(1) EIA). With respect to the Dutch merging entities, the members of the SNB are appointed by the works council, central works council or group works council, as the case may be, set up by such entities and their relevant subsidiaries and establishments (Art. 1:10(2)–(5) EIA). If no such works councils have been set up, the members of the SNB are elected by the collective employees employed in the Netherlands (Art. 1:10(6) EIA).

75.   Each member of the SNB has one vote (Art. 1:14(1) EIA). In principle, decisions of the SNB must be taken by an absolute majority of the members representing an absolute majority of the employees (Art. 1:14(2) EIA), except for the following decisions which require a two-thirds majority of the members of the SNB representing at least two thirds of the employees, including the votes of members representing employees employed in at least two Member States (Art. 2:333k(4) DCC):

(i)   a decision not to initiate negotiations or to terminate negotiations already initiated (see nos 76 to 79 of this chapter); and

(ii)   a decision to approve an agreement leading to a reduction of employee participation rights, if such participation covers at least 25 per cent of the aggregate number of employees of the merging entities (Art. 1:14(3) EIA).

6   Negotiation procedure

76.   Negotiations commence with the first meeting of the SNB and may continue for a period of six months thereafter. The negotiating parties may decide to extend negotiations until up to one year from the first meeting of the SNB (Art. 1:17 EIA).[53]

77.   The negotiations are initiated with a view to entering into a written agreement on the application of an EPS (Art. 1:11(1) EIA). In the event that the surviving entity is a Dutch entity, the EPS does not necessarily have to be the structure regime.

78.   The SNB can decide not to initiate negotiations or to terminate negotiations already initiated; such a decision will terminate the negotiation procedure (Art. 2:333k(4) DCC). Although the DCC does not explicitly state this, in the event

---

53 Where reference is made in this chapter to the 'negotiation period' without further specification, this should be understood to mean the negotiation period as referred to in Art. 1:17 EIA.

that the negotiation procedure is terminated by the SNB, the EPS operating in the Member State where the surviving entity has its corporate seat will apply.

79. The general meetings[54] of the merging entities may decide not to initiate negotiations. In such a case, the standard rules (*referentievoorschriften*) for employee participation in respect of the surviving entity, as laid down in Art. 1:31(2) EIA, will be applicable (Art. 2:333k(3) DCC).[55]

7   Standard rules

80. The standard rules stipulate that, following the merger, the employees of the surviving entity must have employee participation rights as referred to in Art. 1:1(1) EIA (see no 66 of this chapter) with respect to at least an equal number of members of the administrative or supervisory organ in respect of which they had such rights in any of the merging entities prior to the merger (Art. 1:31(2) EIA). In the event that more than one EPS is operating in the merging entities, the SNB may decide which EPS should be applied by the surviving entity. If (i) the SNB does not take such a decision, (ii) the surviving entity is subject to Dutch law, and (iii) any of the merging entities is subject to the structure regime, the structure regime will be the EPS applicable to the surviving entity (Art. 1:21(4)–(5) EIA).

81. The standard rules will only apply if, prior to the merger, one or more EPSs were operating in any of the merging entities covering at least one third of the aggregate number of employees of such entities (Art. 2:333k(2) DCC in conjunction with Art. 1:21(2)(a) EIA). If that is the case, the surviving entity will be subject to the standard rules under the following circumstances (Art. 1:20 EIA):

   (i)   the negotiating parties agree to apply the standard rules; *or*
   (ii) no agreement on the application of an EPS has been reached within the negotiation period, provided that:

   - each merging entity consents to the application of the standard rules; *and*
   - the SNB has not decided not to initiate negotiations or to terminate negotiations; *or*

   (iii) the general meetings of the merging entities have resolved not to initiate negotiations (Art. 2:333k(3) DCC).

82. The standard rules will apply to the surviving entity as from the date that the merger becomes effective (Art. 2:333k(3) DCC and Art. 1:20 EIA).[56]

---

54 Art. 16(4)(a) Dir. refers to the relevant organs of the merging entities, rather than to the general meetings, as referred to in Art. 2:333k(3) DCC.

55 Where reference is made in this report to the 'standard rules' without further specification, this should be understood to mean the standard rules as referred to in Art. 1:31(2) EIA.

56 Art. 2:333k(3) DCC incorrectly refers to the registration of the merger as being the moment as from which the standard rules are to be applicable. Art. 2:333k(3) DCC should be interpreted

8   Applicable EPS

83.   The applicable EPS resulting from Art. 2:333k DCC, which can be the structure regime or any other EPS, must be laid down in the articles of association of the surviving entity if the latter is subject to Dutch law (Art. 2:333k(5) DCC).[57] Consequently, since the surviving entity's articles of association as they will read following the merger must be set out in the merger proposal, the relevant EPS should be part of the merger proposal as well (Art. 2:312(2)(b) DCC).[58]

    If, at the time that the general meeting of a Dutch merging entity adopts its resolution to enter into the merger, the outcome of Art. 2:333k DCC is still unclear, the general meeting may make the resolution subject to the condition that it approves the EPS resulting from the application of Art. 2:333k DCC (Art. 2:333k(6) DCC).

84.   If a surviving entity participates in a domestic merger or cross-border merger within a period of three years after a previous cross-border merger to which Art. 2:333k DCC was applicable became effective, Art. 2:333k DCC will apply, *mutatis mutandis*, to the subsequent merger (Art. 2:333k(7) DCC).

IX   Tax treatment

85.   Even prior to the entry into effect of the Cross-border Merger Directive, both the Merger Tax Directive[59] and purely domestic provisions on tax rollovers already made it possible, in many cases, for cross-border mergers to take place without adverse tax consequences. In some respects, however, the Merger Tax Directive and the legislation implementing it in the Netherlands have a more restricted scope than the Cross-border Merger Directive. Firstly, the Merger Tax Directive applies only to EU Member States (i.e. it does not apply to

---

as referring to the merger becoming effective, since the registration of the merger does not necessarily have constitutive effect. It would not be in line with Art. 16 Dir. if the standard rules were (intentionally or otherwise) kept inapplicable by not registering the merger. See also Art. 1:20 EIA which refers to the registration of an SE, which is the moment of formation of the SE (Art. 27(1) SE Regulation).

57 Complexities can arise in the event that the EPS resulting from Art. 2:333k DCC is incompatible with Dutch law; it would be *contra legem* to include such an EPS in the articles of association of a Dutch surviving entity.

58 In practice, this may turn out to be impractical if, for instance, negotiations on the applicability of an EPS are still ongoing at the time the merger proposal is drawn up. As the outcome of Art. 2:333k DCC cannot be predicted with any level of certainty, in practice, the EPS which will apply to the surviving entity pursuant to Art. 2:333k DCC should be determined prior to the depositing of the merger proposal.

59 Council Directive 90/434/EEC of 23 July 1990 on the common system of taxation applicable to mergers, divisions, transfers of assets and exchanges of shares concerning companies of different Member States, as amended by Council Directive 2005/19/EC of 17 February 2005 (the 'Merger Tax Directive').

Liechtenstein, Norway and Iceland, which are members of the EEA but not the EU). Secondly, the merging entities must be resident in an EU Member State for tax purposes and be subject to a profit tax there that is explicitly mentioned in the Merger Tax Directive. Thirdly, they must not be considered as resident in a non-EU Member State pursuant to an applicable tax treaty. Therefore, for instance, a Dutch entity that has its place of effective management in the Netherlands Antilles and is the disappearing entity in a merger with a French entity cannot benefit from the rollover provisions.

1   Taxation at the level of the merging entities

86.   For Dutch corporate income tax purposes, upon a merger involving a Dutch disappearing entity, the Dutch entity will be considered to have sold all of its assets and liabilities at fair market value to the surviving entity immediately prior to the merger and, in principle, to have thus realised a taxable capital gain. However, pursuant to rollover rules under the Merger Tax Directive and the legislation implementing it in the Netherlands, the Dutch tax authorities may, at the request of the merging entities, determine that the disappearing entity will not be deemed to have realised a capital gain. In such a case, the surviving entity will not be able to step up the basis of the disappearing entity's assets and liabilities to their fair market value, but will continue with the old tax book-values of the disappearing entity. This treatment is only awarded subject to certain conditions. One condition that is specifically relevant for cross-border mergers is that the rollover facility only applies with respect to assets and liabilities that remain taxable in the Netherlands, i.e. assets and liabilities that constitute a Dutch permanent establishment or are deemed to be a permanent establishment of the surviving entity (e.g. real estate located in the Netherlands). Consequently, if no permanent establishment remains in the Netherlands, a Dutch disappearing entity will be taxed on any capital gains on its assets and liabilities. However, if the only assets are shares (e.g. in the situation where the disappearing entity is a Dutch holding entity and the surviving entity is a subsidiary) any capital gain realised on the shares should generally be exempt from corporate income tax under the Dutch participation exemption.

No dividend withholding tax will be due in the event of a cross-border merger involving a Dutch disappearing entity. Consequently, if the disappearing entity has any deferred liability in respect of Dutch dividend tax, this will not be triggered.

Finally, if the disappearing entity's assets consist of real estate located in the Netherlands, Dutch transfer tax, at a rate of 6 per cent, will, in principle, be payable by the surviving entity. However, in many cases a merger exemption may apply.

Upon a merger involving a Dutch surviving entity, the Dutch entity may acquire a permanent establishment or a deemed permanent establishment in another EU Member State if the disappearing entity has real estate or a business remaining in that Member State. The future profits of such an establishment should be exempt from Dutch corporate income tax pursuant to applicable tax treaties or, as the case may be, unilateral rules. The Dutch entity will generally be allowed to step up the basis of all of the disappearing entity's assets and liabilities to their fair market value for corporate income tax purposes, regardless of whether a permanent establishment remains in the other EU Member State.

For Dutch dividend withholding tax purposes, the paid-up capital on any newly allotted shares pursuant to the merger (see no 28 of this chapter) will only be recognised up to an amount equal to that paid up on the shares in the disappearing entity. Consequently, the merger may effectively create a deferred Dutch dividend tax liability in respect of profit reserves generated outside the Netherlands.

2   Taxation at the level of the shareholders

87.   Upon a merger involving a Dutch disappearing entity, the Dutch entity's shareholders will, in principle, be considered to have sold their shares at fair market value and thus to have realised a capital gain. Depending on the shareholder's tax status (e.g. place of residence, type of shareholding), this gain may, in principle, be subject to Dutch personal or corporate income tax. However, like the disappearing entity itself, its shareholders will generally be able to benefit from rollover provisions. In such an event, a shareholder will not be deemed to have realised a capital gain, but will have its new shares in the surviving entity valued at the tax book-value of its old shares in the disappearing entity. However, the rollover provisions will not apply to shareholders resident outside the Netherlands that:

(i)   hold what is known as a substantial interest in the disappearing entity (a statutorily defined term: generally an interest of 5 per cent or more in a separate class of shares, held alone or together with a partner or other related persons), where the interest in question does not form part of the assets of an enterprise; and

(ii)   are not protected against Dutch capital gains taxation under a tax treaty.

For individuals, the payment of tax in this respect can generally be postponed. The income tax will then be imposed on the basis of a suspended tax assessment and will only become payable if the shares in the surviving entity are disposed of within a period of ten years.

A merger involving a Dutch surviving entity will, in principle, not give rise to any tax implications for the shareholders in that entity, as they will retain the shares they already held. However, since new shares in the capital of the surviving entity can be allotted to the shareholders of the disappearing entity (see no 28 of this chapter), the stake of the existing shareholders in the Dutch surviving entity will be diluted. This dilution may have consequences for the tax status of such an existing shareholder. For instance, if the stake of a corporate shareholder is diluted to below 5 per cent, this may result in the Dutch participation exemption no longer being applicable to the benefits derived by that shareholder from its shareholding.

X   Conclusion

88.   Although the Implementation Act brings certainty to the expanded realm of possibilities for Dutch entities which was implied by the *SEVIC* case, certain provisions of the Implementation Act, as well as provisions of the DCC which have been left unaltered in the implementation process, are ill-considered and give rise to equivocality and incertitude. It is unlikely that this will lead to cross-border merger procedures screeching to a halt or to companies or law firms dismissing a cross-border merger as a viable option altogether, but it will certainly require some mental agility from the individuals advising on the merger to avoid the pitfalls created by careless codification. On a positive note: no cross-border merger, once effected, can ever be declared null or void!

15
Poland

MICHAŁ BARŁOWSKI
Wardynski & Partners

I   Introduction

1.   The Cross-border Merger Directive has been implemented in Poland by
the Act of 25 April 2008. The Act amended the Commercial Companies
Code by introducing a new section on cross-border mergers. To the extent
that the new section does not state otherwise, the provisions on internal
merger of Polish companies stipulated by the Commercial Companies Code
apply.

II   Scope of the new rules

2.   The new rules on cross-border mergers apply to three company types governed by the Commercial Companies Code. These are: limited liability companies, joint-stock companies and joint-stock limited companies (Art. 491 Commercial Companies Code).

In accordance with the Commercial Companies Code, a merger can take place in the following ways:

(i)   one or more companies transfer all their assets and liabilities to another acquiring company, in exchange for the issue of securities or shares representing the capital of that company to their members and, if applicable, a cash payment;

(ii)   two or more companies transfer all their assets and liabilities to a company that they form, in exchange for the issue of securities or shares representing the capital of the new company to their members and, if applicable, a cash payment.

In addition, the result of a cross-border merger with the participation of a joint-stock limited company may only be an association of capital. The surviving company may never be a partnership.

3.   The mechanism of cross-border merger does not apply to a company whose corporate purpose is the collective investment of capital provided by the public, which operates on the principle of risk-spreading and whose units may, at the holder's request, be purchased or redeemed, directly or indirectly, out of the company's assets (Art. 516^2 Commercial Companies Code). An investment fund can be an example of such an entity. Cross-border merger does not apply to any cooperative.

Under provisions of Polish law, companies in liquidation cannot take part in a domestic merger. The assets and liabilities of a company which ceases to exist are transferred on the date of dissolution without liquidation of the disappearing companies. No merger of a company is, however, possible in case of its liquidation or when such company has started distribution of its assets or has been declared insolvent.

III   Cash payment

4.   Merger takes place through a transfer of assets and liabilities of a merging company to a newly formed or an acquiring company, in exchange for the issue of securities or shares representing the capital of that company to its members. Additionally shareholders may be entitled to a cash payment in the amount of 10 per cent of the nominal value or the accounting par value of the shares or securities representing capital of the surviving company. At the same time, the surviving company may issue securities or shares to the shareholders

subject to payment upon subscription applicable to the subscription to new shares issued to shareholders.

IV   Legal consequences and enforceability of a cross-border merger

5.   A cross-border merger results in transfer of all assets and liabilities to the surviving company by operation of law. It has the same legal effects as an internal (domestic) merger, i.e.:

    (i)   the merging companies (with the exception of the surviving company, if no new company is established) cease to exist;

    (ii) the shareholders of the companies which cease to exist become shareholders in the surviving company; and

    (iii) all assets and liabilities, including rights and obligations, are transferred to the surviving company.

All administrative decisions, e.g. licences, permits or reliefs, are also transferred to the surviving company, unless particular provisions of law or the administrative decision itself provide otherwise. The authority that issued the licence or a decision for a financial institution may, however, object to the transfer within a month from publication of the draft cross-border merger terms (Art. 494 Commercial Companies Code).

6.   A cross-border merger is effective as from the date of the court registration. The merger shall be announced a day after the registration in the *Monitor Sądowy i Gospodarczy* (Court and Commercial Gazette) or any other gazette stipulated in the company articles.

7.   Furthermore, any real property and other rights *in rem* assigned to the surviving company must be recorded at the appropriate register.

8.   Rights and obligations resulting from employment contracts and employment relations existing on the date of completion of the cross-border merger are transferred on that date by operation of law to the acquiring company or the new company formed for the purpose of the merger (Art. 23^1 (1) Labour Law Act). Members of the management boards of the merging companies shall inform the employees of the intended changes in their employer's ownership structure.

V   Procedure

1   Draft terms of cross-border merger

9.   The management bodies of the merging companies shall prepare draft cross-border merger terms. This document does not need to be in notarised form (Art. 516^3 Commercial Companies Code).

The draft terms of a cross-border merger must be filed with the commercial court of the judicial district where each merging company's registered office is located. In addition, the draft terms shall be published at least one month prior to the general meeting deciding thereon in the manner prescribed by the articles of association of the merging company. However, each merging company is responsible for fulfilling publication requirements separately; in case more than one Polish company participates, it is possible to file a common publication petition (Art. 500(3) Commercial Companies Code).

2   Management report

10.   The management body of each merging company must prepare a written justification report for the company's shareholders. This report should provide a legal and economic explanation and justification for the merger, explain the implications of the merger for shareholders, creditors and employees, the proposed share-exchange ratio, and describe difficulties encountered in the valuation process (Art. 516^5 Commercial Companies Code).

In the event that employee representatives prepare an opinion on the merger and this opinion is submitted to the management in a timely manner, it must be attached to the management report.

The shareholders and the employee representatives or, in the absence thereof, the employees themselves are entitled to examine the management report at the latest one month before the general meeting called to approve the draft cross-border merger terms. The documents should also be available at the company's registered office at their direct request.

3   Auditor's report

11.   The draft terms of a cross-border merger shall be filed with the commercial court along with a motion to appoint an auditor. The management bodies of the merging companies may jointly file a petition to the court to appoint one or more auditors. In such a case, the petition is filed with a Polish court or with an office competent with respect to the place of residence of the foreign company. The purpose of an audit is to report on the draft terms of cross-border merger.

The above-mentioned report does not need to be prepared if all shareholders of all merging companies in the cross-border merger unanimously decide that no report need be drafted and the draft cross-border merger terms need not be examined by an auditor (Art. 516^6(3) Commercial Companies Code). An auditor's report is also not required in the event of absorption of a wholly owned subsidiary by its parent company (Art 516^{15} Commercial Companies Code).

In its report the auditor should certify whether, in its opinion, the share-exchange ratio is applicable and reasonable (Art. 503(1) Commercial Companies Code). The auditor's report should also at least indicate the methods used to determine the share-exchange ratio and the particular difficulties, if any, encountered in the valuation process. The auditor may request any information deemed necessary from the merging companies in order to prepare the report.

After completing the report, the auditor is responsible for filing it and the draft terms of cross-border merger with an appropriate commercial court as well as the management of each of the merging companies. The auditor's report shall be made available to the shareholders of the merging companies before the general meeting called to approve the draft terms of cross-border merger.

4   General meeting of shareholders

A   Information for shareholders

12.   Considering the significance of the act of expressing approval for a cross-border merger, Polish regulations provide for special general meeting notification rules. The management board should notify shareholders of the intended cross-border merger twice prior to the general meeting called to approve the draft merger terms. A first notification should take place not later than one month before the general meeting. A second notification should be made after an interval of at least two weeks. The notification should indicate the reference number from the *Monitor Sądowy i Gospodarczy* issue where the draft cross-border merger-terms were published as well as the place and time of availability of merger related documents, e.g. the draft cross-border merger terms, balance sheet, management report for the last three years and auditor's report. The documents should be made available to shareholders at least one month before approval of the terms of the merger (Art. 504 Commercial Companies Code). Each shareholder may request a copy of any of the above-mentioned documents free of charge.

The shareholders of the merging companies should also receive an oral presentation of significant elements of the draft cross-border merger terms, management report and the auditor's report directly before approval of the merger by shareholders.

B   Shareholder approval

13.   Finally, the general shareholders' meeting must approve the merger and the draft terms of a cross-border merger. However, shareholder approval is not required for the absorption of a wholly owned subsidiary by its parent company (Art. $516^{15}(3)$ Commercial Companies Code).

The merger must be approved by a special majority of three quarters of the votes. Public company merger requires a majority of two thirds of the votes. In both cases, however, the articles of association may provide for a larger majority (Art. 506(1) Commercial Companies Code). In order to duly approve the cross-border merger, at least 50 per cent of the share capital must be present or represented.

A cross-border merger involving a joint-stock limited company requires approval of all its shareholders.

14.   In the event of the existence of different classes of shares in a joint-stock company, i.e. shares with different voting rights, a resolution granting approval for a cross-border merger should be adopted in separate groups representing each kind of shares. The respective voting majorities apply to each group.

15.   The merger resolution should include approval of the draft cross-border merger terms as well as amendments to the articles of the acquiring company or new articles of the company formed for the purpose of the merger. The general meeting of each Polish merging company must be held before a notary, and the minutes must be prepared in notarised form subject to a clause of nullity (Art. 506 Commercial Companies Code).

Effectiveness of the merger may depend on a resolution of the general shareholders' meeting to approve participation terms for employee representatives in the surviving company (Art. 516^8 Commercial Companies Code).

5   Pre-merger certificate

16.   Shareholder approval is followed by a verification of the cross-border merger at the level of all merging companies. Each Member State is obliged to verify the legality of the cross-border merger as regards the merging companies obeying merger rules imposed by domestic law. The commercial court is the competent authority to carry out such audit actions in Poland. The management board of a Polish merging company shall file a petition to the court for issue of a certificate of conformity with the standards of Polish law (Art. 516^{12}(3) Commercial Companies Code). The court shall issue the certificate without delay and make an appropriate entry in the register.

The described rules apply to Polish companies. Merging companies from other countries are obliged to apply for the certificates to an authority competent according to their domestic regulations.

6   Effects of the decision

17.   The issued certificate of conformity shall be an indispensable component of the cross-border merger procedure, since the authorities of the Member State of the surviving or the newly formed company require this to verify completion of the cross-border merger.

Under Polish regulations, the management board of the surviving company shall notify the commercial court appropriate to the location of the surviving company's registered office about the merger. Respectively, if the merger takes place through transfer of assets and liabilities to a new company, the management board or any other governing body of the merging companies shall notify the commercial court appropriate to the location of the new company's registered office of the merger. The notification should be filed along with a number of attachments, i.e. certificates of competent authorities attesting to the legality of the cross-border merger issued to all merging companies within the last six months, the draft terms of cross-border merger, excerpts from the shareholders' resolution expressing approval for the merger, and an agreement containing employee participation terms, if applicable. The court will in particular examine the documents in terms of acceptance of the draft cross-border merger terms by all of the merging companies equally. If applicable, the employee participation terms will also be subject to verification.

18.   A cross-border merger enters into effect as from registration of completion of the merger on the basis of the pre-merger certificates and other documents evidencing the merger. The court will without delay notify the courts that kept registers of the incorporated or the merged companies about the cross-border merger. As from the effective date of the cross-border merger, it cannot be declared void by a court (Art. 516[17] Commercial Companies Code). The publication of the cross-border merger takes place upon application by the company that is the final effect of the merger.

VI   Minority shareholders' protection

19.   Although approval of a cross-border merger expressed in a resolution adopted by majority vote is binding on the company's minority shareholders, a shareholder of a Polish company may object to the merger. In the event of a cross-border merger through transferring assets and liabilities of a Polish company to an existing foreign company or to a newly formed foreign company, the Polish company shareholder may demand buyback by the company of his shares provided that this objection was recorded in the minutes' of the shareholders' meeting. The written buyback demand should be lodged with the Polish company within ten days from the general shareholders' meeting. The company may acquire securities and shares on own account, the total nominal value of which together with securities and shares hitherto acquired by it, its subsidiary companies or cooperatives, or by other persons acting for it does not exceed 25 per cent of the share capital. Shares or stocks may be bought by the company on the company's or the remaining shareholders' account. Polish joint-stock company participation in the cross-border merger requires stock documents or a certificate of deposit of a public joint-stock company to be attached by the shareholder along with the buyback demand (Art. 516[11] Commercial Companies Code). Under Polish regulations, where a Polish company is the acquiring company no minority shareholders' protection is stipulated as a result of the cross-border merger.

VII   Protection of creditors

20.   Polish law stipulates two groups of protection rules for the merging companies' creditors. The first group allows for protection after the merger, provided

that the Polish company is the surviving one. Creditors of the Polish merging companies whose claims existed prior to the merger are entitled to request their relief within six months from publication of the merger. A request made in a timely manner results in the obligation to administer assets of the merging companies separately until the creditors are paid or their receivables secured. During that time, the said creditors are entitled to repayment of their liabilities from the original debtor, with precedence over creditors of other merging companies. The creditors may also demand that their receivables be secured within six months from publication of the draft cross-border merger terms, so long as they can substantiate that the debt repayment may be impossible after the merger (Arts. 495–6 Commercial Companies Code).

The second group of rules allows for protection of creditors of the Polish company prior to the merger, provided that the foreign company is the surviving one. Creditors of the Polish company may demand that their receivables be secured within a month from publication of the draft cross-border merger terms, so long as they can substantiate that the debt repayment may be impossible after the merger. Any dispute between the company and the creditors on establishment of the security shall be resolved by the court appropriate to the place of residence of the Polish company. The court decision shall be adopted within two months from publication of the draft cross-border merger terms. A commercial court may issue a certificate attesting to the legality of the cross-border merger despite the dispute. Such a solution does not weaken the creditors' protection significantly, but it is vital for stability of the merger. It is possible that the dispute might not be resolved until completion of the merger procedure. In accordance with general succession rules, the surviving company will be competent to establish security over creditors' receivables. In other words, the liabilities that originally belonged to the Polish company will now become the foreign company's responsibility.

VIII   Employee participation

21.   With respect to employee participation, the Cross-border Merger Directive has been implemented in Polish law by the Terms of Employee Participation in a Company Resulting from Cross-border Merger Act, which entered into force on 25 April 2008 (the 'TEP').

1   Employee participation in companies established in Poland and resulting from a cross-border merger

22.   The Commercial Companies Code does not provide for employee rights to sit on the management bodies of surviving companies that are established in Poland. The forms of participation as provided by other laws and regulations concentrate on granting the right of election or appointment of a certain number of members of the supervisory board, the right to recommend a

person for the post of supervisory board member or the right to object to such candidacy.

2   Special negotiating body ('SNB')

23.   Establishing rules of employee participation in the surviving company requires formation of a special negotiating body. The purpose of the SNB is to represent employees in terms of concluding an agreement with the competent management bodies of the merging companies. It should be formed shortly after publication of the draft cross-border merger terms. The merging companies may, however, avoid establishing an SNB by adopting standard employee participation rules that are stipulated in the TEP. In such case, the rules are to be obeyed as from the registration of the company resulting from the merger.

The SNB members are appointed in each merging company's Member State and according to its law. Polish law provides for its own rules. Such members are appointed through an election organised amongst the employees of the merging companies. The merging companies establish the number of members of the body at the beginning of the procedure. The number depends on the total number of employees in the merging companies.

3   Protection of employee representatives

24.   Members of the SNB and of the representative body, or the representatives on the surviving company board, are entitled to certain protection measures while exercising their mandate.

Firstly, this concerns the requirement for trade union consent in case of an employer's attempts to terminate their employment contract. If the employee is not represented by the union, consent is required from a competent labour inspector (Art. 49 TEP).

Secondly, the employer cannot make unilateral amendments to the terms of employment and remuneration to these employees' disadvantage without the trade union's or the labour inspector's consent.

IX   Tax treatment

25.   Cross-border mergers involving a Polish company and a company that is resident in another Member State are tax neutral under Polish income tax law. Income tax neutrality is achieved by implementation of community directives regulating company and tax law treatment of cross-border company reorganisation. This means that mergers do not cause any taxation of yet unrealised gains and apply to both acquiring company and target company shareholders. However, income tax neutrality does not facilitate tax avoidance as income is still taxed but it is postponed until the assets or shares are sold.

Directive 90/434 of 23 July 1990 on the common system of taxation applicable to mergers, divisions, transfers of assets and exchanges of shares concerning companies of different Member States, as amended by Directive 2005/19 of 17 February 2005, hereinafter the 'Merger Tax Directive', which established the income tax neutrality of all types of company reorganisation involving companies of two or more different European Union tax jurisdictions, was implemented in the Polish Corporate Income Tax Act and applied from 1 January 2004.

26.   Under the Polish Corporate Income Tax Act, after implementation of the Merger Tax Directive, there are three major principles of cross-border mergers affecting income tax neutrality.

Firstly, all types of company reorganisation have to be completed for 'valid commercial reasons' such as the restructuring, or reorganisation, of the activities of the companies participating in the operation. Otherwise, it could be assumed that the principal objective of the transaction is tax evasion or tax avoidance.

Secondly, a surplus of the value of assets of a target company is excluded from taxation for an acquiring, or newly formed, company. A surplus above the nominal value of shares allotted to shareholders of a target company is not treated as income for the acquiring company. However, the principle does not apply when an acquiring company holds less than 10 per cent of the initial capital of a target company. In that situation, a surplus of value of assets acquired equivalent to the percentage share in the initial capital of a target company over the costs of acquisition of shares in the target company by an acquiring company determines income for the acquiring company.

Finally, in a merger of companies, the revenue of a shareholder of the target company constituting the nominal value of shares allocated by an acquiring, or newly formed, company is not considered to be taxable revenue. Taxable revenue for those shareholders will occur in the future when there is a transfer against payment of the shares acquired in a cross-border merger.

16
Slovak Republic

MICHAELA JURKOVA
Čechová & Partners

I   Introduction

1.   The Cross-border Merger Directive has been implemented in the Slovak
Republic by the Amendment to the Commercial Code of 27 November 2007,[1]

---

[1] Act of 27 November 2007 No 657/2007 Coll., amending and supplementing Act No 513/1991
Coll. the Commercial Code, as amended, and amending and supplementing Act No 530/2003
Coll. on the commercial registry, as amended, published on 31 November 2007 in No 277/2007
of the Collection of Laws of the Slovak Republic, effective as of 1 January 2008.

which has introduced a new general section into the Commercial Code on cross-border mergers of companies in the territory of the European Economic Area Member States (Art. 69aa Commercial Code), as well as certain special provisions on cross-border mergers of joint-stock companies (public limited liability companies) into the section of the Commercial Code regulating joint-stock companies (Art. 218a to 218lk Commercial Code). The provisions regulating mergers of joint-stock companies shall apply to cross-border mergers of other types of companies as well, unless otherwise stated in the provisions regulating particular legal forms of companies.

2.   If the surviving company (the company resulting from the cross-border merger) is a company with its registered seat in the Slovak Republic, the provisions of Slovak law regulating the establishment and creation of the given legal form of a company or cooperative must be complied with as well.

II   Scope of the new rules

3.   In the Slovak Republic, all types of commercial company established under Slovak law can be involved in cross-border mergers, i.e. general partnership (*verejná obchodná spoločnosť*), limited partnership (*komanditná spoločnosť*), private limited liability company (*spoločnosť s ručením obmedzeným*), joint-stock company (or public limited liability company, *akciová spoločnosť*), as well as the European Company (SE) and the European Cooperative Society (SCE). This results from the fact that the provisions implementing the Cross-border Merger Directive in the legal regulation of joint-stock companies shall apply accordingly to all other legal forms of companies.

4.   Under the Slovak rules concerning domestic mergers, only companies with the same legal form may merge (Art. 69(2) Commercial Code). The only exception is absorption of a (private) limited liability company by a joint-stock company, in which case the merger is allowed (the limited liability company ceases to exist and the joint-stock company is the surviving one).

In cross-border mergers, all companies which cease to exist and the surviving company must have a similar legal form; whether a Slovak participating company and a foreign participating company have a similar legal form will be examined and decided by the registry court. The Commercial Code stipulates that the provision on similar legal form shall not apply if the legal regulations of the Member States, in the territory of which the participating companies have their registered seat, allow merger of different legal forms (Art. 69aa(1)(e) Commercial Code). However, this provision seems not to be applicable if one of the companies participating in the cross-border merger is a Slovak company, as under the Commercial Code the merging companies must have a similar legal form.

5.   Unless expressly stated otherwise, rules described below on cross-border merger apply to both:

   (i)   merger by absorption/acquisition (in Slovak *'zlúčenie'*) when one or more companies are dissolved without liquidation while their assets and liabilities are transferred to another, already existing, company which thus becomes the legal successor of the dissolved companies; and

   (ii) merger by formation of a new company (in Slovak *'splynutie'*) when two or more companies are dissolved without liquidation, while their assets and liabilities are transferred to another, newly established, company which becomes the legal successor of the dissolved companies upon its incorporation.

The process whereby a wholly owned subsidiary is absorbed by its mother company is considered as a merger with certain simplified procedure.

III   Cash payment

6.   Under Slovak law, in domestic mergers, the total amount of cash payment paid to the shareholders of companies participating in the merger (in addition to the delivered shares) must not exceed 10 per cent of the nominal value of shares issued by the surviving company to the shareholders of the participating companies (Art. 218a(1)(b) Commercial Code). There are no special provisions in this respect concerning cross-border mergers; therefore the 10 per cent limit for the cash payment shall apply also to cross-border mergers.

IV   Legal consequences of the merger and enforceability of a cross-border merger

7.   In case of domestic mergers, the merger becomes effective upon its registration with the commercial registry. Upon such registration: (i) the assets of the companies being dissolved are transferred to the surviving company; (ii) the shareholders (members) of the companies being dissolved become shareholders (members) of the surviving company; (iii) the companies being dissolved cease to exist; and (iv) in case of merger by formation of a new company, the new company is created (Art. 69a(1) Commercial Code). The registration of the creation of a new company or the registration of the merger by absorption and deregistration of the dissolved companies from the commercial registry are to be made as on the same date.

8.   In case of cross-border mergers, deregistration of the Slovak dissolved company and registration of the newly created company or registration of the merger with the surviving company shall also be executed as on the same date provided the surviving company will have its seat in the territory of the Slovak Republic. Otherwise, the Slovak dissolved company shall be deregistered from

the commercial registry without delay after a notification of the foreign registry that the cross-border merger has become effective has been received by the
Slovak commercial registry; the registration will be executed as on the date
when the cross-border merger became effective according to the law applicable to the company resulting from the merger.

9.   The cross-border merger that has become effective in compliance with the
above-mentioned cannot be declared null and void (unlike in domestic mergers, where the decision of the general meeting which has approved the merger
can be declared void under standard conditions, as can any other decision of
the general meeting).

10.   The data registered with the commercial registry are effective towards third
parties as of the day of their publication. The content of documents, which
must be published, is effective towards third parties as of the day when the
notice on deposition of such documents into the collection of deeds of the
commercial registry has been published. The aforesaid does not apply if the
registered entity proves that the third party was informed of the registered data
or the content of the documents. The registered entity cannot refer to such data
or content of such documents towards third parties until fifteen days following
the day of their publication, if the third parties prove that they could not have
been aware of such data or documents.

   If there is any discrepancy between the data or documents published and those
registered or deposited with the commercial registry, the registered person cannot object towards third parties the published data or documents. Third parties
may refer to published wording unless the registered entity proves that such third
parties knew of the registered data or deposited documents. Third parties may
always refer to documents or data which have not yet been registered or deposited
with the commercial registry, unless such data or documents become effective
only upon their registration or deposition with the commercial registry.

   In general, all documents must be submitted to the commercial registry in
Slovak, the official language of the Slovak Republic. If there are discrepancies
between the Slovak wording of documents deposited in the collection of deeds
and their wording in another language, third parties may rely on the wording
in the Slovak language. Third parties may refer to the wording in a language
other than Slovak, unless the registered entity proves that the third parties were
aware of the wording in Slovak (Art. 27 Commercial Code).

V   Procedure

1   Draft terms of cross-border merger

11.   Under the rules governing domestic mergers, companies participating in a
merger shall prepare draft terms of merger, which must contain the following
information:

    (i)   business name, registered seat and identification number (if only) of participating companies; in case of merger by formation of a new company also the legal form, business name and registered seat of the company to be created;

   (ii)   shares of shareholders of participating companies in the surviving company, or the amount of contributions of shareholders in the surviving company, as applicable;

  (iii)   draft memorandum of association or memorandum of foundation (foundation agreement) and articles of association of the company to be created by merger;

   (iv)   the date as of which the acts of companies being dissolved shall be considered for accounting purposes as acts of the surviving company;

   (v)   the time as of which the shareholders of companies being dissolved will acquire the right to participate in profits of the surviving company as its shareholders;

  (vi)   members of the statutory body, and the supervisory board if applicable, of the company to be created by the merger, if the surviving company is a limited liability company or a joint-stock company.

Apart from the above, the draft terms of cross-border merger must contain the following information:

    (i)   the likely repercussions of the cross-border merger on employment;

   (ii)   the draft amendment to the articles of association of the Slovak surviving company, if necessary, due to the cross-border merger;

  (iii)   where appropriate, information on the procedures by which arrangements for the involvement of employees in the management of the surviving company shall be determined;

   (iv)   the assets and liabilities that are being transferred to the surviving entity;

   (v)   the date of the financial statements of the participating companies, on the basis of which the terms and conditions of the cross-border merger have been determined.

12.   The draft terms of cross-border merger must be deposited in the collection of deeds of the commercial registry (*'zbierka listín obchodného registra'*) at least thirty days prior to the date when the general meeting that shall decide on the merger shall take place.

13.   In addition, the Slovak participating company must arrange for publication of the following data in the Commercial Bulletin (*'Obchodný vestník'*):

    (i)   the business name, legal form and registered seat of each of the participating companies;

   (ii)   the name of the commercial registry or another similar register where each of the participating companies is registered, and its identification number in such register, if there is one, or another number of registration with a commercial registry or in another register, if the law of the country governing the respective participating company imposes the obligation to be registered with a commercial registry or in another register;

(iii) reference to arrangements adopted for protection of creditors' rights and minority shareholders' rights, mentioning the postal address and website address, if applicable, where the above information can be obtained.

14. Each Slovak participating company must make public the following documents at the address of its registered seat, as well as on its internet page (see under (iii) above), at the latest sixty days before voting on approval of the draft terms of cross-border merger:

(i) information that the company, as a result of the cross-border merger, will move its registered seat outside the territory of the Slovak Republic if the surviving company will have its registered seat outside the territory of the Slovak Republic;

(ii) information in the Slovak language on the legal form of the surviving company, together with reference to particular legal provisions regulating such legal form, if the surviving company will have its registered seat outside the territory of the Slovak Republic;

(iii) financial statements (annual accounts) of all participating companies, or their legal predecessors, if applicable, for the last three years;

(iv) interim financial statements drawn up as at a date not preceding the first day of the third month preceding the date of the draft terms of cross-border merger, if the latest financial statements relate to a financial year which ended more than six months before that date;

(v) the name and surname of the notary who will issue the pre-merger certificate, the address of its office, and other contact details, if applicable.

2   Management report

15. In the case of joint-stock companies, boards of directors of all participating companies must prepare a written report explaining from an economic and legal point of view the merger and the information contained in the draft terms of merger, especially the share-exchange ratio, including any special difficulties which have arisen in determining the share-exchange ratio. In the case of a cross-border merger, the report must, in addition, contain the presumed consequences of the merger for shareholders, creditors and employees of the Slovak participating companies (Art. 218b(1) Commercial Code).

The supervisory board of a Slovak participating company shall examine the planned merger, the draft terms of the merger and the management report, and shall submit its statement to the general meeting (Art. 218b(2) Commercial Code).

16.   In the case of private limited liability companies, the management report is not required if all shareholders waive the right to be provided with the management report in writing, or if their waiver has been recorded in the minutes of the general meeting (Art. 152a(5) Commercial Code).

17.   The board of directors and supervisory board members of the participating companies who have breached their legal duties in preparing and executing the merger are jointly and severally liable for the damage incurred by the shareholders (Art. 218g(1) Commercial Code). An individual member of the management or supervisory board is not liable for the damage if he/she proves that he/she has acted with professional care and in good faith that he/she was acting in the interests of the company. They are not liable for damage incurred by the company as a result of implementation of a resolution of the general meeting, unless such resolution is in conflict with the law or the company's statutes (articles of association). The members of the board of directors cannot be released from their liability by the fact that their actions were approved by the supervisory board (Art. 194(7) Commercial Code).

Any agreements between the company and a member of its board which limit or exclude the latter's liability are forbidden. The articles of association cannot exclude or limit the liability of the board members. The company may waive its right to damages or conclude a settlement agreement only after three years from when the damage occurred, and only upon the approval of the general meeting, while no contesting opinion of shareholders holding at least 5 per cent of the registered capital has been recorded in the minutes of the general meeting.

3   Independent expert's report

18.   Draft terms of merger must be examined for each of the merging companies by an independent expert, independent from the company and appointed by the court upon the proposal of the board of directors. Based on a proposal made by all participating companies, the court may appoint one or more common experts for all companies (Art. 218a(2) Commercial Code).

The expert shall draw up a report, which shall contain in particular the following:

(i)   the expert's statement whether the share-exchange ratio and the cash payments, if applicable, are appropriate;
(ii)   an indication of the method or methods used to determine the share exchange ratio;
(iii) statement whether the methods used are adequate for the case at hand, and an indication of the share-exchange ratios using each of the methods and of the importance given to each of the methods in determining the share-exchange ratio proposal;
(iv)   any special valuation difficulties which have arisen (Art. 218a(3) Commercial Code).

Each of the appointed independent experts has the right to be provided with all information and documents from all participating companies which are necessary for preparation of the report, and to execute any necessary control in such companies (Art. 218a(4) Commercial Code).

In the case of merger of joint-stock companies, the expert's report is not required if this is agreed by all shareholders of all participating companies (Art. 218a(5) Commercial Code).

In the case of merger of private limited liability companies, the expert's report is required only if it is requested by any of the shareholders of any of the participating companies (Art. 152a(6) Commercial Code).

19.   The independent experts of each of the participating companies are liable for damage incurred by the shareholders due to the breach by the experts of their duties. They may be released of their liability under the same conditions as the board of directors or supervisory board members (Art. 218g(2) Commercial Code).

4   General meeting of shareholders

20.   Draft terms of cross-border merger must be approved by all shareholders of those participating companies which do not create mandatory registered capital (general partnership, limited partnership). In the case of companies which do create mandatory registered capital (private limited liability company, joint-stock company), the draft terms of cross-border merger must be approved by two thirds of shareholders present at the general meeting approving the terms, unless stricter conditions are stipulated by law, the foundation agreement or the articles of association of the company (Art. 69aa(6) Commercial Code). If more types of shares have been issued by the company, the two-thirds majority of each type of shares is required (Art. 218c(1) Commercial Code).

21.   In the case of a joint-stock company, the general meeting's decision must be executed in the form of a notarised instrument (Art. 218c(1) Commercial Code).

22.   The general meeting of a Slovak participating company may reserve the right to make implementation of the cross-border merger conditional on express ratification by it of the arrangements decided on with respect to the participation of employees in the company resulting from the cross-border merger; in such a case the notary may issue the pre-merger certificate (see no 27 of this chapter) only after such ratification has been made (Art. 218c(1) Commercial Code).

23.   If the memorandum of association of a private limited liability company being dissolved by the merger allows for a transfer of its business share to a third party, and the memorandum of association of the surviving private limited liability company does not allow for such transfer, all shareholders of the company being dissolved must approve the draft terms of the merger (i.e. the two-thirds majority does not apply – Art. 152a(3) Commercial Code).

24.   The following documents must be made available at the seat of the company to the shareholders and the employees' representatives of a Slovak company participating in a cross-border merger at least thirty days before the general meeting that shall decide on the merger takes place:

    (i)   draft terms of cross-border merger;
    (ii)   financial statements and annual reports of all participating companies (or their legal predecessors) for the last three years;
    (iii)   interim financial statements drawn up as at a date not preceding the first day of the third month preceding the date of the draft terms of cross-border merger, if the latest financial statements relate to a financial year which ended more than six months before that date; the interim financial statements must be prepared using the same methods as the latest regular financial statements;
    (iv)   management reports for all participating companies;
    (v)   independent expert's reports for all participating companies, or the common experts' report (Art. 218c(2) Commercial Code).

    Each shareholder has the right to request that the documents be sent to him, and the company must provide such documents for free. This right of the shareholders must be mentioned in the invitation to the general meeting. In the case of cross-border merger, the board of directors must arrange for the translation of the documents concerning the foreign participating companies into Slovak (Art. 218c(4) Commercial Code).

25.   In the case of private limited liability companies, the above-mentioned documents must be sent to the shareholders together with the invitation to the general meeting, and therefore, need not be made available to the shareholders in the seat of the company.

26.   If the merger requires changes to be made in the articles of association or memorandum of association of the surviving company, such changes must either be included in the draft terms of merger, or approved by the general meeting together with the draft terms of merger. Such changes are subject to the same voting rules as the approval of the draft terms of merger (Art. 218c(5) Commercial Code).

    In domestic mergers, the draft terms of merger must, after they have been approved by the general meetings of shareholders, be executed by the statutory bodies of the merging companies as a merger agreement in the form of a notarised instrument. Since there are no specific provisions in this respect applicable to cross-border mergers, it can be concluded that the merger agreement in the form of a notarised instrument must be executed also in the case of a cross-border merger.

5   Pre-merger certificate

27.   Fulfilment of conditions stipulated for cross-border merger shall be examined and certified, before the registration of the merger with the commercial

registry, for a Slovak participating company by a notary who will issue a certificate in the form of a notarised instrument.

The notary may issue the certificate if the proceedings initiated by the creditors (see no 45 of this chapter) have been duly terminated, or if the draft terms of cross-border merger contain an agreement on jurisdiction and governing law under which the creditors of the Slovak participating company may claim their rights against the surviving company before Slovak courts and under Slovak law.

If there are any ongoing proceedings initiated by the creditors, the notary shall state this in the certificate. The jurisdiction of Slovak courts in such proceedings remains even after the cross-border merger becomes effective and even if the surviving company has its seat outside Slovakia.

6   Effects of the decision

28.   The deregistration of a Slovak dissolved company and registration of a newly created company or registration of the merger with the commercial registry shall be executed as on the same date if the surviving company will have its seat in the Slovak Republic. Otherwise, the deregistration of the Slovak dissolved company from the commercial registry will be executed without delay after the receipt by the Slovak commercial registry of the notification of the foreign registry where the surviving company is registered that the cross-border merger has become effective; the deregistration will be executed as on the date when the cross-border merger became effective.

The cross-border merger which has become effective cannot be avoided.

29.   Before registering the company created upon the cross-border merger by formation of a new company, or before registration of changes related to the company resulting from the cross-border merger, with the commercial registry, the registry court shall, among others, examine the following:

   (i)   whether the participating companies and the surviving company have a similar legal form (unless certain exceptions stipulated by special laws apply);
   (ii)   whether the participating companies have approved the draft terms of cross-border merger in the same wording;
   (iii) whether all Slovak participating companies have complied with legal requirements for cross-border merger, the fulfilment of which shall be proved by submission of the certificate issued by the notary (pre-merger certificate);
   (iv)   whether all foreign participating companies have complied with requirements for cross-border merger stipulated by legal regulations of the Member State of their seat, which shall be proved by submission of a certificate or another public document issued in accordance with laws of the respective Member State;

(v) whether the agreement on employee participation in management of the company, if required, was concluded in accordance with law (Art. 7(16) Act on Commercial Registry).

30. If the above conditions are met, the registry court shall make the registration of the cross-border merger within thirty days following the submission of the application. If the application contains the date as on which the registration shall be made, the registry court will make the registration as on such date. If the registry court performs the registration later, or if the application does not contain the date as on which the registration shall be made, the registry court will make the registration as on the date following the day of registration (Art. 8(1) Act on Commercial Registry).

31. In the case of a cross-border merger where the surviving company has its registered seat in the Slovak Republic, the registry court will notify without delay the foreign commercial or other similar registries in which each of the participating companies had to deposit the documents, that the cross-border merger has become effective (Art. 10(5) Act on Commercial Registry).

32. After registration of the merger with the commercial registry, the board of directors of the company resulting from the merger shall arrange without delay for the exchange of the shares in the surviving company for the shares in the dissolved companies or payment of the cash payment (Art. 218e(1) Commercial Code).

No shares in the company resulting from the merger may be issued for the shares held by: (i) the company resulting from the merger or a person acting on the account of the company resulting from the merger; or (ii) the company being dissolved or a person acting on the account of the company being dissolved (Art. 218e(2) Commercial Code).

VI Minority shareholders

33. Those minority shareholders who voted against the draft terms of cross-border merger or were against the share-exchange ratio or amount of cash payment are protected in principle in the same way as the minority shareholders in domestic mergers (Art. 69aa(6) Commercial Code).

1 Adequate cash payment

34. If the share-exchange ratio or cash payments, if applicable, as determined by the draft terms of cross-border merger are not adequate, each shareholder who (i) was a shareholder of any of the Slovak participating companies at the time when the general meeting deciding on the merger took place; (ii) was present at such general meeting; (iii) requested its disapproval of the share-exchange ratio and/or cash payments, if applicable, to be recorded in the

general meeting minutes, has the right against the Slovak participating company to be paid an adequate cash payment. The shareholders must be informed of this right in the general meeting invitation (Art. 218ja(1) Commercial Code).

The above right is subject to two additional conditions: (i) the respective shareholder has not sold any of its shares held in a company being dissolved or in a surviving company before submitting the petition to the court; and (ii) the respective shareholder has not waived its right to adequate cash payment (Art. 218i(2) (d) and (e) Commercial Code). Each shareholder may waive its right to cash payment either in a written document delivered to the company, or at the general meeting by recording its waiver in the general meeting minutes. Such waiver is then effective also towards any subsequent transferee of the respective shares (Art. 218i(3) Commercial Code).

The petition asking the court to resolve that the share-exchange ratio or cash payment have not been adequate must be submitted to the court within one year after the registration of the merger with the commercial registry, otherwise such right ceases to exist (Art. 218i(4) Commercial Code).

35.   The Slovak participating company shall send to the shareholder (who has objected to the share-exchange ratio and/or the cash payment) a proposal for an agreement determining a new share-exchange ratio or an exchange ratio with additional cash payment, within thirty days following the general meeting which has approved the cross-border merger (Art. 218i(5) in conjunction with Art. 218ja(2) Commercial Code).

Such proposal must contain, among others, the value of individual shares to be exchanged and the period for accepting the proposal, not being less than fourteen days following the receipt of the proposal by the shareholder (Art. 218i(6) Commercial Code). If the shareholder does not submit the petition to the court to examine such proposal within the period given for acceptance of the proposal, such proposal is deemed accepted by the shareholder. The competent court is the one having jurisdiction over the respective Slovak participating company (Art. 218i(7) Commercial Code).

36.   If the shareholder does not agree with the amount of the cash payment suggested in the proposal by the company, the definitive cash payment will be determined in the court proceedings using, if necessary, the relevant experts, the costs of which will be paid in advance by the respective Slovak participating company. The court shall determine the expert from the list of experts (maintained by the courts under special legal regulations).[2] The value of the cash payment will be determined as the difference between the value of shares of the respective participating company and the value of shares of the company resulting from the merger (Art. 218i(8) Commercial Code).

---

2 Act No 382/2004 Coll. on experts, interpreters and translators, as amended.

37.   The adequate cash payment must not be lower than (i) the value of the cash payment provided to any other shareholder for the same share; and, at the same, time must not be lower than (ii) the difference between the value of shares of the participating company and the value of shares of the company resulting from the merger, while the value of shares cannot be lower than the value of the net equity capital attributable to one share according to the latest financial statements; and, at the same time, the value of shares of the participating companies whose shares are traded on a regulated market cannot be lower than the average share price of those shares at the stock exchange attained during the twelve months preceding the submission of the draft terms of merger to the collection of deeds of the commercial registry (Art. 218i(9) Commercial Code).

38.   The court's judgment giving the right to a shareholder to adequate cash payment is binding upon the respective Slovak participating company also with respect to all other shareholders, and the respective Slovak participating company must pay the same cash payment to all other shareholders (Art. 218i(11) Commercial Code).

        In case the share-exchange ratio has not been adequate, the shareholders are not obliged to return the shares received; however, this is without prejudice to the provisions on unjustified enrichment and liability for damage (Art. 218i(12) Commercial Code).

39.   The notary shall not issue the pre-merger certificate if the Slovak participating company has not sent a new proposal with a new share-exchange ratio or with a cash payment, in compliance with the above-outlined provisions. The notary may issue the certificate only if all court proceedings initiated in this respect have been terminated, or if the draft terms of cross-border merger contain an agreement on governing law and jurisdiction, under which the shareholders of the Slovak participating companies may claim their rights (to have the share-exchange ratio and cash payment examined by the court) against the company resulting from merger under Slovak law and before Slovak courts, and a consent of all participating companies to such additional settlement. In the latter case, the notary's certificate must contain the information on such pending proceedings (Art. 218ja(3) Commercial Code).

        The Commercial Code imposes on the shareholders and the Slovak participating company the duty to provide due cooperation to the notary in issuing the certificate (Art. 218ja(4) Commercial Code).

2   Repurchase of shares

40.   Each shareholder of a Slovak participating company who (i) was a shareholder of any of the Slovak participating companies at the time when the general meeting deciding on the merger took place; (ii) was present at such general meeting; and (iii) requested its disapproval of the share-exchange ratio and/or

cash payments, if applicable, to be recorded in the general meeting minutes, together with its request to be sent an offer for repurchase of its shares, has the right to have its shares purchased by the Slovak participating company for an adequate consideration. The shareholders must be informed of this right in the general meeting invitation (Art. 218jb(1) Commercial Code).

41.   The respective Slovak participating company must send to the shareholder a proposal for a purchase agreement within thirty days following the date of the general meeting which has approved the merger (Art. 218j(2) in conjunction with 218jb(2) Commercial Code).

   The proposal for a purchase agreement must contain, apart from the other prerequisites stipulated by a special law, the following: (i) the offered consideration which must be adequate; (ii) the time for accepting the proposal, not being less than fourteen days; (iii) the procedure for repurchase of shares; and (iv) an ownership reservation clause (Art. 218j(3) Commercial Code).

42.   The amount of adequate consideration must be the same for all shares, while the adequate consideration cannot be lower than: (i) the highest consideration provided to individual shareholders for the same share; (ii) the value of the net equity capital, including the value of intangible property of the company attributable to one share, determined according to the latest financial statements prepared prior to the elaboration of the draft terms of the merger; (iii) the average price of shares of those companies participating in the merger whose shares are traded on a regulated market, attained on a stock exchange during the twelve months preceding submission of the draft terms of merger to the collection of deeds of the commercial registry (Art. 218j(4) Commercial Code).

   If the entitled shareholder does not submit to the court a petition requesting examination of the proposal by the court, within the period given for acceptance of the proposal, the proposal shall be deemed accepted. In case of court proceedings, the court competent according to the seat of the respective Slovak participating company shall have jurisdiction (Art. 218j(5) Commercial Code).

43.   If the entitled shareholder does not agree with the proposed consideration, or if the consideration is not adequate, the shareholder can request the court to examine the consideration within one year after the registration of the merger with the commercial registry, otherwise its right ceases to exist (Art. 218i(4) in conjunction with Art. 218j(6) Commercial Code). In the proceedings, the court may appoint an expert to determine the adequate consideration. The court's judgment is effective towards all other shareholders (Art. 218i(11) in conjunction with 218j(6) Commercial Code).

44.   Again, the notary shall not issue the pre-merger certificate if the company has not sent to shareholders (who so requested) the proposal for purchase of shares within thirty days following the general meeting which has approved the merger. The notary may issue the certificate only if all court proceedings

initiated in this respect have been terminated, or if the draft terms of cross-border merger contain an agreement on governing law and jurisdiction, under which the shareholders of the Slovak participating company may claim their rights (for an adequate consideration) against the company resulting from the merger, under Slovak law and before Slovak courts, and the consent of all participating companies to such additional settlement. In the latter case, the notary's certificate must contain the information on any ongoing proceedings (Art. 218jb(3) Commercial Code).

VII   Protection of creditors

45.   Creditors of the Slovak participating company who have undue receivables against the company as on the date when the draft terms of cross-border merger have been approved may request that their receivables be secured in an appropriate manner. If the creditors do not come to an agreement with the Slovak participating company as to the appropriate security, it shall be determined by court. The security shall be considered appropriate if the cash in the amount of the due receivables has been deposited with the notary (Art. 69aa(5) Commercial Code).

46.   The owners of exchangeable or priority bonds, or other securities with special rights issued by the companies being dissolved, must obtain against the surviving company the rights equivalent to those which they had towards the companies being dissolved. This does not apply if all such owners agreed to the change of their rights or if the surviving company has the obligation to purchase those securities from them (Art. 218f(2) Commercial Code).

VIII   Employee participation

1   Employee participation in companies established in Slovakia resulting from a cross-border merger

47.   If, in a cross-border merger, the company resulting from the merger has its seat in the Slovak Republic, the employees of the company have the right to participate in its management under the conditions stipulated in Article 200 of the Commercial Code, applicable to joint-stock companies.

48.   Article 200 of the Commercial Code provides for the rules under which the employees' representatives become members of the supervisory board of a Slovak joint-stock company. The supervisory board is a mandatory supervising and controlling body of a Slovak joint-stock company. It must have at least three members, natural persons, appointed for the term stipulated in the articles of association, but not exceeding five years.

Under Article 200 of the Commercial Code, two thirds of the members of the supervisory board shall be elected and dismissed by the general meeting and one third by the company's employees, provided the company has more than fifty employees at the time of the election. The articles of association of the company may provide for a higher number of members to be elected by the employees, which however cannot exceed the number of members elected by the general meeting. The articles of association may stipulate that the employees are entitled to elect a certain number of supervisory board members even if the company does not have more than fifty employees.

The elections of the supervisory board members by the employees shall be organised by the board of directors in cooperation with the labour unions, or, if no labour unions exist, in cooperation with the employees entitled to elect the supervisory board members ('entitled electors'). The rules for election shall be prepared and approved by the labour unions, or by the board of directors in cooperation with the entitled electors if the labour unions do not exist in the company. Any proposal for election or dismissal of a supervisory board member can be submitted to the board of directors either by the labour unions or by at least 10 per cent of entitled electors. For the effective election or dismissal, the decision must be adopted by at least half of the entitled electors or their representatives.

49.   The above provisions will not apply to a cross-border merger if:

(i)   at least one of the participating companies has more than 500 employees six months before submission of the required documents to the collection of deeds in connection with the cross-border merger and the employee participation in this company is arranged in accordance with a special law; or

(ii)   the participation under Article 200 of the Commercial Code is smaller than that which existed in any of the participating companies, while the extent of participation is determined by the number of employee representatives in the companies' bodies; or

(iii)   employees of the branches of the company resulting from the merger, located in other Member States, do not have the same right of participation as the employees of the company resulting from the merger located in Slovakia (Art. 218la(2) Commercial Code).

In the above cases, the merger can be registered with the commercial registry only if the agreement on employees' participation has been concluded, or if the special negotiating body (see no 50 *et seq.* of this chapter) has adopted a resolution not to start or not to continue negotiations on employee participation, or if the period stipulated for negotiations has lapsed in vain (Art. 218la(3) Commercial Code).

2   Special negotiating body ('SNB')

50.   Employee participation in the company after merger shall be determined in a written agreement resulting from negotiations between the special negotiating

body formed of employees' representatives of participating companies and their branches, and the statutory bodies of the participating companies. The statutory bodies may unanimously decide, without entering into negotiations with the SNB, that the standard rules (see no 60 of this chapter) will apply to employee participation.

51.   The statutory body of each participating company must, without undue delay after publication of the draft terms of cross-border merger, take measures necessary to start negotiations with the employees' representatives of participating companies and their branches, on future employees' participation, and to provide the employees' representatives, or all employees, as applicable, with information on the seat and legal form of all participating companies and their branches, on the total number of employees as at the date of publication of the draft terms of cross-border merger, on the number of employees having the right to influence the composition of participating companies' bodies and on the manner and scope of such influence (Art. 218lb Commercial Code).

52.   The number of SNB members shall be determined so that each 10 per cent of employees of participating companies and their branches employed in one Member State, out of the total of all employees of participating companies and their branches in all Member States, will be represented by one member of the SNB for the respective Member State; the number of employees as at the date of publication of the draft terms of cross-border merger shall be decisive (Art. 218lc(1) Commercial Code).

The total number of SNB members shall then be adjusted so that the employees of each participating company being dissolved are represented by at least one member. The total number of SNB members in such case, however, shall not be increased by more than 20 per cent.

53.   The employees from the Slovak Republic can be represented in the SNB also by a natural person who is not an employee of a Slovak participating company or its branch, if such person is empowered by the employees' representatives.

Members of the SNB representing the employees of the Slovak participating companies are elected according to the rules stipulated by a special law (regulating appointment of members into a special negotiating body in connection with formation of a European works council),[3] notwithstanding in which Member State the company resulting from the merger will have its seat. The members representing employees from other Member States will be elected in accordance with the respective Member State law.

It must be evident from the allocation of the places in the SNB how many employees each member represents. Each appointed member of the SNB must notify the SNB without delay after his appointment how many employees he represents, from which Member State and which participating companies.

---

3   Art. 244 of Act No 311/2001 Coll. the Labour Code, as amended.

54.   The companies participating in the cross-border merger must ensure sufficient funds for the SNB and its members for their activity (including travel and accommodation costs, translations and interpretation, fees of external advisers, etc.), as well as material and organisational resources. The SNB members have the right to be compensated for costs incurred efficiently for their activity; however, they are not entitled to a remuneration. The SNB may invite professional advisers for the negotiations; the participating companies, however, must cover the costs only for one expert per area (presumably, each sector of advice).

55.   The SNB adopts its decisions by a majority of votes of all its members representing the majority of employees of all participating companies, each SNB member having one vote.

56.   Any agreement on employee participation which would lead to reduction in participation must be approved by at least a two-thirds majority of votes of all SNB members representing a two-thirds majority of all employees of all participating companies, from at least two Member States. This shall not apply in case less than one third of all employees of all participating companies have the right to elect members of the companies' bodies.

    The SNB may decide not to start negotiations, or to terminate negotiations. In such a case, the rules applicable to employee participation in the Member State where the surviving company has its seat will apply.

57.   The surviving company's employees have the right of participation under the terms and conditions stipulated by law and the articles of association of the company. The articles of association must be in compliance with the agreement on employee participation concluded between the SNB and the statutory bodies of all participating companies. In the case of any discrepancies between such an agreement and the articles of association, the board of directors of the surviving company must amend the articles of association in compliance with the agreement.

58.   The agreement on employee participation must contain, especially, the following information:

    (i)   the scope of application of the agreement;
    (ii) the manner and scope of employee participation in the management of the company, especially the number of supervisory board members to be elected by the employees or employee representatives, and the manner in which this right is to be executed;
    (iii) the date when the agreement becomes effective and its term;
    (iv) cases when new negotiations must be initiated and the respective procedure.

Unless mentioned otherwise in the agreement, the standard rules for employee participation, as mentioned below, do not apply to the agreement.

59.   The negotiations on employee participation start on the day of appointment of
        the SNB and shall not take more than six months. The SNB and the statutory
        bodies may agree to extend the period to up to one year.

60.   The standard rules of employee participation shall apply to the employees of
        the surviving company having its seat in the territory of the Slovak Republic,
        provided (i) it is stipulated in the agreement on employee participation, or
        (ii) the statutory representatives of participating companies have decided to
        apply the standard rules without entering into negotiations with an SNB, or
        (iii) the negotiating parties do not enter into agreement on employee participa-
        tion within six months (or within one year, as applicable).

        The standard rules shall not apply if employee participation in manage-
        ment existed before the cross-border merger only in the participating com-
        panies employing less than one third of the total number of employees of all
        participating companies.

        Under the standard rules, employees have the right of participation to
        the extent corresponding to the most favourable extent in any of the merging
        companies. If the employees of any of the participating companies did not
        have that right, none of the surviving companies will be entitled to partici-
        pation unless stated otherwise in the articles of association of the surviving
        company.

61.   If employee participation is governed by Slovak law, a special body, the
        employees' committee, shall decide on allocation of places in the supervisory
        board among the employees' representatives from different Member States, as
        well as on the procedure as to how the employees of the surviving company
        may recommend or object to the appointment of supervisory board members.
        The employees' committee consists of employees or employees' representa-
        tives, while the rules regulating composition of the SNB shall apply to the
        composition of the employees' committee.

62.   The SNB members, their professional advisers, employees' committee mem-
        bers, employees' representatives and the employees must keep confidential
        all information they learn in connection with the negotiations which was
        indicated as confidential. This applies also after the termination of their
        function.

        The supervisory board may refuse to provide information if its provi-
        sion, according to objective criteria, would jeopardise the operation of the
        surviving company or its subsidiary, or it may identify certain informa-
        tion as confidential. The SNB or the employees' committee may request
        the court to determine that the information was identified as confidential
        without appropriate grounds; this applies to Slovak participating companies
        even if the surviving company will have its seat in the territory of another
        Member State. The SNB and the employees' committee have the capac-
        ity to become participants in the court proceedings for this purpose, even

if the surviving company has its seat in another Member State, providing the respective organisation unit has its seat in the territory of the Slovak Republic.

3   Protection of employee representatives

63.   The SNB members, members of the employees' committee and the employees' representatives in the supervisory board who are employed by participating companies or their branches and who are employed in the territory of the Slovak Republic have the right to the same protection and guarantees in performance of their function as are applicable to the employees' representatives in the Slovak Republic. The employees employed in the territory of other Member States are subject to the protection and guarantees provided by the laws of the respective Member States (Art. 218lj(1) Commercial Code).

The protection of the employees' representatives relates especially to their presence at the meetings of the SNB, employees' committee and supervisory board. The SNB members and employees' committee members have the right to protection against discrimination and to work leave with salary compensation in the amount determined by the Labour Code. The work leave and the salary compensation shall be provided by the Slovak participating company, even if the company resulting from the merger will have its registered seat in another Member State.

IX   Tax treatment

64.   The Slovak Republic has implemented the provisions of the Merger Tax Directive in Act No 595/2003 Coll. on income tax (the 'Income Tax Act'), effective as of 1 January 2004.

Under the Income Tax Act, the income resulting from acquisition of new shares or from exchange of shares when a company is dissolved without liquidation is not subject to income tax, even if the merger also includes the assets of a company which has its seat in another Member State of the European Union (Arts. 3 and 12 Income Tax Act).

In case of dissolution without liquidation of a company with double-entry book-keeping, the tax base shall be adjusted, as on the day of dissolution, with reserves and adjusting entries, including the adjusting entry to assets acquired for consideration, future receipts, proceeds, expenses and costs, except for those items which are taken over by the legal successor of the dissolved company if they relate to rights and obligations of the company which has its seat or place of real administration[4] in the Slovak Republic. The same procedure

---

4 The place of real administration is defined as the place where the managing and business decisions of statutory and supervisory bodies are taken, even if the address of the place is not registered with the commercial registry.

shall apply in case of merger or division of a company or cooperative if it also covers assets of a company or cooperative which has its seat in a European Union Member State. If the legal successor has its seat in the European Union Member State, the adjustment described above shall not apply if the rights and obligations which are taken over by the legal successor relate to assets belonging to a permanent establishment located in the territory of the Slovak Republic (Art 17(13) Income Tax Act).

17

United Kingdom

IAN SNAITH

University of Leicester and Cobbetts LLP

I   Introduction

1.   The Cross-border Merger Directive has been implemented in the United Kingdom by the Companies (Cross-border Mergers) Regulations 2007.[1] These regulations are made by the Secretary of State for Business Enterprise and Regulatory Reform using powers conferred by section 2(2) of the European

---

1 SI 2007/2974.

Communities Act 1972 and sections 1102(2), 1105(2)(d) and 1106(2) of the Companies Act 2006. The Regulations amend the Employment Rights Act 1996, the Employment Act 2002, the Employment Tribunals Act 1996, the Insolvency Act 1986 and the Insolvency (Northern Ireland) Order 1989, and apply various provisions of the Companies Act 2006 in order to implement the Directive. The regulations came into force on 15 December 2007 and contain, in regulation 4(6) and Schedule 1, transitional provisions to deal with those sections of the Companies Act 2006 which had not yet come into force on that date. In this report it is assumed that the Companies Act 2006 is fully in force.

II   Scope of the new rules

2. The new rules on cross-border mergers apply to mergers involving a 'UK Company' or an unregistered company (regulations 2 and 5 of SI 2007/2974).

3. A 'UK Company' is one meeting the definition of a company in section 1 of the Companies Act 2006, other than a company limited by guarantee which has no share capital. This includes a company formed and registered under the Companies Act 2006, one formed and registered under the Companies Act 1985 or under the Companies (Northern Ireland) Order 1986, or one formed and registered under pre-1985 legislation which falls within the definition of an existing company in the Companies Act 1985 or the Companies (Northern Ireland) Order 1986 (regulation 3 of SI 2007/2974 and section 1 of Companies Act 2006). Since 22 December 1980 in Great Britain and 1 July 1983 in Northern Ireland, it has been impossible for a company to be formed as, or to become, a company limited by guarantee with a share capital, so all companies limited by guarantee formed after those dates and those formed earlier which do not have share capital are excluded from the Regulations (section 5 Companies Act 2006 and regulation 3 of SI 2007/2974). This applies the cross-border merger rules to all companies limited by shares – including unlimited companies. They do not, however, apply to partnerships created under the Partnerships Act 1890, limited liability partnerships registered under the Limited Liability Partnerships Act 2000, or limited partnerships registered under the Limited Partnerships Act 1907.

4. The regulations apply to unregistered companies as they apply to UK companies (regulation 5 of SI 2007/2974). An 'unregistered company' is a body to which section 1043 of the Companies Act 2006 applies. That includes corporate bodies incorporated in the UK with their principal place of business there apart from those incorporated under other public general Acts of Parliament; those formed for a purpose other than carrying on a business with the object of profit for the body or its members; and open-ended investment companies (section 1043(1) of Companies Act 2006). Essentially this will include corporate

bodies established by royal charter or private Act of Parliament which operate a business to make a profit.

5. Cooperative societies registered under the Industrial and Provident Societies Acts 1965 to 2003 or registered as companies limited by guarantee without share capital are excluded by these definitions but a cooperative society registered as a company limited by shares would come within the scope of the UK cross-border merger rules.

6. Open-ended investment companies are excluded from the application of the cross-border merger rules by this definition as they are incorporated under regulation 3 of the Open Ended Investment Company Regulations 2001 SI 2001/1228 and not under the Companies Act 2006 or earlier company legislation. Such companies are permitted, in accordance with those Regulations and subject to the regulatory powers of the Financial Services Authority conferred by the Financial Services and Markets Act 2000, to buy back their own shares in ways that other companies cannot so that participants can redeem all or part of their shareholding in the collective investment scheme operated through the company.

7. UK companies in liquidation cannot take part in a cross-border merger (reg. 3(1) of SI 2007/2974). Although, unlike the Domestic Merger Directive (Arts. 3(2) and 4(2)), the Cross-border Merger Directive does not provide that the Member States can exclude companies in liquidation, the UK excludes a company in liquidation from participation in a purely domestic merger in accordance with the provisions of national law implementing the Merger Directive (section 902(3) Companies Act 2006). A company subject to the corporate rescue administration procedure under the Insolvency Act 1986 as amended by the Enterprise Act 2002 is not excluded from participating in a cross-border merger and, indeed, SI 2007/2974 amends paragraphs 73 and 74 of Schedule B1 of the Insolvency Act 1986 and the Northern Ireland equivalent to facilitate a proposal for a cross-border merger in the case of a UK company subject to the administration procedure (regulations 65 and 66 of SI 2007/2974).

III   Cash payment

8. A cross-border merger is possible even if the cash payment exceeds 10 per cent of the nominal value or, in the absence thereof, the accounting par value of the securities or shares representing capital of the surviving company, provided the law of the Member State of one of the participating companies so allows (Art. 3(1) Dir.). Under UK law, mergers involving a cash payment exceeding the 10 per cent limit can benefit from the rules applicable to cross-border mergers, as the consideration for a transfer in the case of either a merger by the formation of a new company or a merger by absorption (other than of a wholly

owned subsidiary) can be, 'if so agreed, a cash payment' (regulations 2(1)(f)(ii) and 2(4)(c)(ii) of SI 2007/2974).

IV   Legal consequences and enforceability of a cross-border merger

9.   A cross-border merger results in all assets and liabilities being transferred to the surviving entity ('the transferee company') by operation of law, without liquidation of the transferor companies. The legal effects are that:

    (i)   the transferor companies are dissolved;

    (ii)   the shareholders (other than the transferee company itself) of the companies which are dissolved become shareholders in the transferee company – except in the case of a merger by absorption of a wholly owned subsidiary; and

    (iii) all assets and liabilities, including rights and obligations arising from contracts of employment, of the transferor companies are transferred to the transferee company (regulation 17(1) of SI 2007/2974).

10.   After the consequences of the cross-border merger have taken effect, the order of the UK court which approved the completion of the merger for the purposes of Article 11 of the Cross-border Merger Directive is conclusive evidence both that the conditions necessary for the order to be made have been satisfied and that all the pre-merger requirements of SI 2007/2974 have been complied with (regulation 16(3) of SI 2007/2974).

11.   In the case of a UK transferee company the consequences of a cross-border merger take effect on the date fixed by the order of the UK court that has scrutinised the merger under regulation 16 of SI 2007/2974 for the purposes of Article 11 of the Cross-border Merger Directive (regulation 17(2(a) of SI 2007/2974). A specific date is fixed by the court when it makes such an order and the date fixed must be not less than twenty-one days after the date on which the order was made (regulation 16(2) of SI 2007/2974). Where an order for the purposes of Article 11 of the Cross-border Merger Directive has been made by the competent authority of an EEA state other than the UK, the consequences of the merger have effect on the date fixed in accordance with the law of that state. The transferee company is required to take all steps required by UK law or the law of another EEA state for the transfer of the assets and liabilities of the transferor companies to be effective in relation to third parties (regulation 17(3) of SI 2007/2974). This will include any necessary formalities in respect of land, ships, aircraft or intellectual property rights under the relevant legislation and the registration of company charges under Part 25 of the Companies Act 2006. The rights and obligations arising from employment contracts of the transferor companies are transferred to the transferee company (regulation 17(1)(b) of SI 2007/2974).

12.   A copy of the order of the UK court approving the completion of the cross-border merger must be sent to any member of the transferee company who requests it and must be delivered for registration to the registrar of companies by the transferee company and every transferor company not more than seven days after it was made, together with details of any register in which a non-UK EEA company is registered (regulations 18 and 19 of SI 2007/2974). UK transferor companies are under a similar obligation in respect of any order of a competent authority of another EEA state approving the completion of the cross-border merger but have fourteen days after the order was made to comply (regulation 19(3) of SI 2007/2974). If the articles or other constitutional documents of a UK transferee company were amended by the UK court order, a copy of the amended articles must be registered with the registrar of companies alongside the court order (regulation 20(1) of SI 2007/2974). Failure to comply with these requirements amounts to an offence by the company and any officer in default and is punishable by a fine (regulations 18(2) and (3), 19(5) and (6) and 20(4) and (5) of SI 2007/2974).

V   Procedure

1   Draft terms of cross-border merger

13.   The directors[2] of the UK merging companies draw up and adopt a draft of the proposed terms of the cross-border merger (regulation 7(1) of SI 2007/2974). The draft terms must include the information described in Chapter 1, no 19 of this book (regulation 7(2) of SI 2007/2974). The draft must also provide that if any securities (other than shares) of a UK transferor company, to which special rights are attached, are held other than as a creditor or a member of the company, the holder is to receive rights in the transferee company of equivalent value, unless either the holder has agreed otherwise or the draft proposal entitles the holder of the securities to have them purchased by the transferee company on terms that the court considers reasonable (regulation 7(4)(b) of SI 2007/2974). In the event a parent company merges with its wholly owned subsidiary, the information mentioned in Chapter 1, no 39 of this book can be omitted (regulation 7(3) of SI 2007/2974).

2   Management report

14.   The directors of each UK merging company must draw up and adopt a report (regulation 8(1) of SI 2007/2974). This report must explain the effect of the cross-border merger for shareholders, creditors and employees of the company and state the legal and economic grounds for the draft terms (regulation 8(2)

---

2 This will generally refer to the board of directors but the term 'director' includes 'any person occupying the position of director, by whatever name called' (section 250 Companies Act 2006 applied by regulation 3(1) of SI 2007/2974).

(a) and (b)(i) of SI 2007/2974). It must also state any material interests of the directors and of the trustees of any deed securing the interests of debentures whose holders will be affected by the merger, whether as directors/trustees, shareholders, creditors or otherwise, and the effect on those interests of the cross-border merger to the extent that it is different from the effect of the merger on similar interests of other persons (regulation 8(2)(b) (ii) and (iii) and (3) of SI 2007/2974).

15.   The directors of the UK merging company must deliver copies of the report to its employee representatives[3] or, if there are no such representatives, to the employees not less than two months before the date of the first meeting of the shareholders, or of any class of the shareholders of the company (regulation 8(5) of SI 2007/2974). If the employee representatives deliver an opinion on the report not less than one month before the date of the first shareholders' meeting or class meeting, any copy of the report issued after the date on which the opinion was received has to include the opinion (regulation 8(6) of SI 2007/2974).

16.   Failure to comply with this and the other pre-merger requirements will prevent the court from making an order confirming such compliance on the application of a UK merging company and so delay or prevent the merger (regulation 6 of SI 2007/2974).

3   Auditor's report

17.   A report on the draft terms of the cross-border merger must be drawn up by an independent expert. That person can be appointed by the board of the UK merging company for that company, or by the UK court for all the merging companies on the joint application of all of them, or by the competent authority of another EEA state for all of them (regulation 9(2) and (3) of SI 2007/2974). The person drafting the report must meet both the requirements as to expertise and professional qualification set out in section 1212 of the Companies Act 2006 and, in respect of all the merging companies, the independence requirements of section 1214 of the Companies Act 2006 as if they were to be appointed as auditor under Part 16 of that Act (regulation 9(7) and (8) of SI 2007/2974). This means that they must not be an officer (other than an auditor) or employee of any of the companies or any of their subsidiaries or holding companies, or the partner of such a person (section 1214 Companies Act 2006). Individuals or firms who are members of the following UK supervisory bodies

---

3 For those employees who have an independent trade union recognised for collective bargaining purposes, this refers to those representatives who normally take part as negotiators in that process. It also includes any other employees elected or appointed as employee representatives to positions in which they are expected to receive general information relevant to the terms and conditions of the employees or about activities of the undertaking that may significantly affect employee interests (regulation 3(1) of SI 2007/2974).

are recognised by the Secretary of State as being eligible to be company auditors under section 1212 of the Companies Act 2006: the Institute of Chartered Accountants in England and Wales; the Institute of Chartered Accountants of Scotland; the Institute of Chartered Accountants in Ireland; The Association of Chartered Certified Accountants; the Association of Authorised Public Accountants; and the Association of International Accountants.

18.   No report need be prepared if all the shareholders of all the companies participating in the cross-border merger unanimously decide that no report is required; or in the event of a merger by absorption of a wholly owned subsidiary; or where there is a merger by absorption and 90 per cent or more (but not all) of the shares (or other securities carrying the right to vote at general meetings) of the transferor company or companies are held by or on behalf of the transferee company (regulation 9(1) and (9) of SI 2007/2974). The Cross-border Merger Directive (Art. 15(2)) allows the Member States not to require an auditor's report in this last case (see Chapter 1, no 39 of this book) and the UK chose to exercise this option.

19.   The independent expert's report should indicate the methods used to determine the share-exchange ratio and the resulting value yielded by each method. It must give an opinion on the relative importance of each method in determining the value eventually decided on and as to whether the share-exchange ratio and the methods used to determine it are reasonable. The report furthermore should describe any special difficulties encountered in the valuation process (regulation 9(5)(a) to (c) of SI 2007/2974). In order to prepare his or her report, the independent expert may obtain from the merging companies and their officers any information deemed necessary and gain access to any documents needed (regulation 9(6) of SI 2007/2974). The independent expert may arrange for any valuation he or she believes to be reasonably necessary to be carried out and for a report to be written to assist with the independent expert's own report. This is to be done either by instructing a person who appears to the independent expert to have the necessary expertise and to be independent of the merging companies or by making use of an existing valuation already carried out by such a person (regulation 9(4) of SI 2007/2974). Where this is done, the independent expert's own report must state the date of the valuation, the name and knowledge and experience of the valuer. It should also describe the assets and liabilities valued and the method used for the valuation as well as stating that it seemed reasonable to the independent expert to arrange the valuation or accept the valuation previously made (regulation 9(5)(d) of SI 2007/2974).

4   General meeting of shareholders

A   Convening meetings when they are needed

20.   When the approval of the shareholders or creditors of a UK merging company (or particular classes of them) is required for the cross-border merger,

it must be given at a meeting summoned by the court for that purpose on the application of the company, its administrator if it is in administration, or a shareholder (for shareholders' meetings or class meetings) or creditor (for creditors' meetings or class meetings) (regulation 11 of SI 2007/2974). Approval at a shareholders' meeting (or class meeting) of the UK transferor is not required in the case of a merger by absorption of a wholly owned subsidiary (regulation 13(3) of SI 2007/2974). If the merger involves an existing UK transferee company it is for the shareholders to convene a meeting if they want one to take place, and if they do not do so no meeting is required providing certain conditions are met.

The conditions are that:

(i)   notice by the registrar of companies of receipt of the documentation about the merger was published at least one month before the first meeting of shareholders of the transferor companies; and

(ii)   shareholders in the transferee company were able to inspect and copy those documents relating to all the merging companies at the transferee company's registered office throughout that period of one month; and

(iii)   it was open to shareholders of the transferee with no less than 5 per cent of the capital of the transferee company with voting rights to require a meeting of each class of shareholders to be called to decide whether to approve the scheme; and

(iv)   no such requirement was made.

(regulation 13(4) of SI 2007/2974).

21.   Approval by meetings of creditors or classes of creditor are only required if a creditor of a UK merging company applies to the court for such a meeting to take place and the court orders that such meeting(s) be summoned (regulation 11(1)(b) and (2)(c) of SI 2007/2974). This aspect of creditor protection is permitted by the Cross-border Merger Directive since it is a feature of the procedure laid down in Parts 26 and 27 of the Companies Act 2006 on mergers and schemes of arrangement applicable to UK companies (Art. 4 Dir.) (see Chapter 1, no 45 of this book).

B   Information for shareholders, employees and the public

22.   Not less than two months before the date of the first meeting of the shareholders, or any class of the shareholders, of the company to approve the terms of the merger, the directors of the UK merging company must deliver to the registrar of companies details of the date, time and place of all such meetings together with a copy of the draft terms of merger, the court order calling the meetings, and details of the name, registered office, legal form, register in which it is entered, and governing law of each merging company (regulation 12(1) and (3) of SI 2007/2974). The registrar of companies publishes notice of receipt of these documents at least a month before

the date of the first meeting of shareholders (regulation 12(3) to (6) of SI 2007/2974).

23. The shareholders and the employee representatives (or, if none, the employees themselves) are entitled to examine at the company's registered office, and obtain free copies of, the draft terms of merger, the directors' report (including any opinion by employee representatives) and the independent expert's report at least one month before the date of the general meeting called to approve the draft terms of cross-border merger (regulation 10 of SI 2007/2974). Failure to comply with this or the other pre-merger requirement will prevent the court from making an order confirming such compliance on the application of a UK merging company (regulation 6 of SI 2007/2974)

24. Every notice of a meeting called by the court to approve the merger which is sent to a shareholder must include copies of the documents mentioned in no 15 of this chapter. If the notice summoning the meeting is given by advertisement then the notice must either include copies of those documents or state where and how shareholders or creditors can obtain copies of them free of charge (regulation 15 of SI 2007/2974). The question of how notice is given is generally a matter for the articles of association of the company calling the meeting, since section 310 of the Companies Act 2006 provides that notice must be sent to every member and every director but also allows the articles of a company to vary that requirement. In general, notice can be given in hard copy, in electronic form such as email or on a website (section 308 Companies Act 2006). In the case of a meeting summoned by the court to approve a cross-border merger, the court will direct how the meeting is to be summoned (regulation 11(1) of SI 2007/2974).

C   Shareholder and creditor approval

25. With respect to the UK participating companies, the draft terms of cross-border merger must be approved by court-convened meetings of each class of shareholders unless the exceptions referred to in no 20 of this chapter for either UK transferee companies or for mergers by absorption of wholly owned subsidiaries apply (regulation 13(1), (3) and (4) of SI 2007/2974).

26. A majority in number representing 75 per cent in value of the shareholders present and voting either in person or by proxy must approve the draft terms of merger at each class meeting (regulation 13(1) of SI 2007/2974).

27. The general meeting (and any class meetings) of the shareholders of a merging company may decide to make their decision subject to express ratification of the arrangements with respect to the participation of employees in the company resulting from the merger or any decision of a competent authority in another EEA Member State which amends the share-exchange ratio in accordance with Article 10(3) of the Cross-border Merger Directive (regulation 13(2) of SI 2007/2974) (see Chapter 1, no 30 of this book).

28.   If a meeting of the creditors or a class of creditors of a merging company has been summoned by the court, the draft terms of merger must also be approved by a majority in number representing 75 per cent in value of the creditors (or class of creditors) present and voting either in person or by proxy at the meeting (regulation 14 of SI 2007/2974).

5   Pre-merger certificate

29.   In the UK, the court is responsible for issuing a pre-merger certificate to the effect that any UK merging company has properly completed the pre-merger acts and formalities. This can be done only after the draft terms of merger, directors' report and independent expert's report have been drawn up and made available for inspection, and the registrar of companies has published notice of receipt of them and of details of any meetings called to approve the merger (regulation 6 of SI 2007/2974).

30.   If the merger is approved at any meetings of creditors or shareholders, or if no such meetings were required, the court scrutinises the legality of the completion of a merger with a UK transferee company. It can make an order approving the completion of the merger on the joint application of all the merging companies as long as the application is made within six months of the date on which the last pre-merger order or certificate was issued for any of the merging companies. However, the court can only make the order if a pre-merger order has already been made in respect of each UK company; a pre-merger certificate has been issued by the competent national authority in respect of each other EEA merging company; the pre-merger certificates or order approve the same draft terms of merger; and any arrangements for employee participation in the transferee company have been determined where that is required (regulation 16(1) of SI 2007/2974).

31.   In the event of a merger with an existing company, the court order approving the completion of the cross-border merger (or the approved merger document itself) can amend the articles of association and any other constitutional documents of a UK transferee company, in which case the company must deliver copies of the articles and other constitutional documents as amended to the registrar of companies together with the other documents referred to in no 33 of this chapter (regulation 20 of SI 2007/2974).

6   Effects of the decision

32.   A cross-border merger only enters into effect on the date specified in the court order referred to in no 30 of this chapter and that date must not be less than twenty-one days after the date of the order (regulation 16(2) of SI 2007/2974).

33.   A copy of the order approving the merger must be given free of charge by the company to any shareholder who requests it (regulation 18 of SI 2007/2974).

Within seven days of the order being made, the UK transferee company and any UK transferor company must deliver to the registrar of companies for registration a copy of the UK order with particulars of the national registers in which all of the non-UK merging companies are registered and their registration numbers (regulation 19(1) and (2) of SI 2007/2974). In the case of an order being made by the competent authority of another EEA Member State approving the completion of a cross-border merger, every UK transferor company must likewise deliver a copy of that order for registration with the registrar of companies within fourteen days of it being made (regulation 19(3) of SI 2007/2974). The registrar of companies must then 'without undue delay' give notice of the UK order completing the merger to the national registers on which each of the other merging companies is registered and remove any UK transferor company from the UK register while placing a note on that register of the date on which the company's assets and liabilities were transferred to the transferee company because the consequences of the cross-border merger came into effect (regulation 21 of SI 2007/2974).

34.   After the consequences of the cross-border merger have taken effect, the order of the UK court which approved the completion of the merger for the purposes of Article 11 of the Cross-border Merger Directive is conclusive evidence both that the conditions necessary for the order to be made have been satisfied and that all the pre-merger requirements of SI 2007/2974 have been complied with so that there can be no question of the merger being declared null and void in the future (regulation 16(3) of SI 2007/2974).

VI   Minority shareholders

35.   A decision to carry out a cross-border merger approved by the majorities discussed under nos 26 and 28 of this chapter and by a court order is binding on the company's minority shareholders and its creditors. They have no choice but to go along with the merger and will receive shares in the surviving or new company.

36.   Under Part 28 of the Companies Act 2006 the Takeover Panel regulates takeovers and mergers from the point of view of protecting the interests of shareholders in the target company in line with the Takeover Directive. In Practice Statement No 18[4] the Takeover Panel has set out how the Takeover Code will apply to cross-border mergers carried out pursuant to the UK Regulations.

37.   The Takeover Code generally applies to takeover offers for UK, Channel Island and Isle of Man registered companies or SEs if any of their securities are admitted to trading on a regulated market or on any stock market in any of those jurisdictions. It also applies to offers for any other companies so

4 See www.thetakeoverpanel.org.uk/new/practiceStatements/DATA/PS18.pdf.

registered (whether public or private) whose central management is in any of those places and which, in the case of private companies, have had their shares traded or listed at some time in the previous ten years ('Code companies') (the Takeover Code Introduction Section 3(a).[5]

38. The Practice Statement applies the Code to cross-border mergers differently depending on the type of merger involved:

(i) In the case of a merger by absorption, the Code will generally apply only if one or more of the transferor companies is a 'Code company', regardless of the status of the transferee company. In that case any transferor company that is a 'Code company' will be treated as the offeree for the purpose of the Takeover Code and the other merging companies will be regarded as offerors. However, if the transferee company is a 'Code company' and, as a result of the merger, one person, or a number of persons acting in concert together, will own 30 per cent or more of the voting rights in the transferee company, a 'whitewash' vote of its independent shareholders may be required under Note 1 of the Notes on Dispensations to Rule 9 of the Takeover Code.

(ii) In a merger by absorption of a wholly owned subsidiary, the Code will not be applied.

(iii) In the case of a merger by the formation of a new company, the Code will apply if one or more transferor companies is a 'Code company'. The transferee company will then be seen as the offeror and the transferor 'Code companies' as offerees for Takeover Code purposes. However, if the Panel is satisfied that the substance of the transaction is the acquisition by a 'Code company' of the 'non-Code company' they may agree that the Code should not apply.

VII Protection of creditors

39. As noted in nos 20 and 28 of this chapter, creditors have the possibility of requesting the court to call a meeting of the creditors, or of particular classes of creditors, in which case they will be able to prevent the cross-border merger if they do not approve it by the necessary majority. If the company was in administration during the cross-border merger process, their interests will, in addition, have been represented by the administrator throughout the process. As a result, creditors are given no special post-merger rights under UK legislation.

40. In addition, the draft terms of merger must provide that if any securities (other than shares) of a UK transferor company, to which special rights are attached, are held other than as a creditor or a member of the company, the holder is to

5 See www.thetakeoverpanel.org.uk/new/codesars/DATA/code.pdf.

receive rights in the transferee company of equivalent value, unless either the holder has agreed otherwise or the draft proposal entitles the holder of the securities to have them purchased by the transferee company on terms that the court considers reasonable (regulation 7(4)(b) of SI 2007/2974).

VIII   Employee participation

41.   With respect to employee participation, the Cross-border Merger Directive has been implemented in UK law by regulations 22 to 64 of SI 2007/2974.

1   Employee participation in companies established in the UK resulting from a cross-border merger

42.   UK law does not make employee participation rights or the right of employees to sit on the management bodies of companies mandatory. Consequently, for a UK transferee company resulting from a cross-border merger, the UK rules will be set aside so as to require employee participation only if such rights existed within any of the merging companies in one of the following ways:

  (i)   a merging company had an average of at least 500 employees in the six months before publication of the draft terms of merger and has a system of employee participation; or

  (ii)   a UK merging company has a proportion of employee representatives amongst its directors; or

  (iii) a merging company has employee representatives among the members of its administrative or supervisory organ or their committees or the management group which covers the profit units of the company (regulation 22(1) of SI 2007/2974).

43.   In such a case, the UK regulations require that information be provided to the employees, or their representatives, identifying the merging companies, and disclosing both any decision to select standard rules on employee participation and the number of employees employed by each merging company (regulations 23 and 24 of SI 2007/2974). The regulations set out standard rules of employee participation. Those rules can be applied either by an initial agreement by the merging companies to do so or if the special negotiating body ('SNB') fails to agree a different set of rules. The standard rules apply to the surviving transferee company at least the lesser of:

  (i)   the highest level of participation in any of the merging companies; or

  (ii)   the use of employee participation in electing, appointing, recommending or opposing one third of the directors (regulations 36 to 39 of SI 2007/2974).

44.   Provision is also made that, in the absence of an initial decision to choose the standard rules on employee participation, an SNB is mandated to reach an

employee participation agreement with the merging companies and the UK regulations lay down the composition of the SNB and the process of negotiation (regulations 25 to 32 of SI 2007/2974). The regulations also deal with the confidentiality of information disclosed by any merging company or transferee company as part of this process and permit information to be withheld if its disclosure would, 'according to objective criteria', harm the functioning of, or be prejudicial to, the transferee or merging company (regulations 41 and 42 of SI 2007/2974).

2   Special negotiating body ('SNB')

45.   Where the rules in force concerning employee participation, if any, in the Member State where the company resulting from the cross-border merger has its registered office are set aside, an 'SNB' must be set up with a view to negotiating arrangements on employee participation, in the company resulting from the cross-border merger, with the management organs of the participating companies (Art. 16(3) Dir.).

46.   The UK Regulations provide specific rules for the appointment of the British member(s) of the SNB (regulations 25 to 27 and 33 to 35 of SI 2007/2974). In general, such member(s) are elected by a secret ballot of UK employees in each merging UK company in which all employees of that company are entitled to vote. Candidates must be employees of the merging UK company which they are to represent but, if the directors of the company agree, a trade union representative who is not an employee of the company may be a candidate. The ballot must be conducted by an independent ballot supervisor using arrangements devised by the directors of the company after consultation with its employees. There is a right for any employee or employee representative to complain to the UK's Central Arbitration Committee (CAC) about the arrangements for the ballot (regulation 33 of SI 2007/2974). The conduct of the ballot is in the hands of the independent supervisor who has power to declare a ballot ineffective if the published arrangements for it were not followed or if other improprieties occurred which he or she believes affected the result. In such a case the board of the merging company must ensure that the ballot is carried out again (regulation 34 of SI 2007/2974).

3   Protection of employee representatives

47.   Any member of, or candidate for election to, the SNB and any employee director or candidate for election to that position who is employed in the UK is protected by the provisions of the UK regulations. In particular, they are entitled to take a reasonable amount of paid time off during working hours to perform their function and are protected from dismissal or other detrimental treatment by the employer as a result of carrying out their role. They have a right to complain to an Employment Tribunal to enforce those rights (regulations 43 to

64 of SI 2007/2974). The employee participation system of the UK transferee company is protected from change as a result of later domestic mergers for a period of three years from the date on which the consequences of the cross-border merger took effect (regulation 40 of SI 2007/2974).

IX   Tax treatment

48.   The UK has implemented the Merger Tax Directive by regulations made under a power conferred by section 110 of the Finance Act 2007. They are the Corporation Tax (Implementation of the Mergers Directive) Regulations 2007 SI 2007/3186 and the Corporation Tax (Implementation of the Mergers Directive) Regulations 2008 SI 2008/1579. These provisions follow the requirements of the directive by amending primary legislation to provide for tax deferral as required but they also take advantage of the permitted anti-avoidance provisions.

PART III

Application in the EEA Member States

18

Norway

STIG BERGE AND HERMAN BONDESON
Thommessen

I   Introduction

1.   Norway is not a member of the European Union, but a party to the EEA
     Agreement. The Cross-border Merger Directive was implemented in the EEA
     Agreement on 22 September 2006,[1] and the Norwegian Parliament approved
     the implementation on 20 March 2007.[2]

---

1 Decision no 127/2006 of 22 September 2006 by the EEA Joint Committee, amending Annex
  XXII to the EEA Agreement by inserting a Section 10e in the annex (*Official Journal* L 333
  of 30 November 2006 p. 59).
2 See St.prp. no 34 (2006–2007), Innst. S. no 139 (2006–2007) and the Norwegian Parliament's
  decision no 380 of 20 March 2007.

The incorporation of the Cross-border Merger Directive into Norwegian law[3] was made through the adoption of the Act of 21 December 2007 no 129 on amendments to the Act on Private Limited Liability Companies, the Act on Public Limited Liability Companies and certain other acts[4] (the 'Amendment Act') and the adoption of the regulation regarding employee representation rights on 9 January 2008 (the 'Employee Regulation').[5]

The Amendment Act inserted a new Chapter 13 VII with the heading 'Cross-border Merger' and a new Chapter 14 III, entitled 'Cross-border Division'[6] into the Act of 13 June 1997 no 44 on Private Limited Liability Companies and the Act of 13 June 1997 no 45 on Public Limited Liability Companies (the latter act is hereinafter referred to as the 'PLLC Act'). The law technique applied in the Amendment Act was to implement the Cross-border Merger Directive in full text in Chapter 13 VII of the PLLC Act with respect to public limited liability companies, and then extend the application of these rules to private limited liability companies through a cross-reference provision in Article 13-25 of the Act on Private Limited Liability Companies referring to the PLLC Act. In this chapter references are therefore made solely to the PLLC Act.

Prior to the adoption of the Amendment Act, the existing domestic legislative framework did not permit mergers between Norwegian companies and companies elsewhere in the European Economic Area to be carried out, since the merger regulation in Chapter 13 of the PLLC Act only governed domestic mergers.[7]

---

3 Norway has taken a dualistic approach to treaties. A treaty has no force and effect within the domestic legal system until the Parliament passes implementing legislation specifically giving effect to the provisions of the treaty. There are generally three methods by which a treaty may be incorporated into Norwegian law: (i) by direct incorporation, i.e. through adoption of an incorporation provision giving the treaty direct effect within domestic law; (ii) by transformation, in which case the rights and obligations of the treaty are transformed into domestic law through the adoption of domestic provisions with the same substance as the provisions of the treaty; and (iii) by so-called passive transformation, i.e. that the rights and obligations of Norway under the treaty are already provided for under the domestic legal framework and, therefore, no implementation legislation is needed. The methods applied for the implementation of obligations pursuant to Council directives are, in general, the transformation principle or the principle of passive transformation, while Council regulations are given effect within Norwegian law by direct incorporation. In the following, the term *incorporation* is used, regardless of the method which has been applied.

4 *Lov 21. desember 2007 nr. 129 om endringer i aksjeloven, allmennaksjeloven og enkelte andre lover (fusjon og fisjon over landegrensene).* The Act entered into force on 21 December 2007.

5 *Forskrift 9. januar 2008 nr. 50 om arbeidstakernes rett til representasjon ved fusjon over landegrensene av selskaper med begrenset ansvar.* The Regulation came into effect on 1 February 2008.

6 The rules regarding cross-border division are described in no 3 of this chapter.

7 Chapter 13 of the PLLC Act implemented the Domestic Merger Directive (the Third Council Directive (78/855/EEC) of 9 October 1978 based on Article 54(3) of the Treaty concerning mergers of public limited liability companies).

II   Scope of the new rules

2.   The new rules for cross-border mergers apply to public limited liability companies (*allmennaksjeselskap*) and private limited liability companies (*aksjeselskap*)[8] as well as European companies (SEs).[9]

Norway has reserved the right under Article 3(2) (see Chapter 1, no 7 of this book) to exempt cooperatives (national cooperatives and European cooperative societies (SCEs))[10] from the scope of the cross-border merger legislation. In the preparatory works to the implementation legislation, the exemption is explained with reference to the lack of efficiency of such rules since several Member States presumably will exempt cooperatives from their regulation on cross-border mergers. The need for cross-border merger legislation for cooperatives is also questioned because cooperatives are entitled to merge in accordance with the rules laid down in the SCE Regulation.[11] Finally, it is emphasised that there are significant differences in structure and legal form between cooperatives in the Member States and that such differences could create difficulties both from a practical and from a legal point of view for the application of rules regarding cross-border mergers for cooperatives.[12]

3.   The Amendment Act also contemplates provisions enabling a Norwegian company to participate in a cross-border division, provided that certain conditions are fulfilled (see Article 14-12 PLLC Act). In the Act, a cross-border division is defined as a division of a company where at least two of the companies involved (the transferor company and/or the company/ies receiving the assets, rights and obligations as a result of the division, the latter hereinafter referred to as the 'recipient company') are governed by the laws of different Member States. Clearly, the introduction of legislation on cross-border divisions in Norwegian law was encouraged by the findings and rationale of the European Court of Justice (ECJ) in the *SEVIC* case.[13] In the preparatory works to the

---

8 *Allmennaksjeselskap* and *aksjeselskap* are the Norwegian companies referred to in Article 1 of the First Company Law Directive (Directive 68/151/EEC of 9 March 1968), see Chapter 1, no 5 of this book. Companies governed by special laws but organised as private or public limited liability companies, such as commercial banks, investment banks and insurance companies, are also covered by the rules on cross-border mergers.

9 The European companies fall within the scope of Article 2(1)(b) Dir., and pursuant to Article 2(1) of the Act of 1 April 2005 no 14 on European companies, the provisions of the PLLC Act shall apply to European companies (unless otherwise stated).

10 Pursuant to Article 9 of Council Regulation no 1435/2003 of 22 July 2003 on the Statute for a European Cooperative Society (SCE), an SCE shall be treated in every Member State as if it were a national cooperative.

11 Council Regulation no 1435/2003 of 22 July 2003 on the Statute for a European Cooperative Society (SCE).

12 Ot.prp. no 78 (2006–2007) *Om lov om endringer i aksjeloven, allmennaksjeloven og enkelte andre lover (fusjon og fisjon over landegrensene)* (proposition from the Law House of the Norwegian Parliament) p. 12.

13 European Court of Justice, 13 December 2005, Case C-411/03, *European Court Reports*, 10805.

Act, the Norwegian Government interprets the freedom of establishment set out in Article 43 of the EC Treaty, and Article 31 of the EEA Agreement in the light of the *SEVIC* judgment, as covering the right to transfer the assets of a company governed by the laws of one Member State to another Member State by way of a cross-border division,[14] and that a general refusal to register a cross-border division would be regarded as going beyond what is necessary to protect legitimate interests.[15] The rules regarding divisions in the PLLC Act, which only allowed for Norwegian companies to be involved in divisions, could therefore not be upheld in their original form. It was acknowledged that the absence of harmonised legislation on cross-border divisions at the Community level would reduce the efficiency of domestic rules for cross-border divisions. Nevertheless, it was emphasised that in the light of the *SEVIC* judgment it appears to be unlikely that the ECJ would accept a general refusal to register cross-border divisions on such grounds.[16] [17]

Article 43 of the EC Treaty does not, however, prevent the Member States from taking measures for the protection of the interests of creditors, minority shareholders and employees, even if such measures imply restrictions on the freedom of establishment.[18] In compliance therewith, Article 14-12(2) no 2 of the PLLC Act states that the companies can only benefit from the new rules for cross-border division if the laws governing the recipient company prescribe employee participation rights that are at least as good as those laid down in Article 16 of the Cross-border Merger Directive. A further condition is that the cross-border division is permitted under the laws governing the other companies participating in the division (Art. 14-12(2) no 1 PLLC Act).

If the recipient company is governed by Norwegian law, the division is carried out in accordance with the rules for domestic division by the formation of a new company (Chapter 2 PLLC Act) or the rules for division by a capital increase following a transfer of the assets of the transferor company to an existing company (Chapter 10 PLLC Act). In addition, certain of the other provisions for domestic divisions in Chapter 14 of the PLLC Act and the provisions regarding cross-border mergers are made applicable to a cross-border division (Art. 14-12(3) and (4) PLLC Act).[19]

---

14 *Ibid.* paragraph 18, where the ECJ observed that 'the right of establishment covers all measures which permit or even merely facilitate access to another Member State and the pursuit of an economic activity in that State by allowing the persons concerned to participate in the economic life of the country effectively and under the same conditions as national operators.'

15 *Ibid.* paragraph 30.

16 Ot.prp. no 78 (2006–2007) pp. 13–15.

17 See *SEVIC* judgment paragraph 26, where the ECJ stated that 'the existence of such harmonisation rules cannot be made a precondition for the implementation of the freedom of establishment laid down by Articles 43 EC and 48 EC.'

18 *Ibid.* paragraph 28.

19 The Norwegian rules for domestic divisions in Chapter 14 of the PLLC Act implemented the Sixth Council Directive 82/891/EEC of 17 December 1982 based on Article 54(3)(g) of

III   Cash payment

4.   As remuneration for the contribution of the assets, rights and obligations, the shareholders of the transferor company are entitled to receive shares in the company resulting from the merger (hereinafter referred to as the 'acquiring company').[20] In addition, the remuneration may consist of a cash payment (Art. 13-2(1), cf. Art. 13-25(2) no 1 PLLC Act). Pursuant to the Cross-border Merger Directive, the cash contribution may, as a general rule, not exceed 10 per cent of the nominal value of the consideration shares. This limit for cash payment does not, however, apply if the laws of one of the involved companies allow the cash contribution to exceed 10 per cent (Chapter 1, no 11 of this book). Article 13-2(1) no 2, cf. Article 13-25(2) no 1, of the PLLC Act allows for a cross-border merger to be carried out with a cash payment of up to 20 per cent of the total consideration payable to the shareholders. If the laws of one of the involved companies so permit, a cash payment in excess of 20 per cent may be contributed.

No consideration is payable in the event of a merger by absorption of a wholly owned subsidiary.

IV   Legal consequences of the merger and enforceability of a cross-border merger

5.   Pursuant to Article 13-33(1), cf. Article 13-17(1) nos 1 to 6 of the PLLC Act, a cross-border merger shall have the same legal consequences as a domestic merger, i.e. the consequences laid down in Article 14(1), (2) and (5) of the Cross-border Merger Directive and described in Chapter 1, nos 16 and 17 of this book. In addition, Article 13-33(1) states that a cross-border merger shall have the effect that the rights and obligations resulting from employment contracts and employment relationships shall be transferred by operation of law to the acquiring company.[21]

---

the Treaty, concerning the division of public limited liability companies, and should therefore be largely harmonised with the regulation on domestic divisions in the other Member States.

20 In the event that the acquiring company is a Norwegian public limited liability company, the consideration shares must be registered on securities accounts in the Norwegian Central Securities Depository (*VPS*). For this purpose the shareholders of the transferor company must open securities accounts with a Norwegian *VPS* registrar. If the shareholders of the transferor company are non-Norwegian they normally have the possibility of having their securities registered through a trustee, see Art. 4-10 PLLC Act.

21 This provision was in reality not necessary since the effect is provided for by Chapter 16 of the Norwegian Labour Environment Act of 17 June 2005 no 62. Furthermore, the provisions in Article 13-17(1) nos 1 to 6 of the PLLC Act, which through the cross-reference in Article 13-33(1) are also applicable to cross-border mergers, have in practice been interpreted to encompass the same effect in respect of domestic mergers.

6.   However, the transfer of the assets to the acquiring company does not become effective against third parties by operation of law. In order for the transfer to be legally perfected, the acquiring company must perform an act of perfection. Registration is the relevant act for transfers of real property (the Norwegian Land Register),[22] vessels (the Norwegian Ship Register or the Norwegian International Ship Register), aircraft (the Norwegian Civil Aircraft Register) and registered financial instruments (the Norwegian Central Securities Depository (*VPS*)). A transfer of movable property or unregistered negotiable instruments is perfected when the acquiring company takes actual possession of the assets, while notification to the debtor is required in order to perfect a transfer of non-negotiable debt instruments.[23]

---

22 The transfer of real property by way of a merger is dealt with as a company name change for registration purposes, and it is therefore sufficient to present a certificate of registration evidencing the merger/the name change of the title holder of the property to the Land Register in order to perfect the transfer, see Directive G-37/90 issued by the Norwegian Ministry of Justice.

23 The legal perfection of the transfer is required in order for the acquiring company to extinguish *prior* (unperfected) rights in an asset covered by the merger. Conflicts with a *later* bona fide purchaser or other third parties deriving competing rights in the assets from the transferor company after the completion of the merger is entered in the Norwegian Register of Business Enterprises (*Foretaksregisteret*) are rare because the transferor company is dissolved upon registration of the merger. If such conflicts nevertheless arise, the third party will not be able to rely on a good faith defence with respect to the acquisition of the rights in the asset, since Article 10-1 of the Act of 21 June 1985 no 78 on registration of business enterprises (the 'Registration Act') prescribes that third parties shall be deemed to have knowledge of documents and information which have been entered in the register. The wording of the Registration Act does not provide for any fifteen-day transition period following registration in which third parties can claim that the merger is not enforceable against them if they prove that it was impossible for them to have had knowledge thereof, *see* Chapter 1, no 37 of this book and Article 3(5) of the First Company Law Directive. Prior to Norway's entry into the EEA Agreement with effect from 1 January 1994, the Norwegian Government took the view that it was not necessary to amend the Registration Act in order to implement the provisions of Article 3 of the First Company Law Directive as the Registration Act, allegedly, safeguarded the interests of third parties and pursued the intentions of the directive, see Ot.prp. no 73 (1991–1992) *Om lov om offentlig støtte og lov om endringer i næringslovgivningen m.v. som følge av EØS-avtalen* p. 13. However, this conclusion is disputable in the light of the transposition obligations laid down in Article 7 of the EEA Agreement, pursuant to which a directive shall 'be, or be made, part of their [the Contracting Parties'] internal legal order'. The compatibility of Article 10-1 of the Registration Act with the First Company Law Directive must be seriously doubted because the Act does not acknowledge any time period for third parties to acquire knowledge of the registration as provided for by Article 3 of the directive. Legal theory has therefore argued that the Registration Act should be interpreted restrictively, i.e. in conformity with the directive, see Søren Wiig, 'Tredjemanns stilling ved signaturberettiget styremedlems fratreden', *Tidsskrift for Forretningsjus* 1997 pp. 84–93 (on pp. 92 and 93). Arguably, such an interpretation would appear reasonable and harmonise with the interpretive technique adopted by the Supreme Court whereby, in the event of conflict with international law, national legislation is construed in conformity with the State's obligations under international law (the so-called 'presumption principle'). However, it remains uncertain as to whether a court will set aside the clear wording of the Registration Act.

V   Procedure

1   Draft terms of cross-border merger

7.   Pursuant to Article 13-26(1) of the PLLC Act, the board of directors of a Norwegian company participating in a cross-border merger shall, together with the competent management organs of the involved foreign companies, prepare common draft terms of cross-border merger.[24]

The draft terms of merger must be prepared in Norwegian, Swedish or Danish or an authorised translation into Norwegian[25] must be provided. The draft terms of merger must also be signed by the board of directors of the companies. Under Norwegian law, there are no other form requirements for the draft terms of merger.

8.   In accordance with Article 5 of the Cross-border Merger Directive, Article 13-26(2) of the PLLC Act prescribes that the draft terms of a cross-border merger shall include at least the particulars mentioned in Chapter 1, no 19 of this book. The Amendment Act did not introduce additional requirements to the content of the draft terms of merger. However, as Article 13-8 nos 1 and 2 of the PLLC Act is made applicable to cross-border mergers,[26] the articles of association as well as the annual accounts, the annual reports and the auditor's reports of all the merging companies for the preceding three financial years must be enclosed as appendices to the draft terms of cross-border merger.

In the event that the cross-border merger takes place through the absorption of a wholly owned subsidiary, the information referred to in Chapter 1, no 39 of this book can be omitted (Art. 13-36 no 1 PLLC Act).

9.   The draft terms of cross-border merger must be filed with the Norwegian Register of Business Enterprises (*Foretaksregisteret*) no later than one month before the date fixed for the general meeting (or the board meeting, as the case may be, see nos 17 and 19 of this chapter) which is to decide on the merger (Art. 13-13(1), cf. Art. 13-25(2) no 5 PLLC Act).

Based on the notification from the company, the Register of Business Enterprises shall publish a notice of the cross-border merger on the Brønnøysund Register Centre's electronic bulletin for public announcements (*Brønnøysundregistrenes elektroniske kunngjøringspublikasjon*)[27] and in a

---

24 The terms of merger to be prepared by the board of directors are referred to in the PLLC Act as the 'fusjonsplan', which can be translated as 'merger plan'. This term seems adequate in the light of the legal status of the document, i.e. a merger agreement conditional on the approval of the general meeting which can only approve or reject the merger plan, not alter it. Since 'draft terms of merger' is the term applied in the Cross-border Merger Directive, as well as the Domestic Merger Directive, it will also be used in this chapter.

25 Art. 4 Regulation of 18 December 1987 no 984 on registration of companies.

26 Art. 13-25(2) no 4 PLLC Act.

27 Following an amendment on 5 September 2003 (Act no 92), Brønnøysund Register Centre's electronic bulletin for public announcements (*Brønnøysundregistrenes elektroniske*

newspaper which is widely read in the area where the registered office of the company is located (Article 13-13(3), cf. Article 13-25(2) no 5 PLLC Act). In addition to the information set forth in Chapter 1, no 20 of this book, the notice shall state that the register has received the draft terms of cross-border merger and that the draft terms are available at the register (Arts. 13-29 and 13-13(2), cf. Art. 13-25(2) no 5 PLLC Act).

2   Management report

10.   In conformity with Article 7 of the Cross-border Merger Directive, the board of directors of the Norwegian merging company must, pursuant to Articles 13-9, cf. Article 13-25(2) no 4, and 13-27(1) of the PLLC Act, prepare a report on the cross-border merger. The report shall provide a legal and economic explanation and justification for the reasons for the merger and the considera-tion to the shareholders in the transferor company. In addition, the report must describe any difficulties encountered in determining the consideration and the implications of the merger for shareholders, creditors and the employees of the company.

11.   The management report shall be made available to the shareholders and the representatives of the employees in the company at least one month before the general meeting shall decide on the draft terms of merger (Art. 13-27(2) PLLC Act).

Pursuant to Article 13-11(4), cf. Article 13-25(2) no 5, of the PLLC Act, any written comments on the cross-border merger received from the employees or the employee representatives shall be appended to the report. The same applies to any statements issued by the corporate assembly of the company.[28]

12.   In general, the managing director, the members of the board of directors, the members of the corporate assembly, the independent expert and the share-holders may be held liable for any damage they cause, or participate in, by intent or through negligence in such capacity (Art. 17-1(1) PLLC Act). The managing director, the members of the board of directors, the members of the corporate assembly and the independent expert may also be criminally sanctioned, by fines or, in aggravating circumstances, by imprisonment of up to one year for any intentional or negligent violation of any of the provisions set out in or pursuant to the PLLC Act (Art. 19-1(1) PLLC Act). These provi-sions for civil and criminal liability will, in principle, be applicable to any failure or misconduct in preparing and implementing the merger, including

---

kunngjøringspublikasjon) is the official state gazette of Norway for the publication of com-pany information.

28 Details of when the company shall set up a corporate assembly are given in no 30 of this chapter.

the preparation of the management report and the independent expert's report.

3   Auditor's report

13.   Article 13-28 of the PLLC Act implements Article 8 of the Cross-border Merger Directive and prescribes that the boards of directors of the companies participating in the cross-border merger shall ensure that an independent expert's report on the merger is prepared. In contrast to the rules that apply to a domestic merger, the rules for cross-border mergers entitle the merging companies to jointly appoint one or more experts to prepare a single report for all the companies (Art. 13-28(1) PLLC Act).

The Act further states that no report is required if so consented to by all shareholders of the merging companies (Art. 13-28(4) PLLC Act). There are no formal requirements to the consent of the shareholders. In order to avoid any dispute as to the existence of consent from the shareholders, it is recommended in the preparatory works to obtain each consent in writing or to record it in the minutes of the general meeting (or the board meeting) deciding on the merger.[29]

Under Norwegian law, an expert report on the merger is not required for a cross-border merger by way of absorption of a wholly owned subsidiary (Art. 13-36 no 2 of the PLLC Act). A report must, however, be prepared if the acquiring company holds more than 90 per cent, but not all, of the shares in the absorbed company, since no simplified procedure has been provided for such mergers under Norwegian law (Art. 15(2) of the Cross-border Merger Directive and Chapter 1, no 40 of this book).

14.   The experts qualified for preparing the report under Norwegian law are state-authorised public auditors and registered auditors (Art. 13-28(2) PLLC Act). Such auditors are subject to authorisation from the Financial Supervisory Authority of Norway (*Kredittilsynet*, to be renamed *Finanstilsynet*)[30] and thus fulfil the requirement under Article 8(2) of the Cross-border Merger Directive, and Article 10(1) of the Domestic Merger Directive, for approval by an administrative authority.

15.   Pursuant to Article 13-28(3) of the PLLC Act, the report must contain the information referred to in Chapter 1, no 22 of this book, and be made available to the shareholders of the company at least one month before the date fixed for the general meeting (or the board meeting) to decide on the cross-border merger. If a joint report for the merging companies is written in a language other than Norwegian, Swedish or Danish, an authorised translation into Norwegian must be made available to the shareholders within the same deadline.

---

29 Ot.prp. no 78 (2006–2007) p. 43.
30 Article 3-1(1) of the Act of 15 January 1999 no 2 on auditing and auditors (the 'Auditors Act').

4   General meeting of shareholders

16.   Pursuant to Article 13-12, cf. Article 13-25(2) no 5, of the PLLC Act, the draft terms of merger, together with the management report and the independent expert's report, must be sent to each shareholder of the company no later than one month prior to the date of the general meeting (or the board meeting) which is to decide on the merger. As mentioned under no 8 of this chapter, the articles of association as well as the annual accounts, the annual report and the auditor's report of the merging companies for the preceding three financial years must be enclosed with the draft terms of merger. These documents will form the basis for the decision of the shareholders regarding the merger.

Under Norwegian law, there are no requirements for the companies participating in a cross-border merger to prepare interim balance sheets because the transposition of the Cross-border Merger Directive, in the interpretation of the Norwegian Government, did not entail an obligation to impose such a requirement on the companies[31] (see Chapter 1, no 27 of this book for the contrary viewpoint).

17.   As a general rule, the resolution on a cross-border merger shall be adopted by the general meeting of the shareholders of the companies approving the draft terms of merger by the same majority as required for an amendment to the articles of association, i.e. by a majority of two thirds of both the votes cast and the share capital represented at the general meeting (Arts. 13-3(2) and 5-18, cf. Art. 13-25(2) no 2 PLLC Act). The requirement for a two-thirds capital majority, in addition to the voting majority, entails that holders of shares or securities representing capital have influence over the merger decision, regardless of any voting right restrictions attached to the shares or the existence of different share classes with unequal voting rights.

There is no quorum requirement for general meetings under Norwegian law.

The decision regarding the approval of the merger in an acquiring company also implies subscription of the shares which are to be received as consideration for the merger (Art. 13-3(3), cf. Art. 13-25(2) no 2 PLLC Act).

18.   The general meeting may reserve the right to make the approval of the merger conditional on ratification by it of the arrangements decided on with respect to the participation of employees in the acquiring company (Art. 13-30 PLLC Act; see Art. 9(2) of the Cross-border Merger Directive and Chapter 1, no 26 of this book).

19.   In the event of a merger by absorption of a wholly owned subsidiary, the approval of the draft terms of merger in the transferor company can be made by the board of directors of that company, cf. Article 13-36 no 3 of the PLLC Act.

---

31   Ot.prp. no 78 (2006–2007) p. 19.

In an acquiring company, the merger decision may be adopted by the board of directors if the capital increase in the acquiring company can be implemented on the basis of a power of attorney granted to the board of directors pursuant to the provisions of Articles 10-14 to 10-19 of the PLLC Act, and which states that it applies to a cross-border merger. Shareholders representing at least 5 per cent of the share capital may, however, demand that a general meeting is held (Art. 13-5, cf. Art. 13-25(2) no 3 PLLC Act).

A simple majority in the board is sufficient in the cases in which the approval of the draft terms of merger can be made by the board of directors. The quorum required for the board approval is that more than half of the board members are present at the meeting (Arts. 6-24(1) and 6-25(1) of the PLLC Act).

5   Pre-merger certificate

20.   Pursuant to Article 13-31(1) of the PLLC Act, a Norwegian company participating in a cross-border merger shall, when the deadline for objections from creditors has expired and the claims from creditors who have submitted objections to the merger have been settled (see no 27 of this chapter), notify the Norwegian Register of Business Enterprises, which has been designated as the competent authority to scrutinise the legality of the cross-border merger in accordance with Articles 10 and 11 of the Cross-border Merger Directive, that it has completed all the pre-merger acts and formalities. Together with the notification, the company must submit documentation required as evidence that the acts and formalities have been fulfilled.

The Register of Business Enterprises shall scrutinise whether the merger conditions under Norwegian law have been implemented. This includes, among other things, that the draft terms of merger, the management report and, if relevant, the expert's report have been prepared, that the general meeting (or the board of directors in certain cases, see no 19 of this chapter) has approved the draft terms of merger and that the claims of creditors who have submitted objections to the merger have been settled. If the completion of the merger is subject to approval from public authorities,[32] the Register of Business Enterprises shall, as a general rule, also scrutinise whether such approval has been granted. The scrutiny shall further extend to whether a prospectus for the offering of the shares has been prepared and approved by the prospectus

---

32 Acts with requirements for approval from public authorities for participation in a merger, or for transfer of the seat of the company to a foreign country, include the Act of 24 May 1961 no 2 on Commercial Banks in Norway (Art. 31), the Act of 10 June 2005 no 44 on Insurance Companies and Pension Funds (Arts. 3-6 and 13-1) and the Act of 10 June 1988 no 40 on Financing Activity and Financial Institutions (Arts. 2a-14 and 3-6). These acts have been regarded as establishing grounds of public interest, according to Article 4(1)(b) Dir., allowing the relevant authorities to oppose a domestic merger as well as a cross-border merger, see Chapter 1, no 15 of this book.

authority (the Oslo Stock Exchange (*Oslo Børs*) or, as the case might be, the Register of Business Enterprises), if this is a condition for the cross-border merger pursuant to the Norwegian Securities Trading Act of 29 June 2007 no 75, which implements the Prospectus Directive (see Chapter 1, no 32 of this book. If the company is required to prepare an information document in accordance with the Continuing Obligations of Stock Exchange Listed Companies adopted by Oslo Børs, the Register of Business Enterprises shall also check that the information document has been approved by Oslo Børs.[33]

Provided that the Register of Business Enterprises finds that the company has complied with all the requirements under Norwegian law for cross-border mergers, the register shall issue a pre-merger certificate attesting to the proper completion of those requirements (Art. 13-31(1) PLLC Act; see Chapter 1, no 29 of this book).

The pre-merger certificate must be sent to the authority which has the competence to scrutinise the legality of the merger pursuant to Article 11 of the Cross-border Merger Directive in the Member State to whose jurisdiction the acquiring company shall be subject, together with the approved terms of cross-border merger, within six months from the issuance of the pre-merger certificate (see Art. 13-31(2) of the PLLC Act).

21.   If the acquiring company in the cross-border merger shall be governed by the laws of Norway, the Register of Business Enterprises shall scrutinise if the requirements for the completion of the cross-border merger have been fulfilled for all the merging companies. This scrutiny shall include checks that (i) pre-merger certificates have been received from all the merging companies within the six-month deadline, (ii) all the companies have approved the terms of merger in the same terms, (iii) if relevant, arrangements for employee participation have been determined, (iv) if relevant, the new company has been legally incorporated, and (v) Norwegian law does not otherwise prohibit the cross-border merger from being registered (Art. 13-32(1) PLLC Act). If these conditions are met, the Register of Business Enterprises shall enter the completion of the merger in the register.

6   Effects of the decision

22.   A cross-border merger where the acquiring company is to be governed by the laws of Norway enters, pursuant to Article 13-33(2) of the PLLC Act, into force when the Register of Business Enterprises registers the merger in accordance with Article 13-32(1) of the PLLC Act.

If the acquiring company is to be governed by the laws of another Member State, the Register of Business Enterprises shall enter the cross-border merger in the register when it receives notice from the competent authority in the other Member State that the merger has come into effect (Art. 13-32(3) PLLC Act).

33 Ot.prp. no 78 (2006–2007) p. 44.

23. In connection with the completion of the cross-border merger, the Register of Business Enterprises shall publish the following information in its electronic bulletin for public announcements (if relevant) with respect to a Norwegian company participating in the merger: (i) the dissolution of the transferor company; (ii) the capital increase in the acquiring company or the formation of a new company; (iii) amendments to the articles of association of the acquiring company; and (iv) the transfer of the registered office of the company (see Article 6-2(1), (5) and (6) of the Registration Act). No other information is published when the merger is completed.[34]

As soon as possible after the registration of the merger, the Register of Business Enterprises shall notify the registers in the other involved Member States that the cross-border merger has entered into force (Art. 13-32(2) PLLC Act).

24. In accordance with Article 17 of the Cross-border Merger Directive, Article 13-35(3) of the PLLC Act prescribes that a cross-border merger which has entered into force cannot be declared null and void.

Prior to the issuance of the pre-merger certificate,[35] legal proceedings on the grounds of invalidity of the company's merger decision may, however, be brought before the court (Art. 13-35(1) PLLC Act). The proceedings may be initiated by the company's shareholders, members of the board of directors, members of the corporate assembly, the managing director, a majority of the employees or by trade unions representing two-thirds of the employees (Art. 5-22 of the PLLC Act).

If legal proceedings are brought before the court in accordance with Article 13-35(1) of the PLLC Act, the court may decide that the proceedings shall have suspensive effect on the issuance of the pre-merger certificate or on the registration of the merger, in which case the Register of Business Enterprises shall not issue the pre-merger certificate or register the merger, as the case may be, until the claim for invalidity has been settled (Art. 13-35(2) PLLC Act). Guidance for the court in the exercising of its discretionary competence to grant a suspension is provided in the preparatory works, according to

34 The Register of Business Enterprises publishes, at a prior stage in the merger proceedings, a notice stating that it has received draft terms of cross-border merger for the companies participating in the merger, see no 9 of this chapter. If viewed together with such prior publication of the draft terms of cross-border merger, the information published in connection with the completion of the merger will enable third parties to acquire knowledge of the companies' participation in a cross-border merger and the completion thereof. In connection with the implementation of the Cross-border Merger Directive, the Norwegian Government took the view that no further legislative initiatives were needed for the incorporation of Article 13(1) Dir., as Article 3 of the First Company Law Directive had been implemented through the Registration Act (see Ot.prp. no 78 (2006–2007) p. 27). All publications are accessible electronically and searches can be made according to companies and chronological order through the website of the register (www.brreg.no).

35 See no 20 of this chapter.

which requests for suspension of the merger procedure should be assessed on a case-by-case basis, taking into account the probability of the legal proceedings being successful, the possible damages or inconveniences the entry into force of the merger could cause to the plaintiffs and the possible damages or inconveniences a suspension of the registration could lead to for the merging companies.[36]

VI   Minority shareholders

25.   Under Norwegian law there are no special provisions designed to ensure protection of minority shareholders who have opposed the cross-border merger (Art. 4(2) of the Cross-border Merger Directive and Chapter 1, no 28 of this book).

In its consultation memorandum, the Norwegian Ministry of Justice had proposed a right for minority shareholders of a transferor Norwegian company who had opposed a merger where the acquiring company would be governed by the laws of another Member State to claim reimbursement of their shares.[37] All the stakeholders who responded to the consultation on this item opposed the proposal. Taking into consideration that, among other factors, a right for minority shareholders to claim reimbursement could create uncertainty for the merger negotiations and increase the risk of shareholders speculating in the shares or retarding the merger process, and further taking into consideration that the minority shareholders are protected by other rules (see no 26 of this chapter), the Ministry of Justice did not follow up the proposal in the proposition to the Parliament.[38]

26.   A minority shareholder will nevertheless benefit from general procedural and material protection rules. To the first category belong the requirements for the preparation and content of the draft terms of merger,[39] the notification to the shareholders of the draft terms of merger,[40] the preparation of the management report[41] and the independent expert's report,[42] as well as the requirement for a majority of two thirds of the votes at the general meeting for approval of the merger terms.[43] Material protection rules include the principle of equality of shareholder rights in Article 4-1(1) of the PLLC Act and the prohibition against the abuse of authority of the general meeting laid down in Article 5-21 of the PLLC Act, pursuant to which the general meeting cannot adopt any resolution

---

36 Ot.prp. no 78 (2006–2007) p. 45.
37 Section 4.11 of the Consultation Memorandum of 14 December 2006.
38 Ot.prp. no 78 (2006–2007) pp. 29–33.
39 Art. 13-26 of the PLLC Act, see nos 7 and 8 of this chapter.
40 Art. 13-12, cf. Art. 13-25(2) no 5, of the PLLC Act, see no 16 of this chapter.
41 Art. 13-27 of the PLLC Act, see nos 10 and 11 of this chapter.
42 Art. 13-28 of the PLLC Act, see nos 13 to 15 of this chapter.
43 Art. 13-3(2), cf. Art. 13-25(2) no 2, of the PLLC Act, see no 17 of this chapter.

which may give certain shareholders or other parties an unreasonable advantage at the expense of other shareholders or the company.

VII   Protection of creditors

27.   The rights of the creditors of a Norwegian company participating in a cross-border merger are protected by the provisions in Articles 13-15 and 13-16 (see Art. 13-25(2) no 5) of the PLLC Act.

Pursuant to Article 13-15 of the PLLC Act, the Register of Business Enterprises shall publish the merger resolution and notify the creditors of the company that any objections to the merger must be submitted to the company within two months. If a creditor with an undisputed claim which has fallen due submits an objection within the two months, the pre-merger certificate cannot be issued before the claim has been settled (Art. 13-16(1) PLLC Act). A creditor with a disputed claim or a claim which has not fallen due may demand that adequate security is furnished. The District Court shall settle disputes about the existence of a claim and concerning whether the security is adequate. The court may reject a claim for security if it is clear that there is no claim or that the merger will not weaken the creditor's possibility of achieving satisfaction for the claim.

In addition, in the financial area special protection rules apply to one group of creditors, namely the customers of commercial banks and insurance companies, cf. Article 31(1) and (2) of the Act of 24 May 1961 no 2 on Commercial Banks in Norway and Article 13-1(1) and (2) of the Act of 10 June 2005 no 44 on Insurance Companies and Pension Funds, pursuant to which a decision to merge or transfer the seat of a commercial bank or an insurance company requires the approval of the King and, in certain situations, also entitles the depositors or the insurance customers to terminate the account or the insurance agreement without any charge.

28.   As mentioned under no 20 of this chapter, a Norwegian company participating in a cross-border merger shall, when the deadline for objections from creditors has expired and the claims from creditors who have submitted objections to the merger have been settled, notify the Register of Business Enterprises that it has completed all the pre-merger acts and formalities. Until such notice is received, the register cannot issue the pre-merger certificate.

VIII   Employee participation

29.   The Employee Regulation,[44] which was brought about pursuant to Article 13-34 of the PLLC Act, implemented the rules pertaining to employee participation in Article 16 of the Cross-border Merger Directive with effect

---

44 See no 1 of this chapter.

from 1 February 2008. The regulation applies to an acquiring company which shall have its registered office in Norway (Art. 2(1) of the Employee Regulation).

In compliance with Article 16(1) of the Cross-border Merger Directive, Article 4(1) of the Employee Regulation states that the acquiring company shall be subject to the rules for employee participation that are in force in the Member State in which it has its registered office.

1   Employee participation in companies established in Norway resulting from a cross-border merger

30.   Under Norwegian law, the employees in a public limited liability company are entitled to representation on the board of directors or on the corporate assembly of the company.[45] The extent of the board representation depends on the number of employees in the company. In companies with fewer than thirty employees, the law does not provide for any right of representation in the management organs of the company. If the number of employees exceeds thirty, the employees are entitled to elect one member and one observer (with deputy members) to the board of directors (Art. 6-4(1) PLLC Act). If the number of employees exceeds fifty, the employees are entitled to elect one third and a minimum of two of the members of the board of directors (with deputy members) (Art. 6-4(2) PLLC Act). It should be noted that the representation on the board of directors is dependent on the employees making a demand for such representation.

When a company has more than 200 employees, it shall, as a general rule and regardless of whether a demand for representation has been made by the employees, set up a corporate assembly in which the employees shall be represented by one third of the members (Art. 6-35(1) PLLC Act). In such case, the board of directors shall be elected by the corporate assembly. One third of the members of the corporate assembly (which is equal to the portion of employee-elected members to the assembly) may, however, demand that the employees be represented by one third and a minimum of two members on the board of directors (Art. 6-37(1) PLLC Act). Pursuant to Article 6-35(2) of the PLLC Act, it may be agreed between the company and a majority of the employees, or trade unions representing two thirds of the employees, that the company shall not have a corporate assembly, in which case the employees are entitled to elect one member (with deputy member) or two observers to the board of directors in addition to the aforementioned representation to which they are entitled pursuant to Article 6-4(2) if the company has more than fifty employees (Art. 6-4(3) of the PLLC Act).

45 The same rules apply to a private limited liability company.

If the company is part of a corporate group, the King[46] may determine, following an application from the group, from trade unions representing two thirds of the group's employees or from a majority of the employees in the group, that the employees of the group are also entitled to elect members of the board of directors in the parent company (Art. 6-5(1) PLLC Act).

2   Special negotiating body ('SNB')

31.   Articles 5 to 15 of the Employee Regulation implement Article 16 of the Cross-border Merger Directive with respect to situations in which the representation rules in force in the Member States where the acquiring company has its registered office are set aside because (i) one of the merging companies has, in the six months before the publication of the draft terms of merger, an average number of employees that exceeds 500 and is operating under a system of employee participation, (ii) the national law applicable to the acquiring company does not provide for at least the same level of employee participation as operated in the merging companies, or (iii) the employee participation rights applicable to the establishments of the acquiring company in other Member States differ from the rights applicable to the acquiring company (Art. 4(2) of the Employee Regulation, see also Chapter 1, no 42, and Chapter 2, no 5 of this book). Due to the extensive employee participation rights provided for by Norwegian law (see no 30 of this chapter), the provision referred to in (ii) above (or more precisely, the equivalent provisions under the laws of the Member State in which the acquiring company will have its registered office) will have the consequence that, when the transferor company is Norwegian, the rules of the Member State to whose jurisdiction the acquiring company will be subject are likely to be set aside. As regards the provision referred to in (iii) above, it should be noted that, under Norwegian law, employees working for a foreign establishment of a Norwegian company enjoy the same representation rights as employees working in Norway. Thus, the provision will have no effect if the acquiring company is to be governed by Norwegian law.

32.   A special negotiating body ('SNB') shall be established if the rules of the Member State where the acquiring company has its registered office are set aside. In the SNB, each Member State shall be represented by one member for each 10 per cent or fraction thereof which the employees of merging companies registered in that Member State represent out of the total number of employees in the merging companies (Art. 5(2) Employee Regulation).

---

46 Delegated to *Bedriftsdemokratinemnda* (the Industrial Democracy Board) pursuant to Article 6, cf. Art. 40 of the Regulation of 18 December 1988 no 1205 on representation in private limited liability companies and public limited liability companies.

The allocation of the seats in the SNB between Norwegian companies and the appointment of Norwegian members to the SNB are governed by Articles 6 and 7 of the Employee Regulation. Pursuant to Article 6 of the Employee Regulation, the seats in the SNB are allocated to the merging Norwegian companies based on the number of employees in each company in descending order, starting with the company with the highest number of employees.

The members of the SNB are appointed by the trade unions if there are trade unions which represent two thirds of the employees. In the absence of trade unions with such representation, or if the trade unions cannot agree as to who shall be appointed, the members are elected directly by and among the employees in Norway in accordance with the Regulation of 18 December 1998 no 1205 on representation in private limited liability companies and public limited liability companies (Art. 7 Employee Regulation).

The task of the SNB shall be to reach an employee participation agreement with the merging companies. For this purpose the merging companies shall provide information to the SNB of the draft terms of merger and the merger process (Art. 8(1) Employee Regulation). The negotiations in the SNB shall be commenced immediately after the establishment of the SNB and may continue for a period of six months after the establishment of the SNB, unless the period is extended by the parties, in which case the negotiations may continue for a period of up to twelve months (Art. 10 Employee Regulation).

Decisions of the SNB are, as a general rule, taken by a majority vote. However, a decision to enter into an agreement which would result in a reduction in participation rights requires a two-thirds majority. The SNB may further decide by a majority vote of two thirds of its members, representing at least two thirds of the employees of the merging companies and in at least two different Member States, not to open negotiations for employee participation arrangements or to terminate such negotiations that have already opened (Art. 8(2), (3), (6) and (7) Employee Regulation; see Chapter 2, no 29 of this book).

An employee participation agreement must be in writing and shall specify its scope, the substance of the arrangements agreed for employee participation, the date of entry into force and the duration of the agreement, under which circumstances the agreement shall be renegotiated and the procedures which shall apply for such renegotiation (Art. 9 Employee Regulation).

If no employee participation agreement is successfully negotiated within the period referred to above, or if the parties so agree, the standard rules of employee participation laid down in the annex to the Employee Regulation shall apply. The merging companies may also choose to apply the standard rules directly without negotiations taking place with the SNB (Art. 11(1) of the Employee Regulation). The standard rules are described in Chapter 2, nos 31 to 35 of this book.

3   Protection of employee representatives

33.   The employees' participation rights are protected in the event of a subsequent domestic merger for a period of three years from the date the cross-border merger takes effect (Art. 2(3) Employee Regulation; Chapter 1, no 44 and Chapter 2, no 43 of this book).

34.   Article 16(3)(f) of the Cross-border Merger Directive (see Art. 10 of the SE Directive) states that the Member States shall ensure that employees' representatives enjoy the same protection and guarantees provided for employees' representatives by the national legislation and/or practice in force in their country of employment. The Employee Regulation does not contain any provision to this effect.[47] However, it is evident that the members of the SNB and the members of the representative body enjoy the same protection and guarantees provided for 'domestic' employees' representatives by Norwegian legislation and practice, namely that any alleged breach by the companies of the employee participation rights may be brought before the courts.

IX   Tax treatment

35.   The EEA Agreement does not extend to tax matters and Norway has therefore not implemented the Merger Tax Directive (see Chapter 3 of this book).

Pursuant to Article 11-2 of the Norwegian Tax Act of 26 March 1999 no 14 (the 'Tax Act'), a merger may be carried through without taxation of the company in question or the shareholders of the company, provided that certain conditions are fulfilled. However, the tax exemption only applies to mergers between companies resident in Norway for tax purposes. A cross-border merger will therefore, in principle, trigger income tax for the shareholders of a transferor company on capital gains derived from the realisation of the shares in a Norwegian limited liability company and a final settlement of the tax positions of the company being dissolved (Art. 11-11(1), cf. Arts. 10-30 through 10-37 Tax Act).

In general, Norwegian corporate shareholders are exempted from Norwegian tax on dividend distributions and capital gains from shares in limited liability companies, provided that the company is resident in the European Economic

---

47 Article 10 of the SE Directive and the similar provision in Article 12 of the SCE Directive have also not resulted in any implementation legislation. Nor are there any remarks in the consultation documents prior to the adoption of the Employee Regulation or the regulations implementing the SE Directive and the SCE Directive as to the need for legislative initiatives for the incorporation of these provisions, see the Consultation Memorandum of 3 June 2004 regarding the SE Directive, the Consultation Memorandum of 21 March 2006 regarding the SCE Directive and the Consultation Memorandum of 8 October 2007 regarding the Cross-border Merger Directive.

Area for tax purposes (Art. 2-38 of the Tax Act).[48] However, individual share-holders do not benefit from this exemption and will thus be liable for such taxes.

36.   Following an application prior to the merger, the Norwegian Ministry of Finance may grant roll-over tax relief, i.e. that the capital gain on the realisa-tion of the shares is deferred when the proceeds are reinvested in the consid-eration shares, and the capital gain becomes liable for tax on a subsequent disposal of the consideration shares (Art. 11-22 Tax Act). In order to be cov-ered by a roll-over tax relief, the shareholders of the company must be able to demonstrate that the merger is part of a reorganisation process which is a necessary measure for increasing the efficiency of the company's business operations. Further, special grounds must be shown to justify a roll-over tax relief. In practice, it is required that the transaction is made conditional upon such roll-over tax relief being granted.

The Norwegian Ministry has tended to approve of roll-over tax relief with regard to mergers provided that the merger is comparable with, and is carried out largely in accordance with applicable Norwegian regulations for, a domes-tic merger. Roll-over tax relief will only be given on condition of continuation of the tax base of the transferred assets by the successor. Thus, the acquiring company must assume the transferor company's tax values and other tax posi-tions related to the assets transferred and the shareholders must retain their values of the shares for tax purposes.

37.   The Ministry of Finance has previously announced that a draft reform bill for the taxation of cross-border mergers would be sent for public consultation by the end of 2008, the objective of which shall be to enable restructuring that is facilitated by company law to be carried through without triggering the need for an application for roll-over tax relief, whilst at the same time securing the Government's fiscal interests.[49] However, as of 1 November 2009 no draft reform bill has been presented.

---

48 Following an amendment to the Tax Act on 12 December 2008, 3 per cent of the annual net income exempted under Article 2-38 shall be recognised as taxable income and taxed at a rate of 28 per cent.

49 See letter from the Norwegian Minister of Finance to the Norwegian Parliament dated 4 December 2007 and Ot.prp. no 1 (2008–2009) *Skatte- og avgiftsopplegget 2009 – loven-dringer* pp. 49 and 50.

PART IV

Annexes

Annex I

25.11.2005 | EN | Official Journal of the European Union L 310/1

I

(Acts whose publication is obligatory)

DIRECTIVE 2005/56/EC OF THE EUROPEAN PARLIAMENT AND OF THE COUNCIL

of 26 October 2005

on cross-border mergers of limited liability companies

(Text with EEA relevance)

THE EUROPEAN PARLIAMENT AND THE COUNCIL OF THE EUROPEAN UNION,

Having regard to the Treaty establishing the European Community, and in particular Article 44 thereof,

Having regard to the proposal from the Commission,

Having regard to the opinion of the European Economic and Social Committee ([1]),

Acting in accordance with the procedure laid down in Article 251 of the Treaty ([2]),

Whereas:

(1) There is a need for cooperation and consolidation between limited liability companies from different Member States. However, as regards cross-border mergers of limited liability companies, they encounter many legislative and administrative difficulties in the Community. It is therefore necessary, with a view to the completion and functioning of the single market, to lay down Community provisions to facilitate the carrying-out of cross-border mergers between various types of limited liability company governed by the laws of different Member States.

(2) This Directive facilitates the cross-border merger of limited liability companies as defined herein. The laws of the Member States are to allow the cross-border merger of a national limited liability company with a limited liability company from another Member State if the national law of the relevant Member States permits mergers between such types of company.

(3) In order to facilitate cross-border merger operations, it should be laid down that, unless this Directive provides otherwise, each company taking part in a cross-border merger, and each third party concerned, remains subject to the provisions and formalities of the national law which would be applicable in the case of a national merger. None of the provisions and formalities of national law, to which reference is made in this Directive, should introduce restrictions on freedom of establishment or on the free movement of capital save where these can be justified in accordance with the case-law of the Court of Justice and in particular by requirements of the general interest and are both necessary for, and proportionate to, the attainment of such overriding requirements.

(4) The common draft terms of the cross-border merger are to be drawn up in the same terms for each of the companies concerned in the various Member States. The minimum content of such common draft terms should therefore be specified, while leaving the companies free to agree on other items.

(5) In order to protect the interests of members and others, both the common draft terms of cross-border mergers and the completion of the cross-border merger are to be publicised for each merging company via an entry in the appropriate public register.

(6) The laws of all the Member States should provide for the drawing-up at national level of a report on the common draft terms of the cross-border merger by one or more experts on behalf of each of the companies that are merging. In order to limit experts' costs connected with cross-border mergers, provision should be made for the possibility of drawing up a single report intended for all members of companies taking part in a cross-border merger operation. The common draft terms of the cross-border merger are to be approved by the general meeting of each of those companies.

([1]) OJ C 117, 30.4.2004, p. 43.
([2]) Opinion of the European Parliament of 10 May 2005 (not yet published in the Official Journal) and Council Decision of 19 September 2005.

(7) In order to facilitate cross-border merger operations, it should be provided that monitoring of the completion and legality of the decision-making process in each merging company should be carried out by the national authority having jurisdiction over each of those companies, whereas monitoring of the completion and legality of the cross-border merger should be carried out by the national authority having jurisdiction over the company resulting from the cross-border merger. The national authority in question may be a court, a notary or any other competent authority appointed by the Member State concerned. The national law determining the date on which the cross-border merger takes effect, this being the law to which the company resulting from the cross-border merger is subject, should also be specified.

(8) In order to protect the interests of members and others, the legal effects of the cross-border merger, distinguishing as to whether the company resulting from the cross-border merger is an acquiring company or a new company, should be specified. In the interests of legal certainty, it should no longer be possible, after the date on which a cross-border merger takes effect, to declare the merger null and void.

(9) This Directive is without prejudice to the application of the legislation on the control of concentrations between undertakings, both at Community level, by Regulation (EC) No 139/2004 (¹), and at the level of Member States.

(10) This Directive does not affect Community legislation regulating credit intermediaries and other financial undertakings and national rules made or introduced pursuant to such Community legislation.

(11) This Directive is without prejudice to a Member State's legislation demanding information on the place of central administration or the principal place of business proposed for the company resulting from the cross-border merger.

(12) Employees' rights other than rights of participation should remain subject to the national provisions referred to in Council Directive 98/59/EC of 20 July 1998 on collective redundancies (²), Council Directive 2001/23/EC of 12 March 2001 on the safeguarding of employees' rights in the event of transfers of undertakings, businesses or parts of undertakings or businesses (³), Directive 2002/14/EC of the European Parliament and of the Council of 11 March 2002 establishing a general framework for informing and consulting employees in the European Community (⁴) and Council Directive 94/45/EC of 22 September 1994 on the establishment of a European Works Council or a procedure in Community-scale undertakings and Community-scale groups of undertakings for the purposes of informing and consulting employees (⁵).

(13) If employees have participation rights in one of the merging companies under the circumstances set out in this Directive and, if the national law of the Member State in which the company resulting from the cross-border merger has its registered office does not provide for the same level of participation as operated in the relevant merging companies, including in committees of the supervisory board that have decision-making powers, or does not provide for the same entitlement to exercise rights for employees of establishments resulting from the cross-border merger, the participation of employees in the company resulting from the cross-border merger and their involvement in the definition of such rights are to be regulated. To that end, the principles and procedures provided for in Council Regulation (EC) No 2157/2001 of 8 October 2001 on the Statute for a European company (SE) (⁶) and in Council Directive 2001/86/EC of 8 October 2001 supplementing the Statute for a European company with regard to the involvement of employees (⁷), are to be taken as a basis, subject, however, to modifications that are deemed necessary because the resulting company will be subject to the national laws of the Member State where it has its registered office. A prompt start to negotiations under Article 16 of this Directive, with a view to not unnecessarily delaying mergers, may be ensured by Member States in accordance with Article 3(2)(b) of Directive 2001/86/EC.

(14) For the purpose of determining the level of employee participation operated in the relevant merging companies, account should also be taken of the proportion of

---

(²) OJ L 225, 12.8.1998, p. 16.
(³) OJ L 82, 22.3.2001, p. 16.
(⁴) OJ L 80, 23.3.2002, p. 29.
(⁵) OJ L 254, 30.9.1994, p. 64. Directive as amended by Directive 97/74/EC (OJ L 10, 16.1.1998, p. 22).
(⁶) OJ L 294, 10.11.2001, p. 1. Regulation as amended by Regulation (EC) No 885/2004 (OJ L 168, 1.5.2004, p. 1).
(⁷) OJ L 294, 10.11.2001, p. 22.

(¹) Council Regulation (EC) No 139/2004 of 20 January 2004 on the control of concentrations between undertakings (the EC Merger Regulation) (OJ L 24, 29.1.2004, p. 1).

employee representatives amongst the members of the management group, which covers the profit units of the companies, subject to employee participation.

(15) Since the objective of the proposed action, namely laying down rules with common features applicable at transnational level, cannot be sufficiently achieved by the Member States and can therefore, by reason of the scale and impact of the proposed action, be better achieved at Community level, the Community may adopt measures in accordance with the principle of subsidiarity as set out in Article 5 of the Treaty. In accordance with the principle of proportionality as set out in that Article, this Directive does not go beyond what is necessary to achieve that objective.

(16) In accordance with paragraph 34 of the Interinstitutional Agreement on better law-making ([1]), Member States should be encouraged to draw up, for themselves and in the interest of the Community, their own tables which will, as far as possible, illustrate the correlation between this Directive and the transposition measures and to make them public,

HAVE ADOPTED THIS DIRECTIVE:

Article 1

Scope

This Directive shall apply to mergers of limited liability companies formed in accordance with the law of a Member State and having their registered office, central administration or principal place of business within the Community, provided at least two of them are governed by the laws of different Member States (hereinafter referred to as cross-border mergers).

([1]) OJ C 321, 31.12.2003, p. 1.

Article 2

Definitions

For the purposes of this Directive:

1) 'limited liability company', hereinafter referred to as 'company', means:

    (a) a company as referred to in Article 1 of Directive 68/151/EEC ([2]), or

    (b) a company with share capital and having legal personality, possessing separate assets which alone serve to cover its debts and subject under the national law governing it to conditions concerning guarantees such as are provided for by Directive 68/151/EEC for the protection of the interests of members and others;

2. 'merger' means an operation whereby:

    (a) one or more companies, on being dissolved without going into liquidation, transfer all their assets and liabilities to another existing company, the acquiring company, in exchange for the issue to their members of securities or shares representing the capital of that other company and, if applicable, a cash payment not exceeding 10 % of the nominal value, or, in the absence of a nominal value, of the accounting par value of those securities or shares; or

    (b) two or more companies, on being dissolved without going into liquidation, transfer all their assets and liabilities to a company that they form, the new company, in exchange for the issue to their members of securities or shares representing the capital of that new company and, if applicable, a cash payment not exceeding 10 % of the nominal value, or in the absence of a nominal value, of the accounting par value of those securities or shares; or

    (c) a company, on being dissolved without going into liquidation, transfers all its assets and liabilities to the company holding all the securities or shares representing its capital.

([2]) First Council Directive 68/151/EEC of 9 March 1968 on coordination of safeguards which, for the protection of the interests of members and others, are required by Member States of companies within the meaning of the second paragraph of Article 58 of the Treaty, with a view to making such safeguards equivalent throughout the Community (OJ L 65, 14.3.1968, p. 8). Directive as last amended by the 2003 Act of Accession.

L 310/4   [EN]   Official Journal of the European Union   25.11.2005

Article 3

Further provisions concerning the scope

1. Notwithstanding Article 2(2), this Directive shall also apply to cross-border mergers where the law of at least one of the Member States concerned allows the cash payment referred to in points (a) and (b) of Article 2(2) to exceed 10 % of the nominal value, or, in the absence of a nominal value, of the accounting par value of the securities or shares representing the capital of the company resulting from the cross-border merger.

2. Member States may decide not to apply this Directive to cross-border mergers involving a cooperative society even in the cases where the latter would fall within the definition of 'limited liability company' as laid down in Article 2(1).

3. This Directive shall not apply to cross-border mergers involving a company the object of which is the collective investment of capital provided by the public, which operates on the principle of risk-spreading and the units of which are, at the holders' request, repurchased or redeemed, directly or indirectly, out of the assets of that company. Action taken by such a company to ensure that the stock exchange value of its units does not vary significantly from its net asset value shall be regarded as equivalent to such repurchase or redemption.

Article 4

Conditions relating to cross-border mergers

1. Save as otherwise provided in this Directive,

(a) cross-border mergers shall only be possible between types of companies which may merge under the national law of the relevant Member States, and

(b) a company taking part in a cross-border merger shall comply with the provisions and formalities of the national law to which it is subject. The laws of a Member State enabling its national authorities to oppose a given internal merger on grounds of public interest shall also be applicable to a cross-border merger where at least one of the merging companies is subject to the law of that Member State. This provision shall not apply to the extent that Article 21 of Regulation (EC) No 139/2004 is applicable.

2. The provisions and formalities referred to in paragraph 1 (b) shall, in particular, include those concerning the decision-making process relating to the merger and, taking into account the cross-border nature of the merger, the protection of creditors of the merging companies, debenture holders and the holders of securities or shares, as well as of employees as regards rights other than those governed by Article 16. A Member State may, in the case of companies participating in a cross-border merger and governed by its law, adopt provisions designed to ensure appropriate protection for minority members who have opposed the cross-border merger.

Article 5

Common draft terms of cross-border mergers

The management or administrative organ of each of the merging companies shall draw up the common draft terms of cross-border merger. The common draft terms of cross-border merger shall include at least the following particulars:

(a) the form, name and registered office of the merging companies and those proposed for the company resulting from the cross-border merger;

(b) the ratio applicable to the exchange of securities or shares representing the company capital and the amount of any cash payment;

(c) the terms for the allotment of securities or shares representing the capital of the company resulting from the cross-border merger;

(d) the likely repercussions of the cross-border merger on employment;

(e) the date from which the holding of such securities or shares representing the company capital will entitle the holders to share in profits and any special conditions affecting that entitlement;

(f) the date from which the transactions of the merging companies will be treated for accounting purposes as being those of the company resulting from the cross-border merger;

(g) the rights conferred by the company resulting from the cross-border merger on members enjoying special rights or on holders of securities other than shares representing the company capital, or the measures proposed concerning them;

(h) any special advantages granted to the experts who examine the draft terms of the cross-border merger or to members of the administrative, management, supervisory or controlling organs of the merging companies;

(i) the statutes of the company resulting from the cross-border merger;

(j) where appropriate, information on the procedures by which arrangements for the involvement of employees in the definition of their rights to participation in the company resulting from the cross-border merger are determined pursuant to Article 16;

331

(k) information on the evaluation of the assets and liabilities which are transferred to the company resulting from the cross-border merger;

(l) dates of the merging companies' accounts used to establish the conditions of the cross-border merger.

Article 6

Publication

1. The common draft terms of the cross-border merger shall be published in the manner prescribed by the laws of each Member State in accordance with Article 3 of Directive 68/151/EEC for each of the merging companies at least one month before the date of the general meeting which is to decide thereon.

2. For each of the merging companies and subject to the additional requirements imposed by the Member State to which the company concerned is subject, the following particulars shall be published in the national gazette of that Member State:

(a) the type, name and registered office of every merging company;

(b) the register in which the documents referred to in Article 3(2) of Directive 68/151/EEC are filed in respect of each merging company, and the number of the entry in that register;

(c) an indication, for each of the merging companies, of the arrangements made for the exercise of the rights of creditors and of any minority members of the merging companies and the address at which complete information on those arrangements may be obtained free of charge.

Article 7

Report of the management or administrative organ

The management or administrative organ of each of the merging companies shall draw up a report intended for the members explaining and justifying the legal and economic aspects of the cross-border merger and explaining the implications of the cross-border merger for members, creditors and employees.

The report shall be made available to the members and to the representatives of the employees or, where there are no such representatives, to the employees themselves, not less than one month before the date of the general meeting referred to in Article 9.

Where the management or administrative organ of any of the merging companies receives, in good time, an opinion from the representatives of their employees, as provided for under national law, that opinion shall be appended to the report.

Article 8

Independent expert report

1. An independent expert report intended for members and made available not less than one month before the date of the general meeting referred to in Article 9 shall be drawn up for each merging company. Depending on the law of each Member State, such experts may be natural persons or legal persons.

2. As an alternative to experts operating on behalf of each of the merging companies, one or more independent experts, appointed for that purpose at the joint request of the companies by a judicial or administrative authority in the Member State of one of the merging companies or of the company resulting from the cross-border merger or approved by such an authority, may examine the common draft terms of cross-border merger and draw up a single written report to all the members.

3. The expert report shall include at least the particulars provided for by Article 10(2) of Council Directive 78/855/EEC of 9 October 1978 concerning mergers of public limited liability companies ([1]). The experts shall be entitled to secure from each of the merging companies all information they consider necessary for the discharge of their duties.

4. Neither an examination of the common draft terms of cross-border merger by independent experts nor an expert report shall be required if all the members of each of the companies involved in the cross-border merger have so agreed.

Article 9

Approval by the general meeting

1. After taking note of the reports referred to in Articles 7 and 8, the general meeting of each of the merging companies shall decide on the approval of the common draft terms of cross-border merger.

([1]) OJ L 295, 20.10.1978, p. 36. Directive as last amended by the 2003 Act of Accession.

L 310/6 | EN | Official Journal of the European Union | 25.11.2005

2. The general meeting of each of the merging companies may reserve the right to make implementation of the cross-border merger conditional on express ratification by it of the arrangements decided on with respect to the participation of employees in the company resulting from the cross-border merger.

3. The laws of a Member State need not require approval of the merger by the general meeting of the acquiring company if the conditions laid down in Article 8 of Directive 78/855/EEC are fulfilled.

Article 10

Pre-merger certificate

1. Each Member State shall designate the court, notary or other authority competent to scrutinise the legality of the cross-border merger as regards that part of the procedure which concerns each merging company subject to its national law.

2. In each Member State concerned the authority referred to in paragraph 1 shall issue, without delay to each merging company subject to that State's national law, a certificate conclusively attesting to the proper completion of the pre-merger acts and formalities.

3. If the law of a Member State to which a merging company is subject provides for a procedure to scrutinise and amend the ratio applicable to the exchange of securities or shares, or a procedure to compensate minority members, without preventing the registration of the cross-border merger, such procedure shall only apply if the other merging companies situated in Member States which do not provide for such procedure explicitly accept, when approving the draft terms of the cross-border merger in accordance with Article 9(1), the possibility for the members of that merging company to have recourse to such procedure, to be initiated before the court having jurisdiction over that merging company. In such cases, the authority referred to in paragraph 1 may issue the certificate referred to in paragraph 2 even if such procedure has commenced. The certificate must, however, indicate that the procedure is pending. The decision in the procedure shall be binding on the company resulting from the cross-border merger and all its members.

Article 11

Scrutiny of the legality of the cross-border merger

1. Each Member State shall designate the court, notary or other authority competent to scrutinise the legality of the cross-border merger as regards that part of the procedure

which concerns the completion of the cross-border merger and, where appropriate, the formation of a new company resulting from the cross-border merger where the company created by the cross-border merger is subject to its national law. The said authority shall in particular ensure that the merging companies have approved the common draft terms of cross-border merger in the same terms and, where appropriate, that arrangements for employee participation have been determined in accordance with Article 16.

2. To that end each merging company shall submit to the authority referred to in paragraph 1 the certificate referred to in Article 10(2) within six months of its issue together with the common draft terms of cross-border merger approved by the general meeting referred to in Article 9.

Article 12

Entry into effect of the cross-border merger

The law of the Member State to whose jurisdiction the company resulting from the cross-border merger is subject shall determine the date on which the cross-border merger takes effect. That date must be after the scrutiny referred to in Article 11 has been carried out.

Article 13

Registration

The law of each of the Member States to whose jurisdiction the merging companies were subject shall determine, with respect to the territory of that State, the arrangements, in accordance with Article 3 of Directive 68/151/EEC, for publicising completion of the cross-border merger in the public register in which each of the companies is required to file documents.

The registry for the registration of the company resulting from the cross-border merger shall notify, without delay, the registry in which each of the companies was required to file documents that the cross-border merger has taken effect. Deletion of the old registration, if applicable, shall be effected on receipt of that notification, but not before.

Article 14

Consequences of the cross-border merger

1. A cross-border merger carried out as laid down in points (a) and (c) of Article 2(2) shall, from the date referred to in Article 12, have the following consequences:

(a) all the assets and liabilities of the company being acquired shall be transferred to the acquiring company;

333

(b) the members of the company being acquired shall become members of the acquiring company;

(c) the company being acquired shall cease to exist.

2. A cross-border merger carried out as laid down in point (b) of Article 2(2) shall, from the date referred to in Article 12, have the following consequences:

(a) all the assets and liabilities of the merging companies shall be transferred to the new company;

(b) the members of the merging companies shall become members of the new company;

(c) the merging companies shall cease to exist.

3. Where, in the case of a cross-border merger of companies covered by this Directive, the laws of the Member States require the completion of special formalities before the transfer of certain assets, rights and obligations by the merging companies becomes effective against third parties, those formalities shall be carried out by the company resulting from the cross-border merger.

4. The rights and obligations of the merging companies arising from contracts of employment or from employment relationships and existing at the date on which the cross-border merger takes effect shall, by reason of that cross-border merger taking effect, be transferred to the company resulting from the cross-border merger on the date on which the cross-border merger takes effect.

5. No shares in the acquiring company shall be exchanged for shares in the company being acquired held either:

(a) by the acquiring company itself or through a person acting in his or her own name but on its behalf;

(b) by the company being acquired itself or through a person acting in his or her own name but on its behalf.

Article 15

Simplified formalities

1. Where a cross-border merger by acquisition is carried out by a company which holds all the shares and other securities conferring the right to vote at general meetings of the company or companies being acquired:

— Articles 5, points (b), (c) and (e), 8 and 14(1), point (b) shall not apply,

— Article 9(1) shall not apply to the company or companies being acquired.

2. Where a cross-border merger by acquisition is carried out by a company which holds 90 % or more but not all of the shares and other securities conferring the right to vote at general meetings of the company or companies being acquired, reports by an independent expert or experts and the documents necessary for scrutiny shall be required only to the extent that the national law governing either the acquiring company or the company being acquired so requires.

Article 16

Employee participation

1. Without prejudice to paragraph 2, the company resulting from the cross-border merger shall be subject to the rules in force concerning employee participation, if any, in the Member State where it has its registered office.

2. However, the rules in force concerning employee participation, if any, in the Member State where the company resulting from the cross-border merger has its registered office shall not apply, where at least one of the merging companies has, in the six months before the publication of the draft terms of the cross-border merger as referred to in Article 6, an average number of employees that exceeds 500 and is operating under an employee participation system within the meaning of Article 2(k) of Directive 2001/86/EC, or where the national law applicable to the company resulting from the cross-border merger does not

(a) provide for at least the same level of employee participation as operated in the relevant merging companies, measured by reference to the proportion of employee representatives amongst the members of the administrative or supervisory organ or their committees or of the management group which covers the profit units of the company, subject to employee representation, or

(b) provide for employees of establishments of the company resulting from the cross-border merger that are situated in other Member States the same entitlement to exercise participation rights as is enjoyed by those employees employed in the Member State where the company resulting from the cross-border merger has its registered office.

L 310/8   EN   Official Journal of the European Union   25.11.2005

3. In the cases referred to in paragraph 2, the participation of employees in the company resulting from the cross-border merger and their involvement in the definition of such rights shall be regulated by the Member States, *mutatis mutandis* and subject to paragraphs 4 to 7 below, in accordance with the principles and procedures laid down in Article 12(2), (3) and (4) of Regulation (EC) No 2157/2001 and the following provisions of Directive 2001/86/EC:

(a) Article 3(1), (2) and (3), (4) first subparagraph, first indent, and second subparagraph, (5) and (7);

(b) Article 4(1), (2), points (a), (g) and (h), and (3);

(c) Article 5;

(d) Article 6;

(e) Article 7(1), (2) first subparagraph, point (b), and second subparagraph, and (3). However, for the purposes of this Directive, the percentages required by Article 7(2), first subparagraph, point (b) of Directive 2001/86/EC for the application of the standard rules contained in part 3 of the Annex to that Directive shall be raised from 25 to 33 1/3 %;

(f) Articles 8, 10 and 12;

(g) Article 13(4);

(h) part 3 of the Annex, point (b).

4. When regulating the principles and procedures referred to in paragraph 3, Member States:

(a) shall confer on the relevant organs of the merging companies the right to choose without any prior negotiation to be directly subject to the standard rules for participation referred to in paragraph 3(h), as laid down by the legislation of the Member State in which the company resulting from the cross-border merger is to have its registered office, and to abide by those rules from the date of registration;

(b) shall confer on the special negotiating body the right to decide, by a majority of two thirds of its members representing at least two thirds of the employees, including the votes of members representing employees in at least two different Member States, not to open negotiations or to terminate negotiations already opened and to rely on the rules on participation in force in the Member State where the registered office of the company resulting from the cross-border merger will be situated;

(c) may, in the case where, following prior negotiations, standard rules for participation apply and notwithstanding these rules, determine to limit the proportion of employee representatives in the administrative organ of the company resulting from the cross-border merger. However, if in one of the merging companies employee representatives constituted at least one third of the administrative or supervisory board, the limitation may never result in a lower proportion of employee representatives in the administrative organ than one third.

5. The extension of participation rights to employees of the company resulting from the cross-border merger employed in other Member States, referred to in paragraph 2(b), shall not entail any obligation for Member States which choose to do so to take those employees into account when calculating the size of workforce thresholds giving rise to participation rights under national law.

6. When at least one of the merging companies is operating under an employee participation system and the company resulting from the cross-border merger is to be governed by such a system in accordance with the rules referred to in paragraph 2, that company shall be obliged to take a legal form allowing for the exercise of participation rights.

7. When the company resulting from the cross-border merger is operating under an employee participation system, that company shall be obliged to take measures to ensure that employees' participation rights are protected in the event of subsequent domestic mergers for a period of three years after the cross-border merger has taken effect, by applying mutatis mutandis the rules laid down in this Article.

Article 17

Validity

A cross-border merger which has taken effect as provided for in Article 12 may not be declared null and void.

335

Article 18

Review

Five years after the date laid down in the first paragraph of Article 19, the Commission shall review this Directive in the light of the experience acquired in applying it and, if necessary, propose its amendment.

Article 19

Transposition

Member States shall bring into force the laws, regulations and administrative provisions necessary to comply with this Directive by 15 December 2007.

When Member States adopt these measures, they shall contain a reference to this Directive or shall be accompanied by such reference on the occasion of their official publication. The methods of making such reference shall be laid down by Member States.

Article 20

Entry into force

This Directive shall enter into force on the 20th day following its publication in the *Official Journal of the European Union*.

Article 21

Addressees

This Directive is addressed to the Member States.

Done at Strasbourg, 26 October 2005.

For the European Parliament	*For the Council*
The President	*The President*
J. BORRELL FONTELLES	D. ALEXANDER

Annex II

1990L0435 — EN — 01.01.2007 — 004.001 — 1

►B

COUNCIL DIRECTIVE

of 23 July 1990

on the common system of taxation applicable in the case of parent companies and subsidiaries of different Member States

(90/435/EEC)

(OJ L 225, 22.9.1990, p. 6)

Amended by:

		Official Journal		
		No	page	date
►M1	Council Directive 2003/123/EC of 22 December 2003	L 7	41	13.1.2004
►M2	Council Directive 2006/98/EC of 20 November 2006	L 363	129	20.12.2006

Amended by:

►A1	Act of Accession of Austria, Sweden and Finland	C 241	21	29.8.1994
	(adapted by Council Decision 95/1/EC, Euratom, ECSC)	L 1	1	1.1.1995
►A2	Act concerning the conditions of accession of the Czech Republic, the Republic of Estonia, the Republic of Cyprus, the Republic of Latvia, the Republic of Lithuania, the Republic of Hungary, the Republic of Malta, the Republic of Poland, the Republic of Slovenia and the Slovak Republic and the adjustments to the Treaties on which the European Union is founded	L 236	33	23.9.2003

Corrected by:

►C1 Corrigendum, OJ L 23, 29.1.1991, p. 35 (90/435)
►C2 Corrigendum, OJ L 16, 18.1.1997, p. 98 (90/435)

▼B

COUNCIL DIRECTIVE

of 23 July 1990

on the common system of taxation applicable in the case of parent companies and subsidiaries of different Member States

(90/435/EEC)

THE COUNCIL OF THE EUROPEAN COMMUNITIES,

Having regard to the Treaty establishing the European Economic Community, and in particular Article 100 thereof,

Having regard to the proposal of the Commission ([1]),

Having regard to the opinion of the European Parliament ([2]),

Having regard to the opinion of the Economic and Social Committee ([3]),

Whereas the grouping together of companies of different Member States may be necessary in order to create within the Community conditions analogous to those of an internal market and in order thus to ensure the establishment and effective functioning of the common market; whereas such operations ought not to be hampered by restrictions, disadvantages or distortions arising in particular from the tax provisions of the Member States; whereas it is therefore necessary to introduce with respect to such grouping together of companies of different Member States, tax rules which are neutral from the point of view of competition, in order to allow enterprises to adapt to the requirements of the common market, to increase their productivity and to improve their competitive strength at the international level;

Whereas such grouping together may result in the formation of groups of parent companies and subsidiaries;

Whereas the existing tax provisions which govern the relations between parent companies and subsidiaries of different Member States vary appreciably from one Member State to another and are generally less advantageous than those applicable to parent companies and subsidiaries of the same Member State; whereas cooperation between companies of different Member States is thereby disadvantaged in comparison with cooperation between companies of the same Member State; whereas it is necessary to eliminate this disadvantage by the introduction of a common system in order to facilitate the grouping together of companies;

Whereas where a parent company by virtue of its association with its subsidiary receives distributed profits, the State of the parent company must:

— either refrain from taxing such profits,

— or tax such profits while authorizing the parent company to deduct from the amount of tax due that fraction of the corporation tax paid by the subsidiary which relates to those profits;

Whereas it is furthermore necessary, in order to ensure fiscal neutrality, that the profits which a subsidiary distributes to its parent company be exempt from withholding tax; whereas, however, the Federal Republic of Germany and the Hellenic Republic, by reason of the particular nature of their corporate tax systems, and the Portuguese Republic,

---

([1]) OJ No C 39, 22. 3. 1969, p. 7 and Amendment transmitted on 5 July 1985.
([2]) OJ No C 51, 29. 4. 1970, p. 6.
([3]) OJ No C 100, 1. 8. 1969, p. 7.

▼B

for budgetary reasons, should be authorized to maintain temporarily a withholding tax,

HAS ADOPTED THIS DIRECTIVE:

Article 1

1.   Each Member State shall apply this Directive:

— to distributions of profits received by companies of that State which come from their subsidiaries of other Member States,

— to distributions of profits by companies of that State to companies of other Member States of which they are subsidiaries,

▼M1

— to distributions of profits received by permanent establishments situated in that State of companies of other Member States which come from their subsidiaries of a Member State other than that where the permanent establishment is situated,

— to distributions of profits by companies of that State to permanent establishments situated in another Member State of companies of the same Member State of which they are subsidiaries.

▼B

2.   This Directive shall not preclude the application of domestic or agreement-based provisions required for the prevention of fraud or abuse.

Article 2

►M1 1. ◄   For the purposes of this Directive 'company of a Member State' shall mean any company which:

(a) takes one of the forms listed in the Annex hereto;

(b) according to the tax laws of a Member State is considered to be resident in that State for tax purposes and, under the terms of a double taxation agreement concluded with a third State, is not considered to be resident for tax purposes outside the Community;

(c) moreover, is subject to one of the following taxes, without the possibility of an option or of being exempt:

— impôt des sociétés/vennootschapsbelasting in Belgium,

— selskabsskat in Denmark,

— Körperschaftsteuer in the Federal Republic of Germany,

— φόρος εισοδήματος νομικών προσώπων κερδοσκοπικού χαρακτήρα in Greece,

— impuesto sobre sociedades in Spain,

— impôt sur les sociétés in France,

— corporation tax in Ireland,

— imposta sul reddito delle persone giuridiche in Italy,

— impôt sur le revenu des collectivités in Luxembourg,

— vennootschapsbelasting in the Netherlands,

— imposto sobre o rendimento das pessoas colectivas in Portugal,

— corporation tax in the United Kingdom,

▼A1

— Körperschaftsteuer in Austria,

— yhteisöjen tulovero/inkomstskatten för samfund in Finland,

— statlig inkomstskatt in Sweden,

▼A2

— *Daň z příjmů právnických osob* in the Czech Republic,

— *Tulumaks* in Estonia,

— *Φόρος Εισοδήματος* in Cyprus,

— *uzņēmumu ienākuma nodoklis* in Latvia,

— *Pelno mokestis* in Lithuania,

— *Társasági adó, osztalékadó* in Hungary,

— *Taxxa fuq l-income* in Malta,

— *Podatek dochodowy od osób prawnych* in Poland,

— *Davek od dobička pravnih oseb* in Slovenia,

— *daň z príjmov právnických osôb* in Slovakia,

▼M2

— *корпоративен данък* in Bulgaria,

— *impozit pe profit* in Romania,

▼B

or to any other tax which may be substituted for any of the above taxes.

▼M1

2.   For the purposes of this Directive the term 'permanent establishment' means a fixed place of business situated in a Member State through which the business of a company of another Member State is wholly or partly carried on in so far as the profits of that place of business are subject to tax in the Member State in which it is situated by virtue of the relevant bilateral tax treaty or, in the absence of such a treaty, by virtue of national law.

▼B

Article 3

1.   ►**M1** For the purposes of applying this Directive:

(a) the status of parent company shall be attributed at least to any company of a Member State which fulfils the conditions set out in Article 2 and has a minimum holding of 20 % in the capital of a company of another Member State fulfilling the same conditions;

such status shall also be attributed, under the same conditions, to a company of a Member State which has a minimum holding of 20 % in the capital of a company of the same Member State, held in whole or in part by a permanent establishment of the former company situated in another Member State;

from 1 January 2007 the minimum holding percentage shall be 15 %;

from 1 January 2009 the minimum holding percentage shall be 10 %;

(b) 'subsidiary' shall mean that company the capital of which includes the holding referred to in (a). ◄

2.   By way of derogation from paragraph 1, Member States shall have the option of:

▼**B**

— replacing, by means of bilateral agreement, the criterion of a holding in the capital by that of a holding of voting rights,

— not applying this Directive to companies of that Member State which do not maintain for an uninterrupted period of at least two years holdings qualifying them as parent companies or to those of their companies in which a company of another Member State does not maintain such a holding for an uninterrupted period of at least two years.

Article 4

▼**M1**

1.   Where a parent company or its permanent establishment, by virtue of the association of the parent company with its subsidiary, receives distributed profits, the State of the parent company and the State of its permanent establishment shall, except when the subsidiary is liquidated, either:

— refrain from taxing such profits, or

— tax such profits while authorising the parent company and the permanent establishment to deduct from the amount of tax due that fraction of the corporation tax related to those profits and paid by the subsidiary and any lower-tier subsidiary, subject to the condition that at each tier a company and its lower-tier subsidiary meet the requirements provided for in Articles 2 and 3, up to the limit of the amount of the corresponding tax due.

1 a.   Nothing in this Directive shall prevent the State of the parent company from considering a subsidiary to be fiscally transparent on the basis of that State's assessment of the legal characteristics of that subsidiary arising from the law under which it is constituted and therefore from taxing the parent company on its share of the profits of its subsidiary as and when those profits arise. In this case the State of the parent company shall refrain from taxing the distributed profits of the subsidiary.

When assessing the parent company's share of the profits of its subsidiary as they arise the State of the parent company shall either exempt those profits or authorise the parent company to deduct from the amount of tax due that fraction of the corporation tax related to the parent company's share of profits and paid by its subsidiary and any lower-tier subsidiary, subject to the condition that at each tier a company and its lower-tier subsidiary meet the requirements provided for in Articles 2 and 3, up to the limit of the amount of the corresponding tax due.

▼**B**

2.   However, each Member State shall retain the option of providing that any charges relating to the holding and any losses resulting from the distribution of the profits of the subsidiary may not be deducted from the taxable profits of the parent company. Where the management costs relating to the holding in such a case are fixed as a flat rate, the fixed amount may not exceed 5 % of the profits distributed by the subsidiary.

3.   ►**M1** Paragraphs 1 and 1a shall apply until the date of effective entry into force of a common system of company taxation. ◄

The Council shall at the appropriate time adopt the rules to apply after the date referred to in the first subparagraph.

▼**B**

Article 5

1. ►**M1** Profits which a subsidiary distributes to its parent company shall be exempt from withholding tax. ◄

▼**M1**

——————

▼**B**

Article 6

The Member State of a parent company may not charge withholding tax on the profits which such a company receives from a subsidiary.

Article 7

1. The term 'withholding tax' as used in this Directive shall not cover an advance payment or prepayment (précompte) of corporation tax to the Member State of the subsidiary which is made in connection with a distribution of profits to its parent company.

2. This Directive shall not affect the application of domestic or agreement-based provisions designed to eliminate or lessen economic double taxation of dividends, in particular provisions relating to the payment of tax credits to the recipients of dividends.

Article 8

1. Member States shall bring into force the laws, regulations and administrative provisions necessary for them to comply with this Directive before 1 January 1992. They shall forthwith inform the Commission thereof.

2. Member States shall ensure that the texts of the main provisions of domestic law which they adopt in the field covered by this Directive are communicated to the Commission.

Article 9

This Directive is addressed to the Member States.

343

▼<u>M2</u>

ANNEX

LIST OF COMPANIES REFERRED TO IN ARTICLE 2(1)(A)

(a) companies incorporated under Council Regulation (EC) No 2157/2001 of 8 October 2001 on the Statute for a European company (SE) and Council Directive 2001/86/EC of 8 October 2001 supplementing the Statute for a European company with regard to the involvement of employees and cooperative societies incorporated under Council Regulation (EC) No 1435/2003 of 22 July 2003 on the Statute for a European Cooperative Society (SCE) and Council Directive 2003/72/EC of 22 July 2003 supplementing the Statute for a European Cooperative Society with regard to the involvement of employees;

(b) companies under Belgian law known as 'société anonyme'/'naamloze vennootschap','société en commandite par actions'/'commanditaire vennootschap op aandelen', 'société privée à responsabilité limitée'/'besloten vennootschap met beperkte aansprakelijkheid', 'société coopérative à responsabilité limitée'/'coöperatieve vennootschap met beperkte aansprakelijkheid', 'société coopérative à responsabilité illimitée'/'coöperatieve vennootschap met onbeperkte aansprakelijkheid', 'société en nom collectif'/'vennootschap onder firma', 'société en commandite simple'/'gewone commanditaire vennootschap', public undertakings which have adopted one of the abovementioned legal forms, and other companies constituted under Belgian law subject to Belgian corporate tax;

(c) companies under Bulgarian law known as: 'събирателното дружество', 'командитното дружество', 'дружеството с ограничена отговорност', 'акционерното дружество', 'командитното дружество с акции', 'неперсонифицирано дружество', 'кооперации', 'кооперативни съюзи''държавни предприятия' constituted under Bulgarian law and carrying on commercial activities;

(d) companies under Czech law known as: 'akciová společnost', 'společnost s ručením omezeným';

(e) companies under Danish law known as 'aktieselskab' and 'anpartsselskab'. Other companies subject to tax under the Corporation Tax Act, insofar as their taxable income is calculated and taxed in accordance with the general tax legislation rules applicable to 'aktieselskaber';

(f) companies under German law known as 'Aktiengesellschaft', 'Kommanditgesellschaft auf Aktien', 'Gesellschaft mit beschränkter Haftung', 'Versicherungsverein auf Gegenseitigkeit', 'Erwerbs- und Wirtschaftsgenossenschaft', 'Betriebe gewerblicher Art von juristischen Personen des öffentlichen Rechts', and other companies constituted under German law subject to German corporate tax;

(g) companies under Estonian law known as: 'täisühing', 'usaldusühing', 'osaühing', 'aktsiaselts', 'tulundusühistu';

(h) companies under Greek law known as 'ανώνυμη εταιρεία','εταιρεία περιορισμένης ευθύνης (Ε.Π.Ε.)' and other companies constituted under Greek law subject to Greek corporate tax;

(i) companies under Spanish law known as: 'sociedad anónima', 'sociedad comanditaria por acciones', 'sociedad de responsabilidad limitada', public law bodies which operate under private law. Other entities constituted under Spanish law subject to Spanish corporate tax ('Impuesto sobre Sociedades');

(j) companies under French law known as 'société anonyme', 'société en commandite par actions', 'société à responsabilité limitée', 'sociétés par actions simplifiées', 'sociétés d'assurances mutuelles', 'caisses d'épargne et de prévoyance', 'sociétés civiles' which are automatically subject to corporation tax, 'coopératives', 'unions de coopératives', industrial and commercial public establishments and undertakings, and other companies constituted under French law subject to French corporate tax;

(k) companies incorporated or existing under Irish law, bodies registered under the Industrial and Provident Societies Act, building societies incorporated under the Building Societies Acts and trustee savings banks within the meaning of the Trustee Savings Banks Act, 1989;

(l) companies under Italian law known as 'società per azioni', 'società in accomandita per azioni', 'società a responsabilità limitata', 'società cooperative', 'società di mutua assicurazione', and private and public entities whose activity is wholly or principally commercial;

▼M2

(m) under Cypriot law: 'εταιρείες' as defined in the Income Tax laws;

(n) companies under Latvian law known as: 'akciju sabiedrība', 'sabiedrība ar ierobežotu atbildību';

(o) companies incorporated under the law of Lithuania;

(p) companies under Luxembourg law known as 'société anonyme', 'société en commandite par actions', 'société à responsabilité limitée', 'société coopérative', 'société coopérative organisée comme une société anonyme', 'association d'assurances mutuelles', 'association d'épargne-pension', 'entreprise de nature commerciale, industrielle ou minière de l'Etat, des communes, des syndicats de communes, des établissements publics et des autres personnes morales de droit public', and other companies constituted under Luxembourg law subject to Luxembourg corporate tax;

(q) companies under Hungarian law known as: 'közkereseti társaság', 'betéti társaság', 'közös vállalat', 'korlátolt felelősségű társaság', 'részvénytársaság', 'egyesülés', 'szövetkezet';

(r) companies under Maltese law known as: 'Kumpaniji ta' Responsabilita' Limitata', 'Soċjetajiet en commandite li l-kapital tagħhom maqsum f'azzjonijiet';

(s) companies under Dutch law known as 'naamloze vennnootschap', 'besloten vennootschap met beperkte aansprakelijkheid', 'Open commanditaire vennootschap', 'Coöperatie', 'onderlinge waarborgmaatschappij', 'Fonds voor gemene rekening', 'vereniging op coöperatieve grondslag', 'vereniging welke op onderlinge grondslag als verzekeraar of kredietinstelling optreedt', and other companies constituted under Dutch law subject to Dutch corporate tax;

(t) companies under Austrian law known as 'Aktiengesellschaft', 'Gesellschaft mit beschränkter Haftung', 'Versicherungsvereine auf Gegenseitigkeit', 'Erwerbs- und Wirtschaftsgenossenschaften', 'Betriebe gewerblicher Art von Körperschaften des öffentlichen Rechts', 'Sparkassen', and other companies constituted under Austrian law subject to Austrian corporate tax;

(u) companies under Polish law known as: 'spółka akcyjna', 'spółka z ograniczoną odpowiedzialnością';

(v) commercial companies or civil law companies having a commercial form and cooperatives and public undertakings incorporated in accordance with Portuguese law;

(w) companies under Romanian law known as: 'societăți pe acțiuni', 'societăți în comandită pe acțiuni', 'societăți cu răspundere limitată';

(x) companies under Slovenian law known as: 'delniška družba', 'komanditna družba', 'družba z omejeno odgovornostjo';

(y) companies under Slovak law known as: 'akciová spoločnosť', 'spoločnosť s ručením obmedzeným', 'komanditná spoločnosť';

(z) companies under Finnish law known as 'osakeyhtiö'/'aktiebolag', 'osuuskunta'/'andelslag','säästöpankki'/'sparbank'and 'vakuutusyhtiö'/'försäkringsbolag';

(aa) companies under Swedish law known as 'aktiebolag', 'försäkringsaktiebolag', 'ekonomiska föreningar', 'sparbanker', 'ömsesidiga försäkringsbolag';

(ab) companies incorporated under the law of the United Kingdom.

Annex III List of national laws implementing the Cross-border Merger Directive

This Annex contains a list of the current national legislation implementing the Cross-border Merger Directive.

Austria

Bundesgesetz über die grenzüberschreitende Verschmelzung von Kapital-gesellschaften in der Europäischen Union

Bundesgesetz, mit dem ein Bundesgesetz über die grenzüberschrei-tende Verschmelzung von Kapitalgesellschaften in der Europäischen Union erlassen wird sowie das Firmenbuchgesetz, das Gerichtsgebührengesetz, das Rechtspflegergesetz, das GmbH-Gesetz, das Aktiengesetz 1965, das Umwandlungsgesetz, das Unternehmensgesetzbuch und das Übernahmegesetz geändert werden (Gesellschaftsrechts-Änderungsgesetz 2007 – GesRÄG 2007, *Bundesgesetzblatt* I Nr. 72/2007

Belgium

Code des sociétés/Wetboek van vennootschappen

Bulgaria

Търговски закон, обнародван в Държавен вестник бр. 48 от 1999 г., с последващи изменения и допълнения

Закон за публичното предлагане на ценни книжа, обнародван в Държавен вестник бр. 114 от 1999 г., с последващи изменения и допълнения

Кодекс на труда, обнародван в Държавен вестник бр. 26 от 1986 г., с последващи изменения и допълнения.

Cyprus

Ο περί Εταιρειών (Τροποποιητικός) (Αρ. 4) Νόμος 186(I)/2007, Επίσημη Εφημερίδα της Κυπριακής Δημοκρατίας Αρ. 4154, παράρτημα πρώτο, μέρος I της 31ης Δεκεμβρίου 2007

Czech Republic

Zákon č. 125/2008 Sb., o přeměnách obchodních společností a družstev. Částka: 40/2008 Sb., na s. 1570, *Rozesláno*, 16.4.2008.

Denmark

Lovbekendtgørelse nr. 649 af 15 June 2006 (aktieselskabsloven) med senere ændringer
Lovbekendtgørelse nr. 650 af 15. juni 2006 (anpartsselskabsloven) med senere ændringer
Lovbekendtgørelse nr. 651 af 15. juni 2006 (erhvervsvirksomhedsloven) med senere ændringer
Lovbekendtgørelse nr. 652 af 15. juni 2006 (erhvervsfondsloven) med senere ændringer

Estonia

Äriseadustiku ja sellega seonduvate seaduste muutmise seadus, 21 November 2007, *Riigi Teataja* I, 13.12.2007, 65, 405

Germany

Zweites Gesetz zur Änderung des Umwandlungsgesetzes, 19 April 2007, *Bundesgesetzblatt Jahrgang* 2007 Teil I Nr. 15, 24.04.2007.

Hungary

2007. évi CXL. törvény a tőkeegyesítő társaságok határokon átnyúló egyesüléséről

The Netherlands

Wet van 27 juni 2008 tot wijziging van boek 2 van het Burgerlijk Wetboek in verband met de implementatie van richtlijn nr. 2005/56/EG van het Europese Parlement en de Raad van de Europese Unie betreffende grensover-schrijdende fusies van kapitaalvennootschappen (PbEU L 310), *Staatsblad* 27.06.2008

Poland

Ustawa z dnia 25 kwietnia 2008 r.o zmianie ustawy – Kodeks spółek handlowych (.Dz.U.08.86.524 z dnia 20 maja 2008 r.)

Slovak Republic

Zakon z 27. novembra 2007 c. 657/2007 Z.z., ktorym sa meni a doplna zakon c. 513/1991 Zb. Obchodny zakonnik v zneni neskorsich predpisov a o zmene a doplneni zakona c. 530/2003 Z.z. o obchodnom registri v zneni neskorsich prepisov, uverejneny dna 31. decembra 2007 v c. 266/2007 Zbierky zakonov Slovenskej republiky

United Kingdom

Statutory Instrument 2007 No. 2974 The Companies (Cross-Border Mergers) Regulations 2007

Norway

Lov 21. desember 2007 nr. 129 om endringer i aksjeloven, allmennaksjeloven og enkelte andre lover (fusjon og fisjon over landegrensene, *Norsk Lovtidend Avd. 1*, 2007 no. 13, p. 1868

Forskrift 9. januar 2008 nr. 50 om arbeidstakernes rett til representasjon ved fusjon over landegrensene av selskaper med begrenset ansvar, *Norsk Lovtidend Avd.* 1, 2008 no. 1, p. 267

Index